John Bradburne:

John Bradburne:
Vagabond of God

DIDIER RANCE

Translated from the French by Malachy O'Higgins
Abridged by David Crystal
Foreword by Jean Vanier

DARTON · LONGMAN + TODD

First published in Great Britain in 2017 by
Darton, Longman and Todd Ltd
1 Spencer Court
140–142 Wandsworth High Street
London SW18 4JJ

First published in the French language in 2012 by Editions Salvator, Paris

Translated from the French by Malachy O'Higgins

ISBN 978-0-232-53-339-2

A catalogue record for this book is available from the British Library.

Typeset by Kerrypress Ltd, Markyate, St Albans

Printed and bound in Great Britain by Short Run Press, Exeter

Contents

Abbreviations

The following abbreviations are used throughout the book, especially in the later chapters:

AFMM: Associazione Femminile Medico-Missionaria.
ANC: African National Council (1971–72).
ARU: Administration Reinforcement Units.
JBMS: John Bradburne Memorial Society.
JOC: Joint Operation Command.
SFO: Secular Francisan Order.
UANC: United African National Party (Bishop Muzorewa).
UDI: Unilateral Declaration of Independence.
ZANLA: Zimbabwe African National Liberation Army (ZANU military branch).
ZANU: Zimbabwe African National Union (Robert Mugabe).
ZAPU: Zimbabwe African People's Union (Josuah Nkomo).
ZIPRA: Zimbabwe People's Revolutionary Army (ZAPU military branch).

Preface

In 1983, John Bradburne entered my life. 'You have been to Africa. Do you think you could raise money for this project?' The project I was being asked to consider by Aid to the Church in Need (ACN) concerned the rehabilitation of a chapel and houses in a leper centre at Mutemwa. I accepted all the more readily, having already worked as a volunteer a few years earlier in neighbouring Zambia on a development programme which included a colony of lepers – I had greatly admired their courage. Two hundred thousand French francs were raised and sent to Mutemwa. The letter of thanks I subsequently received was accompanied by a booklet entitled *John Bradburne of Mutemwa, 1921–1979*, written by Father John Dove, which gave a brief account of the life and death of this English lay Franciscan tertiary. Reading it filled me with enthusiasm for this extraordinary person! Apart from the many reasons for loving John, which I hope will be shared by the readers of this book, there were several points of personal convergence: the lepers; Africa; wanderings; flute; poetry; Franciscan Third Order (Franciscan secular order since 1979), even if I was well aware of the gap between this life all given to God and mine.

Ten years later, John Bradburne (in this book I have called him simply John) was still in my heart when I had a lunch at ACN headquarters with a missionary from Zimbabwe, Father Tim Peacock. The first thing I asked him was whether he had heard of a man called John Bradburne. By way of reply he said he was organising an annual pilgrimage to Mutemwa! As the conversation continued, he told me Father Dove had published in Ireland a book of reminiscences about John. A few weeks later *The Strange Vagabond of God* arrived in the post, and I eagerly read it, resolving to translate it into French one day and make John known in France. In the meantime I gave some lectures on him to groups of Franciscans, and spoke about him to the Pontifical Commission of New Martyrs in Rome, as I was participating in its work. When in 2001 I published *Un Siècle de Témoins* ('A Century of Witnesses'), a compendium of research and publications on the martyrs of our time, John and his friend Luisa Guidotti figured among the names of martyrs on the cover, and received attention in the work itself. In 2004, I devoted a chapter to John in a book on the prayer of twentieth-century martyrs.

In 2008 I decided to honour my promise about John Dove's book, and headed for England to meet the members of the John Bradburne Memorial Society (JBMS). They received me with great courtesy, informing me that since this book numerous other testimonies and documents relating to John had appeared, including almost all his poems, running into thousands of pages, as well as numerous letters. As a result, the need for a full-scale biography of John made itself felt, which would draw on this rich mine of documentary resources, including of course Father Dove's own testimony on John. Trained as a historian, and having written some 15 books on martyrs and witnesses to the faith in our time, I decided to rise to the challenge and write, not a hagiography of John, but a full and rounded biography of the real man that people had known (both hagiography and biography have their own legitimacy, but they belong to different literary genres).

Supported by the JBMS, I set off in the footsteps of John in England, Italy, Belgium and Africa, visiting the places where he lived (using also my own memories of the Holy Land and India), meeting those who knew him, gathering their recollections, or completing those they had already written. I also got in touch with other sources, studied the writings of those close to him, and those who were interested in him, especially Judith Listowel, the archives of the JBMS, and the articles and testimonies in the JBMS Newsletter. I also studied John's letters and his many poems, which yield precious biographical data but have to be handled with care: not only was he a poet, but even if John's memory was astonishingly sharp, it could sometimes play him false. This book has emerged from this vast corpus (tens of thousands of pages), and allows us to follow with a degree of accuracy, sometimes even from day to day, the life of John Bradburne, though details and dates sometimes conflict, including in John's own writings. It is slightly shorter than the French original text, but all the omitted material can be found on the JBMS website: www.johnbradburne.com.

At this point, in a long adventure which started more than 30 years ago, where do I stand with John? From reading certain accounts, his life and death would seem like a meteorite from Voragine's *Golden Legend*, bursting into the twentieth-century, he himself like a saint from an ancient stained-glass window, or a cardboard saint. In fact the thousand pages of poems and letters which he left behind and the many testimonies reveal a man of flesh and blood. The stuff of human nature, with its weaknesses and its limitations, and not least its grandeur, has replaced the icon. But we must have no regrets, for – in Michael O'Halloran's words – 'the last thing we want is the kind of person who is presented with no human failings'. On the contrary, the light that shines through the sometimes opaqueness of concrete individual human lives is greater than that which passes through stained-glass windows, even if they are in Chartres Cathedral or Paris Sainte-Chapelle. If John manifested the 'heroic virtues' of which saints are made (the Church will tell us), his whole life was a long struggle to achieve them. Far from stifling his essential humanity, this struggle for holiness has if anything blossomed it, as has been made clear by many who knew him, such as Father George Webster: John was 'a most interesting character, a fully-rounded person, larger than life... He enjoyed company... drank some cheap local brandy... We would talk and drink together. He was a very happy person, he showed his humanness but was a person of deep spirituality, a mixture of prayer and humour.'

The enthusiasm which John stirs in me is not the same as that in 1983 – it is greater.

Foreword by Jean Vanier

After my visit to Zimbabwe in 1982 I wrote the following to my community in l'Arche (*Our Life Together: A Memoir in Letters,* p. 270): 'During my visit several people spoke to me about John Bradburne, an Englishman who had lived a life similar to that of Benedict Labre. During the last years of his life he lived in a small hut at the centre of a leprosarium caring for the lepers, praying with them, bringing them the Eucharist and, at times, angrily defending them against those who tried to steal from them. He lived a very poor life amongst them and he was always surprised that the lepers welcomed him with such kindness and allowed him to stay with them. He was murdered by unknown assassins in September 1979.'

And so I had a glimpse of the kind of person John was, and was even lodged in a hut near Harare where he had lived. However, this excellent book has helped me to know John in a new way. It is with joy and a certain emotion that I write a foreword to this deeply moving book, in the hope that readers will get to know this exceptional Englishman.

He was exceptional from several points of view. His father was a priest of the Anglican Communion. In 1939 John was commissioned an officer in the British army and fought in a terrible war against the Japanese in Malaya and Burma, both ex-British colonies. From hand-to-hand fighting with the enemy to forced marches through the jungle without food, stricken by serious illness, facing near death several times, this young 20-year-old spent several months in hell. He had rare gifts of intelligence in poetry, music and a love of nature. He had a difficult character, at once funny, rich, serious and given to practical joking, and he became a seeker after God and the absolute. After a number of years searching he entered the Catholic Church, a man enthralled by holiness, poverty and the things essential to the Church. He was a true follower of God, and called himself Christ the King's jester, the mystical spouse of the Virgin Mary. The richness of his nature, but perhaps also the harrowing things he had experienced in the war, unsettled him, turning his life into an endless quest. He entered monasteries, only to leave them again a few months later because he hadn't found the absolute he was looking for. For a time he considered spending his whole life in Israel converting the Jews. He then became a vagabond of Jesus, a busker in London playing his recorder along the Thames Embankment.

He spent time as a sacristan in a little church in southern Italy, living in the organ gallery, then as caretaker of the house of the Archbishop of London. He made many pilgrimages and was passionately devoted to Lourdes. He was certainly a mystic, but of a rather peculiar kind! He had received the grace to be able to describe in poetry his adventures, his humours and his love of Jesus and Mary. He was quick to get angry, but just as quick to become soft again. He had a deep love of eagles, and for a time lived with an eagle who flew while attached to its perch by a fishing line a hundred yards long. He became also a great lover of bees. He loved to climb trees. He was a serious man, but knew how to make others laugh out loud. He made friends through music and reading, especially the writings of the mystics. He was a strange, sometimes disconcerting man, but most of all he was a man in search of God, a man of prayer, who wanted to live a life of poverty like Francis of Assisi.

Where did this searcher find his God? In a leper centre in Zimbabwe. From his first visit he immediately knew that this was where God meant him to be. He moved in with these afflicted men and women, sharing their food, caring for them with kindness and gentleness, bathing them and, above all, offering them his friendship. These men and women, thrown on the scrap heap of humanity, rejected by all, regarded him as their father, brother, friend – Baba John. In a short while he transformed this leper centre into a community, a place of laughter, friendship and tenderness. His life with these men and women did not prevent him from living his life of prayer. He sang the Office of vigils at midnight for an hour, and was up at six o'clock in the morning for another Office. He rebuilt the chapel in the centre and, with the permission of the Archbishop, administered communion to those who wished it. He consoled the lepers, accompanying them in the painful last hours of their journey towards their final end. He brought doctors in to care for them. He also invited other people to visit this 'unspeakable' place, who brought all sorts of presents, but who mostly came to befriend those stricken by leprosy.

A man like John, with his thirst for the absolute, also made enemies, especially the health professionals, who did not like the Christian spirit and wished to enclose the residents in institutions ill adapted to their deeper needs. John, who found God among the rejects, became himself a reject from this place of peace. When this happened he pitched his tent close by the centre and continued to visit his friends and console and support them as best he could. He was not only excluded from the leper colony as a white man in a country torn apart by a war between races. He was bothersome. In Southern Rhodesia at that time the Whites made up 4 per cent of the population, controlling all the power and all the wealth. John was abducted, then killed, by the insurgents. He found Jesus among the poor. He died alone. He was murdered, far from his brothers and sisters the lepers, alone, like Jesus.

Didier Rance, who wrote this book, is a distinguished and painstaking historian who has undertaken long research to produce this lively and accurate account of the life of John Bradburne, against the background of his religious upbringing in England, the war in Southern Rhodesia, and the Far East. He has a passion for truth and an impressive grasp of reality. But this is above all a religious book. The story of John's life has touched me heart and soul, and brought me closer to God. It has revealed to me a God wonderfully full of surprises, better, more intelligent, more creative than we could imagine. An extraordinary God who cannot be confined in rational concepts or in an 'ordinary' religious life. John, God's jester, has confirmed me in my life in L'Arche, with men and women who have been marginalised by society on account of their handicap.

Jean Vanier
March 2017

Chapter 1

Between Eden and the Cross, 1921–1929

Lucky may many people seem
In places of their birth
But we were born nigh Eden stream,
No fairer runs on earth.
(*Jack-o'-lantern*, 1969)

John Bradburne was born on June 14th 1921 between Eden and
the Cross – or more exactly, East of Eden and at the foot of the
Cross. Eden is the name of the mountain river which flows close
to Skirwith, the village where he was born, and the Cross is Cross
Fell (at 2930 feet the second highest mountain in England), the
mountain overlooking the town. From Paradise to Golgotha: the
geographical metaphor seemed to proclaim a singular destiny,
even if many other children besides John Bradburne were born
in Skirwith.

On this day, in this remote north-western corner of England,
close to the Scottish border, while the country was experiencing a
three-month drought which would be recorded as the most severe of
the century, the Reverend Thomas William Bradburne and his wife
rejoiced in the birth of their third child, ten days before the feast of
the saint whose name he would bear, and after whom the church
where his father was the vicar was named. The birth took place in
the vicarage, as did that of the two elder children, assisted by a young
woman sent by Edward Parker, the village squire. Six weeks later, on
July 31st, the infant John Randal Bradburne was christened.

Thomas Bradburne had been vicar of Skirwith since September
1913. He had been nominated and appointed by the Parkers, who
held in perpetuity the right to nominate the incumbent of the
village church, built half a century previously by the Parker family.
For Thomas, like the Parkers a High Church Anglican, the generous
dimensions of the vicarage garden had been a determining factor

in his decision to accept the appointment. Born in 1875 in the Midlands, son of a clergyman, he had like his father turned his back on high responsibility and settled for a quiet country life. After Pembroke College Cambridge and Wells Theological College, followed by a spell in a working-class parish at Oldham in Lancashire, he came down with tuberculosis, as a result no doubt of his visits to the lowly houses of his parishioners. Having recovered his health, after a three-year break in Australia he was appointed vicar of the parish of the Holy Saviour in Notting Hill, at the time a sleepy suburb in West London, where one of his parishioners, an India-born widow, fell in love with him.

Mabel Higgins had previously been married to Arthur Hill, who had gone to India to make his fortune. When she arrived in England in 1900, she had been a widow for five years, and was now living with her daughter Erica, who was born in Lucknow in 1894. She was being supported by her family, in particular by her cousin Evelyn, who had married William Rattigan, born in India to an Irishman from Kildare. William had risen to become Chief Justice of the Punjab and had been raised to the peerage by Queen Victoria (family lore had it that he was the inspiration for Kipling's eponymous hero, Kim). Despite her straitened circumstances, Mabel had no intention of retiring from the social scene; she had acquired a number of Samoyed dogs, recently made fashionable by the Prince of Wales, had enrolled Erica at a school for young ladies and arranged piano lessons for her, and had taken her on regular visits to the theatre and to the Russian ballets of Diaghilev. Soon the creditors came knocking at the door, obliging the elegant widow to marshal all her charms to keep them at bay.

She regularly invited the young vicar, and he took the young Erica for trips on his bicycle. He for his part cherished no romantic feelings towards the widow, and the years went by. Embittered by thwarted passion, Mabel sought solace in resentment and alcohol. Meanwhile her daughter grew up, and found herself the object of the vicar's passion, to which she responded in kind. Not daring to announce their love to the widow, the vicar continued to pay regular visits to the house, which Mabel believed were for the pleasure of her company. When the hapless widow finally discovered the truth, she confined her daughter to the house. The lovers continued to meet in secret, in faraway Bushey Park and Richmond Park. In 1913 Erica reached the legal marriage age, but Mabel still withheld her consent.

After Thomas accepted his appointment at Skirwith, he did not forget Erica. However, Mabel remained adamant and so, in 1916, the lovers decided to get married secretly in London. When they announced the *fait accompli* to Mabel, to their surprise she offered them her congratulations. Because of his age, Thomas escaped conscription to the trenches of Northern France by one month, and the couple settled down in Skirwith. Philip was born in 1917, Mary in 1919, John in 1921, and Audrey in 1924. On the occasion of each birth a present arrived from Mabel, who died in 1924.

A very English family

On a living of £250 per annum, the Reverend Bradburne found himself and his family hovering somewhere between a lower middle-class and a skilled working-class subsistence income, although they lived rent free. Despite his athletic build, Thomas was not a healthy man and was plagued by asthma, a result of his tuberculosis, and this was not helped by his smoking habit. Subject to chronic anxiety, he suffered regular attacks of 'melancholy', of whose onset he warned in advance with the words 'Deep sea, deep sea', quoting from Robert Burton's *Anatomy of Melancholy*. The children would react with terror, while Erica would offer him the cigarette that she knew would calm him. He also experienced long periods of serenity, when everything was 'simply fine'.

In that long portrait gallery of country clergymen, familiar to readers of the English novel, Thomas belonged to the category known as 'gardeners'. He supplied his family with regular fresh vegetables and raised chickens, as well as a pig called Dinah, who chased after the children. In due course the revenue from poultry helped defray the children's school fees.

> The garden was his happy span
> If the parish not his waltz.

> He gloated when surrounded
> By his chickens and his coops.
> (*Prologue to the next possible exit,*1979)

The children took great delight in feeding the chickens, sometimes helping themselves in the process. When bored by visitors, they would ask to be allowed to feed the chickens in order to be excused; this became their agreed password to escape outside to the garden. Thomas's vegetable patch was surrounded by trees, which included a tall willow, gooseberry bushes, flower beds of daffodils, and other flowers of various kinds. An enormous lawn led to the fields beyond and the path to the church, alongside the banks of the Beck (a small brook) – a green paradise for the children. John greatly admired his father, whom he nicknamed Fist, who was for him the voice of authority and wisdom. He later said: 'My father was an honest man / who hated all things false'. But at the same he felt that he was different from him:

> I said to him when I was five,
> 'Father, could anyone
> Jump off the roof of home alive?'
> He said, 'A fool, my son!'
>
> From that time forth a deep regard
> For fools grew up with me.
> (*Prologue to the next possible exit*, 1979)

He also felt he owed his capacity for attention to his father:

> Then Father said:
> 'Watch the dark clouds
> Forms most amazing are theirs;
> See as they come
> One after one,
> Like camels and dragons and bears.'
> (*Skirwith*, 1949)

Erica, unlike the capricious Mabel, turned out to be an even-tempered mother, attentive to her household and with a strong sense of order. Her children rarely saw her angry, even when sorely provoked; she had little time for childish sulking or quarrelling, and was always anxious to calm any storms. Shy, innocent but insightful, she was a wonderful homemaker, but not very good in extended company. Generous to a fault, she often played hostess to the Bradburne clan, sometimes welcoming up to 14 guests at a time around the family table, even though Thomas refused to increase her budget for such occasions. She saved constantly and sometimes even sold off pieces of jewellery. Though often tired, she would never rest, and her only indulgence was a glass of Dubonnet at six o'clock in the evening. Nicknamed Mist by John, Erica was a well-read woman familiar with the Victorian novelists, and she also painted and dabbled in pottery. She never forgot her childhood in India, and while bathing the children she would sing melodies to them in Hindi, thus developing in them an aptitude for languages and memory. The children grew up feeling closer to their young mother than to their middle-aged father.

Mrs Groves the governess, nicknamed Ninnie, laid down the law, being old enough to be Erica's mother. Far from taking offence, the young mother was pleased at the way Ninnie kept a keen look-out for her children and carried out the household chores. But when Ninnie retired, Erica discovered a new freedom, and showed herself to be a capable housewife and mother.

Philip, called Broibe by John, was the eldest of the children, and enjoyed the privileges that went with his older brother status. He was soon accorded his own bedroom and was the first to leave home for boarding school at Seascale in 1925, after which his ascendancy over his younger siblings would never be the same. Mary (known as Mare) shared her bedroom with her younger brother John until she too left for Calder Girls School in 1927. The two grew very close, no doubt in solidarity against the older brother. Mary, kind and sensitive, seemed to realise that John was special, and developed a protective attitude towards him. Audrey (Audre) kept to herself and showed little inclination to join in their games. She suffered from a slight handicap in one foot, and could not always keep up with them. As a result she developed a tendency toward self-effacement and introversion.

John would became aware that on both sides of the family he was linked by a long line of ancestors to a thousand years of his country's history – and owed his first names to two of these. Among these ancestors were to be found descendants of William the Conqueror, servants of Crown and Church, an archbishop, but also a businessman, a nail merchant, an adventurer, clergymen gardeners, a crypto-Catholic, several ne'er-do-wells, and even a young Jewess from Venice – a whole swathe of humanity that John gradually discovered, and that would crop up in more than one future poem. The Bradburnes were acutely family conscious and much given to hospitality. Charles Bradburne came down to Skirwith to rest when weary of life in London. More than 30 years later John, crossing the bridge over the Eden, would remember (in a letter to his mother) 'the place where Uncle Charlie fell in whilst fishing'. Henrietta, a sister of John's father, visited regularly, accompanied by her husband Peter Comber and their four children, older than their cousins but quick to organise games.

From Erica's side of the family, the vicarage played host to her cousin Peter Murray Hill, who later married the actress Phyllis Calvert, and her aunt Lucy 'Mabel', married to the enormously wealthy Joseph Townsend. The latter's sister Catherine had married Harold Soames, from a landed gentry background, who had become one of the wealthiest brewers in the country. Although herself a rare visitor, her daughter Olave was very close to Erica, even if her various commitments occupied most of her time. Married to Robert Baden-Powell, her senior by 32 years, she accompanied her husband on his many travels promoting his worldwide Boy Scout movement. Her brother Arthur was the father of Christopher Soames, born a year before John, and destined to a long political career; Winston Churchill's son-in-law, he was to become in turn Ambassador to Paris, cabinet minister, and the last High Commissioner of Rhodesia. On Erica's mother's side, Evelyn Rattigan, 'aunt Rat' to the children, sent gifts regularly, but became depressed when her son Frank was sacked by the Foreign Office after his mistress Princess Elizabeth of Romania procured an abortion to enable her to marry the King of Greece (she was credited with declaring: 'I have committed every vice but one, and I do not intend to die before I have killed a man'). John was a playmate of Frank's handicapped son, Brian.

Conversely, the Bradburne children sometimes travelled to visit their uncles and aunts. Their favourite destination was their Aunt Mabel's at Troon in Scotland. She had orange-coloured teeth, which fascinated the children, but also a Rolls Royce with a chauffeur, and Philip delighted the children by playing with the intercom.

They got up to all sorts of mischief, which was later recalled in an enigmatic quatrain:

> Unstable Boys, Aunt Mabel ruled you well
> And though mine English Aunt was not the rage
> Bad Cain enables you for naught but Hell,
> For cabbages is all your pilgrimage!
> (*Paradise Tossed Aside: Incipit Lamentatio...* 1978)

The old lady gave them presents, among them G. E. Farrow's *The Wallypug of Why*, full of fantastic wordplay, in which John first discovered the witty style at which he later became so adept. The children also went holidaying in the farming county of Smalley, near Morecambe Bay in the Lake District. John was excited by everything he saw, and Mary had to scold him all the time for talking with his mouth full. On their rambles they came across a tramp who travelled 30 miles every day on foot in all weathers, 'not to talk / To less than The Divine' (*Idyll*, 1977). This encounter opened John's mind to 'strange life', the tramp being 'the oldest member / Of the strangers in my mind'. He also spent some time with Ninnie's family on the coast of the Irish Sea, with its vast dunes, pine trees, endless beaches and seaside resorts, which John found sinister.

A forgotten village

Skirwith was fairly typical of the old England of country mansions, quaint vicarages and thatched cottages set in a countryside far removed from the bustle of great industrial cities, in which J. B. Priestley found the quintessence of that 'Englishness' to which John remained so attached. The village seemed to have been bypassed by the modern world. Leaving behind the hamlet of Langwarthby, the tiny lane winds its way between forests on either side and soon gives way to a road, which after a few hundred yards crosses another road. This is Skirwith, and with a slight lapse of attention one could miss it altogether. Like many English villages it had its own green, divided in two by the Beck, with its fast-flowing current which could swell and flood without warning. At the time the village had a population of 280 inhabitants, living in a few dozen red-brick houses and a few more of stone, as well as the church, the vicarage, the Methodist chapel, the Sun Inn (whose construction had been funded by the Parkers), the Hall (a Georgian style farmhouse), and the Abbey, the manor of the Parkers. The school, which was next to the church, had an enrolment of 70 pupils, not including the Bradburnes, who, apart from church or vicarage visits, or chance encounters in the street, had hardly any contact with children of their own age.

The climate was harsh, although the sun was known to shine in the warmer seasons. Dampness pervaded everywhere, and Cross Fell boasted both the highest rainfall and the lowest temperatures in the whole of England. Sometimes snow fell in summer. Skirwith, uniquely in the British Isles, had a wind with a name of its own, the Helm, whose stormy visits would be heralded by black clouds above Cross Fell. As a child John had heard tales of the Helm, and had seen with his own eyes the ravages it could cause as it hurtled down the mountain at speeds of up to 100 miles an hour, destroying crops, mowing down sheep, and sometimes carrying them off, its roaring wind a source of terror to the villagers, fuelling his father's depression, and that of others no doubt. Some claimed to have witnessed carts spiralling into the swirling wind, never to be seen again. One could never know how long the storm would last, whether a single night or weeks on end, during which time all would be confined indoors: 'When the Helm comes down and the dogs bark / Close your doors before it's dark', as local lore had it. In the 1920s, meteorologists had yet not cracked the mystery of this unusual wind, and the people of Skirwith continued to attribute to it some sort of supernatural origin. John learnt that 'the Scourge', as it was known, was a henchman of Satan; that once upon a time St Paulin had travelled from York to defy the demon of the Fell (then called the Devil's Mountain), though with limited success.

Life was hard for the small farmers of Skirwith. Yields were uncertain, and in times of severe cold, incessant rains or a prolonged Helm took their toll. Sheep and subsistence farming were the main sources of livelihood. The thin and sandy soils of Skirwith lacked the fertility of those of the neighbouring villages of Culgaith and Kirkland, and the Helm had devastating effects. Moreover in the mid-1920s a foot-and-mouth epidemic decimated the livestock;

whole herds had to be slaughtered, and their carcasses burned –
a distressing spectacle for a young boy. The population survived,
living from hand to mouth from their own produce, making
their own clothes, gathering firewood for fuel, and making for
themselves their small everyday life tools. Every family, including
the Bradburnes, raised a pig, and housewives did their own weaving
in the home. Skirwith nevertheless kept in touch with the outside
world with the help of the local newspaper: *The Mid Cumberland
and West Cumberland Herald.*

Skirwith vicarage, built at the same time as the church, was in
the 'Anglican' style, to use the label coined by Osbert Lancaster: in
essence, mock Tudor – as English at that time as smog and cricket.
Its architecture blended the public and the private spheres: the
vicar's office, the choir room and the children's bedrooms, similar
to those we encounter in Victorian novels. The sandstone houses
testified to the harshness of the climate, with their pointed roofs
and narrow latticed windows. The rooms were spacious but damp,
the bedrooms heated by a portable oil stove, which was carried
from room to room – a constant fire risk which sometimes
materialised, though the house miraculously escaped serious
outbreaks of fire. After dark, acetylene lamps cast long shadows
across the rooms, while of course ghosts played at night on the
landings and corridors. Nobody claimed to have seen one, but the
Bradburne children believed in them in the same way they believed
in witches. Lingering superstitions from a long-departed pagan past
were alive and well in Skirwith: the cawing of a crow could herald
the arrival of a stranger; a speck of dust in a candle wick could
mean a letter on the way; a burning ember falling from the hearth
meant a funeral in the offing; and no one must ever move house
on a Friday. At Halloween the children hollowed out turnips from
the garden and placed a candle inside, casting grotesque shadows
and shapes to guide the steps of dead souls back to their former
earthly dwelling. In winter they espied on Cross Fell will-o'-the
wisps, which they called 'Jack o'- Lanterns', lying in wait for their
victims.

The rhythm of life at the vicarage was inviolable. Tuesday to
Friday were 'ordinary' days, Saturday to Monday 'extraordinary'.
On Saturday the vicar set about his duties, and the rest of the family

devoted themselves to preparing Sunday lunch. Sunday was a working day for Thomas Bradburne, but also a day of rest according to venerable tradition. Monday was washing day, the washing done by Mrs Hardy, a ritual as familiar to the children as the liturgy of the day before, with its impressive array of materials: mangle, washing board and table, wooden bucket, surface for scrubbing clothes, and laundry basket. The operation took all day, as did the day set aside for baking bread. Young John discovered also that the annual spring clean took its place alongside the great religious feast days, the children becoming almost like gypsies when the house was turned inside out, and everything swept, beaten and cleaned. The whole operation, always close to Easter, instilled in the children an awareness of a cosmic rhythm of renewal.

An enchanted childhood

As a child John was something of a tearaway – what nowadays would be called hyperactive – who seemed unable to sit still, constantly charging around and climbing everything in sight. He was nicknamed 'Red Chicken' by his older brother and sister – always bleeding from some fall or collision. He seemed to be accident prone, tripping and scraping his knees, and in need of constant care, which he usually got from his sister.

At the vicarage in summer time the day began with the pleasant smells of drying linen and apple blossom drifting through the bedroom window. John was intoxicated by these and had difficulty getting up in the morning, even when the sun poured through the red curtains of his bedroom. Listening to the cooing of the pigeons, he made up from it a prayer he would remember in later life:

> Soon I did sleep,
> Slept till the sun
> Wakened the ring-doves again;
> Listened as they
> Welcomed the day
> Roucouling this gentle refrain: –
>
> 'Thanks be to Thee
> Maker of all,

Lord of the country and farm!
Pray shew us corn
Early this morn
And keep us from peril and harm'.
(*Skirwith*, 1949)

Every day at midday and in the evening, the Bradburne family sat down to eat together. Usually their meat diet was restricted to pigeon, rabbit or chicken, with home-grown vegetables from the garden. As an occasional treat they got rook tart – a Scottish dish, thanks to Thomas, an accomplished hunter – and sometimes pheasant or grouse from the Parker's estate or donated by parishioners. The neighbours were aware that the vicar had a large family and many mouths to feed.

When the Helm blew and it was too cold to venture outside, the children played in the nursery, a vast playroom whose Oriel windows looked towards the Fells. The custom was that the children played there accompanied by Ninnie, and the parents almost regarded it as out of bounds to them. The toy farms and Philip's train set were usually scattered across the floor. John loved to join in the games, and always managed to gather a bigger herd of farm animals than anyone else. He gradually took over more and more floor space, and proceeded to defend his territory against all comers.

The vicar, possessed of a fine singing voice, used it to advantage in church, and Erica, when she had the time, played the nursery harmonium. Music appreciation played a natural role in the educational culture of their social milieu. It was customary to impart the basics to young children, allowing them subsequently to follow their own bent. The Bradburnes were committed to encouraging their children according to their talents and potential. Philip early on seemed attracted by the clavier; Mary learnt to play the cello, and continued to do so for the rest of her life; and Audrey took up the violin. John seems to have inherited his father's singing voice, though he also improvised on the piano from time to time. He quickly learnt to sing in different voices, and hummed at will any air that came into his head, accompanying himself on the harmonium. During a visit to Aunt Catherine in Hutton, in Essex, herself a self-taught and versatile pianist, John's natural talent as a singer became apparent to all.

He continued to develop his musical sense with the help of the recently acquired 'Aeolion, a gramophone with an enormous loudspeaker – a gift, along with eight records, to Thomas Bradburne. The children played the records over and over until the needles were worn out. John's and Mary's favourite were Mendelssohn's *Hebrides* and its touching melodies; other favourites were *Midsummer Night's Dream, Siegfried Idyll,* the *Tannhäuser Overture* and the *March of the Toreador* from *Carmen*. At this time young John devised his own party piece, which he would never tire of performing: at the opening notes of *Carmen* he would disappear under the table and re-emerge wrapped in a red carpet and proceed to charge around the room like a bull. Later, when Mary had learnt to read musical scores, she initiated her younger brother into Handel's *Messiah* and other works of the repertoire. Brother and sister would often spend hours singing together.

The Bible held the place of honour in the Bradburne household, though it played no major role when it came to reading lessons. The vicar himself, and sometimes Ninnie, taught the children to read, using Favell Mortimer's nineteenth-century best-seller *Reading without Tears, or A Pleasant Mode of Learning to Read*. Though of evangelical inspiration, this guide to reading was full of terrifying stories. John was a reluctant pupil, however, and averse to sitting still for any length of time. He would go into hiding at the appointed hour, as often as not by climbing up a tree. On the other hand, he enjoyed the stories read to him by his mother on the sofa every day after lunch: the Brothers Grimm, Beatrix Potter, and especially Kipling, beloved of Erica the Indian. This 1907 Nobel Laureate had almost become one of the family. Having failed at Oxford, he headed for India; en route he was smitten by one of the Higgins girls, and proposed to her on the boat. He was unsuccessful, being considered an unsuitable match, and one can only imagine Mary's reaction on learning that her aunt had turned down a future Nobel prizewinner.

Erica also read Shakespeare and Dickens to her children, her even, soft voice never faltering, even when Nancy was battered to death in *Oliver Twist*. *A Tale of Two Cities* terrified the children, and

Mary later found, in a chimney of the doll's house, the guillotined remains of one of the dolls. Philip was the suspected executioner, possibly with the complicity of John. John's favourite readings were *The Jungle Book* and *Boy's Own Annual*, in which cousin Baden Powell often wrote in praise of 'clean, manly and Christian lives'. *Boy's Own Annual* appeared every year under the auspices of the Religious Tract Society to instil the principles of muscular Christianity in its youthful readership. Each year this sizeable volume would bring household stories of derring-do, articles on nature study, games, competitions, and suchlike. It was aimed at readers from the middle and upper classes, and its stories were often set in public schools. Its contributors included Jules Verne, Arthur Conan Doyle and Rudyard Kipling. On the other hand, John's poetical gift had no precedent in the Bradburne family.

The older children spent most of the day in the open air. Their parents insisted on their playing outside after breakfast, allowing Erica to look after her baby, even in winter, so that by lunchtime their hands were numb with cold. The children's daily destination was the large garden, with its many flowerbeds, plants and shrubs, where they ran around playing hide-and-seek, or cycled around the paths, with John no doubt climbing the trees. He liked tree climbing with a passion, and assigned it a centrality in his personal existence.

Saturday was Pat Lowther day. This burly, lately settled, rag-and-bone gypsy sold second-hand clothes, and delivered sacks of grain and flour to the Bradburne family. Always dressed in black, he would arrive in his gaily painted cart drawn by his imperturbable dray horse. He fascinated the children, who demanded to be told gypsy lore, which he was often reluctant to do, not wishing to consider himself of gypsy stock, of whom he was inclined to speak disparagingly. When it was time for him to go, the children were allowed to climb up with him in the cart or on the horse's back and accompany him as far as the junction for Blencarn and Culgaith, 500 yards to the south, from where they made their own way home on foot.

John knew that the gypsies often camped not far from the village. Sometimes caravans passed by the vicarage on the way to Appleby Fair – which they had done for generations, as is attested by an engraving of 1849 – or they would see the caravan of Bramwell Evens, a gypsy apostle to the gypsies, who cut a fine evangelical figure. At night, after lights out, John and his sister told each other tales of kidnapped children, which in turn nourished visions of freedom and wild adventure. Together they imagined being kidnapped, or running away, building themselves childish caravans painted in bright colours and joining up with the grown-up gypsies. These reveries reflected the stereotypes of their time, like the romantic notions of gypsy life to be found in Walter Scott and Wordsworth. The gypsies continued to haunt the imagination of John, and he later recalled what they meant to him, in a poem with a title borrowed from Bach: *Air on G's String*.

When they were young, the Reverend Bradburne often took his three eldest children for a ride on his bike, which was a great thrill for them. Their parents allowed them to roam the countryside at will, and they quickly became acquainted with every corner of the village, inhabited – with the exception of the squire, the vicar, the Slacks from the Hall, the innkeeper and the grocer – by a community of farm labourers. John loved to watch

> The snow-white geese below Crossfell,
> On Skirwith Green in Cumberland:
> Most solemn they did ever seem,
> About the bridge which spanned the stream –
> Most loud and clear their cry!
> (*Ut Unum Sint*, 1956, stanza 1799)

Every morning churns of milk were delivered from the big farm beyond the vicarage, to the great delight of the children. They loved to visit the farm and watch the cows being milked, sometimes making their way to the mill which had been built in 1860 on the Beck, or built dams on the river, or huts on the islands, where John dreamt of flowers...

> Glowing rare orchids, growing fair in dreams of June
> Mid summered heating, tended as with angel-hand
> By wisdom's Merlin-man in wild East Cumberland
> To whom came cuckoo, falcon, fox, – fearless,
> unbanned
> (*Beck-Mill*, undated)

Sometimes they visited Willie and Annie, the brother- and sister-in-law of Ninnie, for afternoon tea. Here they would be offered bread and butter as a prelude to Annie's iced cream cakes. And once a month the Bradburne family paid a visit to the Abbey for tea with the Parkers. Despite its name suggesting medieval origins in the time of the Knights Templars, this large country mansion of cut stone went back no further than the eighteenth-century. Approached by a large tree-lined driveway with lawns on either side, the house itself was accessed by steps with a handrail leading up to the front door, which never failed to impress the children. The Parkers lived a somewhat withdrawn existence since the death of their son at the Battle of Ypres, aged 27. Edward Parker owned two game reserves, through which flowed a river rich in catch. Both the game and the fish often found their way to the Bradburne dinner table. Mrs Parker was no less generous. No young Bradburne birthday passed without a present arriving from her.

On visits to the Parkers the children were obliged to don their Sunday best, which by no means pleased John, given his propensity for climbing trees. When their parents went upstairs with the Parkers, the children enjoyed cucumber sandwiches and cake with the kitchen staff. Tea, always Lapsang Souchong, was served in the china set that so impressed Mary. On departure, Mrs Parker never failed to fill the children's pockets with chocolates.

Once a week Thomas Bradburne took the children on a trip to Penrith, the local market town. With its population of 8200, and its narrow streets of identical red-brick houses and shops, Penrith must have seemed quite a metropolis to the young visitors from Skirwith. Here John received his first history lesson on a visit to the imposing ruins of the fourteenth-century castle, once extended by the future Richard III. The town retained its associations with Wordsworth, who was born nearby and attended school there. Reverend Bradburne, having dropped Mary off at her dancing class, would go to the deanery to confer with his colleagues. Invariably John insisted on being taken to the toyshop, where he spent his meagre pocket money. One day, taken there by his mother, he caused some embarrassment by asking in a loud voice: 'Can I have two Shire stallions, please?'

The vicar drove a Durant A22 (a red and black contraption with visible engine). His son recalled much later, in a letter to his mother on March 5th 1969:

> Tar-macadam was rare and the cars had souls
> That careened tween the fields with a marvellous
> power
> At fastest twenty-five miles an hour.

The windows could be wound down in good weather and every trip was an adventure, the vicar being somewhat absent-minded behind the wheel, and accidents were not infrequent. Furthermore he could only drive in daylight, but insisted in carrying on 'as long as I can see'. On one occasion he ran over a young sheep, the recollection of which often gave the young John nightmares.

From time to time the family enjoyed picnics at Stainmore, or in one of the valleys in the Fells. Other attractions were the fairs at Whit weekend and the feast of St Martin, as well as Appleby with its throngs of gypsies, and Penrith and Brough, which John, four at the time, attended with his parents. Seated on a low orchard wall John looked on, beaming with pleasure. In the same letter to his mother, he writes:

> For I watched and I watch the passing show
> Of the beasts that to Brough or to Penrith go,
> Untold went wonders quadruped by,
> Right through the day in a daze sat I.

> Yearling calves and yearling lambs
> And yelling men and belling rams
> And bawling bulls and enormous Shires
> Groomed with care for the swearing Squires!

> No screaming brakes but squealing pigs
> Netted in carts and jig-a-jig gigs,
> Poultry too in a wealth of crates
> And A-doodle-doo by the vicarage gates!

> An occasional car with a Squire inside
> Or a Farmer far too fat for pride

> Or a Parson praps in a lapse from zeal
> For the Galilean walkaday weal.

Ousby and Culgaith also boasted their own fairs. Here local farmers met in the Fox Inn or the Black Swan for food and drinks, where tea-rooms catered for the ladies and teetotallers, and farm workers offered their labour for hire on the day.

As the years passed, the children became hardy from climbing on the mountain. In winter the slopes of Cross Fell were covered in snow, and they delighted in hauling their sledge up the mountainside and sliding down at speed. In summertime they were allowed to climb Cross Fell, provided they got home before sunset. John got lost several times, but was not to be put off: he loved heights, and couldn't resist a climb. With his elders, and then with Mary when Philip had left for Seascale, he roamed the fields and the pathways, or scrambled up the dry slopes (at one stage they had a mountain pony), enchanted by everything he came across: waterfalls, streams, all the sounds of nature.

Colours changed with the seasons, from the white of winter to the carpets of flowers in June, though green and grey dominated. The cycle of colours became ingrained in John's memory – gorse, buttercups, mossy saxifrage, alpine lady's mantle, great burnet, sneezewort, cottongrass, knapweeds, and 'rhododendrons gay' (*Prologue to the next possible exit*, 1979). Birds were no less various: wheatears, pipits, warblers, larks, kestrels, sparrow hawks hovering in search of prey, lapwings, curlews, golden plovers, woodcocks, crows, swallows and swifts. Sometimes the children came upon a dead sheep that had fallen down the mountainside, or had been carried away by the Helm, and would baptise him 'Mr Guts'. Bypassing the bothies, they arrived on the plateau at the top of the mountain, which was often shrouded in mist. From there they enjoyed breathtaking views: other summits in the Pennine Range, Alston Valley with its lead mines, the Lake District and its peaks, and, at their feet, Skirwith and its church spire. They often returned home with a bird, too injured or too young to fly – a hawk, a buzzard or an owl – or a mouse, a lizard or tadpoles, which they would nurse back to health or keep at home (for a while John walked around with a mouse under his cap).

John also liked to wander down to the Eden, where he spent hours watching the current carrying away the waters of this providentially named river (celebrated by more than one English poet, including Michael Drayton in his 1612 *Poly-Olbion*):

> Many the names of the rivers that run to the sea,
> Indus and Amazon, Tigris and Jordan and Thames,
> Ganges and Jumna, Euphrates and Tweed, but to me
> Eden is fairest, so rare as with Paradise stems.
> (*Edensong*, undated)

> Scents of rose
> And lawngrass newly mown are here, whilst flows
> Leisurely by the garden-wall Life's stream
> Which is to me, throughout Life's endless theme,
> The river Eden, and for evermore
> I'll watch the flow which as a child I saw.
> (*Ut Unum Sint*, 1956, stanza 1864)

'Suffer the little children to come unto me'

John was born into the household of an Anglican vicar. At that time the Church of England was seen as a pillar of the Establishment. Ever since George Herbert's *Country Parson*, the vicar was expected to play a key role in maintaining social stability, his primary obligation being never to call in question the established order. The old system of patronage was still in place and was still being lauded as 'the best possible system' by Bishop Hanson in the 1930s. A patron (the local squire, the Crown or a university) had practically the right to propose the vicar of the parish over which he had patronage, coupled with the obligation to pay him a fixed income. This right could be transmitted from generation to generation, sold or mortgaged. It ensured the independence of the vicar, but if, as in Skirwith, the stipend was insufficient, the parish, the Bishop and the patron could leave him and his family to flounder in poverty without a twinge of conscience (fallen into disuse, the system has never been formally abrogated, but was amended in 1986).

Thomas noted in his parish journal the death of Lieutenant Thomas Parker on the Western front, the celebrations of peace in

1919, and his arguments with local Nonconformists, including those who were offering cut-price baptisms – the Established Church was not alone in serving Skirwith. Catholics had disappeared centuries before, but Nonconformists (Methodists) were numerous. They attracted poor farmers, who thereby gained social status. From Penrith, the Methodist pastors served 40 communities in the valley and, since 1868, owned a chapel at Skirwith. The unimpressive building stood opposite the Anglican church, across the Beck. John could see it from the vicarage and thus discovered the reality of Christian division.

Behind his calm exterior, the vicar possessed an unsuspected willingness to enter the fray in defence of issues he considered important, a trait he passed on to his son. He took a dim view of 'modernist' developments in his own Church, such as the eugenic ideas of Archbishop Barnes of Birmingham, or those who waged open war against the High Church tradition to which he belonged. Although the family atmosphere was deeply religious, John did not strike his family as being overly religious in his attitudes, even though religion, it must be said, was often a matter of social and moral reflex. He later wrote (exaggerating, no doubt):

> Crossfell rose over up behind the place
> Where I was born to be a parson's son
> Haunted by prayer where never made I one.
> (*Of a district*, 1970)

The church was the Reverend's second home. With its sumptuous Lazonby stone and squat spire ('built / Well to withstand The Helm', wrote John in *Prologue to the next possible exit* (1979)), it was justly called 'the Cathedral of the Fells'. The care brought to its construction, decoration and furnishing recalls Emerson's jibe at the Gospel then being preached by Anglicanism: 'By taste are ye saved' (*Journal*, 15 May 1853). Passing through the church doors the visitor is enveloped in an atmosphere of peace. There is a stained-glass portrayal of John the Baptist, John's patron saint, and two of the Virgin Mary – not so frequent in Anglican churches – including one which bears a striking resemblance to Erica with baby Audrey in her arms. But the attention is quickly drawn to the great stained glass window above the choir, framed in three sections, depicting Jesus standing in a grassy plot blessing three children. He is holding one of them in his arm, dressed in a robe with gilt cross-shaped decorations in the same design as the hem of the robe of Christ himself. At his feet we see more children, standing or sitting with their mothers, being introduced to Christ by bearded apostles. The figure of Jesus, the clarity and sharpness of the image and the serenity of the colours, induce an effect of peace, even if the style has a certain mawkishness.

It is likely that here, looking at this glass window, John beheld an image of Jesus for the first time, and learnt to attach a face to a name, the face of someone unmistakeably good, a sort of bearded Thomas Bradburne, fond of children. Here he discovered a different supernatural figure from the redoubtable Helm when it blew against the church. Later he was able to decipher the words from St Matthew's Gospel inscribed on the window ('Suffer little children to come unto me, and forbid them not: for of such is the kingdom of God'). Thus he discovered that there was a kingdom other than that of King George V, to which Jesus could guide you, and that he himself, as a young child, would receive a welcome there. But the church contained another Jesus, hanging on the great cross with quatrefoils, suspended above the nave. He did not seem to be suffering greatly, but his wounds were visible, and his position was clearly uncomfortable. In this way John learnt that this person who loves children like him had suffered and died on the cross. Favell Mortimer's book, in which he was learning to read, had pointed out that it was because of him, when he misbehaved, that Jesus died.

Every Sunday John sat with his brothers and sisters on a cushion at the foot of the altar, leaning against the marble pillar eating sweets, or in the front row with his mother, or further back beside Ninnie. The Parkers occupied their privileged pew, and John knew that at the end of the service he would be given a bar of chocolate, always the same black Velma Suchard. The offices were conducted with the solemnity appropriate to the High Anglican rite, with Gregorian chant and coloured vestments. Skirwith was the only parish church of its kind in the county. For the parishioners it was their vicar who conducted the service, but for John it was Papa, who sang in a beautiful voice and, seated in his carved wooden chair, intoned big, complicated words hard to understand. Some unexpected scenes would indelibly mark young John's memory, such as when Father interrupted the middle of a sermon and said: 'Will the little girl in the blue hat please give her attention?' John's childish gaze often no doubt strayed upwards to the ceiling of the church, or towards the still unfinished new chapel of remembrance, or the immense parish Bible with its red leather cover where one could read in golden letters the name of the church and the date, 1859. He would have been frightened or amused by the neo-Gothic sculptures which sprouted from the walls or the pillars, with round chubby faces, virtuous, pensive or grotesque, a veritable bestiary to feed his imagination; or angels playing celestial music, to remind him of another world.

When the service ended, the Bradburne children helped to put away the liturgical vestments, the cassock and the other items which played a role in the service. Then the family made their way back across the graveyard to the vicarage, a mere stone's throw away. At home, as on every other Sunday, Erica read aloud from J. A. Douglas' *The Young Christian's Progress,* an adaptation of Bunyan's *Pilgrim's Progress,* published in 1911. The chapter recounting Jesus' meeting with the leper, and the illustration showing a young Christian carrying a leper on his back, especially filled Mary and John with terror, particularly when Erica told them about what she had seen in India as a child. The children also learnt local religious history: St Paulin on the Fells, St Cuthbert of Lindisfarne, missionary and hermit, who had been ordained bishop against his will.

John looked forward to Christmas and Easter with great excitement, in anticipation of presents. Once, Mary and he resolved to stay awake and surprise Father Christmas. Another year, he was so excited on waking up that he fell out of bed and gashed his forehead. Nothing daunted, he dashed to the sitting room where the presents awaited them, streaming blood. Presents from their parents were modest but always surprising, Erica being naturally inventive, as were presents from Aunt Rat, who always sent them boxes full of Easter eggs in brightly coloured wrappings.

Explosive outbursts

If young John gave no inkling of the spiritual itinerary he would eventually embark on, he nevertheless already showed certain character traits that would blossom later: a sense of humour, natural kindness and generosity. He was 'absent-minded', according to Mary, who went on to add:

> The term 'free spirit' was never more appropriate to anyone than to John. He was never 'run of the mill'. And he devoted himself to things – like home-life, birds, pets and adventurous undertakings.

According to his brother Philip, John had an extremely loving nature, and was ultra-sensitive and easily hurt, but had a violent temper (Philip added: 'more violent than mine'). He also noted that John was not without a certain vanity: 'Pass the jam to the famous and glorious John', he might say, perhaps in imitation of his older brother, given that Philip himself demanded that his younger siblings addressed him as 'lord of all he surveys'.

John was also given to explosive outbursts. When laughed at or teased by his elders he leapt to the attack, and even when very young did not hesitate to attack Philip, four years his senior, who considered him 'a damned nuisance'. Passionate by nature, John loved or hated without nuance. When negative emotions took hold of him he lost all self-control, foaming at the mouth, to the horror of the older brother and sister. In these situations Mary would accompany him for a ride on his bike to calm him down. Another sign of internal turbulence was how quickly he wore out new shoes: he couldn't resist kicking out at stones, and destroyed a pair of shoes in no time.

A single handwritten record of these early years has been preserved, dated 1928, the year that John's childhood at Skirwith came to an end, at seven; six pages of a ragged little notebook, barely legible, a strange blend of precocity and childishness with no reference to religion but which suggests a degree of moral turmoil:

> Good points are fairly frequents in my character but I think that they are more than the bad points

which are comparatively few. I have a fiery temper when it is thoroughly aroused is horrid, and if when I am at the height of my rage someone chooses to annoy me seven more devils, each ten times as bad as the first find room in my heated heart. All this is from no fault of my parents bringing up and training of me. Sometimes I may have nothing to do, or shall I say had a craze for looking like a 'shopwalker' a favorite term used by mother or as termed by my indulgent parent father 'an undertaker's assistant'. That is to say I 'smarmed' my hair down with revolting Woolworth's hair oil, and I took great care of my appearance.

Through the trees in the garden the children could see the graveyard, and watching burials gave them an awareness of death. John liked to frighten himself with tales of ghosts and gypsies, and sometimes he really was afraid – of the dark, of death. But mostly his early childhood was happy and contemplative. He remained profoundly attached to these early years for the rest of his life, and convinced himself that he was predestined to be born in Skirwith, between Eden and the Cross, and to live his early years there.

Chapter 2

The Fall into Time, 1929–1939

Having enjoyed the rudiments
Of marvel-archery
I went to the schools: Cumberland's, Kent's
And Norfolk's ... heavily –
I hated going back to school
Until I was thirteen.
(*A Game of Buried Names*, 1978)

The years 1928 to 1933 are the most obscure in John's life. In 1929 he joined Philip and Mary at Seascale, some 60 miles to the west of Skirwith. The arrival of the railway had transformed this old port into a popular seaside resort. The headmaster of its school was Frank Burnett, an Oxford graduate with pronounced modern ideas, who even dispensed the rudiments of sexual education, but imposed a regime where discipline was strict.

School fees at this time accounted for almost a third of the Reverend Bradburne's income. In common with 40 or so other boarders, John studied mathematics, English and history; science classes were non-existent. Even though accompanied by his brother, departure for school was always a most traumatic occasion for John, free-spirited and untamed as he was. On arrival at the school, for the first few days he would spend hours next to the fireplace, head in hands, and cried himself to sleep every night. He missed Skirwith terribly, and made no secret of it. Predictably he was jeered and bullied as a result, and Rachel Burnett, the headmaster's daughter, became his tormentor. To get himself expelled, John tried to shock his teacher Miss Jackson by resorting to all his 'naughty language – some of it really advanced' (*Letter to mother*, 30 January 1941), but to no avail. His only solace was the holidays and return to the vicarage, where he resumed his games where he had left off, and became happy again for the duration. But when the new term loomed he would succumb to fits of rage; Philip recalled that 'he had never seen someone cry so heartrendingly as John when it was time to return to school'.

In the autumn of 1929 Thomas Bradburne was offered a parish, by his old Cambridge college, at Tilney All Saints in Norfolk, with an annual living of £350 and five acres of land. His youngest child, Michael – nicknamed Lamp Post by his brother – was born there in 1931. John found his new environment depressingly featureless, with fields of cereal and beetroot stretching as far as the eye could see. The village itself was situated in the heart of loamy and fertile fenlands, which had gradually been reclaimed from the sea over the centuries. A little more than four miles from King's Lynn, Tilney was home to 600 inhabitants and eight large landowners, including the Hickmans on Islington estate, and Sir Richard Bragge, a veteran of the Boer Wars. It lacked everything that was dear to John's heart, except when summer brought the countryside to life, and later the harvest turned it to gold and the laden carts brought home the mown hay.

Tilney is famous for its grave of the Saxon giant Thomas Hyckathrift, reputed to have slain a local ogre, and to have followed Richard the Lionheart on his Crusade. The oldest parts of the church went back to the eleventh-century and could accommodate 300 parishioners (the Reverend Bradburne's congregation fell far short of this number), but here the stained-glass windows depicted not Jesus and the little children but dead soldiers from the recent war. The vicarage had at one time been the scene of the murder of a young girl, and a hanging from the rafters of the kitchen ceiling. The popular press reported stories of haunted vicarages, especially at Borley ('the most haunted house in England') and at Stowmarket in neighbouring counties (Agatha Christie published her *Murder at the Vicarage* in 1930 and Dorothy Sayers her *Nine Tailors* in 1934). The children convinced themselves that their house was haunted too. For these and other reasons, including his incarceration at Seascale, far from his family, John's unhappiness continued unabated:

> Lyrical Fall below the Fells! then slid
> Suddenly all that background into Fen...
> (*The Pen of Peter Pan*, 1974)

> None held out hatred more towards the sea
> However it might ripple to beguile
> Than, exile by one hundred miles times three,
> Me in an eight-year-old unmoulded style;
> Then sea I would escape and seascape shun
> Being at Seascale in West Cumberland
> So far away from holiday and fun.
> (*Zebulon's Pendulum*, 1971)

Highly strung and difficult, he was still liable at any moment to outbursts of uncontrolled tantrums. But around this time he began to develop a talent for mimicry, inherited from his mother, which was a source of great amusement in the family, and music sessions continued to give him pleasure. And he discovered, not far from Tilney, a fragment of his lost paradise: Islington. A colony of grey herons had nested there in an acre of oak trees, and John spent his summer holidays bird watching with his brother Philip, who recalled: 'One day, John – only eight years old, said to me: "Doesn't it fill you with a sort of longing?"'John looked back fondly on Islington in later life:

> Else it is greed, for money and for land,
> That makes a desert of God's wide wild Eden;
> When I was young a Heronry did stand
> With three-score nests and ten twixt earth and
> heaven:
> It stood in Norfolk near King's Lynn until
> Cut down to grow potatoes: growing still?
> (*Paradise Tossed Aside: Incipit Lamentatio...* 1978)

John was nine when his father switched his sons from Seascale to the King's School at Ely, some 25 miles to the south of Tilney. Founded in 970, and nowadays housed in a cluster of medieval buildings in the shadow of the cathedral, King's proudly proclaimed itself one of the oldest schools in the world, and was just as proud of its choir. John developed his singing voice at King's, but seemed if anything even unhappier than he had been at Seascale. He ate little and dreamt of escape. However, the school reports signed by the Headmaster, T. J. Kirkland, from September 1930 to April 1933, recorded respectable marks and all- round integration:

> He is showing a marked improvement in all his work... His Divinity is always good, and he is working steadily and conscientiously... He is a well-mannered, attentive boy, always neat in his appearance, and most anxious to please. He is showing promise of good work in the future.

Suddenly, in the spring of 1933, John ran away from school and walked the 25 miles home! He did not return to Ely.

Kent and Norfolk

How was one to deal with this 12-year-old tearaway? The Reverend Bradburne decided to send his son to a 'crammers' school, which would hopefully prepare him for entrance to a public school. Laurence Sargent, an acquaintance of the family, agreed to take him at Up Pantiles, of which he was the headmaster, in Thanet on the outskirts of the Victorian seaside resort of Westgate-on-Sea. Sargent was a retired major and a member of the Society for the Promotion of Roman Studies, a passion which he hoped to finance from the proceeds of the school. Here John seemed to fit in better, and the headmaster held out some hope to the vicar of John gaining a scholarship, even though he was ranked far below average for his age. It was not to be, and John shone only by his mediocrity: 'On that of Thanet made no crammer glad' (*Balladey School Report*, 1974). But he did make some friends, including Robin Oates, a relative of the explorer of the Zambezi River, who told him tales of far-off southern Africa. If he received any religious instruction at Thanet, he never afterwards spoke about it.

Whether because of the haunted house or the petty snobbery of the locals, none of the Bradburnes liked Tilney, and in 1933 Thomas moved to Cawston parish, still in Norfolk, 40 miles east of Tilney. Here John rediscovered somewhat more of the nature that he loved. Although flat – relieved only by church spires – Cawston abounded in fields, woodlands and hedgerows, and at the time had a population of a thousand. A royal manor was recorded here at the

time of the Norman conquest, and the village had achieved fame
of sorts on two occasions: firstly by its association with Richard
Pole, Chancellor to Richard II, who built St Agnes' Church, and
again in the eighteenth-century, thanks to the wool from its black
sheep and its annual fair. But in recent years it had become a
sleepy backwater, not so different from the country at large where,
despite the gathering storm, inertia and pacifism held sway: in 1938
the Munich Agreement was widely welcomed and Chamberlain
proclaimed 'Peace in our time'.

St Agnes' Church was a vast edifice whose 150-foot spire
dominated the countryside. Its architecture was Gothic, and
attracted lovers of beauty by its wooden vaults, its luminosity,
its sculptures and the inscriptions recording popular wisdom
down through the ages which decorated its walls, and its lofty
fifteenth-century chancel. Apart from St Agnes', there were two
Nonconformist chapels, and a strong Nonconformist presence in
the region, which accounted for half of the baptisms. In contrast,
Catholics were here the least numerous in all England, at one per
cent of the local population.

The vicarage was not far from the church. The old two-storey
house was covered in ivy, and in the garden there were abundant
shrubs, which appealed greatly to John. Thomas Bradburne planted
flowerbeds and flowerbanks, and built a pond, and was surprised
to see his son spending up to three hours at a time gazing idly at
the water and the calm movements of the fish below the surface.
Even if he still yearned for Skirwith and seemed reluctant to grow
up, he loved Cawston and rediscovered there his love of play. One
day he would write to his sister Mary:

> You had a Doll's House, I'd a Noah's Ark
> And both of us played Ghosts when it was dark.
> (*In loving memory of lawns and shrubberies*, 1978)

Mrs Bradburne was helped with the housework by Edith, the cook,
and Mrs Burke and her daughter Gladys. All hands were required
because the vicarage was large, and being nearer to London it often
played host to uncles, aunts and cousins. While the vicar spent his

time in the garden, Erica received and returned invitations to the lord of the manor, Herbert McDougall, among others.

Thomas Bradburne carried out his duties with conscientious zeal. Even though he was a ritualist, he was nevertheless a stickler for accuracy and truth, even at the risk of confusing his congregation, as John later recalled:

> My father, Rector of a Norfolk village,
> Scanning a wonted prayer at Matins read
> One time at least considered it a pillage
> Upon the truth to say it as 'tis said;
> 'Lord, who to the beginning of this day
> Hast safely brought us', read nigh twelve o'clock
> Seemed once to him a dunceish thing to say
> So said he 'to the Middle' ... shook the flock!
> Unless they were asleep and dreaming that
> The beef was over-roasting and the fire
> Was likely to ignite the habitat
> But, as to that, no matter to enquire:
> My mother well remembers, anyway,
> His saying 'To the Middle of this day'!
> (*Day-Mattins*, 1974)

On top of his normal round of duties, the vicar celebrated the silver jubilee of George V in May 1935 with a religious service, festivities and various sporting events. Mrs Bradburne presented every child in the village with a silver goblet. The King died the following year, and the shock waves caused by the abdication crisis were gradually stilled in the early months of the reign of the stuttering and dutiful new King George VI. His coronation provided the occasion of another celebration at Cawston, with a religious service, a parade and tuba fanfare which had been rehearsed at the Bell Inn, a display featuring local dances, a coronation cup for the children and a meat dish and pint of beer for the parents. ('Will Grown-ups kindly bring a knife and fork' said the invitation card.) At 7 o'clock in the evening, silence descended as everybody listened to the new King's hesitant speech, and the evening came to a close with prize-giving, followed by a ball.

Gresham's School

In 1934 John was 13 years old. His clear, calm voice was deceptively mature: he had still not gained control of his violent outbursts. At the end of the summer holidays he became a boarder at Gresham's School in Holt. A generous friend of the family had offered to pay the school fees (which at £166 in 1938 were far beyond the pocket of the Bradburnes). Holt was about a 12-mile cycle ride from Cawston across fields and country lanes for John on his Raleigh bike. He was to spend five years there and, for the first time, he seemed to settle down.

Gresham's was run on the 'house' system, each house having its own living quarters. Intended to recreate a family atmosphere, the house offered a stable emotional and social environment, where the boys could mix freely in a relaxed and harmonious atmosphere. Each house had its own housemaster, but responsibility was gradually handed over to the boys as they progressed from year to year. House selection was random, and John, along with another 50 boys, was assigned to Farfield, a large red-brick pile built in 1911, whose badge was the Owl of Minerva. His housemaster was G. R. Thompson, a brilliant mathematician of undistinguished appearance, compensated for by his cheerful buxom Irish wife. In 1936, he was succeeded by another mathematician, Bruce Douglas, nicknamed 'the Bird' by the boys. Douglas was a veteran of the trenches, good at sport, and something of a philosopher:

> My housemaster once said to me
> In gambolling days so light and free –
> 'Get wisdom, the most precious thing':
> ('Twas long ere I besought the King).
> (*Ut Unum Sint*, 1956, stanza 876)

Farfield House could boast some distinguished past pupils, such as Benjamin Britten and W. H. Auden. This caused John some pride, and he later ironically recalled:

> Benjamin Britten, Wystan Auden, me
> And other mummers, number mongst her goods
> She may and she is fruitful even though

> She writes my name in golden letters not!
> (*Alma Mater*, 1969)

Today, he is present in the 'Hall of Fame' of the monograph on Gresham's: Steve Benson's *I will Plant Me a Tree: An Illustrated History of Gresham's School*.

John was happy at Farfield. He was popular, became friends with Tony Foster and other boys, and impressed his classmates by mimicking the teachers, which earned him the nickname 'Take-off'. He couldn't resist telling jokes, but these were never malicious, according to another boy, Michael Stern, who later also went to Southern Africa and set up a multi-racial school. His keen insight and sense of the ridiculous explain his talent for mimicry: he unfailingly saw the funny side of situations and people, and when the going got tough this talent acted as a bulwark against despair and despondency. To his peers he seemed cheerful and easygoing.

The teaching staff included some formidable characters, with only two women, one of whom, Miss Bristow, taught arts and crafts. But women were by no means absent from the school, including the wives and daughters of the masters, as well as non-teaching staff. Certain poetic efforts of John at the time suggest an awakening of interest in girls. He alludes frankly to early exploits, including pursuing a staff member through the laundry in the hope of a kiss:

> But when I went to Holt in Norfolk, ah,
> Love for a Janet (or, a matron) had
> Been no delight if unrequited; mad
> For joy of it!
> (*Balladey School Reports*, 1974)

Cultivating his oddities: Shakespeare, trees and bugles

John's record as a student at Gresham's was undistinguished, even if the school is now proud to boast of him as a past pupil. He won no prizes, wrote for no school magazine, and his examination results were at best mediocre.

> I'll never be a scholar, Lord,
> So slow am I to learn.
> (*School*, 1949)

But he developed a passion for literature, above all Shakespeare, who became a lifelong companion: numerous Shakespearian references are to be found in the poems. Dozens of these poems were devoted to the 'Baconian Theory' which John inherited from his father ('Did Sir Francis Bacon write Shakespeare's plays?'). His acquaintance with Shakespeare served him well in school exams. He also read widely in medieval and Tudor literature, and had a special affinity for the troubadours, the madrigalists and Shakespeare's clowns. He imagined himself as a knight, and developed a passion for heraldry. He also tried his hand at writing poetry of his own, and in an interview 30 years later he was able to quote a quatrain he wrote at Gresham's, in which wordplay and multiple punning abound:

> When Bluff King Hal discovered that the Pope
> Pronounced him as a limb without a hope,
> 'I'll be supreme (quoth he), betroth more wives
> To keep me warm while Reformation thrives'...
> (Then trundled off and had a game of fives).

His love for Shakespeare also led to a passion for theatre. In common with the other houses, Farfield held its annual field day, when students presented selections from plays, as well as sketches and various musical offerings. Every year the school put on an open-air production of a Shakespeare play, attended by parents, Shakespeare lovers and invited journalists. Auden first drew attention as an actor, and many budding theatrical careers date from this period at Gresham's, including Peter Brook and Michael Aldridge, who distinguished himself here in the role of Hamlet in 1937, and later as Othello, gaining honourable critical mention in *The Times*. In 1939 *The Night of Kings* was played to acclaim, and was often cited as a highlight in the memoirs of contemporaries such as Ben Travers. John got supporting roles in these plays, as well as in modern plays like *Journey's End* by R. C. Sherriff (the author of *Goodbye, Mr Chips*):

> When I was but a boy at school
> Amidst a leafy wood
> I played in Shakespeare like a fool
> At any part I could.

> Deaf-Mute I took in Hamlet once
> And once in Henry Five
> A soldier's part befell the dunce
> Inane as aught alive.
>
> Twelfth Night bestowed Antonio
> On one who'd never been
> To sea, to sea, so let me flow
> With MARIA, SEAS, The Queen!
> (*Regina Reginarum*, 1978)

Music was also one of John's passions, and he found an exceptional teacher in Walter Greatorex, composer of *Woodlands*, who according to Auden played the organ better than Albert Schweitzer. 'Gog' or 'Greatox' (as Greatorex was called) was at the time at the pinnacle of his creativity, but was also of a sensitive disposition, and homesick or otherwise unhappy pupils sought him out as a confidant:

> In music-lesson none too keen
> I talked the time away when able:
> My master said – 'You should have been
> A bricklayer on the Tower of Babel'!
> (*Ut Unum Sint*, 1956, stanza 976)

John sang as a tenor in the school choir – his only prize at school was as a member of the choir. He also learnt to play a number of wind instruments, including the bugle, the clarinet and the recorder. With his friend Tony Foster he became a member of the OTC (Officer Training Corps) band, he as bugler, Tony on drums. He was not particularly good at the clarinet, but playing it gave him, and others, great pleasure, and the recorder, like Shakespeare, was to become a lifelong companion. At Gresham's he picked up the essentials of his musical culture, up to then limited to the record collection at the vicarage and the liturgical music of Sunday church services. The choir had its Renaissance and Baroque repertory, and John became an admirer of Gregorian chant, as also of Dowland, Tallis, Byrd, Morley and Purcell. John's favourites were Bach and, among the moderns, Brahms. Back home in Cawston he often sang with his sister Mary, or sought out places where he could allow the bugle its full resonance:

> The echoes came from Cawston Tower oft
> On summer evenings when a certain fool
> Practiced his silver bugle which, but soft,
> Should have been left behind, resigned at school.
> (*The Last Post*, 1977)

He occasionally slipped in to St Agnes' to play the organ, even though he was a less gifted player than Philip.

Sport had by this time become a national religion in England and already in 1923, 200,000 spectators had converged on Wembley stadium for the first FA Cup Final. Sport played an important role at Gresham's, but less so than in some other public schools. John played rugby, hockey and cricket, once threatening the life of Bruce Douglas with an erratic bowl. His sporting talents were modest, and he failed to make it to any of the numerous school teams, though he did manage to tog out for Farfield in the inter-House Rugby league. He also took archery lessons:

> It really felt the decent thing
> To bear a bow, rare like a King!
> The arrows went their chosen way
> Wherein my grin had little say.
> (*Archery*, 1971)

For a while he tried his hand at falconry, but the falcon escaped, never to be seen again. Later he trained some mynah birds, but these too disappeared without trace.

His favourite diversion remained tree climbing. He spent hours perched in a tree, more interested in birdwatching than in the cricket matches being played out below, like Calvino's Cosimo Piovasco di Rondò in *Il Barone Rampante* ('The Baron in the Trees'), not published until 20 years after John had set the example! Most of the poems about Gresham's or Cawston evoke this singular passion for tree climbing. Often accompanied by his friend Tony, he would head for the Monarch, a magnificent 300-ft high pine tree in the wood half-a-mile from the school:

The tallest tree we called The Monarch, and
From ninety-seven feet I Norfolk scanned...
I'd sit there with a friend, we'd perch for hours,
Swaying as brothers, weighing what we thought
Of wasting summertime sublime and powers
Of climbing forearm on that static Sport
Called Cricket!
(*Alma Mater,* 1969)

Cawston I remember well –
Laburnum, lilac, yew,
And golden hours in copper-beech
With hayricks in the view.
(*Ut Unum Sint,* 1956, stanza 960)

The passion was not without its risks. Fifteen years earlier a boy at the school had died when he fell from a tree, inspiring one of Auden's earliest poems. But John was fearless, even though his favourite tree was by no means an easy climb.

Life for John seemed to consist of sitting at the top of the Monarch, or the purple beech at Cawston, where he often dragged his sister Mary (who had no head for heights herself). This passion for trees astonished both his schoolmates and his family (John had 'a phenomenal head for heights' and was an 'inveterate tree-climber' according to Mary), and earned him the nickname *Hornbeam*. Why Hornbeam? The origin of the name is explained in a John Bradburne Memorial Society Newsletter (Winter 2003):

> Once as John and his sister Mary stood on a high grassy slope leading down to a stream bordered on one side by trees, she asked: 'What are those trees called, John?' He replied 'I think they are hor..hor.. hor.....' And as he slid down the slope doubling with mirth... 'Hornbeam!' he cried. Ever after, Hornbeam stuck as a nickname for John.

Jack Dunn has suggested another origin of the nickname, going back to when John was working as a forester (Newsletter, Summer 2000):

> He said that he was carrying a log out of the woods
> and he asked what sort of timber it was. On being
> told it was hornbeam, he repeated the word,
> tripping and falling as he did so, so that what
> came out of his mouth was a rather shrill and long
> drawn out 'Hornbeam', to the merriment of all
> within hearing distance. And so he was stuck with
> that nickname, amongst the woodsmen anyway.

The two versions are not contradictory.

John discovered that trees were not deserts, but protectors
of a variety of wildlife, and friends to man. It was above all the
fascination for heights and the views from the top which urged
him on, as well as the climb itself, whether at Cawston or its
neighbourhood, not only in trees but also in the churches, with
their immense spires, or on the rooftops, as on Cross Fell in earlier
days in Skirwith. One day while Mrs Bradburne and Mary were
arranging flowers in the church they observed John arrive and
proceed to climb the narrow rood screen, to a height of 15 feet
from the ground. Terrified ('We halted our breath,' wrote Mary),
they scarcely dared to breathe as the boy made his way, heedless of
any danger, across the narrow ledge before making his way back to
earth at the other side. At other times he would take a stroll along
the roof of the church, or the nearby one in Pole:

> One evening, at the twilight hour
> Of summer harvest-day,
> Some folk perceived me on that roof
> And almost ran away!
>
> For (as my sister then observed)
> They thought I was a ghost:
> (But no, my dears, a goblin-boy,
> And most substantial, most!).
> (*Ut Unum Sint*, 1956, stanzas 962-3)

> Some people dream they fly like doves and larks
> And even that they soar as eagles can,
> One Daedelus and Icarus remarks

As something falling short of thoughtful plan;
I clapped my wings at least three times a year
Whilst fast asleep with pigeons from the tower
Of London not but Cawston, to be clear
That stands in Norfolk, rises like a Power;
I lit upon the pantiles of the stable
And still I'll sit roucouling on the roof
And I shall cane you if you are unable
To stop yourself from asking me for proof:
Faith is the substance of things hoped-for and
The evidence of things unseen at hand.
(*Ibid: I bid for it,* 1978)

At Gresham's the boarders were allowed out on Sundays after morning chapel, on condition that they reported back at teatime for evening service, but John often breached the curfew. The region was covered in maritime pine trees and other conifers, and its invigorating climate made it a natural location for the nearby sanatorium at Kelling. To the west the wooded hills of Spout provided ideal walking conditions along its many grassy trails. To the east he was attracted by the medieval ruins of Baconsthorpe Castle, where he scribbled on the outer walls light-hearted verses, one of which evoked once again his passion for trees:

Alas, alack, I am undone,
I want to eat a currant-bun;
But God is good,
He told me so,
The trees are swaying to and fro.
(*Excelsior,* 1971)

(They have of course long disappeared from the wall. Later, John gave a Eucharistic meaning to the quatrain.)

For longer walks there was the sea coast. The ancient ports of Holt, Cley-next-the-Sea and Wells-next-the-Sea are now landlocked, but immense salty marshland stretches as far as the sea. Over this region from time immemorial the wind has blown in gusts across the sea lavender, piling up cloud banks along the coast, a refuge for herons and white seagulls. Periwinkle gatherers, running to escape the advancing tide, mark the only visible signs of human presence. In the company of Mary or some schoolmate, John sometimes stopped in one or other of these villages to drink a glass of cider or play the organ in the local church. Later they would go for a swim, but John preferred to spend the long afternoons birdwatching or exploring the woods. He had a somewhat reckless taste for adventure: one day he threw a clod of mud at a bull to see whether it would make him charge, like he himself used to do from under the table at Skirwith. He escaped with his life after a hectic flight across a field, scrambling across a fence at the point of being gored by the enraged beast!

During the holidays John invited two friends from Gresham's to join him on the Broads. Famous for its rivers and canals, the region boasts nearly 125 miles of navigable waterway and more than 60 lakes – a paradise for pleasure boats and canoes, and a natural reserve of wild fowl, dragonflies and fish. The boys glided along the waters, observing the birds, water lilies and insects. On one occasion, having consumed too much cider on a visit to a pub, John presumed on the way back to give a lesson on how to crew a university eight, losing the oars in the process, necessitating a late-night search in the murky water with the aid of a torch.

There were also family visits. John's godmother Mary Comber was matron at the Dragon School in Oxford, which was under the aegis of the Lynam dynasty, who had managed it for half a century. John went to spend a few days at the school, and on Sunday was invited to the headmaster's table for lunch. Any other boy might have felt intimidated in the presence of a man regarded as one of the two or three most eminent figures in British education, but not John. When Mrs Lynam (nicknamed 'Mrs Hum' by John and his sister) put the Sunday roast on the table he exclaimed: 'I know what's coming next: fruit salad and custard!' As silence descended on the table, and Mrs Hum's face assumed a wrathful expression, John tactfully added: 'But so delicious', thereby flattering Mrs Lynam in her threefold pride as cook, Englishwoman and traditionalist – whereupon she congratulated the young visitor.

Like many public schools, Gresham's boasted an Officers Training Corps (OTC), suppliers to the officer class since 1908. The institution had found Gresham's to be a fertile recruiting ground, and the school was proud to have fostered some notable military vocations. His housemaster Douglas himself took charge of the OTC and made a significant contribution from his experience of service in the Great War. But in the pacifist thirties, enthusiasm for the OTC had waned somewhat. John quickly found here his own cosy niche:

> I joined perforce the O.T.C.
> But, being a clown at musketry,
> Soon took to higher strategy
> By bugling for His Majesty.
> (*Ut Unum Sint*, 1956, stanza 877)

The young recruits wore uniform and every weekend engaged in basic training, in which parade-ground drill and camping played an important role. Strategic and tactical studies as such had little place in a regime focussed mainly on discipline. An examination took place at the end of the training period. Though optional, it could open the door to a military career.

The crossroads

As for religion, at Farfield house students attended evening prayer organised by the prefects, which comprised hymns, readings and prayers, ending with the ritual 'Goodnight, boys', and boys present at the weekend were obliged to attend morning and evening prayers on Sunday. Religious instruction classes were dispensed, and there was even a resident chaplain, the Reverend E. H. Habershon, who remained at the school until 1946, though he does not merit mention in the otherwise very comprehensive *History of Gresham's*. As for the chapel, rebuilt between 1912 and 1916, Sunday attendance was compulsory, but by the time John arrived at Gresham's the building was in a dilapidated state and had to be shut down for repairs, which seemed to drag on forever. Religion was certainly a feature of the school, but it was mainly preoccupied with moral conduct, rather than Christianity as such. Many pupils drifted away from Christianity at Gresham's, an example being Auden, who had been a devout, even strait-laced boy: at Gresham's he discovered Freud and Marx, and turned his back on his faith. While such was not the case with John, he gave no sign of regarding faith as a personal matter.

John left Gresham's with an A rating, and though he had seemed destined to go up to Oxford, he sat for and passed the entrance examination to Sandhurst in June 1939. By this time, at the age of 18, he had passed through adolescence as if without noticing it. He later used the word 'mad' to describe himself at this stage of his life, but everything suggests that Gresham's was for him part of a maturing process. The emotionally unstable child had become a young man, no doubt different from others and living in his own world, but one who had embraced his own eccentric ways. After 1935 he had learnt to curb his impulsiveness and his angry outbursts. Moreover, living in the treetops did not prevent him from developing his own sense of responsibility, and he became a sub-prefect in his last year at school.

His new-found self-mastery even took the form of arrogance, perhaps sharpened by a certain jealousy towards his older brother, now like their father before him a student at Cambridge. Philip was hard-working, conscientious and demanding (he had taught himself Arabic). He also played the organ in church, and when his younger siblings accompanied him on outings they were obliged to labour over the bellows. But Philip was very conscious of what constituted 'good form' and was not a 'free spirit' like his brother, and was embarrassed by what he considered the social failure of his father. John admired and envied his brother but gradually grew away from him, perhaps out of a sense of inadequacy. Mary wrote to Philip: 'He was very envious of your height, good looks and social aplomb, always denigrating his own physical defects (short legs, long body).' At home in the vicarage both brothers seemed determined to have the last word, and rows were frequent, with Erica and Mary often obliged to restore calm. John had a simple method of driving home his point: he would keep repeating it *ad nauseam*, whether the discussion was about music or history. Though a bad loser, he was often right, backing up his arguments from an amazingly well-stocked memory. However, though he aspired to perfection in all things, he lacked the critical spirit, and beneath the bluster he was tortured by a great fear, the fear of death:

I knew such odd and morbid fear
Of death that till my nineteenth year
Wary before I went to bed
Nearly each night for hidden dead
Thereunder I would look, for bones,
Hideous forms decayed, lest groans
In deep of night from sleep might wake
Suddenly me who then might shake
Terror-struck, trembling swell the moans
O necromantic fool! and why?
Only because not death did die.
(*To the Warworn School*, no date)

In the summer of 1939 John found himself at a crossroads. Given his independence of mind, his absence of ambition, his love of trees, of birds, of nature, of Shakespeare and of music, it would have been difficult to predict what the future held for him. Climbing trees doesn't get anyone a job, though the idea of actually looking for one was foreign to him. But was it not the case that he was already on his way, given that he had been offered a cadetship at Sandhurst, where officers were moulded like peas in a pod?

Chapter 3

A Reluctant Hero, 1939–1945

Burma and Malaya are
Sung enough by Public Bar,
Browsed upon by chimney-corner.
(*Furthermore*, 1971)

Events were about to take a new turn. On September 3rd 1939
Britain declared war on Germany. Two of the first measures to
follow would affect John: conscription, and the closing down of
Sandhurst for the duration of the war. It remained to him to await
his call-up. In the meantime he set out for Twyford with Stephen
King, a friend of his brother Philip, with whom he had formed a
bond. They sold seeds in this horticultural village on the banks
of the Thames, and spent their free time walking and listening to
music: Byrd, Bach, lots of Brahms, Delius and Vaughan Williams:

I stretched my legs in Berkshire
From Reading to the brink
Of writing poems full of fire
On what I could not think:
Is it so hard to be a bard?
(*Strolling*, 1972)

The seeds sprouted and the months passed. On the BBC, on May
13th 1940, Churchill broadcast his 'blood, toil, tears and sweat'
speech; on the 24th, the British army was encircled and forced to
take to the sea at Dunkirk. On June 24th Britain found itself alone
face to face with Hitler and John received his call-up to an OCTU
(Officer Cadet Training Unit):

They made me a lance-corporal and crowned
My ignorance by sending me from Reading

To something called an OCTU which was found
On Salisbury Plain, at Bulford – Deadening!
(*Military Memoirs,* 1979)

He began four months of training in August, shortly after a visit to the camp by George VI. He did not take kindly to the constraints of military routine, and amused himself in horseplay and making friends with his young fellow officers. The British army was in no shape for combat after the long interlude from 1918 to 1939, and John learnt nothing about warfare, nor about the men he would be called upon to command. At weekends he left the camp to join up with Stephen King, and together they listened over and over again to Bach's suite in C minor until the record eventually became inaudible.

On December 20th 1940 John received his commission as second lieutenant, almost at the same time as his brother. They were both posted, at their own request, to the Indian Army, in the country of their mother's birth, and set off to board ship at Liverpool. However, their convoy was not ready to sail, so they invited themselves to stay with Frank Burnett at Seascale, where their sister had become a teacher at her old school. Philip delivered a learned discourse on Persia to the children at the school, but John declined to offer his services on the grounds that 'little girls never were my cup of tea to the extent that they are Philip's!', as he wrote to their parents. The older ones, on the contrary, had begun to interest him more and more, beginning with Rachel Burnett – the former tomboy having metamorphosed into a delightful teenager – whose sense of humour had much in common with his own ('What funny birds frogs are'). The pair went on long cycle trips together, and on one occasion John climbed to the top of a beech tree for her benefit, 'just to be a boy...' in Rachel's eyes. Back in Liverpool the brothers checked into the Adelphi Hotel to await embarcation – a pair of 'chocolate soldiers', as John wrote in a letter home (30 January 1941), with little military bearing, and with eyes rather for the girls.

With the Gurkhas

At the beginning of February 1941, the two brothers boarded SS *Mulberra* along with a group of 30 or so newly made officers. John looked dashing in his army hat, very much the fresh-faced 20-year-old. They shared a cabin, sunbathed, learnt some rudiments of Urdu, and boldly flirted with any single young woman who happened to be on board. According to Philip, religious thoughts seemed to be the last things on his younger brother's mind, who was more inclined to play cocky rooster, amusing himself at the expense of his fellow passengers, to such an extent that he felt obliged to rein his younger brother in. In fact John was the source of a falling out which led to the formation of two opposing groups among the young officers aboard the *Mulberra*, who refused to speak to each other.

Their ship was part of a convoy which, to steer clear of German U boats, sailed along the coast of Iceland and Nova Scotia before heading south to Cabo Verde and on to Freetown and the Cape. John later wrote:

> I'd hated sight of sea because
> No green tree upon it was.
> (*Maritime Notes*, 1971)

But he enjoyed the stop-offs, which were his first contacts with Africa.

On April 15th *SS Mulberra* finally docked at Bombay. The shock of the Orient bewildered John, who was overcome by the smells, the noises, the crowds and the extreme poverty. Here he discovered for the first time that people in other places of the world related differently to time and existence. Philip and he soon left for the suburb of Hyderabad, the great metropolis on the Deccan plateau. Philip was posted to the 27th infantry brigade headed for the Middle East, and John to the 28th, in the 2nd battalion of the 9th Gurkha regiment (2/9th). The brothers would not see each other again for the rest of the war. John wrote to his mother on April 27th:

> India is a weird country – the people give me the
> impression of being passively miserable, and they
> just seem to exist without any particular love or
> interest in anything. Their predominant quality
> seems to be of absolute refusal to do anything for

nothing. But the East is interesting, even if it isn't alluring.

The Indian Army was made up of indigenous regiments commanded by British officers, and since 1903 had been one of the two components of the British Army in India (the British Indian Army comprising regiments drawn from the home country). Its 200,000 men in 1939 would soon swell to almost a million, a third of whom would be sent to serve in North Africa, the Middle East and Malaya, another third remaining in situ, and a final third still in training. Many of its officers were colonials (tea planters or engineers), the young British officers were products of OCTUs, while the rank and file (in Gurkha regiments) were Nepalese. John got to know the Nepalese Gurkhas, often described as 'the finest soldiers in the world', 'the gentlemen from the mountains', but also 'the world's most feared soldiers', who formed the backbone of the Indian Army. He was deeply impressed by these faithful men, and enjoyed playing basketball with them, despite the difference in height. While he got on well with them, they soon found his ways strange, when, at every opportunity, he went tree climbing and, having got to the top, spent long hours playing his recorder. Down on the ground the Gurkhas were amused and whispered to each other (in Nepalese) about the strange Englishman whose behaviour was not of the kind expected of a British officer. No one, however, took any notice of his flirtatious way with the ladies.

The Malayan Campaign

John was assigned to command a mortar platoon, and received training in the use of artillery. But his stay in India was short-lived and, in August, he was sent to Bombay, from where he sailed on the 22nd for Malaya. On September 3rd the 750 men of 2/9th Gurkha, including his company commanded by James Hart, a planter from Assam, disembarked at Port Sweetenham, and set out immediately for Taiping, 125 miles to the north. John was smitten by the jungle landscapes of 'palms and aphrodisiac', and wrote to his family (11 October 1941) that Malaya was 'one of God's own countries with one of the Devil's own climates... We are surrounded by high hills, covered in equatorial forest. Colours are really vivid... All in all, I like it very much, ten times as much as India.'

Lt Colonel Ray Selby, head of the battalion, took charge of training – marches through the jungle, and familiarisation with living conditions in the region. Like the other young British officers, John was a slow learner when it came to grasping Gurkhali, to the amusement of the Gurkhas. Some of them couldn't even distinguish between the kitchen knife and the famous kukri. Side by side with his men, John made his way upstream along riverbeds clutching his bayonet, chopping a path through dense vegetation in burning heat, or crossing rubber plantations where European planters lived with no contact with the native population. He crawled on all fours through impenetrable mangroves and jungle forests where the sun never reached the ground, and which were home to wild animals – tigers, leopards and panthers (familiar from the *Boy's Own* of his youth, though he only rarely caught a glimpse of them), but also gibbons, callaos, fairytale birds with fabulous plumage, cicadas and butterflies.

October passed, then November, without the British making any effort to take defensive measures against an impending Japanese threat, in which their superior officers still didn't believe. Thus, when in the course of an exercise, 2/9th Gurkhas, acting as the enemy, easily crossed through a plantation and took up position three miles behind 'the front line', the experts declared the manoeuvre to be 'totally unrealistic'. When a Singapore newspaper reported on Japanese troop movements, it found itself rapped on the knuckles for publishing 'alarmist' news. And when an expert arrived from London to impress on the top brass the strength of the Japanese army he was accused of 'defeatism'. Worse, when warned of the imminence of a Japanese attack, the chiefs-of-staff decided to make limited defensive steps so as not to appear too strong, thereby missing an opportunity to impress the enemy at little cost. This wilful blindness would in due course leave John furious.

On their side, the Japanese continued to build up their offensive. Conscious of the numerical superiority of the British, as well as their superior fire and naval power, they were relying on their planes and their tanks. Their troops had experienced tropical warfare in China, and would be backed up by aircraft taking off

from newly built airstrips in occupied Indochina. At the beginning
of December 1941 two Japanese convoys sailed from the Chinese
port of Samah, heading south towards Singora in Siam and from
Kota Bharu in the north-west of Malaya. Bad weather and poor
visibility gave them cover from British reconnaissance aircraft. On
the 8th, two hours before Pearl Harbour, the 28th Japanese division
disembarked at Kota Bharu, and the majority of British aircraft
were destroyed on the ground. Despite ten-foot-high waves, the
landing was a success. The same night an armoured detachment led
by Colonel Saeki headed south from Singora towards north-west
Malaya, sweeping aside British defences and advancing six miles.
On the 10th the *Prince of Wales,* pride of the British Navy, was sunk
by Japanese air attack. In the space of two days the British had lost
almost their entire air force and navy in Malaya. Having witnessed
the rout of the Indians guarding the Siamese frontier, Colonel Tsuji,
commander of Japanese strategy, decided on a lightning offensive.
By the 10th the Japanese had nearly reached Jitra, some 20 miles
south of the border.

John was discreet about his involvement in this campaign, and
his later campaign in Burma. He generally refused to talk about it
and, in 1972, he ridiculed in his poem *Furthermore* those who 'sung
enough at Public Bar' or 'browsed upon by chimney-corner' about
the two major episodes of World War 2 in which he participated.
But letters to his parents, some poems, and confidences to friends,
as well as recollections and stories by those who fought beside him,
have made it possible to build up a picture of these years.

John's battalion was moved forward as reinforcements, but his
own company was kept behind in reserve. British High Command
was still so complacent that it pulled back its troops to avoid any
losses. Japanese tanks, having reached Jitra in less than an hour
and a half, immediately invaded the city during the night (another
British belief was that the Japanese were not disposed to fight at
night). The British withdrew in chaos after minimal resistance,
leaving behind vehicles, petrol supplies and stocks of ammunition.

On the night of the 12th and 13th, two companies from 2/9th
Gurkha received the order to blow up the bridge across the river
Kedah, but the Japanese had already arrived before them and
charged with cries of 'Banzai'. The Gurkha battalion fought on in

the dark but eventually pulled back with the loss of 30 men. Further south, at Alor Star, it was the same story. Here the battle lasted several hours, with the Gurkhas again retreating, this time losing 70 men. The battalion found its way back to Gurun on the 14th, in a state of complete exhaustion. Orders were still to pull back with a minimum of casualties, the High Command still convinced that the Japanese Army would soon collapse. But within a week the Japanese had pushed forward by almost 75 miles. Selby, by now at the head of the 28th Brigade, was forced to move back south to Bagan Serai in order to establish a bridgehead. The 2/9th Gurkha and its new commander Major Maurice Allsebrook managed to retreat southwards under driving rain, harassed all the way by the Japanese advance guard. John was still further south, with orders to bring forward reinforcements. This was the moment at which he finally came face to face with war and death:

> One eve, upon the edge of war
> Where to Battalion went before
> While I with Reinforcements First
> Remained at Base (and not athirst
> For fame at bottom let me say
> Hearing our booming guns at bay
> Back driven by the Japanese) –
> One eve, a lorry came wherein
> A hero was (as fit to win
> As any) and a corpse of one
> Whom over-nigh his wheels had run,
> And all the night unburied lay .
> That victim of the foeman's day
> And haunted me the thought of It
> Wrapped in a blanket to befit
> An unknown warrior's demise
> As onward came the Japanese:
> Of being killed was less my fear
> Than of Death's Presence, parcelled near,
> Compassionate there rolled no tear
> But cried that night
> Like Tempest of Affright,

'All hell is empty
All the fiends are here!'
(*To The Warworn School*, undated, with echoes
of Shakespeare's *The Tempest*, 1.2)

He nevertheless succeeded in his mission, and received his baptism of fire on December 22nd. On that date, according to the regimental history, 'reinforced by a second draft under 2/Lieutenant J. R. Bradbourne [*sic*]', the Gurkhas destroyed a railway bridge and occupied the crossroads at Blanja.

John did not stay long at the front line. By Christmas he had already been moved further south (perhaps to procure mortars). On the 27th, the Japanese renewed their assault, but the British had by now decided at last to stand their ground at all costs. The Gurkhas made up the front line of defence, while the bulk of the British Army retreated towards the River Slim 50 miles further south, in an attempt to establish an impassable barrier to the Japanese advance. On the 28th, John and his company received the order to deploy new mortars. But someone had forgotten to provide platforms, and the makeshift wooden replacements collapsed at the first salvo, forcing the battalion to retire in a tropical storm under the command of Allsebrook. When Allsebrook's car overturned, he continued on a borrowed bicycle, and having fallen off that, made his way on foot! When the battalion got to Sahun they were greeted by a hail of British shells captured by the enemy. The sight of mangled bodies, at Sahun and elsewhere, moved John to write this epitaph:

O Jesus, Son of Mary, grant I pray
A place of life and peace in lasting Day
To those who fell, and never journeyed more
Along the road that led to Singapore.
(*Ut Unum Sint*, 1956, stanza 1409)

By December 30th, the Japanese were attacking Kampar, where the Gurkhas had dug in, in a battle that went on for four days. John Sharpe, a young British officer, described as a 'medieval vision' the advance of a Japanese company led by an officer brandishing his sword in front of his men, screaming 'Banzai!' But elsewhere contact was less medieval, as Japanese tanks broke through British lines, leading to hand-to-hand engagement.

On New Year's Day, the Japanese launched an amphibious attack on the coast in an attempt to take the enemy from the rear. The British commander, understanding what was happening, ordered another retreat. Again 2/9th Gurkha provided cover while the men dug trenches under enemy fire. When the Japanese advanced, John and his comrades were relieved by the Scots Yeomanry, who launched a counter-attack singing 'Rule Britannia, the British will never be slaves'. The Japanese then drew back. Was this to be the turning point? The next morning Tsuji was wondering whether he should delay the assault, but when he discovered that the British High Command had given the order to retreat he decided to press forward. At the same time the Ando regiment had made its way around British positions in the marshy jungle, and on January 2nd began to encircle the British from the south, thereby accelerating their retreat. On the 4th, the Gurkhas abandoned their position and fell back:

> Malaya's impact on retreating soles
> Of soldiers in Strategic a Withdrawal
> As Whitehall's walling stony might announce,
> As if I cared!
> (*Land of Hope and Glory*, 1972)

John and his battalion joined the other British troops at the River Slim, some 200 yards wide, at a particularly dense point in the jungle, the last obstacle before Kuala Lumpur and Singapore. The troops redeployed under fire from Japanese planes: the Indians to the north, in the dark and dense jungle; the Scottish Highlanders in the rubber plantations; while the Gurkhas were tasked with defending the bridges. John's C Company remained stationed south of the plantations at the junction with the 2/2nd Gurkhas.

'The worst disaster and largest capitulation in British history'

At dawn on January 7th, Major James Stephens was shaving, taking care not to alert Japanese aircraft with his mirror, when he spotted a glare in it, which turned out to be a Japanese tank. As he tried to work out what an enemy tank was doing ten miles behind British lines, the Gurkhas found themselves under heavy fire. Three hours earlier the decisive battle had begun in the light of the moon. Major Shimada, who had only arrived at the front the evening before, unleashed Lieutenants Wanatabe and Morokura with 30 tanks in a lightning advance under cover of darkness. A rain of fire descended on the sleeping Indians, sowing widespread panic and forcing them to flee into the jungle. The Scottish Argylls, hampered by the fleeing Indians, witnessed their defences collapsing in turn. Thus the Japanese had arrived near the railway bridge just at the moment when Major Stephens became aware of them.

Their tanks proceeded to demolish the British headquarters and push past the Gurkhas, who had no anti-tank weaponry, their superior officers not having envisaged an offensive of this kind. Desperate efforts were made to regroup, but it was too late. Day had dawned on the rubber plantations, by now swarming with fleeing soldiers, which the Gurkhas were powerless to stop. John's C Company was soon cut off from the rest of the battalion, as the Japanese rushed towards the road bridge, arriving at the same time as the Gurkhas, who were marching quietly along the road. Another massacre ensued, with survivors sprinting for the bridge. The Japanese beat them to it and sent forward a reconnaissance south of the river before halting, finally stopped in their tracks by the batteries of the 155th Field Regiment.

Shortly before noon, a new group of Japanese tanks arrived on the road, followed by a troop of infantry, who fanned out across the plantations. The Gurkhas fought courageously, but a patrol sent out towards the river returned with alarming news: the bridge had been taken, and the Japanese had deployed on both banks of the river. In such circumstances crossing the river would soon become impossible, because only the railway bridge, about half a mile to the west, and whose sleepers had been destroyed, was still free. Allsebrook gave orders to the two companies under his direct command to retreat. Wooden planks were placed along the railway bridge and the Gurkhas began crossing as evening fell, pounded by Japanese artillery (only 149 men succeeded in escaping, and 500 men failed to answer the call). News from the two other companies, brought by Lieutenant Cooper, was even worse. D Company had headed west to cross the river by a badly damaged footbridge and was surprised by the enemy, and all but a few of its members wiped out. C Company was reported as missing.

In fact John's company had had no contact with the enemy until the order to fall back received by Captain Hart. Under Hart's command the company headed for the railway bridge, but becoming aware of what was happening it changed direction west, bringing with them two companies from 2/2nd Gurkha. They decided to cross the river by using felled tree trunks, their only protection being a guiding cable formed from their rifle straps. A number of soldiers slipped from the trunks, were carried away by the current and drowned. The remaining troops joined up on the far side of the river and sought refuge in the forest, climbing to the top of a wooded hill to get their bearings, and down the other side in the direction of the road, intending to join up with the rest of the battalion. But the Japanese were already in control of the road, so Hart decided that the men would proceed through the jungle in separate small groups to reduce their chances of detection. In spite of their exhausted state each group, at an order from their officer, set out, one after the other, and disappeared into the jungle in an orderly fashion, until only Captain Hart and John remained. Then, according to the *Regimental History*, 'Captain Hart and Lieutenant Bradbourne, because of their height and colouring, elected to travel alone', so as not to put in danger any Nepalese who might have accompanied them.

The casualties suffered by the British at Slim River were disastrous: hundreds dead, 700 lying wounded in the plantations, and 1200 taken prisoner, a number which would exceed 3000 in the ensuing days. Only a small percentage of men escaped death or capture. The 11th Division, the crack unit of the British army in Malaya, had all but ceased to exist. Seventy pieces of artillery, 50 armoured cars and more than 500 other vehicles had been abandoned in the plantations, along with stocks of ammunition and fuel supplies for more than a month, which enabled the Japanese to reach Singapore.

On arriving in Malaya on January 7th, General Archibald Wavell, Commander-in-Chief of allied troops in South-East Asia, decided to pull out of Malaya in order to defend the Singapore peninsula, the centre of British power in that part of the world. The survivors of the 11th Division regrouped and took part in the defence of Singapore (the Gurkhas who had survived the Slim disaster were the last to surrender). But the Japanese were unstoppable, and on February 15th the British Army surrendered at Singapore: 130,000 Britons were taken prisoner, 9000 having died in the course of the campaign (against 3500 Japanese). Churchill in his *Memoirs of the Second World War* described it as 'the worst disaster and largest capitulation in British history'. The myth of Western invincibility had died in Asia, routed by 30 tanks and the audacity of two junior Japanese officers.

In the midst of extreme distress, a lone star glitters

One month after the Slim debacle, John's parents received a telegram from the Foreign Office informing them that their son was missing in action. A week later a second telegram informed them that he had reappeared in Sumatra. What had happened? Unlike their men who, after they entered the jungle, headed in a south-easterly direction in an attempt to reach the road, only to be mopped up by the Japanese, Hart had decided that he and John would go south-west towards the coast – some 40 miles as the crow flies, 60 by crossing the Sungai Tengi and then following the winding course of the Sungai Selangor. They had no food and were at the mercy of predatory wild animals, reptiles and mosquitoes. Their progress was very slow, three to six miles a day at the most. They lived off roots, wild fruits and perhaps some rice supplied in villages along the banks of the Sungai Selangor (without which they would probably not have survived), unaware that the Japanese had distributed leaflets and sent out patrols letting it be known that any aid granted to fugitives, or failure to denounce them, was punishable by death. (On occasion, whole families were executed on suspicion of having harboured British soldiers, even though for Malayan farmers it was an ancestral custom of the Kampung to welcome and offer food to strangers, whom they regarded as sacred guests.)

John discovered that he could survive without food, but he soon began to shiver, and suffer from nausea and headaches, all symptoms of malaria. He had in fact contracted cerebral malaria, the most virulent form, usually fatal if not treated rapidly. He began to lag behind, but Hart was determined not to abandon him, and they kept going as best they could, John weakening all the time and becoming delirious. It was at this point, at the nadir of distress, that he looked up at the star-filled sky and experienced a sort of vision:

> The brightest Westward, beckoning afar;
> It seemed to me a sign from Christ the King,
> Who out of chaos joy and peace doth bring.
> (*Ut Unum Sint*, 1956, stanza 1408)

Was he thinking at this moment of Jesus as he used to see him in the stained-glass window at Skirwith? In any event this rediscovery of Christ led him to a second discovery (reported in a memoir by Shirley James): 'I felt for the first time that there is something beyond us – if only we could get in touch with it', and that he himself possessed as it were a sixth sense to perceive this 'beyond'. He rarely mentioned it again, and the expression 'sixth sense' is open to various interpretations; but the important thing was that it was linked to the joy and the peace that Christ can bring to the afflicted soul. Several poems invoke this 'sixth sense': *INRI* (1973), *Atonement* (1974), *Nimrod* (1974), *On the Feast of Corpus Christi* (1978) and *Maria* (1979). John believed it can grasp a supra-sensible but nevertheless present reality higher than that perceived by the bodily perceptions, and connected to God, Christ, the Virgin Mary and love.

After a month's march through the jungle, supported by Hart, John and his fellow officer arrived at the sea not far from Kuala Selangor. The Japanese were by this time more than 150 miles to the south, still mopping up stragglers to their rear, but Hart decided to keep going, even though his companion's health was becoming more worrying by the day. He came upon a sampan, requisitioned it from its owner, and with John aboard set out for Sumatra, more than 60 miles to the west, the two men sharing the rowing. But the frail craft was caught up in the tail of a typhoon, frequent in that season, and washed up on the Malayan coast, where it sank. Both men were astonished to be still alive:

> we stole a boat, we rowed
> Into the straights of a terrific wrath
> Which whirled about us as we hurled, 'Be blowed!';
> We held to fishers' break-gale stakes, we owed
> Our lives to them... 'these things do greatly please,
> Port after stormy sea'.
> (*A Ballade of a Triple Vigil*, 1977)

The two men continued their journey, searching for another boat along the rain-and-wind-battered coast, eventually coming across a group of Highlanders as bedraggled as themselves after their ordeal in the jungle. Together they requisitioned another sampan, this time forcing its owner at gunpoint to take them to Sumatra. At sea John suffered from heat and sunstroke and became completely delirious. He drifted in and out of consciousness, and while conscious succumbed to black depression, a sure symptom of cerebral malaria, though he had not forgotten his double discovery in the jungle, which continued to haunt him. A somewhat obscure poem recalls those fateful days:

> I too have sojourned in a war
> (Dare soldiered say I not for, Lor,
> A sorry warrior and strange
> Noteworthy not) but on that range
> Decidedly I leaned from East
> Delirious; malarial,
> Orientated more to Priest
> Not necromantic but of Feast
> Expatriating funeral.
> (*To the Warworn School*, undated)

The sampan eventually arrived in Sumatra near Banga Siapi Api, a small fishing port built by the Chinese a century and a half before. The group made straight for the nearest hospital to secure medical care for John. Their arrival on June 15th coincided with the fall of Singapore, but also with the Japanese attack on Sumatra. Hart sent a telegram to report that they were still alive. The doctors at the hospital were so concerned by the gravity of John's condition that they arranged for him to be transferred to the hospital at Medan, unaware that the city would soon be shelled by the Japanese. There he was cared for by Dutch doctors, but was becoming more and more delirious. At the height of his illness, as he recalled 25 years later, he lost consciousness and for three days hovered –'immured' as he put it – between life and death. When he finally came round it was with a firm conviction of what would shape his future life, a single-minded search for God:

> I know not what disease I had
> But in Sumatra I went mad
> (With sunstroke and malaria
> Maybe) – O blest hysteria!
>
> O blest delirium that told
> Me clearly that to find The God
> Was all I really wanted! odd.
> But thus He called me to His Fold.
> (*Ut Unum Sint*, 1956, stanzas 1410–11)

A further religious experience occurred at this time. During his delirium it appears that John had a vision, which he subsequently identified with the Virgin Mary.

Ten days after this near-fatal episode, John's convalescence began, and he was able to leave bed and walk around. But he and his companions were soon obliged to flee again, as the Japanese advance necessitated the evacuation of all British still in Sumatra. Still very weak, John was transferred to Padang, some 400 miles to the south-west. Here the *Tenedos*, an old First World War destroyer, one of the few ships to have survived the destruction of the British fleet, had already been overrun and filled when James Hart arrived on the quay, carrying rather than supporting John. The already overcrowded boat had just begun to raise the gangplank. Hart got a grip on it, and, 'just as the gangplank was being lifted', shoved John, 'slung over his shoulder', on board. Ignoring the 'No more, no more, we are listing' of the crew, he managed to fight his way on board just as the boat moved away, once again saving John's life. The boat lurched its way out to sea, heading for Ceylon, just as Sumatra fell to the Japanese. Managing to elude Japanese air surveillance it docked at Colombo, where Hart and John were transferred to the

Chitral, an Australian vessel requisitioned by the Royal Navy, which took them to Bombay. Shortly afterwards the *Tenedos* was sighted by the Japanese and sunk, with the loss of 33 lives.

Indian interlude

The two men arrived in Bombay in mid- March. On the 16th, John sent a telegram to his parents: 'I am safe and well.' He stayed for a time at The Taj Mahal, the city's top hotel, from where he wrote on the same day a letter to his parents, which reflects both his ill condition and his new state of mind:

> The Malaysian tragedy you know of. I was there, and there is much that I would say, but cannot now. Let it suffice that I have been very lucky having passed from Malaya to malaria, from malaria to a mind more nearly right than ever before... The first stage of my malaria amounted to lunacy, combined as it was with sunstroke. But it is something for which I am extremely grateful. I believe that having touched rock bottom, my reason is now surely founded on a desire for two things: honesty and simplicity.

The letter rambled on somewhat, before returning to the war and John's plans for the future,

> on the prayers of Ignatius Loyola; on the same creed as yours; on the aim of the democracy – Christianity – and on the firm belief that magic is confined to Popery and Buddhism – nothing to do with us...

before concluding:

> Our war is a fight against the Antichrist, with the weapons of the Antichrist. And when it's over I'll go to Wells, in a country where the sun shines, to prepare for a loyal fight. I call Father

> Fist reluctantly – but now I realise that he always
> fought loyally.

These words suggesting a priestly vocation in the Anglican
Communion must have brought joy to the heart of the Reverend
Bradburne. But what followed could only have renewed his concern
for his son: a scrambled stream of consciousness, with burlesque
undertones, which might have tempted him to doubt his son's
sanity, with a postscript running commentary on the etymology
of Bradburne ('broad river') and Bach ('river' in German), and on
the Cross.

A fighting unit lost in battle is never reconstituted, and shortly
after convalescence John was assigned to 3/9th Gurkha and posted
to Dehra Dun. The battalion, formed in October 1941, comprised
20 or so officers and 900 men. The epic tale of his survival in Malaya
made John a hero, even if he himself remembered it with a great
sense of humiliation. A month later he was appointed battalion
Adjutant, opening the way to a future position of command. He
was put in charge of general organisation, looking after the 'library'
and discipline – office work for him after the Malayan hell.

His stay with 3/9th Gurkha was short-lived. A new battalion, the
5/9th Gurkha, came into existence on July 15th 1942, to which John
was appointed as Adjutant, an indication of a satisfactory report. He
wrote to his parents: 'Life at present is as good as I've ever known
it, twelve hours work a day, good friends and lovely surroundings.'
To battalion second-in command Captain Peacock, John came
across as 'a fleeting impression of a very likeable young man'. He
was soon promoted to the rank of Captain, and joined the battalion
in training manoeuvres in the forests around Saharrapur, and on
the banks of the Yamuna. In December 1942, most of 5/9th Gurkha
left for Raipur, and then on to the North-West Frontier. But John,
tired of office work, asked to be sent back to 3/9th Gurkha to take
charge of a mortar platoon. From then on he worked with a very
capable *jemadar* (military assistant) who organised manoeuvres
while John passed his time climbing trees, birdwatching, singing
and praying after his own fashion.

Shortly after his arrival in Dehra Dun, he made the acquaintance
of another young officer, John Thurston Dove, from 1/9th Gurkha,

who came knocking on his door one day to ask if he could play a light-music record on John's gramophone, only to be forced to listen to Bach's 'Jesus, Joy of Man's Desiring'. From that moment on the two became lifelong friends.

> Of friendship best I'd not rejoice
> Neither would I voice desire
> For any friend I'd less admire.
> (*Tatterdemalion*, 1971)

John Dove (for John successively 'Thurston', 'Critch', 'Guru', 'the Dove', and then simply 'Dove'), a year younger than John, was the son of an English country gentleman who lived off his annuities in Somerset, hunted in the winter season, and played polo in the summer. His Irish mother was a devout Catholic, his father somewhat indifferent when it came to religion, except for his emphatic anti-Catholicism, though their marriage was 'happy and solid, and so my childhood was happy and without great concerns'. The father agreed to his children being brought up as Catholics, and on Sunday remained at home while the rest of the family took off to Mass. At 20 years of age, when John first met him, his friend was chiefly interested in polo and young women. Good looking, he did not share the mystical imaginings of his new friend, but was happy to join him in long discussions, nature walks, and in flirting with the ladies. He was an uncomplicated Catholic, not given to theological speculation, 'with a simple devotion to Mass and the Sacraments ... at school and in the army finding instinctively my way to Mass on Sundays'.

The two young officers were soon sharing a military bungalow at Birpur with an ex-banker from Kenya, a burly Scot, a Wellington College old boy, and a rough-and-ready tea planter. They were well supplied with domestic assistance: a *dhobi* (washerman) for their laundry; a *bhisti* (water-carrier) for their bathwater; a house cleaner; a *mali* (gardener) to look after the garden, and each officer with an individual batman. John's batman was Dhil Bahadur, helped by his son, whose principal task was to arrive in the morning with a cup of tea, intoning in a deep voice: 'Paune che, Sahib' – 'quarter to six, Sir.' It was his father's job to make sure the young officer's uniform was permanently in impeccable condition, and to defend his interests among the competing domestic staff.

Day began with Bach or a Beethoven symphony, John gradually winning over John Dove to his own classical musical tastes. After work, which lasted until lunchtime, the afternoons were devoted, theoretically at least, to the study of Gurkhali. A teacher was supplied, at their own expense, and attended their bungalow to dispense lessons to the two young Englishmen sprawled on their beds, while he did his best to instil some of the finer points of Gurkhali grammar in the minds of his pupils, soon sweating in the damp heat of the monsoon. Sometimes after about ten minutes John would get up and declare: 'Enough of that. Now, Sahib, you must learn to appreciate Bach.' The unfortunate man had no choice but to sit and listen in silence to the music, which was then followed by John's enthusiastic commentaries.

Afternoons were rounded off with a parade, after which the two friends played tennis or, in Dove's case, polo. Mostly they went for long walks, or sometimes horse riding. Behind the colonial-style buildings of the military academy, which trained thousands of future Indian NCOs, they climbed up through the forests of sals (incense trees) and deodars, the kings of the Himalayan forests with pagoda-style pyramids of branches. One day a shepherd they met along the way gave John a present of a small local flute, which he treasured for years to come. At the weekend they sometimes climbed Mussorie, the 'Queen of Mountains', from where the health resort gave splendid views over Himalaya and the Siwaliks.

John also went for walks with his cousin Peter Comber, who had arrived from Tobruk. Peter often wrote to Mary Bradburne, whom he married after the war, recounting their trips on horseback together, and how his cousin was once thrown from his horse and, with his ankle caught in the stirrup, dragged for a mile along the ground, frightened but not injured by the experience; or the time he found John, by following the sound of his recorder, perched at the top of a tree. John often spent hours admiring the Indian sky, the blood red sunsets, the clear bright dawning day, the change of seasons, the rude winter, and the semi-parched season, followed by the explosion of the monsoon in almost indecent profusion.

Come evening, the two Johns usually dined together in the officers' mess, one of the finest in India, which overlooked a deep valley against the background of the Messorie Hills and the Himalayan summits, which seemed to them like so many flowerbeds deluged with hibiscus and canna lilies. Dinner always began with a toast to the King, and when the commanding officer, a colonel, was present, all officers wore dress uniform, while Indian musicians played the regimental bagpipes. When the colonel withdrew, the young men sometimes changed into sports gear and played rugby with a ball made from tiger skins.

On occasion, women were admitted, and the Kenyan ex-banker always made sure that his fellow lodgers in the bungalow were supplied with escorts. John stood out by his sense of humour and his mimicking skills, and according to John Dove he was invariably the 'life and soul of the party'. Rum flowed freely, and John often brought back a supply of rahski to the bungalow for his Scottish friend, who seemed permanently broke. On another occasion the banker from Kenya, dead drunk, had to be carried back to the bungalow on the shoulders of an obliging young parachutist.

John was no slouch when it came to drink, and was known to overindulge, and also drew attention to himself with other eccentricities. He sometimes didn't bother to shave, which was in breach of regulations (that in any case were not to his taste); and when he travelled to the Dehra Club by tonga (a two-wheeled horse-drawn trap) he sat beside the driver, and woe betide the latter if he hit the poor horse: John would retaliate by hitting him! But, like his friend Dove, John was happiest in female company. The women in question were mostly the daughters and nieces of their senior officers, and the two young gentlemen would when possible arrive to visit them in a tonga. According to John Dove, his friend was not very successful in love; he was quick to fall in love and blurt out his feelings, which were invariably unrequited. The young women were entertained rather than attracted. According to other witnesses, John was not always so unsuccessful.

John later spoke of his Indian interlude as 'two years which were idled away / In the clubs and the pubs and the profitless play' (*Ut Unum Sint*, 1956, stanza 1422). His desire for God nevertheless continued to grow. Despite what he had written to his father in

May 1942, his religious feelings were mainly of the cosmic variety: love of nature, the sun rising and setting, mountains and forests and birds, and silence, all of which found expression in his letters of that time, where for example he can switch from contemplating clouds to a reflection on the truth of Eternity. It was as if he were trying to put into place the pieces of a puzzle connecting the tragedy of Malaya and the revelations which came to him in the face of death. John Dove recalls that they often discussed religious questions, 'quite naturally, as we discussed other subjects, and that remained between us. Our differences left unaffected our good relationship – we discussed so freely, so naturally.'

At the time John regarded himself as a High Church Anglican, but in the eyes of his friend, 'one did not notice any formal or institutional approach to religion in him', and John's beliefs seemed to be confused with religious emotions associated with nature and music. The fervour of his emotions struck his friend when, with him one day in a bookshop in Mussorrie, John came across a dusty gramophone recording of the *Nunc Dimittis* by Dufay, and a pre-Elizabethan *Gloria*. At this stage, John had no interest in Catholicism, in spite of his vision in Medan, and his friend made no attempt to influence him. The Nonconformist chaplains of the regiment had also been struck by the young man, and one of them tried to recruit him, but without success.

Then John 'discovered' the Orient. Prayer wheels and repetitive forms fascinated him by their spiritual power. One day returning home with his friend from a call on some young women, he experienced a flash of insight:

> I heard a sound of singing, saw a sole
> Sadhu at praise... into the fane did stroll
> And felt myself a fool and vain, no role...
> (*Retrospective Retrograde*, 1974)

At this point his attention turned towards the religions of India. At first Hinduism captivated him with its Brahmins, its Sanyassis, or its simple devout villagers, whom he saw in their thousands passing along the Yamuna towards Yamunotri and its sanctuary of sacred springs at a height of some 13,000 feet, one of the four great places of pilgrimage in the Himalayas. He was also fascinated by the Buddhist mantra 'Aum mane padme hum'. But he remained unimpressed by yoga, and was faintly amused by a fellow officer who practised it when returning from parade. His oriental fervour, however, was short-lived. In fact the seed sown in the Malayan jungle and at Medan had taken root. And if, as he wrote in the same poem, 'back I did go to Bach and Bacchus mixed', the Christian influence of the former was beginning to weigh more and more. His meditative listening to Cantata BWV 147 ('Jesu, Joy of Man's Desiring') played an essential role in his search. On May 23rd 1943, he wrote to his parents: 'My life is dedicated to Christ once and for all.'

At that time he was considering a vocation in manual work and a Christian apostolate in the world directed towards those he met on his way, leaving open the question of ordination. As the months went by, according to John Dove, 'discussions of a religious nature took more and more a greater place in our relationship and mutual affection'. Seeing his friend going off to Mass in a Catholic church every Sunday, John began to question him about his religion. Unable to help him, John Dove sent him to the Franciscan parish priest at Dehra Dun, who lent John the book *Now I See* by Arnold Lunn. An accomplished athlete, the inventor of the slalom, novelis, and controversialist, Lunn had written a pamphlet on the idiocy of Catholicism in 1924, which led to a public debate with Ronald Knox, and in turn to Lunn's own conversion to Catholicism in 1933. This first contact left John unconvinced, although he did write to his parents that reading the book had increased his interest in the Catholic Church. He continued to draw inspiration by collecting miscellaneous Hindu and Christian prayers and hymns which made up the 'Office' which he chanted every day, while at the same time thinking of an ecclesiastical career in the Anglican Communion, or even studying at Oxford.

In May 1943 the friends were granted leave, and decided to spend it on the shores of Lake Naini at Nainital. The surrounding landscape was breathtakingly beautiful, with Nanda Devi, the second highest summit in the Himalayas, in the background, a magnetic tourist attraction since it was 'discovered' by the British in the nineteenth-century, as well as being the summer residence of the Governor of the United Provinces. The two young officers stayed in the residence of the local Police Commissioner, overlooking the lake, and spent three weeks playing tennis, climbing China Peak, walking and horse riding, drinking in The Boathouse, and going to the club with well-bred young women. One evening, impressed by the exertions of the *dandy* porters (the dandy was a sort of rickshaw pulled by four porters) John took the place of one, told him to sit up on the seat, and took his turn pulling with the other three for about half a mile:

> Labouring coolie,
> As lean as he's tired,
> Drawing a rickshaw by heavyweight hired ...

> O European,
> These lines are not written
> Merely for purpose of preaching a sermon
> People are all
> Bound one to another,
> And each of us somewhat depends on his brother.

> Privileged people,
> For sake of the hired
> May his employer observe when he's tired:
> Let each respect
> The lot of the other
> For all are God's children, regardless of colour.
> (*Ut Unum Sint*, 1956, stanzas 1438–40)

I am a Chindit

As a result of their lightning victory in Burma in 1942, the Japanese were now face to face with India, whose stability within the Empire was being undermined by the nationalist campaigns of Ghandi and regular famines. At this point the war seemed to be bogged down in the trenches at Arakan, but in the autumn of 1943 the Indian interlude of the two friends was coming to an end. John Dove parted for the European front (Italy, later Greece), while his friend, along with six other officers and 150 men from 3/9th Gurkha were sent to the training camp of the Chindits, founded by Orde Wingate, at Mynamatti in West Bengal, in preparation for Operation Thursday, which would involve the dropping of commandos behind enemy lines in Burma.

For Wingate, training was the key to success, and he had deliberately brought African troops with him to prove his point. But Wingate wanted no truck with Gurkhas, whom he regarded as lacking in initiative, and he was only prevailed upon to accept them by the insistence of his second-in-command, Michael Calvert. Along with his fellow Chindits, John underwent the rigorous training required to strike the enemy by surprise and disappear again into the Burmese jungle, in stark contrast with the amateurism he had known in Malaya. On September 16th, Admiral Mountbatten, now Allied Commander in Chief, came in person to deliver a pep talk to the assembled Chindits. His prime intention was to halt the spiral of defeatism, and while he was perhaps addressing the newsreel cameras as much as the soldiers, his athletic appearance and the ease with which he bounded on top of a barrel, not to mention his infectious optimism, produced the desired effect. Moreover, he spoke a few sentences in Gurkhali, and hearing the King's cousin speak their language went down well with the Nepalese.

Training continued through Christmas, on warm days and cold nights. Every evening on parade each soldier had to swallow his Mepacrine (antimalaria pill), even though rumour had it that it led to impotence. At Christmas the whole battalion celebrated, and John took part in a dinner of Chinese goose washed down with Indian gin, rum and whisky. This was followed by a football match between the Gurkhas and British officers, which the British won.

Though he took part in the training, John's heart was elsewhere. Rare were those who, like Scott Leathart (in *With the Ghurkas*), shared his passion for nature to the point of declaring: 'My general interest in natural history made my life more interesting than that of my colleagues.' Like him, John loved to watch the night flight of thousands of sterlites, listen to the noisy chatter of Bengal cicadas, and the cries of predatory owls. He continued to climb trees and play his recorder, but was also happy to share the life of his men and listen every evening at the setting of the sun, as they sang to the rhythm of their drums nostalgic melodies about their faraway

homes, their ageing parents and the wives and children they had
left behind. They continued to haunt his memory and would later
inspire this ballad:

> From mountain airs of Himalayas,
> O sad departing!
> From homes 'neath lairs of shaggy bears,
> And we come laughing.
>
> To sunbaked plains or jungle rains
> Or lonely dying,
> Though great the pain, we follow fame,
> Our loved ones sighing.
>
> From lands of flowers and fresh'ning showers,
> And cowbells ringing;
> Near temple towers sweet peace was ours
> With sadhus singing!
> (*The Gurkhas,* 1949)

His thoughts about the future were deepening, and he came to a
decision which he shared with his parents in a letter of December
8th: 'Being known as a most thriftless cub', he had become 'John
the Miser', because he had started putting aside some money every
month to finance his projected studies at Oxford. Two months later
he had changed his mind, and decided he wanted to be ordained
as soon as possible. The decision was, he wrote, the fruit of two
years of reflection and persuasion, and of reading *A Serious Call to
a Devout and Holy Life* by the eighteenth-century Anglican divine,
William Law.

In the New Year of 1944, John continued his training at Fenua,
to the north of Chittatong, in a jungle similar to the one in Burma,
then returned to Siadpur near Dehra Dun. While admiring a
caravan of 50 camels passing through the hills, he thought of the
three Magi. Calvert, nicknamed Mad Mike, outlined to the Chindits
the grandiose plan devised for them by Orde Wingate: they were
to be airlifted by gliders behind Japanese lines, where the 'floater
columns' would spread out 'like the fingers of one's hand, and then
concentrate in bunching the fingers together into a fist to strike

the enemy' (recounted in his memoir, *Prisoners of Hope*). John and 3/9th Gurkha learnt that their mission was to defend the principal stronghold, code-named Broadway.

At the end of February 1944, the Chindits arrived at Hailakandi in West Bengal, and camped beside the airport. They performed their final exercises with planes and gliders, and long marches carrying up to 33 kilos on their back. John received his combat uniform, corps jumper, green jungle shirt, breeches, a jacket with no indication of rank (Chindits didn't salute, because to do so would alert snipers to their rank, and enable them to pick the officers off at will), and a soft hat nicknamed IWT, 'I was there'. Shortly before D-day, Wingate himself inspected 3/9th Gurkha. He announced that he would arrive at ten o'clock in the morning, and Adjutant Scott Leathart was given instructions: 'I was to arrange the digging of a 30-foot square sandpit which was to be marked by one-foot grid squares, and by tapes stretched across both ways... much digging in the hot sun, the jemadar Adjutant and me were able to look upon this handicraft with some pride.'

At 10 o'clock sharp, John and his battalion saw a decidedly scruffy-looking Wingate arriving at full gallop on a pony, wearing a filthy bush shirt and carrying an old non-regulation Weston, followed by his aide 'immaculately dressed'. To the fury of Leathart, Wingate ordered the men at ease and told them to sit as they wished, while he himself stood where they had been expected to sit, in 'peremptory disregard of all our hard work on his express orders'. But the men were galvanised by his pep talk, impressed by the way he seemed to be on top of everything; in full command of exactly how the mission would unfold, how the Japanese would react, and how his men should respond.

When he finished talking, Wingate inspected the men, stopping when he came to John, shaking his hand and addressing him at the top of his voice: 'Congratulations, Captain Bradburne, on your escape', adding he had recommended him for the Military Cross. He then mounted his horse and was gone, while everyone hailed the conquering hero. John soon forgot about the medal, which in the event he never received. (Wingate was probably sincere in promising John an MC, as he did to many others, but it was the last thing on his mind on the eve of D-day, and certainly after the operation was launched. Less than a month later he was dead.)

Operation Thursday

The operation was scheduled for Thursday March 15th 1944, just before the night of a full moon. Wingate had chosen the Burmese region of Indaw, 140 miles behind Japanese lines, to build the two strongholds, Broadway and Piccadilly. He wished to send out 10,000 men, and it was to be the greatest airborne operation of the war before Normandy. He had managed to muster 80 giant Waco CG-4 gliders for the operation, each capable of carrying weights of one-and-a-half and even two tons of equipment and personnel. On March 4th he spoke to his men for the last time, telling them: 'Many of you will be killed or wounded or will die from illness. All of you will endure sufferings beyond anything you have ever imagined.' This was according to a French military historian (but according to Harold Atkins, who was there, Wingate spoke quite differently: 'No man need worry if he was wounded; he would not be left behind'); and, according to John Mattinson, another Chindit, it was Lt Colonel Philip Cochran, head of the American Air Force Commando, who said to the Chindits: 'I know that some of you will not come back'). That night the Nepalese of 3/9th Gurkha got blind drunk. When a British officer asked them why, Sinbahabadur Lumbu answered: 'That damned sahib with the beard told us we were all going to die tomorrow, so why not drink all the rum now. Otherwise we will have to lug it around on our backs.'

On the morning of the 5th, General William Slim, Commander of the 14th Army, landed at the camp. Having circled overhead, he described the men on the ground as looking 'like busy ants round captive moths', ready for the 'biggest and most hazardous operation of the war'. He was far from convinced of the wisdom of the operation, and resented the fact that Wingate had got the go-ahead from Churchill over his head. John had been chosen to go in with the first wave of gliders. He and his companions spent the whole day resting in the shade of the gliders talking with Cochran's American pilots (who incidentally included Jackie Coogan, Chaplin's *Kid*). According to one of John's companions,

Bill Towill (in *A Chindit Chronicle*), 'some of us with strong religious beliefs – and no doubt others who would not openly admit to such beliefs – silently committed ourselves to God's keeping'.

The end of the afternoon presented a spectacular sight. As the Dakotas lined up with their nylon pulleys, a stream of men emerged from the shadows and advanced as if in a much-rehearsed ballet. The Dakotas revved their engines to the limit and waited for the order to take off. Suddenly, barely an hour before departure, a plane landed on the runway. Despite orders (Wingate wanted total blackout), Charles Russhon had made a final reconnaissance flight over the landing areas and discovered that the Piccadilly zone was covered in blocks of teak. He had photos to prove it, and an exasperated Wingate was obliged to take note. Had the Japanese been alerted? Were they lying in wait for the gliders at Piccadilly, or even at Broadway? Or was it woodcutters who had cut down the trees? Wingate was forced to consider calling off the whole operation, which would have been the end of the Chindits. But he decided to take a risk: all the gliders would head for Broadway, led by Calvert, and Wingate ordered his adjutant to send a radio message on landing: Pork Sausage if all went well; if not, Soya Link.

John and his companions climbed into the gliders, and the leading Dakotas, each one pulling two gliders – another risky innovation – took off. The nylon ropes went taut, and the planes took off in wide loops to gain height before heading east. Viewed from the ground the operation seemed to get off to a bad start. Several gliders crashed, including one carrying the future commander at Broadway, Lt Colonel George, and 15 others were rapidly forced to return to base while the remaining planes were still trying to get off the ground. Finally silence fell as the planes disappeared east into the night, and American fighter planes created a diversion by attacking enemy airports in another direction.

From the confined space in the Waco, John could make out the hills of Nagaland, and beyond the Chindwin plain, its river lit up by the light of the full moon. By now they were gliding silently over enemy territory, across hundreds of miles of inhospitable jungle stretching all the way to China. Then, still with no enemy aircraft in sight, the Dakota slowed down and prepared its descent to the site of the planned stronghold, Broadway. From the air the landing site, lit up by fires, resembled a slag heap ravaged by torrential rainfall, or a black crab on a vast carpet of green. The nylon pulley suddenly fell away, and with a shudder the glider prepared to land. The spot chosen to land looked tiny to John from the air, but he knew that 200 yards was enough to land. What he didn't know was that the non-existent runway was very uneven, with two deep trenches and two trees right in the middle of it. The glider in front crashed straight into the trees, killing all the transport mules aboard. John's glider landed without mishap, but a mere 32 gliders out of 67 made it to Broadway that night.

Exiting his glider, John beheld an appalling spectacle: the remains of wrecked gliders strewn on all sides or caught in the trees, the cries of the dying and the wounded trapped in fuselages, while the unscathed made pathetic efforts to clear the terrain by hand and unload the damaged gliders. But they were unable to drag the heavy Waco gliders clear of the landing strip as the next wave arrived with the regularity of clockwork, only to smash into wrecks in their path or be impaled in the trees in their desperate attempts to avoid them. Calvert tried desperately to make radio contact with Wingate to prevent further departures. Finally at 4 o'clock in the morning he managed to get through and pronounced the fateful Soya Link. Back in Hailakandi his commander broke down on hearing the news and immediately suspended all take-offs, but just after another wave of gliders had set out on their doomed mission. Operation Thursday was a disastrous failure. Wingate's despair was so dramatic that Derek Tulloch, one of his adjutants, forced him to go to bed.

At break of day on March 6th 1944, Broadway, at last visible, looked 'a beautiful open space', according to Peter Heppell of the Lancashire Fusiliers, even if strewn with wrecked Waco gliders. Calvert set about gauging the extent of the disaster: 32 dead, 31 badly wounded, 200 other wounded. In other words, half of the 539 men who landed at Broadway were already unfit for combat, meaning he had at his disposal a mere quarter of the projected number of men. Worse, the landing strip was so potholed that the men had no chance of levelling it off with their shovels in time for the next wave of gliders before nightfall. Operation Thursday had all the appearances of a resounding failure.

At this point Calvert picked up the sound of an approaching engine, imagining it as a Japanese plane. It turned out to herald the arrival of one of the Americans driving a small bulldozer. A miracle! There were even two of them, as well as a roller rescued from the debris of the crashed engineering gliders, and Lieutenant Brockett lost no time in putting them to work. Calvert, with a new lease of life, immediately sent off a radio message: Pork Sausage. Back at Hailakandi it was time to rouse Wingate. Calvert gathered the 30 tons of equipment they had managed to land in one spot and the men set to work, most of which was done by Gurkha 3/9th, including John, who were still able-bodied. One of the two bulldozers and the roller, pulled by the latter, set about levelling the land, backed up by men with picks and shovels. For hours on end the men dug, filled in potholes, flattened the surface, while others went about building shelters with the broken tree trunks, or digging trenches. Air defences were put in place, and Calvert sent more men to the nearby stream to bring back water supplies. Others, including Fusilier Peter Heppell, were detailed to burn the crashed gliders, with dead bodies inside, wedged in the trees. Heppell was also told to burn the dead bodies, which he couldn't bear to do, distraught at the idea of seeing his dead comrades immolated. Another man was assigned the duty.

Meanwhile, in the surrounding jungle, there was only 'the babbling brook and the sleepy sounds of the chirruping of myriad cicadas which clustered on the trees and looked at us unafraid with their saucer-like eyes', as one of the Chindits (Bill Towill) remembered later. By early afternoon, when 12 American L5s appeared on the horizon (one with Jackie Coogan on board), having crossed Burma at near zero altitude, the landing strip was ready to receive them. Calvert welcomed the pilots in his makeshift headquarters on the edge of the jungle and arranged for the evacuation of the more seriously wounded, after which the planes immediately took off again. Later in the evening the landing strip was ready for the Dakotas. Wingate was among the first to land. Within a couple of hours the battalion at Broadway had doubled in size, and canons and mortars were in place. Wingate informed his second-in-command that the next day his men were to blow up a nearby railway line and cut off the supply line leading north to

Burma, while 'floater columns' were to be deployed permanently around the stronghold.

John used the time during the aircrafts' round trips to write a letter to his parents. Understandably, because of censorship, he made no mention of the stronghold, but referred to his spiritual preoccupations and his religious plans with surprising detachment, considering his present circumstances. In an about-turn he explained that he had changed his mind about his recent decision to enter a seminary, which he now regarded as presumptuous and hasty, and gave two reasons why. In the first place he identified his unfortunate inability to organise his life, even though a spiritual impulse was urging him to serve God alone. But the second problem was a new one, destined to worry his father:

> The other problem is the Roman Catholic Church,
> but that must be faced thoroughly later on; at this
> time I have the deepest respect for that Church;
> it seems to me that all those things we hold dear
> are native to her, whilst foreign to the Church of
> England

By March 11th, thanks to about 600 Dakota airlifts, Broadway was garrisoned to the tune of 9000 Chindits, 1359 pack mules, fowl, seeds for a vegetable garden, and 254 tons of equipment (in all 30,000 Chindits and 5000 mules were airlifted behind Japanese lines). So far the Japanese had made no appearance, preoccupied as they were by their preparations for an imminent attack on India. John assembled his mortar platoon with his *havildar* (sergeant), and spent his time surveying the landscape from a tree-top. The floating columns set out on patrol every morning, while six Spitfires remained on standby against attacks from the air. The seeds were planted, and chicken runs built. In the evenings John strolled through the teak trees, wondering what God was planning for him, reading a few pages of Law, and listening to the rhapsodies of the cicadas. Major Shead, another Chindit, was approached one day by John, who asked him: 'Do you know what they are saying?', only to provide the answer to the question himself: 'plenty of corpses here, here, here...'. Shead was puzzled, but John was right.

On March 13th, as reported in Derek Tulloch's *Wingate in Peace and War*, Wingate issued a first order of the day, delivered in Napoleonic style:

> Our first task is fulfilled. We have inflicted a complete surprise on the enemy... Let us thank God for the great success he has vouchsafed us and we must press forward with our sword in the enemy's ribs to expel him from our territory... It is an enterprise in which every man who takes part may feel proud one day to say: I WAS THERE.

But on the same day a Japanese reconnaissance plane overflew Broadway for the first time. The Japanese immediately dispatched a squadron of 30 planes to attack the stronghold. These were quickly repulsed by the Spitfires, who brought down six of them. General Tazoe, Commander-in-Chief of the Japanese air force contacted Lt General Renya Mutaguchi, Commander-in-Chief of the Japanese Army, who had more important matters on his mind: the invasion of India was due to begin two days later with an assault on Imphal and Kohima, the gateways to Bengal. A column was nevertheless despatched in the direction of Broadway, and the following day Nar Bahadur, a Gurkha who had strayed from the stronghold, was taken prisoner (the Japanese usually shot British captives, but sometimes spared the Nepalese for forced labour).

On the 23rd, a high-spirited Wingate returned to congratulate the Chindits. He left that night, but on the way back his plane crashed into the side of a hill, with no survivors. This was a dramatic development for the Chindits, especially when General Slim made a surprise choice to replace him not by Calvert but by the relatively unknown 'Joe' Lentaigne. The Chief of the 14th Army had never believed in Wingate, and did not like him. Had he also heard tell of an eccentric Englishman who spent his time at the top of some tree or other? He later wrote in his memoirs: 'This cult of special forces is as sensible as to form a Royal Corps of Tree Climbers and say that no soldier, who does not wear his green hat with a bunch of oak leaves stuck in it, should be expected to climb a tree.'

The war dragged on, and on March 27th the battle for Broadway began in earnest. At dawn a Gurkha reconnaissance patrol stumbled across a Japanese camp and opened fire. On the following night the Japanese launched a hand-grenade attack not far from the landing strip. Jamadar Chandrabahadur and his men engaged the enemy hand to hand, using bayonets, kukris and even their boots. As they pulled back they were caught in an ambush and all but one were massacred, including the wounded. The fight continued all night, and John and his men did their utmost with the mortars. A handful of Japanese even tried to confuse the Gurkhas by charging the landing strip from the north, shouting in English. At dawn the enemy withdrew. The stronghold had lost 14 men (as against at least 100 Japanese losses), with 36 wounded, but this baptism by fire had the effect for the Chindits that they no longer believed the myth of the invincibility of their enemy.

What the British discovered in their counter-offensive advance was truly frightful. The Gurkhas who had been taken prisoners had been used as dummies for bayonet practice; others had been decapitated during bushido sessions by Japanese officers. Limbless corpses and, around the stronghold, severed heads and eviscerated entrails began to putrify. Soon an overwhelming stench of rotting flesh led to chronic vomiting. In the midst of this horror, with Broadway surrounded and liable to fall at any moment, John found the time to write a letter to his parents on the 28th, letting them know that he had deposited the 200 rupees, which he was saving each month, in the Bank of Norwich, adding, in his regular and careful handwriting that 'the very first ambition in my life is making itself felt in me – viz., to get a first in English at Oxford. Nothing like aiming high in such things, I think.' He also told them, in an indication of his growing attraction towards the Catholic Church: 'St Thomas Aquinas is the man I want to read most at the moment, but I can't obtain...' And with good reason.

The Japanese returned to the attack next day, determined to bring matters to a head. Their snipers raked the stronghold with machine-gun fire from tree-tops. Jamadur Yambahadur and his mortars eventually dislodged them, as John's mortar position relentlessly pounded the attackers. It was possibly at this moment that an incident recorded by Major Shead occurred. Mortar crews were obliged to operate from their trench without cover from the infantry and under enemy fire. Suddenly John leapt from the trench with his arms stretched wide and shouted at the Gurkhas: 'God will protect you.' Another officer told John Dove that he had to force John to keep down in the trench at the height of battle. Could this be a reference to the same incident? For his part, Captain Coultart, at the head of his men, counter-attacked with flamethrowers and fixed bayonets. He was killed, but the Japanese were driven back.

Under cover of darkness, the Japanese received supplies by air, but the British managed to shoot down one of their planes. On the 30th, shelling and fighting continued throughout the day. The following night a huge storm created an atmosphere verging on the apocalyptic: flashes of lightning, driving rain, hurricane-force winds, branches torn from trees crashing to the ground. Against this Wagnerian background, bombs rained down, Japanese and British mortars crisscrossed the skies, hand grenades were flung, and bursts of machine-gun fire mingled with human cries without interruption. Bill Towell later described this night: 'it seemed as if the Almighty and his creatures were all engaged in a desperate contest to see who could make the most noise and cause the greatest mayhem.'

The next day Colonel George managed to get American air backup. A colour smoke bomb was fired at the Japanese position to provide bearings for the pilots and soon the defenders felt the ground shudder beneath their feet. Then Captain Blaker, a medical student of John's age, and a mortar platoon, were sent forward to attack, only to discover that the Japanese had fled, and that the area around the airstrip was littered with the mutilated bodies of dead Chindits. Humiliated by this setback, the Japanese High Command decided to form an army corps with four divisions and a mixed brigade, which had been pulled back from the final assault on Imphal and Kohima, to take on the Chindits. On April 6th, a massive attack was launched on White City, the stronghold Calvert had set up 25 miles south-west of Broadway. During the attack the Japanese lost hundreds of men, at least 700 from a single battalion, while the Chindits lost 100. The stench of dead bodies was such that the American pilots used it to find their bearings for White City.

But the strongholds held out, and the Japanese, thwarted, withdrew from the zone.

The month of April was calm, except for frequent bombardments. The garden bloomed, nature became beautiful again, and John found time for prayer and reflection, often pen in hand, to write to his parents a letter saying a Dakota was on the way with letters, and to pick up the ones from himself and his comrades. He learnt that his brother Philip had got married in Baghdad to Esme Williams, 20 years his senior. His parents had been hostile to the marriage, but their oldest son, newly promoted captain and deputy political advisor to the great tribe of the Dulaimi, had his way. In his letter of April 10th, John also referred to his own situation: 'A lull for me just now, perhaps the last for some time. There must be a storm soon, but I trust the Ark I'm in.' Concerning his own spiritual quest he resorted to a metaphor:

> As time hurries on, and I try to stand where
> real Christians stand and have stood, knowing
> that I must concentrate on God as a tight-rope
> walker concentrates only on his own feet, and
> slowly slowly loving reliance on Him, cynics and
> cynicisms, 'brilliant' atheists and their devil darts
> fall one by one into their fitting places.

On April 18th, speaking of his own war, he described himself as 'somewhat of Aesop's fly, who sitting on the axle-tree of the chariot saith "What a dust do I raise".' He informed his parents that he had provisionally become a lieutenant again, linking this to his change of regiment (although this had taken place the year before, so his explanation was unclear). On the 24th, he wrote to say that he had no complaints about his situation, which was good, except that he was not allowed to let his beard grow, as he would like to. He made reference to travelling by air 'from necessity', but none to gliders or Broadway. He mentioned in passing that his only reading was the Bible and Boswell's *Life of Samuel Johnson*, whose implicit Christianity appealed to his taste. On May 3rd he wrote that he was in good health even though he found the heat oppressive, but felt that he was living such that 'I don't feel myself to be near or far from anywhere.' He added, for the first time, 'I am what the News calls a Chindit', and that he was consoled by reminding himself that before becoming one he was himself, and that therefore he had preserved his individuality, such as it was.

The long march

At the beginning of May 1944, the Allied High Command had decided to abandon the strongholds and use the Chindits in a more conventional infantry role, under the command of the American General Joseph Stilwell, a strong critic of Wingate's ideas and an Anglophobe to boot, despite the fact that the Chindits were neither trained nor equipped for this kind of warfare (90 per cent of their casualties during the Burma campaign date from this change of role). The 111th Brigade, to which the Chindits belonged, received the order to abandon Broadway and move north to Blackpool, a stronghold near Hopin. Some of the officers protested vehemently: Broadway stronghold was holding out well and was doing a good job blocking the Japanese advance. Moreover the Chindits were suffering from exhaustion. The officers suggested they be repatriated for a period of rest before undertaking a new offensive. The request was flatly declined by High Command.

Colonel George, seriously ill, was evacuated, and Colonel Alec Harper took his place. This cavalryman had asked to be transferred to the Gurkhas to be at the heart of the action, and from May 9th to 13th took charge of the evacuation for Blackpool. He divided his men into two columns, supplied with five days of rations. Attached to a column of 900 Gurkhas, Nigerians and British officers, John set off on a gruelling march north across the Gangaw hills, having crossed the river Namyin Chaung just before it was in spate. Each day began at dawn with a mug of tea, a breakfast unit of K ration (American daily combat food – powdered milk, cheese and ham, biscuits, sugar and dates). Some of the men mixed them up and swallowed the lot together: disgusting, but nevertheless it kept the body warm. The menu was more or less the same at midday and evening meals.

Before starting out, the mules had to be loaded, the site cleaned up, and kitbags weighing 30 kilos hoisted on backs, feeling heavier to undernourished and chronically weakened bodies. The demeanour of troops laden down with kit became known later in the the Indian Army as the 'Chindit stoop'. The advance was punctuated by ten-minute breaks every hour, meaning that a day's march averaged at best twelve miles. The men in front navigated by compass, while the rest followed in single file, sometimes along a track (but these usually didn't last, at which point kukris were used to chop a way through creepers, bamboos and scrub to open a path for men and mules). Not many were minded, like Scott Leathart, Bill Towill or John, to appreciate the colour spectrum of teaks and other jungle trees, deer bellowing in the dense undergrowth, birds taking flight from the tree-tops (a good tree can shelter up to 10,000 birds, according to a Burmese proverb), and apes shrieking their mocking cries:

> Gibbons, compete
> Ere roaming I fall to the cries which you call in the heat
> Burmese.
> (*A monk is a man who has given up all*, 1967)

The jackals screeched in the distance and, above the tree-tops, the Chindits heard the muffled sound of reconnaissance aircraft trying to pinpoint their advance. Thankfully the teaks kept them invisible from the enemy. But most of the men were indifferent to the splendour of the jungle, and even the legendary toughness of the Gurkhas was reaching its limits.

Like the rest, John strained to scale steep hills, where many men fell backwards, dragged by the weight of their kit bags, while the mules had to be alternately pushed and dragged to the top. There were also many dangerous swamps to be crossed. At nightfall a camping spot had to be found away from all trails, hidden and invisible from the sky in the trees; leaves had to be gathered for bedding, and a water source located, which was difficult, as the dry season was coming to a close – with the added hazard that the Japanese were searching for the same water. Sometimes the Gurkhas managed to rob nests and make themselves an omelette. On one occasion the column was lucky to get airborne supplies after dark, having lit fires to guide the Dakota to an agreed dropping location, even if some parachutes had to be searched for in the jungle.

At night the men slept with their boots on, for fear of sudden attack, the snoring of the Gurkhas drowned by the braying of elephants in the distance. Leeches clung to shirts and skin, sucking blood, but the men got used to it, and resigned themselves to the bites, the mushrooms on their skin, and the malaria attacks. One night, according to Scott Leathart, a nervous sentry opened fire at a lemur that jumped out of a tree. John, ever receptive to the forest cries, recorded many of them in his poems.

From time to time the column passed through a typical Kachin village, with lavender growing along the edge of its river, men labouring in the rice fields, buffaloes drinking from the stream, chickens and pigs wandering around the compound – when the Japanese had not taken them away or shot them on the spot. It was an oriental pastoral idyll, almost like a Gainsborough painting of a strange landscape, except for little altars at the entrance with their dried flowers, a buffalo skull, and swarms of butterflies with giant multi-coloured wings which John would later remember:

> The Burmese Buddhists think that butterflies
> Are representative of souls a-sleeping,
> Not with the sleep accounted his who dies
> But rather with the sleep from which a-leaping
> To yet another daydawn come one may
> If rising thence betimes; this thought Burmese
> Doth greatly please, is cogitation gay.
> (*Butterflies*, 1968)

The Kachins, also at war with the Japanese, were not hostile to the column, and the village chief offered them some tsaku – the local home brew – and looked forward to their next visit. But the column could not delay its departure. The villagers prayed to their protective guardians, and the column vanished once more into the jungle.

On the tenth day of the march the column arrived at a railway line, beyond which the camp at Blackpool was visible in the distance. Mortar fire could be heard because the Japanese were already attacking. Harper ordered a rapid advance, which drew no gunfire, since the Japanese had not been expecting an attack from that side. The Chindits made it unscathed to the lines of Danert barbed wire and the minefields, and were warmly greeted by the beleaguered Blackpool defenders.

Situated on a slight ridge along the Bumrawung Bum chain, dominating two valleys and a small plain with a landing strip, Blackpool was far removed from typical Wingate textbook operations, with no real stronghold and no floater columns. The 3/9th Gurkha dug in on the Western zone on the flank of the hill facing the landing strip. Relations with the Blackpool commanding officer John Masters – 'cool and distant, rather pompous and self opinionated', according to Bill Towill – proved to be difficult, a far cry from the egalitarian camaraderie which the Chindits were used to. Morale was rock bottom, and the Blackpool garrison, who had seen Colonel Harper's column as their last hope, soon realised that it was totally inadequate against the enemy.

On May 22nd, the monsoon broke, in a deluge that lasted for eight hours. Once more the Japanese attacked, while the Dakotas landed with their latest – and last – food supplies, less than 300 yards from the fighting. Once again the Gurkhas found themselves engaged in hand-to-hand fighting, but in conditions much less favourable than at Broadway, on top of which they had had little time to recover from their exhausting march through the jungle. The battle raged for three days in a muddy swamp amid dead bodies and scattered human body parts. The Japanese were held at bay with great difficulty, and an attempt to wrest a strategic ridge from them ended in failure.

The battle continued through the night in considerable confusion, the brunt of the fighting being absorbed by the Gurkhas, since the landing strip had been taken by the Japanese, who by now were inside the camp. Japanese squads continued to move forward fighting to the last man to gain a yard of ground, then followed by the next wave, setting up their machine guns on the piled-up corpses of their fallen comrades. John found himself in a foxhole for two sleepless nights, hungry, thirsty (water was rationed), among the stench of rotting corpses, gunpowder, cordite and excrement, with skin-devouring diseases, the roar of mortars flying overhead, and the shouting and roaring from both sides to inspire courage among themselves and terrify the enemy:

> I only reached a shelter just in time
> To hear Nigerians upon the march
> Boom 'John Brown's Body' in an Eastern clime.
> (*Land of Hope and Glory*, 1972)

(John, as always, did not give any indication of place and date, and these lines could be an allusion to another episode – as others quoted in this chapter.)

Masters had given the order to keep firing until ammunition ran out. Despite another onslaught of malaria brought on by the monsoon, which he himself was treating with quinine, John continued to man a mortar position – a rare photo from the Blackpool archives shows us a hirsute emaciated figure loading a mortar that could well be John. Artillery rained down without respite. Was it at this moment that an incident occurred which caused shock and horror to his second-in-command Tirth Bahadur Thapa and his men, and which John evoked in a poem mentioning the various ranks alongside him (although this poem refers to both Burma and Malaya)?

> At battle once and in command
> Of Three-Inch mortars I
> Mounted them under the spreading wand
> Of the jungle twelve yards high:
>
> My Havildar was horrified,
> My Subedar shot off,
> My Jemadar who stood beside
> Just gave a gentle cough
> And said in perfect Urdu, 'Sarb,
> Not friend but foe is owed the barb'...
>
> But I'm a donkey and the lob
> Of the mortar didn't miss.
> (*Donkey-drops*, 1976)

On the 24th, 3/9th Gurkhas, the last line of defence of Blackpool, fell back on the hill. For every hundred Japanese killed, another hundred moved forward to replace them, but when a Gurkha fell, there was no replacement. A silent refrain began to flow through the ranks of the defenders: 'If Wingate were still alive, he would be at our side.' Masters requested permission to fall back, but no reply was forthcoming. Already, not counting the dead (nobody was counting any more), there were 150 seriously wounded and in need of care, and by the 25th there remained ammunition for one more day. Masters took it upon himself to order an evacuation for the next day, indicating as objective Mokso Sakan, 15 miles north. During the night it was decided to destroy everything that would have to be left behind. The mules were let go, and the commanding officer of Blackpool had Maggy, his own mule, put down.

At dawn on May 26th, after another night of hell, the evacuation got under way through the mud in torrential rain, as the Japanese poured into the camp. The question arose as to the fate of the wounded who were unfit to travel. Masters, following the advice of Wingate in the matter, decided that they should be killed to spare them the horrors which would befall them at the hands of the enemy. Many of the wounded had already requested this. John took no part in this horrific exercise, but when a wounded British soldier begged him to finish him off, he was incapable of granting his request, which was carried out by someone else.

The soldiers of 3/9th Gurkha were assigned to cover the retreat of the 2000 men from the camp. They set out like sleepwalkers, two men often holding up a third wounded. Some were still in uniform, others in motley. Masters ordered that the mortars be disabled and left behind. When a Subedar refused, and Masters insisted, he declared that if he could not take it with him his men would not leave the camp, at which point Masters backed off. The same went for the mules, which the Nepalese took with them in defiance of orders. The evacuees were down to one day of rations, and Masters had no idea whether they would be replenished by air: a furious Stilwell had by now written off the Chindits. With no protection, and 350 wounded, including 200 on stretchers, the column pulling out of Blackpool made an easy target for the Japanese. Mercifully the latter showed no interest in pursuing them, no doubt because they too were in a pitiful state. The 15 miles to Mokso Sakan were undertaken in driving rain, causing immense suffering to those on stretchers, and scarcely less for those carrying them. The terrain was rough, muddy and so slippery that it was often necessary to dig steps to minimise exhaustion in the uphill advance, followed by treacherous swampy valleys. The mules were finally abandoned. The men were staggering from lack of food and sleep. At the top of the hill the Gurkhas came across Nigerians, wandering around naked and dazed, having thrown away their tattered uniforms, which caused some eyebrows to be raised among the Gurkhas.

On May 29th, after a three-day march, Mokso Sakan and Lake Indawgy became visible from the top of a ridge, but the men were too exhausted to climb down the hill, except for the Gurkhas of 3/9th, who kept going. A veritable army of the living dead, they eventually arrived at a small encampment of Gurkha 3/4th. The latter had not received supplies for a week and were forced to survive on roots and any fruit to hand, while the fitter among them hunted animals. Fortunately on the following night they were spotted by RAF and USAF pilots who had been searching for the column since its evacuation of Blackpool, and who dropped fresh supplies for the famished contingent. At the same time seaplanes were urgently dispatched to Lake Indawgy. Blackpool army doctor Desmond Whyte observed that the men were now beginning to drop like flies, from minor wounds, a bout of malaria or a sudden chill.

From the next day, 150 survivors on stretchers and 450 other critically injured men began to be airlifted by seaplane, at a rate of about 25 per flight – John, who continued to treat his malaria with quinine, held back – while a field hospital was set up on the shore of the lake. Since the Japanese were for the time being showing no signs of life, the Blackpool survivors set up camp around the lake, building bamboo huts where they could at last sleep eat, and heal their wounds, close to herds of wild elephants. A religious service for the dead and missing was celebrated. Masters first had refused a service with 'thanksgiving' but allowed 'a service of intercession... as long it was neither too godamned gloomy nor too goddamned cheerful'. The Catholic chaplain nevertheless did offer thanks: 'The hand of God has been with us, enabling us to disengage from the block in such conditions', adding: 'We have been defeated, but not in spirit' (reported in John Masters, *The Road Past Mandalay*). The dead were then buried, each with a little cross indicating the spot.

How did John pass the time? There are no surviving letters, and the poems are silent concerning these days at Indawgy. Probably he recited his Office. The elephants certainly fascinated him. In a poem about his experience in Burma he claimed that:

> The higher life is lived by elephant,
> Yet, they're ahead of men, even of monks.
> (*Trunk-call to Burma*, 1976)

Apart from food and fresh uniforms, the column received weapons, mortars and ammunition by parachute drop: the war was not over and it was soon time to move on. On June 3rd, 3/9th Gurkha was in battle order, the mortars deployed to prevent the Japanese from taking position in Kar Maing valley. On the 7th, Calvert received the order from Stilwell to attack Maugung with his remaining 2000 Chindits, now in a condition as pitiable as the Blackpool survivors, who were ordered to back them up, dozens of miles to the east. As they prepared for the assault they learnt that the invasion of Normandy was underway. The news was meant to boost their morale, but they were beyond all consolation. Many baulked at the order, and some deserted, though none from the ranks of the Gurkhas.

The Battle for Point 2171

On the 9th the men once again set off. John's platoon had been supplied with two new three-inch mortars, and was accompanied by a dozen elephants. In the swamps and in torrential rains the leeches took their toll on already exhausted bodies, as the men slowly and painfully advanced through elephant grass ten feet high. On the 11th the Gurkhas walked into an ambush at Lakhren, losing a company commander, but having taken the position they found that most of the enemy were already dead, probably from hunger. The march went on, passing through a long litany of villages with strange names: Padigatawng, Ngushharawng... Enemy attacks were frequent and hard fought. On one day 50 Japanese were killed, on another 20. Captain Blaker distinguished himself in eliminating a Japanese mortar platoon which had been pinning them down. In the pockets of enemy dead, soldiers found pictures of Fuji-Yama or of trees shrouded in mist, but also pornographic photos.

On June 20th Masters' column finally arrived at Maugung to back up Calvert, while the Japanese began to fall back from Imphal and Kohima, leaving behind 53,000 dead and wounded. On the same day John wrote a letter to his parents telling them that he was a captain again (the letter was lost). On the 27th Calvert gathered together the remainder of his fit men and launched a successful attack on Maugung. Stillwell instructed him by radio to carry on to Myitkina, but Calvert refused and switched off his radio. Deaths from cerebral malaria and exhaustion continued, but the men had no option but to keep on the move.

On July 5th, 3/9th Gurkha arrived at the Sahmaw Chaung and waded across the river before scaling the ridge where Harper organised a bivouac for the night. Suddenly a deluge of 105mm shells rained on the battalion, causing little damage, the ground being so waterlogged that the shells failed to explode, much to the amusement of the Gurkhas. A strong Japanese force had dug into individual foxholes and trenches above the Gurkha position on point 2171, in preparation for the latest deadly assault, which began after three days. On July 9th Captain Blaker raised the siege, losing his life as he charged into a hail of machine-gun fire to capture the Japanese flag. He was posthumously awarded the VC.

But the battle for the hill continued. The Gurkhas dug in to the positions they had taken, and the battle raged for eight days, for the most part hand to hand. The Chindits were by now dying on their feet from exhaustion. Manbahadur Rai from the medical corps searching for the wounded came upon a hole where a Gurkha and two Japanese soldiers lay side by side, all three dead from exhaustion, apparently without a fight.

As this battle at Point 2171 raged, John's mortar platoon caught the admiring attention of Bill Towill, positioned nearby. John and his men had dug in on the edge of a ditch in a field of Indian corn and were bombarding Japanese positions, and at the same time forced to protect themselves from Japanese fire coming from the other side of the valley. Other Gurkha officers came down the hill from time to time to discuss the situation or just to rest or grab a bite of corn on the cob. On the 18th the Japanese spotted their position, and landed a grenade in the ditch, luckily wounding nobody from John's platoon. Tirth Bahadur Thapa, his second-in-command, continued to fire at the enemy while the others defended the position, until the Havildar himself, weapon blazing, charged at the enemy and put them to flight, for which he won a well-merited Military Cross. According to Bill Towill, John Bradburne was 'equally courageous'.

On the same day when the order to pull out finally came through, those fit to march numbered scarcely 70, with 100 wounded. Masters requested the Americans to carry out a medical inspection. The first report was devastating: of the 2200 original Chindit survivors, only 118 were deemed fit for combat. A decision was taken to repatriate all of them to India. The men set out slowly for Pohok at the rate of four miles a day. According to Desmond Whyte, these men had lost the will to live: 'Every man has his breaking point, and we were reaching it. You could see people going downhill. Some even died in their sleep', and they died one after the other mostly from malaria, despite the quinine injections. In spite of everything, on the 19th, Stilwell accused Lentaigne of evacuating too many men, a serious act of disobedience. The head of the Chindits defended himself, and the Medical Commission backed him up.

On arrival at Pohok on the 21st, the most seriously wounded were airlifted to Mogaung and from there on to India. The rest of the battalion, including John, set off on foot for Myitkyina, the capital of Kachin country, some 40 miles north-east. On the 25th the Medical Commission submitted its final report: a third of the Chindits were to be hospitalised as a matter of urgency. The report concluded: 'The British wounded had obviously been through an ordeal... Statistically considered, Special Force met a more dangerous enemy in disease than in the Japanese Army. Clinically analysed, it was more severely injured by malaria and dysentery than by bullets and grenades.' The Nepalese soldiers had fared better than their British officers: photos of the time show the latter with emaciated, prematurely aged, haggard features, while the Nepalese look comparatively unscathed.

The end of the war

John was among those evacuated. On August 3rd the 3/9th Gurkha wounded were airlifted from Myitkinya to Bengal, from where they took the train to Dehra Dun. They arrived just before midnight on August 8th at the garrison-town railway station, where they were greeted by the regimental orchestra and bagpipes. The women of the volunteer service served refreshments, after which a bus took officers and men to the military camp at Birpur, while in the meantime the remaining able-bodied Nepalese set off on leave to their homes in the valleys. John wrote to his parents that he was about to set off for four weeks to Ranikhet, a high-altitude resort well known for its pine forests, oaks and deodars. He mentioned leave, but this was most likely an allusion to an obligatory rest or even hospitalisation at Hyderabad 19th Regiment facilities. Once there, he gradually recovered his strength after his exhaustion and malaria bout and went back to Dehra Dun.

In September 1944 he met Howell Parry, an officer from 4/9th Gurkha who had joined 3/9th for a projected third Chindit campaign which never happened, and they shared experiences. This young Englishman was avowedly agnostic, and John refrained from mentioning his own religious quest, but Howell remarked that his new friend radiated 'an aura of simple goodness and integrity of soul that I found irresistible'. He further noted his tendency to focus on what was positive, beautiful or good. It seems that John had not lost his originality – not to mention eccentricity. One evening they decided to go to an open-air screening of a film starring the forces' favourite pin-up, Betty Grable (of whom John was a great fan at the time). As the night was cool Howell Parry had put on two pullovers under his battle fatigues, when John, according to Howell Parry, 'Turned up in his dressing gown. Conversation: "You can't wear that, John." "What's wrong with it? I had it in school." "That makes no difference; it's just not the thing an officer wears in public." "Nonsense – it'll show everybody I've been to school."'

In October and November John again wrote home. He repeated his desire to be rapidly ordained an Anglican priest, and his wish to return to England for this reason. At the end of November he left Dehra Dun and met up with his cousin Peter Comber in Bengal. They were both posted to a brigade which was due to return to the front. While changing trains en route, John lost his recorder, which affected him deeply. He was soon in Burma. His letters of February and March 1945 tell us little about his activities during this period, no doubt due to censorship. The British at this stage were approaching Mandalay. In a February letter he compared the song of the curlews at Skirwith to that of the lapwing that he heard every night in the jungle in Asia. Neither the *Regimental History of Gurkha 9* nor poems nor confidences give any indication about John's activities at this time.

But by March 27th he was already back in Dehra Dun, once again evacuated for health reasons, and installed in the military hospital at Poona. From there he wrote to his parents that he had more or less been engaged in guerrilla action in Burma. He insisted so strongly on his good health that there is little doubt that he was putting on a brave face. He learnt by return that Philip and Esme had had a little girl called Pamela, and that they had chosen him as godfather. He was then sent to convalesce at Dehra Dun, as the war in Burma was winding down: Mandalay had fallen in March, and Rangoon would follow in May. On April 22nd John wrote home to announce three 'miracles'. First, 'I am so strong and fit that I could outrun an Olympic runner in the 100 yards.' Second, after a heavy cold he now possessed a fine baritone voice:

> For a long time I have been praying for a really
> good voice. Three weeks ago I was suffering from
> catarrh and bloody phlegm. Now I have a voice – a
> baritone, which has a wide range: the production
> is excellent and natural. ... The volume is terrific
> and the control excellent. I have been asked to join
> the Dehra Dun Church Choir – and congratulated
> on having the voice of a professional.

He had been invited to join the choir at the church in Dehra Dun – on the strict condition that he must not sing too loud, for fear the church roof would fly off. Third: 'I can write freely in English, and poetry at times flows as fast as I can write it.' He felt ready to go up to Oxford where he would shine, and thanked God for the gifts he had bestowed upon him.

In reality John was no longer fit for combat, and had been relieved of military duties after an examination by the ad hoc committee at level A (reservists to be called up only in case of extreme urgency), which said a lot about his state of health. His war was over. Had he been a war hero, even if a reluctant one? In any case he was on standby for his passage back home, just as the war was coming to an end in Europe, if not yet in Asia. In June he visited Lucknow, his mother's birthplace, from where he wrote his earliest surviving poem (except the two quatrains from his days at Gresham's):

> Sacred bulls of lumb'ring size,
> Mooching 'mongst the stalls;
> Varied smell or merchandise
> This Englishman enthralls.
> Children play as children do
> Ignoring time and space.
> (*Indian Bazaar*, 1945)

From there he set out for Bombay to embark for England. During a stop that seemed to last forever, he got out of the train and discovered to his surprise a swarming hornets' nest just above the stationmaster's head. He asked the Indian how he managed to stay calm, and received the following reply:

> a blissful ray
> Of soft irenic humour marked his glee:
> He answered, 'Sarb, there is no need to fuss,
> We do not speak to them nor they to us'!
> (*Nota Bene*, 1974)

The memory stayed with him, and is mentioned several times in the poems. A battleship whose name John forgot was waiting for him, as Japan surrendered. Stretched out in a deckchair on the bridge, he read *The Romany Eye* (1857) by George Borrow, who, in all his books, gloried in fulminating 'against Rome with all his heart, with all his mind, with all his soul, and with all his strength'. John, more or less convinced, believed the 'Catholic problem' resolved as far as he was concerned:

> In homeward battleship I read
> George Borrow, and quite lost my head
> In being sure that never I
> Would countenance the Papacy!
> (*Ut Unum Sint*, 1956, stanza 1412)

Looking back: a vision?

Did John experience a vision of the Blessed Virgin during his stay at the hospital at Medan, as he confided to his friend Jack Dunn in 1946 or 1947?

> He told me that he started to get interested in Catholicism when he was in hospital in the Far East and had a vision of Our Lady. To my shame I do not recall the details but I know that I did not question the fact that he had a vision. He asked me not to mention it, but I suppose there is no point in maintaining that confidence now.

In Rhodesia 20 years later John spoke of it to a friend (Joan, see p. 276) and told her:

at the time I went out of my mind and for three days I was locked up. When I was at the bottom of my insanity, I had a vision of Our Lady. This and my newly found faith led me out of the Abyss.

This 'vision' could of course been caused by his delirious state at the time, which John made no attempt to hide.

The two accounts were independent of each other. A problem is that his friend, confessor and first biographer, John Dove, never mentioned it. I put the question to him in Harare in September 2010, and he said:

> I think that there was a vision, but I can't recall it at the moment. What is certain is that he told me everything, that he was guided by the Blessed Virgin and knew it. John was a good man, upright and saintly. Moreover I wasn't particularly religious in India, as I became later, and I could have forgotten.

John's poems make no mention of it either, except maybe a possible allusion in some obscure lines in *Cure for Psychosis* (1974 – but here the reference is to Malaya not Sumatra, and involves hearing rather than vision):

> Hail the Maid who aprons thus,
> In the rubber bowled be player
> On the word heard well by us –
> Maid Immaculate, conception
> Of the way this lay might shape
> Had I not, thy light direction
> Skating thinly wins the tape.

Looking back: the soldier

How did John really conduct himself during the war? Did he fight, or did he spend his time in the tree-tops, or contemplating flowers and watching birds? The isue is contentious, because John himself said little and the accounts of others vary. As far as Malaya is concerned, we know that from December 22nd he was on the front with his mortar platoon. In general these platoons were not engaged in hand-to-hand fighting, but could be if the front line gave way, which happened. In his poems John came across as a sort of Fabrice at the Battle of Waterloo.

> Having spent in the trees all my youth, overseas
> I was sent to engage with the fierce Japanese:
> From Secunderabad this impossible lad
> Was despatched to Malaya, as officer clad –
> But clothing was all the resemblance I bore
> To my brothers who fought to defend Singapore.
>
> ...
>
> A thriftless cub, a clueless scout
> Who knew not what 'twas all about –
> The war, the mortars and the guns
> Still less the Regimental funds.
> (*Ut Unum Sint*, 1956, stanzas 1401, 1403)

Did he subsequently, while in India, make a vow to save the injured from danger, to climb the highest trees in order to collect intelligence, to engage in the most dangerous missions, but never to kill, as he was about to set off for Burma with the Chindits, who had been trained to do just that? This is what we read in the draft of a biography by Judith Listowel, though backed up by no references.

Where does the truth lie? We can be sure that he did not choose to join the Chindits, but he passed through all stages of his training, even though there was a 70 per cent dropout rate, and he knew that the fighting would be fierce and bloody. Moreover reports of fighting in Burma, apart from that of Major Shead quoted above, describe him as a 'highly effective and brave officer' (Rex Newton-House), and 'equally courageous' (Bill Towill). On the other hand, several officers who fought alongside him told Howell Parry that he seemed totally indifferent to bullets and shells, as if oblivious to everything around him. Did he not on one occasion, according to Parry, under a hail of bullets say to a fellow fighter: 'I say, Reggie, come and look at this wizard bush!'? The style and tone of his letters, and some recollections of him, show moreover that the hell in which he found himself did not prevent him from saying his Office, nor from advancing in spiritual maturity, nor from reflecting on his future, however desperate his situation. Furthermore John suggested in the above poem that his relations with his men were not always easy, and the report referred to below confirms this. And what are we to make of his demotion from captain, a rank to which he was later re-promoted? Was this connected to a disciplinary matter or an incident with the men under his command? The Nepalese Gurkhas were soldiers to the core, and must sometimes have been shocked by this unsoldierly and 'stupid' (as he described himself) Englishman who was their commander:

> They sent me to Burma a 'Chindit' to be –
> To make war once again on the fierce Japanee!
> There, gormless as ever, I followed the band,
> Completely oblivious of all which was planned:
> We squelched through thick mud, heard the music of
> shells
> On occasions...
> (*Ut Unum Sint*, 1956, stanzas 1422–3)

How do we reconcile all these differing perspectives? One officer must have been near to the truth when he judged that John was extraordinarily brave, but lacking all taste for the weapons of war. A reluctant soldier, a hero in spite of himself? Let us leave the last word, and the last sally, to John himself:

> My absent-minded presence at a war
> Earned me Report, an Adverse – here's the score:
> 'Personal courage very high, but can
> Keep neither temper nor control of man,
> No good relations with the rank and file...'
> 'Personal courage very high' – I smile
> Because I have a creaking fear of bulls
> And thought of public-speaking downwards pulls
> My soul to hell! concluded adverse chaff
> 'For staff-job recommended' (hollow laugh
> From Alec Harper...)
> (*On Easterside*, 1974)

Chapter 4

Stages on the Journey, 1945–1950

We are all lost children until we find our heavenly Father, or, more
truly, until we allow ourselves to be found by Him.
(*Wild Geese changing their ground*, 1949)

The war was over for the 4,635,000 men and 437,200 women who had
served in the British armed forces with John, when he arrived home
in 1945. These numbers posed a huge challenge for the new Labour
government, which had just swept to power against all expectations.
But the slogan of the victors, 'Labour for Future', with its twofold
meaning, proclaimed another ambition: to create a new socialist
Britain. The majority of Labour MPs were committed to realising
this project – a mixture of party Marxist 'experts' and a Messianic
Christianity shared by a substantial number of the Anglican clergy,
for whom industrial private property was 'contrary to natural justice'.

The ambition of the Welfare State was to provide citizens with
social security 'from the cradle to the grave', even if for the moment
poverty and rationing were the order of the day. In 1946 the Health
Service was nationalised, and education was due to follow soon.
Decolonisation was also on the agenda; the British Empire, which
in 1945 controlled 200 colonies, dominions and possessions, was
soon to lose India and Burma, and would only hold on to Malaya
after a bitter and costly war.

'Heavenly Devonshire'

At the beginning of October 1945, John came home:

I gloated for my country and I thought her
The fairest sunlit isle where one may stand;
I strolled her in my soul...
(*For a Feast of Christ the King*, 1975)

His parents celebrated his homecoming to Cawston in Norfolk, but were shocked by his gaunt appearance and bewildered by his refusal to talk about his wartime experiences. The now retired Reverend Bradburne had aged and was in ill health, and the family was on the point of moving to Devon. Mary had just got married to Peter Comber, also back from Asia, and had found a house for her parents near Ottery St Mary. Increasingly depressed, Thomas waxed sarcastic about his children, which was distressing for Erica, who insisted on standing up for them. He was particularly scathing towards Michael, who had emerged from Eton with catastrophic examination results.

The family moved to Devon scarcely four days after John's arrival. There being no room for him in the car, he decided to hitch-hike, despite the remonstrations of his father. Before they could move into their new home, the family stayed for a time in Sidford, six miles or so east of Ottery. John quickly rekindled the warm relationship he had with his mother prior to the war, but the Reverend Bradburne failed to understand why his son had no immediate plans to go to Oxford or Wells, and was bewildered by his affinity for oriental notions of mysticism, which were alien to him, and was suspicious of what he sensed was John's drift towards Roman Catholicism.

John spent only ten days with his parents before heading to a military hospital in Dumfries in Scotland for a medical check-up. On October 21st he wrote to thank his mother for 'the best holiday I have ever known', and told her the doctors had given him the all clear. By the end of the month he was in Aldershot, where he was supplied with the regulation civilian suit, overcoat and hat to which he was entitled as a member of his regiment. He then went to stay with the Combers, and shocked Mary by his emaciated appearance. He refused to talk about the war, continually diverting the conversation to amusing incidents of one kind or another.

By the time he returned to Devon, his parents had moved into Fir Grove, which John was not slow to rename Fir Grave. Their new residence was a fine brick house in an ancient hamlet on the Baron Kennaway estate, surrounded by woods, which was now being developed for residential purposes. John did not join them, but rented a room in Sidbury, keeping his distance from his father, and cycling regularly to West Hill while remaining his own master. His sole preoccupation seemed for the time being to be nature, young women and religion. At 24 he looked young for his age. He considered himself gauche and unattractive: too long body, too short legs, feet too wide, head too big, protruding ears (though he appreciated their natural susceptibility to the sound of birds singing in the trees); according to himself he looked like a donkey, 'but unlike the donkey I lack natural dignity', as he would write later on (in *A Wandering*, 1968).

Nevertheless he was attractive to young women, and soon struck up an acquaintance with Ruth Williams, a general's daughter, and later Anne Hardwicke – a 'dark beauty', as he would write 30 years later to a friend. The latter became his girlfriend. Anne's mother Cecil, a warm-hearted woman, quickly became a second mother to John. He also became close to Anne's brothers, Adrian and Patrick. Every day he visited the Hardwickes and paid court to Anne under the benevolent eye of Cecil. He went for long walks on his own and got to know every nook and cranny of Sidbury: its pub, its cider and its church; Otter valley; woodlands, fields, rivers and streams. He became enchanted by the fields, the pathways enclosed by hedgerows and wild flowers, the gentle hills, the mild climate of 'heavenly Devonshire', as he would write to his mother in June 1969, to describe which he could not find enough adjectives of praise, and which became his paradise regained.

Like every year, Ottery St Mary was in a fever of excitement on November 5th 1945 for the Feast of Flaming Tar Barrels, the local variation of Guy Fawkes Night. At midnight, burning tar barrels bedecked the town centre, where the effigy of Guy Fawkes was burnt to universal acclaim. John felt far removed from these festivities, with their vestiges of anti-Catholic feeling. In fact, his 'Catholic problem', briefly anaesthetised by reading George Borrow, was gnawing at him again. Thomas Bradburne had begun to understand that his son was drifting away from him for ever, and John still refused to consider going to Oxford, or even to look for a job. Like hundreds of thousands of other demobilised soldiers he felt alienated in post-war Britain, and with life in general (suicides were commonplace, and James Hart, his erstwhile saviour in the jungles of Malaya, reportedly threw himself into the Thames in 1949 or 1950).

But it was necessary to earn money. John did odd jobs here and there to supplement his meagre army gratuity, and for a while worked on a ward in Exeter Hospital. His relationship with Anne and his religious quest took up most of his time. He had already abandoned the idea of a career in the Anglican Church, but did not know where to turn. 'Om mane padmi hum' continued to ring in his ears. He reread Swedenborg and Montaigne, then Arnold Lunn, and again Borrow, arch-enemy of the Catholic Church, and everything became even more confused. Where did the truth lie? He still could not shake off the demons of his war experience, and one day he felt an urge to visit Skirwith, to see again his birthplace, the old Abbey and Ninnie's house. The church had scarcely changed, although there was more space in front of the altar, and Jesus in the stained-glass window bestowed the same welcoming smile. He was amused to see his father's name in the list of past vicars on the plaque installed in 1935. But he came back more torn than ever between his Anglican roots and his growing conviction that the Catholic Church was the one true Church of Christ.

One day shortly afterwards he entered a church in Ottery – not the Anglican St Mary's but the modest Catholic Chapel of St Anthony, in an old refurbished coach house. Ottery was still – although this was not to last – a Nonconformist stronghold, but a Catholic community had existed there for ten years, and John was not slow to seek out its discreet place of worship in Mill Street. He entered the chapel one morning and was impressed by the Mass and the Holy Sacrament, which caught his eye for an instant. Mass was being celebrated by an Irish priest, Father Patrick Dunne, for a handful of sisters and a small lay attendance. The Marist sisters, who ran the local Dolforgan school at the centre of the small town, were quick to notice the unknown young man at the back of the chapel who knelt right through the Mass but never approached the altar for communion.

Sister Ernest was impressed by his evident piety, and Sister Camilla, who was training at Ottery before going to Exeter University, thought that he was even more pious than her brother, who was about to enter the Franciscan Order. The nuns debated among themselves, especially since the morning when Father Dunne, from the pulpit, advised them to take this young man as an example. No one dared to look around to see his reaction, but John left hurriedly, and they declared that such a pious young man must be close to God. They came to a decision to take him in hand, and one day at the end of Mass they invited John to join Father Dunne for a cup of coffee, which he declined with profuse apologies. The proposal became a daily rite, and the nuns soon discovered that their devout young visitor was the son of the Reverend Thomas Bradburne who gave a helping hand to the Anglican clergy of Ottery.

'To clear the cobwebs of the war from my mind'

In the event, John was still searching for his way. His friend Dove was still in the Gurkhas, and when he tried to open up to his father, it inevitably led to a row, which made it preferable to say nothing. The months passed, and the odd jobs at Sidbury continued, but towards the end of spring in 1946 choice could no longer be deferred. There was Anne, of course, who debated at length with him 'the Catholic question', though with less enthusiasm than he. There was also the Oxford option, not to mention difficulties with his father. And there were those 'cobwebs of the war in my head'.

Then a solution presented itself to clear them, propitious for one who loved trees. The Forestry Commission was recruiting trainee woodcutters to work in the forests of the Quantock Hills in neighbouring Somerset. John applied, in the hope that the hard labour involved would heal his inner confusion, and signed up, on his twenty-fifth birthday, on June 14th 1946. To his father's raised eyebrows he replied that he enjoyed climbing, and that where he would be working there were many tall trees. Before leaving he proposed to Anne: At half-past-nine one night in June

It seemed as bright as day,
The cuckoo yet was set in tune
And fragrant was the hay:
I said to Anne,
Do be my Queen
And she said Yes.
(*At the Sign of the Nine Muses*, 1976)

The register, headed by the coat of arms of George VI, records the name of John Bradburne as forester, social security number W7U 16025348. He had given as his address Quantock Hotel (which didn't exist), Nether Stowey. Was this by way of a joke? Or did 'Hotel' designate his lodging above the Post Office and grocer's shop, which he sometimes shared with other demobbed soldiers who worked with him in the Commission as suggested by Jack Dunn and Harry Wheeler)? He soon found a room at Cockercombe in the valley leading to the Forest House.

He was quickly smitten by the Quantock Hills, which offered breathtaking views of the surrounding countryside, its rocky landscape, slopes, woodlands, rivers and lakes, changing constantly with the weather. The area's fame, less than 40 square miles, largely derives from its historical associations with Roman Britain, and later Saxon resistance to the Viking invaders:

> Pleasance of pasturing cattle,
> Old terrain of knights and great kings;
> Site of green England's last battle,
> And scene of the chivalrous things
> Is that vale between Quantock and Mendip,
> Where cuckoo so merrily sings.
> (*Avalon*, 1949)

But it was above all the poets who had made Quantock famous. In the course of his long forest walks with Wordsworth, it was here that Coleridge meditated on *The Ballad of the Ancient Mariner*, familiar to John as to every English schoolboy. The poet settled in Nether Stowey in 1797, walked the forest along the trail that today bears his name, and wrote his poems checking his inspiration against the evidence of his eyes. John himself often did likewise, and shared Coleridge's conviction that man's life on earth was a search for the redemption and salvation promised to the righteous by the life of Christ.

Quantock Forest had been a royal hunting reserve for many centuries, and later a rich source of timber, but had been taken over by the Forestry Commission in 1919, which preferred to cultivate pine trees rather than the oak or hazel which had grown there for centuries. Among the team of foresters in 1946 were several local professionals, such as the Dobles, Palmers and Bellamys. The trainees were mainly recently demobbed ex-servicemen at a loose end, taking time out before settling back into civilian life. John quickly became friends with Syd Cosgrove, who shared his love of music and poetry among other things, and Harry Wheeler. Jack Dunn, who had served in the Navy, and who signed up at Quantock to gain some experience before applying for forestry school, also became a firm friend. He later wrote about John:

> I thoroughly enjoyed his company because he was such a humorous, generous and gentle person, full of fun and yet very interesting and serious in conversation... Some of the outstanding memories I have of John from the forestry days were the lunchtime barbecues in the forest, when we toasted our inevitable cheese sandwiches over the embers and John always managed to burn his black, but he would down the lot saying that 'charcoal is good for the teeth, old boy'... A number of times, when the crack was good in the gang around the fire, John would go quiet and with a far-away look in his eyes, he was quite literally not with us.

John often sang Orlando Gibbon's madrigal 'More geese than swans now live, more fools than wise', or played the recorder. Jack Dunn remembers Syd Cosgrove and John listening over and over again on an old gramophone to 'something on a theme by Thomas Tallis' (the *Fantasia on a Theme by Thomas Tallis* by Vaughan Williams). He also liked to take off the characters of the popular *ITMA* radio programme of the time, to the great delight of his fellow workers. On Saturday and Sunday evenings all would adjourn to Cranleigh Social Club at Bridgwater, some eight miles away, and enjoy a hot bath, a snack and copious amounts of beer and cider. On these occasions it seems John was as good as the rest when it came to bending the elbow.

John was supposedly a trainee in view of a future career as a forester, but it is doubtful if he ever entertained this ambition seriously. Like many of the others he was there, remember, to 'clear the cobwebs from his head'. Cutting trees was exhausting enough, but by the autumn of 1946 John had achieved a degree of physical and mental fitness, helped no doubt by working outdoors throughout the glorious summer months. Some 20 years later he wished for Cecil Hardwicke 'a summer like 1946'.

Their foreman was 'a morose Scots-Canadian', recently home from Canada, 'somewhat eccentric, given to telling tall stories about his days in Canadian forests – how he outpaced ravenous wolves, and how he used to plant trees on steep mountainsides by firing the young plants like arrows from a bow' (as Jack Dunn recalls). In the eyes of these war veterans this 'old cow' felt intimidated in their company, and tried to impress them by boasting about his own past exploits. He was the only person that John didn't get on with at the time, though this was perhaps because he was the boss, and because John always had difficulty with authority figures. Moreover the latter's accommodation was next door to John at Cockercombe, and he continued to regale John with tales of his own glory after working hours, at a time, as Jack Dunn remembers, when 'there was no TV then to keep people in their houses'.

Though he loved to climb trees, where he could pray in peace, John proved somewhat less talented when it came to cutting them down, and displayed no aptitude for his new work, or for anything mechanical. He was, moreover, aware of his own incompetence, and the first to admit it himself, as we can see from a letter he wrote to Jack Dunn shortly after his departure, in which he remarked wryly that he 'always passed the hammer when asked to pass a screwdriver'. In fact his attention seemed preoccupied by anything except the job on hand. But he made up for his awkwardness by his self-deprecation, his kind-heartedness and his sense of humour, working with teams whose make-up changed from day to day, and explained to all his nickname *Hornbeam* (see p. 35), complete with demonstration.

The outdoors allowed John to loosen up, but his religious questionings only became more acute. Jack Dunn was a Catholic, and in the course of working together John probed him about his religious beliefs. This disconcerted Jack who, though a cradle Catholic, took his religion for granted and was not the questioning type. John's constant probing indicated the seriousness of his quest, but Jack felt powerless to help him. Fortunately, in the autumn of that year John Dove was demobbed from the Gurkhas and finally arrived home at his parents' house, a mere ten miles from Quantock. He soon looked up his friend at the Bridgwater Club, and found John 'wearing a roll neck, breeches, wool stocking, and forester's boots. He looked fine, well and strong.'

John was invited to the Dove household at North Curry, a handsome late-eighteenth-century manor in a wooded valley near Taunton, and quickly baptised the large bedroom where the two friends slept 'the Trappists' dormitory'. On the mantelpiece reposed a statue of St Anthony carrying the Infant Jesus, which John Dove gave to his friend. They often got together to drink beer and cider, and John explained why he had taken up the job of woodcutter, how much he liked the open-air life of the hills and forests, and how it gave him time to think and pray. John Dove confided that he too was searching for his way, and that such questions had come to occupy a central place in his life. The two men, anxious to know God and serve him in his Church, exerted a mutual influence on each other, the one by his radicalism, the other by his convinced Catholicism. Later they would banter about who was the greater influence, and who was and remained whose guru; for now they shared equally their enthusiasms, their thirst for God, and their questionings. For John Dove, who always loved the company of women, the question soon arose as to whether he was called to the religious life; for his friend, it was whether to become a member of the Catholic Church to which he felt God was calling him.

The winter of 1946–47 was the coldest Britain had experienced for three centuries. Livestock died in the fields; crops failed. Two million industrial workers had to be laid off for want of energy supplies, and many poor people died. The Quantock Hills, in common with other areas of the country, were covered in snow for months on end, resembling a landscape from Breughel. Life for the foresters, working in the open air, was particularly harsh. One evening Jack Dunn informed John that he couldn't take any more and had decided to leave. The doughty John gave him a serious talking to and persuaded him to stay on, for which Jack remained grateful to him for the rest of his life.

Just before Christmas John Dove paid a visit to Fir Grove, and was impressed by the High Church cultivated atmosphere prevailing in the Bradburne household. At the time, with Labour in government pursuing its socialist programme, people from a family background such as that of the two Johns, whose social status was being eroded, often reacted by exaggerating their social difference in accent and manner – a polished Oxford accent, and abstruse literary allusions casually dropped into conversations. John probably conformed to this trend during those years: an upper-class accent, Shakespeare allusions and a certain taste for adventure. For him and his like, the venerable and well-tried institutions had survived the test of time and must be respected, even if they might at times rail against them, like his cousin Terence Rattigan, the son of Frank, on the way to becoming a successful playwright in the West End of London; and it was against this backdrop that they played out their individual private adventures.

At weekends, John was spending less and less time in the company of his workmates at Bridgwater, as the call to God became more and more insistent:

> The Voice is God The Holy Ghost and He
> Haunts us in Taunton, Bridgwater may be.
> (*A Full Appreciation of the Queen's Shadow*, 1977)

He continued to discuss religion with Jack Dunn while cutting timber, and with John Dove whenever they met, but he often went off to Taunton on Saturdays. He had asked Canon Richard Iles, of St George Catholic Parish, for instruction in the Catholic faith, and often spent the weekend at his house. Anne had difficulty in sharing his enthusiasm, even though she too was receiving instruction in preparation for entering the Catholic Church. Nevertheless the two seemed to be still in love, though John rarely returned to Sidbury.

'Buckfast was my Bethlehem'

The exceptionally cold winter was followed by widespread flooding. Staples like bread and potatoes became scarce, and daily power cuts of up to five hours were common. To head off bankruptcy, the Labour government increased exports, despite an already reduced production base, while continuing to forge ahead with its project of 'undermining the foundations of capitalism'. Energy, public transport, iron and steel, and the Bank of England were all nationalised, while British bureaucracy soon rivalled that of the Soviet Union: 46 forms and 42 signatures for a few gallons of oil, with the Labour Party publishing a pamphlet lauding the latest Soviet achievements.

It was in this gloomy spring that John discovered the Benedictine Buckfast Abbey, some 60 miles South of Quantock, and it was love at first sight.

> Well blew the balmy breezes and I goaled
> By Buckfast Abbey's happy door. Tale's told
> And truly.
> (*Retrospective Retrograde*, 1974)

St Mary's Abbey at Buckfast stands on the edge of Dartmoor Forest, a vast region of plateaux, wooded hills and barren moors. It gets its name from the deer that used to come down to graze and breed in its park. At this time it was at the peak of glory in its recent history; the fame of Dom Vonier, whose idea it had been to rebuild the medieval church, and the apiary of Brother Adam, had made it a tourist attraction. Its imposing church, whose construction had been completed ten years before, combined Cistercian austerity with a richly decorated interior, including porphyre and ancient stones brought back from Ephesus and Egypt, and stained-glass windows copied from Chartres.

John made a return visit with John Dove at Pentecost, when the scene bore some resemblance to a picture of a pilgrimage to one of the popular shrines of the Middle Ages, only the majority of the pilgrims appeared more curious than pious. But for John it was different. Here the pull of the Catholic Church was becoming irresistible. Far from rejoicing, he became alarmed, imbued as he was with the deep suspicion of many English to all things Catholic. Thomas Bradburne, who shared this suspicion, convinced his son to attend a retreat at Mirfield run by the Fathers of the

Resurrection, an Anglican order with a liturgical spiritual, and missionary orientation, to whom successive rectors at Skirwith had always been close (the latest Parker would soon bestow on them the patronage of the parish). John made his way to Yorkshire for a private retreat conducted by the Reverend Denys Shropshire, a former missionary in Rhodesia (who maybe spoke to him about the colony). The retreat was based on the Exercises of St Ignatius of Loyola, the Offices were in English and Latin, and the music was an eclectic mixture of Gregorian and contemporary.

But all to no avail. It was here that John discovered Newman who, as he said in *Retrospective Retrograde* (1974), 'detained me, really made me think'. He read the *Apologia* in a 'desultory' fashion, and this road-map to Rome became his guide, even if the itineraries followed by the two men were by no means the same: Newman had traced his through the jungle of the Church Fathers, John Bradburne through the jungles of Malaya and Burma! He did not find in the *Apologia* the answers to his questions about Rome, having already found them for himself, but its frank and lucid account of the issues satisfied John's conscience: the great Oratorian became for him a figurehead. Newman showed him the way to become that new man which he yearned to be:

> What a head
> That New Man had who gladly worked
> Out either side and neither shirked!
> (*Of All the paths*, 1971)

Then Thomas Bradburne, having in vain urged his son to remain faithful to the Church into which he had been born, decided to play his last card: his nephew Tom, also an ecclesiastic but closer to John in age. The Reverend Thomas Comber, older brother of Peter, was working in a parish in South Africa. His uncle Thomas Bradburne wrote to him, and then to John who, suddenly hesitant at the moment of decision, fired off an SOS to his cousin:

> I wrote to High-Church Cousin Tom and asked
> Him pip me at the post and on the brink
> Of Popeing.
> (*Retrospective Retrograde*, 1974)

> I wrote, and Cousin Tom replied,
> 'I might, if I were at your side,
> Be able to convince you that
> Anglo-Catholic habitat
> Bespeaks your spirit truly still;
> Since I am not, supply I will
> Address of one, my best of friends
> Whose mind is mine in holy trends,
> With whom at Cambridge wended I
> From Pembroke to The Trinity'.
> (*Of All the Paths*, 1971)

John decided to 'shelve Peter', and set out on his bike 'to go to Paul', the Reverend Paul Osborne, who was living in nearby Dorset. He discovered a country vicar not unlike his father, except that he kept a herd of cows. Their first meeting had a certain drama, as he recounts in *Of All the Paths*:

> Albeit clergyman, with charm
> And calmly kept a pleasant farm
> Whereon I walked to seek him out
> Until arrested by a shout:
> 'I take it you are used to Bulls!
> That's not a cow up coming...'
> Out I pulls!

The absent-minded John took appropriate precautions and explained to the vicar, surrounded by his herd, the purpose of his visit, only to hear this response (versed in *Retrospective Retrograde*):

> Then he said softly, whimsically glad,
> 'My licence as a preacher is suspended,
> My Lord of Dorchester is rather sad,
> I'm on a pilgrimage with yours is blended.'

The Anglican clergyman immediately offered to teach John the rosary – a pious papist practice if there ever was one! The two men spent the whole afternoon talking, and at the end the Reverend Osborne invited John to stay the night:

Together with his wife we supped, as free
Of heavy care as summer fair's for glee.

That night John had 'papist' dreams, but peaceful ones. The following morning, the feast of St Barnabas, he attended 'the Roman Mass' in English celebrated by the Reverend Osborne, in the company of three parishioners, which made a profound impression on him and confirmed him on his way:

'twas a step ahead:
A certain step towards the home
Of England's Faith: the path to Rome
Was entered on more surely then.
(*Ut Unum Sint,* 1956, stanzas 1298–9)

The Reverend Paul Osborne himself took another seven years before making up his mind to go over to Rome. Later he wrote to John: 'Don't try more fast to go / Than will The Holy Ghost (who haunts me so!)...'

John, on the other hand, as he pedalled his way light-heartedly back to Devon, had already made up his mind. But what of his engagement to Anne, who seemed strangely absent from the scene during these days leading up to his dramatic decision? He did in fact return for a time to Sidbury, and announced his decision to his less than enthusiastic fiancée. As for the Quantock Hills, John's tree-cutting days were over. The records of the Commission do not give the date of his retirement, indicating simply 'terminated'. But his departure was celebrated with a night of revelry at Bridgwater Club:

I asked the Barmaid of the Freest House
If she would mind if I, combined, should bray
Praises to Christ Mine Host: 'At most, no grouse!'
(*A Full Appreciation of the Queen's Shadow,* 1977)

John left to work for a time at Exeter Hospital and on local building sites, followed by a week sailing on the Broads with his friend Stephen King, to whom he confided his intentions. Then in the summer months he rented a room in Buckfastleigh, the village surrounding the Abbey, where Dom Raphael prepared him for his reception into the Church. This Benedictine monk took charge of pilgrims, as well as the Catholics of the village, and those following the path to Rome. A gentle giant with a heart of gold, erudite, this veteran had lost an eye during World War 1, which didn't deter him from enlisting as a chaplain for the second, where he served in West Bengal and Burma. He and John would have much to talk about. John described him in *Ut Unum Sint* (stanza 1301) as 'a winged spirit swift in flight' when replying to his final questions about the Catholic Church.

Dom Placid Hooper was the novice master, and he too followed John's progress; originally from Taunton, he was one of the first English recruits to the Abbey. To all appearances a retiring intellectual type with his enormous glasses, he too had seen action on the battlefields of Europe and the Middle East. His love of the liturgy and his inexhaustible memory made him a precious guide for John, who attended the Abbey every day, and met Abbot Dom Bruno Fehrenbacher. Dom Bruno, of ascetic appearance, and with a vague resemblance to Pius XII, hailed from South Germany and had joined Buckfast while very young, having heard about its reconstruction. Buckfast Abbey had one of the strictest – some would say most rigid – rules in the country, but at this time when John was becoming acquainted with it the Abbot was moving away from the old regime's toughest rules, and would soon do away with the tonsure.

The memory of Dom Anscar Vonier was still very much alive, and his memorial could be seen in the church, erected by Benno Alkan, a German Jewish sculptor, a refugee in England and sheltered by the Abbey. Not only a builder in ancient stone, Abbott Vonier also left behind many intellectual and spiritual monuments as a thinker and theologian, and was one of the most influential writers on Catholic spirituality of his time. His writings demonstrate 'how rigorous – and yet religiously exhilarating – the best Catholic theology can be' (A. Nichols in *Anscar Vonier: A Key to the Doctrine of the Eucharist*). His spirituality left its mark on John – not that of the Thomist revival, to which Buckfast Abbey, a kind of medieval reincarnation in the twentyieth-century, made a significant contribution, but its theme of the dimension of mystic 'clownish' madness which Christianity can accommodate. The lesson was not lost on John. His devotion to the Eucharist was founded on reason, which the convert would make his own: the union of the highest spirituality with the most ordinary situations from everyday life, as well as his belief in 'the People of God' (a notion Dom Vonier had proposed in 1937 and which the Second Vatican Council would adopt). We can discern Dom Vonier's influence in the reasons John gave for his conversion in an interview in *The Shield* in 1965: 'There was in me a great desire to belong to a society which could embrace a maximum, and not an exclusive minimum, of people on their way to Heaven.'

On his arrival John rented a room in the village. While he received instruction, he helped out the monks in the garden and in the upkeep of the cemetery, in return for meals. His constant readiness to offer a helping hand was much appreciated by the monks and there was certainly plenty of work to do, whether in the workshop, where the famous tonic wine was produced from Spanish grapes, or with Dom Norris cutting marble slabs to lay in the church choir, or with Brother Adam in the apiary. John spent long hours with the latter, observing him closely as he went about his work:

> The bee to Brother Adam flies,
> The cuckoo in the mead
> Bobs trebly low to emphasise
> The Tenor in the lead
> But the Bourdon, seven tons, replies
> 'I'm no less muffled: Heed!'
> (*The Ballad of Buckfast*, 1978)

From him he acquired practical knowledge of the world of bees: each bee in the hive is unique, but all have a sense of order and precision, and a remarkable capacity to adapt. Brother Adam often praised the even, peaceful temperament of his charges, in terms which recalled, and went further than, the words of the Indian stationmaster overheard by John two years before (p. 89): 'It is up to us to understand her ways and adjust ourselves to her truly marvellous nature, not attempting the impossible task of "mastering" her, but rather doing all we can to serve her needs.'

From this German monk John learnt that we must not only respect the bees, but also love them: though humans will never be able to make them into domestic pets like cats or dogs, they can learn to live alongside them, and among them. These lessons were not lost on John.

Although he was fed at the Abbey in return for these odd jobs, John was nevertheless obliged to look for work elsewhere, and found a job as an assistant bricklayer. His upper-middle-class accent grated on his fellow workers at first, but they were soon won over by his affability and his sense of humour. Which is not to say that he never made mistakes, such as passing the hammer when asked for the trowel, or when he lost his balance on the scaffolding and dropped his load of bricks on a roof that had just been completed. His co-workers covered up the incident and he escaped being fired.

After work, John – when he was not with Dom Raphael – often joined his workmates in the pub. He also became friendly with the villagers and guests at the Abbey, such as Philip Bridge, a retired schoolmaster and a great friend of the Benedictines, as well as with a well-known local eccentric and his mother:

> His mother was a Carmelite,
> Third Order dressed in brown
> With over it a cloak of white:
> She was ninety ... ne'er a frown,
> Never a wrinkle! was her name
> Elizabeth? embraced Our Dame.
> (*Ring-a-Ring-a-Rosary,* 1977)

John particularly enjoyed the company of the local bank manager, Hugh Symons, his senior by a generation, a gentleman to his fingertips, generous but discreet. This Anglican and former freemason had been received into the Catholic Church at Buckfast in 1942. He joined Dom Raphael in helping John to overcome any lingering scruples and difficulties, and to discover the riches of the Catholic faith. They often got together in the pub after compline and exchanged jokes. Hugh was quick to spot John's minor weakness. When the two Johns visited the Abbey together he would warn them: 'Now, you two, behave yourselves in the Monastery, and do

not drink too much cider in front of my dear friend the Abbot!'
When the monk judged that the young convert was ready, he asked
Hugh to be his godfather:

> Now meet my Godfather – good Hugh:
> At Buckfast he enlarged my view,
> And he it was taught brother ass
> That few things beat a quart o'bass!
> (*Ut Unum Sint*, 1956, stanza 1349)

John continued from time to time to join his old Quantock friends
at Bridgwater, especially Jack Dunn, who was preparing to set out
for the forestry school at Dean in Gloucestershire. The latter was
delighted to hear of his friend's impending conversion. John was
particularly happy to see John Dove again, who was becoming more
and more attracted to the idea of joining the Society of Jesus. The
Dove parents now considered John Bradburne to be a bad influence
on their son; for John Dove senior, the Jesuits represented all that
was quintessentially 'non-English', whereas the Reverend Thomas
Bradburne was of the opinion that it was John Dove who was
leading his son down the path of Catholicism!

By Christ the King

John was received into the Catholic Church by Dom Raphael Stones
on October 26th 1947, the feast of Christ the King (at that time
celebrated on the last Sunday of October), shortly before second
Vespers. Hugh Symons and Philip Bridge were his godparents, John
Dove not being able to get away for the occasion. The ceremony
took place in the vaulted Chapel of St Anne, a vestige of the ancient
medieval Abbey. It was not a conditional baptism, and John was
overjoyed that the baptism he had received from his father (the
certificate at Buckfast states: 'cf. no. 274, Skirwith Anglican Parish
Register, Cumberland, August 31st, 1921') was not called into
question, although he had been prepared to renounce it if necessary.

The ceremony was private, as laid down by the decrees of the
1852 Synod of Westminster. Dom Raphael followed to the letter
the 1917 ritual, and began the ceremony seated in front of the

altar, on the Epistle side, wearing a surplice, head covered, next
to John. Then both knelt, and sang the *Veni Creator*. Dom Raphael
recited a prayer, and sat down. John, still kneeling, recited before
him the profession of Catholic faith. The monk held a book of
the New Testament on his knees and, after a penitential psalm,
stood up and, turning towards the altar, chanted the *Kyrie Eleison*.
He then sat down and John, still kneeling, was absolved from
excommunication, confessed, and received a plenary indulgence.
All then intoned the *Te Deum*, and the monk gave the new Catholic
his blessing with the sign of the cross.

John made his first communion during the Mass which followed,
which was served by Hugh, deeply impressed by the demeanour
of his godson throughout the ceremony. John confided to him at
this time his deepest wish, which was that 'he hopes that his end
on earth would be a martyr's'. According to Hugh, 'whilst his head
was in Heaven, his feet were firmly planted on earth. One could
not help loving him – he in some ways resembled to me a young
pedigree bouncing sheepdog.' Two days later John was confirmed,
probably by the new Bishop of Plymouth, Francis Grimshaw. He
considered the date of his reception into the Catholic Church as a
gift from Christ the King, and believed that he had been called to
be a knight in the service of Christ; henceforth he saw Christ as his
royal lord, and himself as Christ's subject and vassal. In the years to
come this vision would be enriched, but it remained anchored in
the memory of October 26th 1947 (the day is invoked in more than
150 poems). And since Christ the King was prominently the King
of the Jews, John would draw from this feast day the inspiration for
what he considered his vocation towards the Jews, as he recounted
in his 1965 interview in *The Shield*:

> My concern for the Jews dated chiefly from my
> thinking about the gospel of that feast – 'Art thou
> the King of the Jews?' I thought what a pity that
> he is not since he was born in Juda.

His joy on the day was marred by two shadows. Thomas
Bradburne was deeply hurt by his son's conversion, as a father,
an Anglican,and a churchman; and Anne was not present. In the

event, John's reception into the Catholic Church spelt the end of their engagement. They still loved each other, but she had no wish to follow him down the road he had taken. In addition, since his arrival in Buckfastleigh he had seriously been considering a monastic vocation, and the moment of truth had arrived. He broke off the engagement, and in the above mentioned poem he attributed the reason to the Virgin Mary:

> I said to Anne, Do be my Queen
> And she said Yes, and might have been
> If Mary had not come between
> Engagement and the fray.
> (*At the Sign of the Nine Muses*, 1976)

Anne had no doubt been expecting the break, which was amicable, and the deep friendship between John and all the Hardwicke family, including Anne, was unaffected. She would have agreed with her mother Cecil that 'it was just great to have been part of his life'.

A wise delay

John was now a Catholic. The Church he had just entered was about to celebrate the centenary of the restoration of the English Catholic Hierarchy, and the many works published around this time were imbued with a feeling of satisfaction at progress made over the last century. But it was towards the monastic life, flourishing in English Catholicism in the post-war period, with its promise of being 'alone to the Alone', that John, like many new converts from Anglicanism, now numerous in monasteries and convents, felt particularly drawn. He wrote on a sheet of paper pinned to the wall of his room the word GOD, followed by the words 'That I should always think of Him and daily love more Him'.

He was convinced that his spiritual pilgrimage, begun six years earlier in the Malayan jungle in the face of death, had led to Buckfast. His reasons seemed substantial: the fervour of the recent convert, his love of prayer and solitude, of Gregorian chant, his good relations with the monks. He confided to Dom Raphael his desire to enter the monastery. But the latter knew his young friend well, and thought differently. When consulted, the Abbot and Dom

Placid agreed with him, much to the chagrin of John, who refused to admit defeat, insisting to his mentor that he was certain of his vocation. He then turned to Hugh Symons and asked him to plead his case with the monks, convinced that they would not dare refuse his request. And it worked. Out of friendship for Hugh, the Abbey accepted the new convert as a postulant, but on one condition: he must wait two years before being admitted to the monastery, as was customary with new converts, to allow a cooling off period and to submit his vocation to the test of time.

To teach a bit of everything at Gaveney School

The year 1948 opened on a more auspicious note than the previous one, and the anticipation of the forthcoming Olympic Games prompted stirrings of national pride, with the spectre of dogmatic socialism seemingly in retreat, and the Marshall Plan having reduced the need for rationing. When in 1949 George Orwell published his *1984*, the collectivist nightmare he had imagined for his country no longer threatened, while the country itself seemed more bent on pursuing the *Brave New World* of Aldous Huxley, a far cry from the aspirations of John and people of like mind.

Accepted as a 'provisional postulant' at Buckfast, the new convert was urged to find gainful employment. He spent in fact several months at a loose end, seemingly content to let the two-years wait drift by. From time to time he stayed with his parents (having worked out a modus vivendi with his father), but they too pressed him to find work; or, more often, at Sidbury with the Hardwickes; and finally took up odd jobs here and there, surviving on a pittance. He would sometimes disappear and spend long periods walking through the countryside. In the end, in the spring of 1948, and probably recommended by Dom Raphael, he applied for a teaching post to Theodore Williams, Headmaster at Gaveney House boys' prep school in Exmouth, some 12 miles south of Sidbury. Here he was asked to take a class of 8-year-olds to 10-year-olds. Like Paul Pennyfeather in Evelyn Waugh's semi-autobiographical novel *Decline and Fall*, John admitted to knowing little about anything, whereupon Williams told him he could teach a bit of everything, and signed him up on the spot. (John himself later compared this episode to *Decline and Fall*, whose hero admits: 'I don't know a word of German, I've had no experience, I've got no testimonials and I can't play cricket', then is told: 'It doesn't do to be too modest. It's wonderful what one can teach when one tries.')

When John started at Gaveney House, private schools had just narrowly escaped being shut down. The government would have liked to nationalise them, but couldn't afford to, and Atlee was not inclined to use force. Like Gaveney House, many Catholic schools were established by private initiative, owned and controlled by their headmaster. The school had originally been established in Hampstead in the 1920s, and included among its past pupils Robert McNair (a hero of the Battle of Britain and a devout Catholic: whenever he shot down a German plane he would ask his crew to pray for its pilot) and future Chindit hero Michael Allmand, whom John might have met. The school was evacuated in 1939 and took up residence in an imposing Georgian mansion in Exmouth, overlooking the town from Highfield. Classrooms were located on the ground floor, with dormitories upstairs. The house was surrounded by high walls, and there was a garden where the pupils played in the shadows of numerous tall trees.

At the end of the war, Williams decided to stay in Exmouth, and the increase in pupil numbers obliged him to take on new staff. Most of the 80 boarders were Catholic, whereas the majority of dayboys were Protestant, and all were hoping to go on to public schools in the region. Standards were high. Williams, a former Anglican clergyman, was an effective if eccentric educationist, especially in the areas of English literature and religion, both of which he considered more important than anything else on one's curriculum vitae. Every day the boys looked forward to Williams' religious knowledge class, not least because he was an excellent storyteller. He had also composed rhymed jingle versions of the rules of grammar, which the boys had to learn off by heart, even before they had grasped their meaning.

John got on well with the boys, and soon discovered the best way to catch their attention – by making them laugh – a revolutionary approach, but one which bore fruit. He soon became friendly with them, especially the younger boys who were far from home. The new teacher was universally liked, and the boys went out of their way to impress him. Nick Lowry, at the time ten years old, became friends with John. He was not in John's class, but in such a small school everybody knew everybody else. He later became editor of the *Brandsma Review* in Dublin and still remembers John. 'Have you ever known a saint? I have, I think... For a brief period one of our teachers was John Randal Bradburne.' Young Nick was struck by a man who could be so amusing and pious at the same time:

> He used to try to draw out whatever talent he thought a boy might have. I recall his training of a small schola to sing *Non Nobis Domine* as a round. He would accompany them on the recorder.

Nick was dumbstruck with admiration for his teacher, but taken aback one day because 'musically, he was skilful but apparently largely self-taught. When one boy he asked to play a duet with him inquired, "What key, Sir?" Bradburne replied, "Heavens, I don't know. I just play it!"' Another time, tells Nick Lowry:

> in the classroom after homework supervised by Bradburne, I fell and bruised my bare shin against the steel leg of a desk. It was surprisingly painful, but another boy, slightly younger than I, pointed and laughed 'ha ha!' like Bart Simpson's tormentor. Enraged, I lashed out and punched him on the nose. A quiet voice summoned me to the teacher's desk. 'I'm surprised at you, Lowry!' said Mr. Bradburne. 'That's a very bad temper.' That was all, but I am still ashamed even 60 years later – for the sole and simple reason, then and now, that I deserved a rebuke from such a man.

John had no difficulty fitting in with the teaching staff. Male and female, and particularly the more mature among the latter, took their boyish newcomer to their hearts. He became friendly with Rupert Pearce, and stood as godfather to his daughter Sarah. He found he had things in common with the teacher whose class preceded his – 'the Babies', as they were called. Margaret Smith, a friend of Williams, was 41, but like John did not look her age. Born in India, she shared his passion for music, including Bach. They attended concerts and often dined together in the town. John was still committed to his monastic vocation and was counting down the months to the autumn of 1949, but this friendship with Mollie, as he would soon call her, made him feel good.

John came to love Exmouth, which, though a small town, was rich in historical associations, including Sir Walter Raleigh and Nelson. At the time of John's stay it still retained its charm as a holiday resort, and was a tourist draw on account of its two miles of golden sandy beaches, cliffs, magical rock pools, and magnolias, imported there for the first time in Europe by John Colleton. He enjoyed the pubs and wrote a poem in praise of the Pilot Inn and its cider. He often walked along the sea front, and took John Dove there when he came on a visit in the autumn of 1948, before leaving for Cape Town – dispatched there by the company he worked for to give him a taste for business. John also liked to go for long walks in the surrounding countryside, always full of surprises, the estuary being a natural reserve of flora and fauna. And the road he cycled to Sidbury and back traversed woodland, meadows and softly undulating hills.

At Exmouth he received an unexpected 'bonus' from his conversion. He had already experimented with verse, but his new inspiration led to a steady stream of poetry that would never diminish for the rest of his life:

> By my twenty-seventh year, had stirred
> In my fancy scarce a single rhyme;
> Then I came to Rome and, homing, spurred...
> Galaxies of brightness at a time!
> Now there is a ladder that I climb, –
> Up I go...
> (*A Ballade of a Lifetime*, 1974)

He regarded this poetic gift as both privilege and duty, as he later revealed in his interview in *The Shield* (1965):

> I never wanted to write, I never felt the impulsion
> to put thoughts into verse until that first spring. I
> also believe that anyone who has a talent however

small or great, once he is a Catholic should use it
for the sake of the Kingdom.

The new poet was anything but self-centred: in June he copied out
and posted to John Dove 40 or so poems, as well as extracts from
biblical and liturgical sources, revealing his wide acquaintance with
literature and the Bible.

The year 1948 passed quickly for John, whether at the bar of the
Pilot Inn, concerts with Mollie, cycle trips, writing poetry, or visits
to Buckfast. He accompanied the children to Mass on Sundays at
the Catholic Church beside Gaveney House, but continued to visit
the Church of St Anthony of Ottery. He was no longer the discreet
shadowy figure at the back of the sanctuary; he was now at home.
The Marist sisters had rejoiced at his reception into the Catholic
Church, and were proud to tell him that their church had been
registered by the authorities as a place of community prayer and the
celebration of marriages, as a further step towards full recognition.

In early 1949 John Dove returned from South Africa and
announced to his delighted friend that he had come to a decision
to enter the Jesuit Order at Campion House in Osterley. They both
set off at Easter for Buckfast, and John would return there for the
Ascension. The celebrations inspired him on the spot to write a
hymn, which he started to compose at the foot of an image of the
Virgin and Child, marking the beginning of that striking mixture
of styles that became characteristic of his work. The hymn included
a discreet reference to the role of the bees in producing the wax
for the Paschal candle in the Latin 'Exsultet', emphasising John's
growing affinity with them:

> In a pub, I was told that a message had come,
> Marked 'Urgent! From all Abbey bees' ...
> 'Twas as follows: 'Dear Bard, tho' we sing not, but
> hum,
> Our life is not given to ease.
> If you look in the Sanctuary, you will observe
> There burns near the Altar a flame:
> 'Tis fed by a pillar of flowers and herbs –
> A wax candle – our title to fame!

To us, lest the world think bees wanting in praise
The Lord gives this work for a sign;
And while others sing canticles marking the Phase,
We cause His memorial to Shine!'
(*A Song to Our Lady of Buckfast*, 1949)

John continued his visits to the Hardwickes, his relationship with Anne having settled into relaxed friendship. He hadn't forgotten his other friends, and wrote to Jack Dunn suggesting a somewhat original campaign of evangelisation: they would both head abroad 'carrying the banner of Christ in front of us', not specifying whether the banner was a literal or a metaphorical one. Poor Jack, feeling perhaps guilty at his own lukewarm missionary zeal, declined on the pretext that he was immersed in his studies, and that in any case he was getting married. The feast of the Sacred Heart prompted John to write a poem of introspection, with echoes of Francis Thompson's 'Hound of Heaven', and suggestive of an inner conflict:

I do not follow Thee, O Lord,
I seek not well Thy will;
And all my life is weariness
And all my love falls ill;
And everywhere is emptiness
Of which I drink my fill;
I do not follow Thee, O Lord,
But Thou dost find me still.

Yet do I seek Thy Face, O Lord,
Thy wonder I would see;
The Maker of all loveliness
All beautiful must be:
Now, overcome by loneliness
I cast my cares on Thee;
This do I by Thy grace, dear Lord,
Thy Spirit follows me.
(*The Sacred Heart of Jesus*, 1949)

A few day days later, what was to be John's last term at Gaveney House, before he entered Buckfast, was due to come to an end. But his friendship with Mollie, unawares to both, had taken a new turn. He was used to showing her his poems, some of them dedicated to her, in which his feelings found indirect outlet. Margaret was by no means indifferent to the charm of her young colleague. Their age difference presented no problem to John, his brother Philip having married a woman even older at the time than Mollie, but to Margaret it represented an insuperable obstacle, and she tried to gently hint that their relationship had no future, while John remained unclear in his mind about his own feelings.

Suddenly catastrophe struck on another front. The boys, accompanied by their teachers, had been bathing on the beach, when one of them narrowly escaped drowning. John was impressed by the alacrity shown by Margaret in running into the water to help a colleague rescue the endangered boy. But worse was to come. When it was time to go home, another pupil, Gerard Orwin, who couldn't swim, was nowhere to be seen. He had been carried away by the current, and his body was washed up two days later. A police enquiry followed. The tragedy was made more poignant by the fact that the boy's father had been killed in the war – his mother had recently remarried. The people of Exmouth were deeply shocked and, 60 years later, elderly women will still bring it up in conversation. One can still see on the beach a dilapidated sign with the warning: 'Bathing and paddling is dangerous for 200 yards each side of this sign.'

John and Margaret were also traumatised, and the event seemed to draw them even closer together. But life had to go on, and a few days later the traditional end-of-year cricket match went ahead. As John and she sat together on the edge of the pitch, he suddenly leaned towards her, told her he was in love with her, and asked her to marry him. She begged him to stop, warning him that 'the little ones have extremely long ears, they will hear and gossip – please stop it'. John however continued to press his suit, until Margaret lost her composure; 'Stop it – you hear me – this is more than embarrassing.' At this John leaped to his feet and took off, and Margaret would never see him again. He failed to show up for afternoon tea, or for dinner that evening. At ten o'clock a worried Margaret knocked on the headmaster's door, and told him all. Williams, already devastated by the death of a pupil, was outraged.

Even Nick Lowry, who considers John a saint, remained shocked to this day by his disappearance, and felt that Margaret Smith 'had the good sense and strength of character not to allow the relationship to develop, realising I suspect that he was not called to the married state'.

Where had John gone? He had walked all afternoon, all evening, and all night, directing his footsteps instinctively towards Buckfast, some 30 miles from Exmouth. He arrived at daybreak and immediately called Gaveney House to tell Williams he was coming back. He was curtly informed that there was no point, given that the term would be over in two days; that he should not even think about coming back in September, and that his belongings would be sent on to him in the coming days. John then went to inform Dom Raphael and Hugh Symons of what had happened. Symons was furious: had he not been bullied into pressing John's case at Buckfast? The novitiate was now out of the question, and his friend Hugh seriously advised John to get a job aboard ship and learn some discipline! In the meantime, John stayed for some time at the house of Mrs Ash in Buckfastleigh, and often at Sidbury. He there gave poetic expression to his bruised feelings:

> World's losses sow the seed of heaven's gain;
> There's ne'er a single severance on earth,
> No death-struck blow, nor parting charged with pain,
> No sadness, but can give to joy a birth.
> Let those who in their heart's desires are crossed,
> And, sore in anguish, would from life retire,
> Believe love's longings never to be lost –
> Misfortune is the soul's refining fire.
> (*In via*, 1949)

It was however in these unhappy circumstances that he discovered St Francis of Assisi, who filled him with enthusiasm. The Franciscan spirit would never abandon him, and in July 1949 he composed a poem in honour of the saint, invoking his medieval ideal of courtesy, the courtly love of God, and universal brotherhood under the cross of Christ:

Bright master minstrel, Bernadone blest,
You have outsong'd the troubadours of France:
Sweet jester of the King, you did advance
The jongleur's art. O fool! God's fool the best,
Being lost in love with Love, you far outran
The muse's measure, overtook the seers
In racing to the fountains whence all tears
Of true repentance flow for fallen man.
So loving Christ, you loved the things He made,
Each living thing, bird, cricket, lizard, beast,
All creatures from the greatest to the least, –
All souls for which the Lord so dearly paid.
O pray Him, send us holy Brother Fire,
To light our hearts in flame of pure desire.
(*To Saint Francis*, 1949)

Stars of the Sea: Lourdes and a voyage at sea

John Dove, hearing of John's misadventures at Gaveney House, asked him to accompany him on a pilgrimage to Lourdes on August 15th, thinking that this might 'heal his disturbed heart'. John gratefully agreed, though up to this point Marian devotion had never particularly attracted him. In his eyes France was a Catholic country, and that was enough. The two friends met in London and joined a band of English pilgrims. Wearing a Sherlock Holmes hat, John cut an entertaining figure with his banter, his sense of humour and his recorder playing. From Paris to Bordeaux, while John Dove marvelled about the new electric trains and read a book, his friend stood in the corridor at the window admiring the countryside. In Lourdes the two friends rented a tiny room, and on August 15th attended the Grotto, along with 200,000 other pilgrims. John was greatly taken by the candle-lit procession, and performed all the rites traditional at Lourdes, drank copiously of the spring water, and visited the baths.

The two friends often wandered away from their group, but the Benedictine in charge turned a blind eye to their absences. They went for occasional walks to Luz and Gavarnie, where John was inspired by the grandeur of the Pyrenees, not to mention the beauty 'Of a graceful lass who seemed to me / More than a queen of nymphs' (*Ballad*, 1979). They also spent long hours at the Grotto praying and (as John Dove wrote) 'happy just to be there, taking in the scene, the River Gave, the pilgrims, the rock, the invalids, the peasants of the world at prayer'. John was particularly fascinated by pilgrims from Eastern Europe who, having lost everything, sought solace in prayer heedless of those around them. He continued to notice pretty young women on all sides; but his heart was drawn in another direction.

At the outset John was made distinctly uneasy by the extravagant display of Marian devotion that characterised Lourdes. Having spoken about it to the Benedictine in confession, he was gently advised: 'Let Mary show herself to you YOUR way' (*Aeronautics*, 1971). (John Dove had a somewhat different remembrance of the sentence: 'Allow her to show herself to you in her way.') For the young Englishman these words opened the door to Marian devotion, and helped him to understand that he was free to pray to the Blessed Virgin in his own way, regardless of others, talking to her when he felt the urge, and listening for her answer in his own heart. Later he recalled:

> Lourdes worked a miracle in my body and soul:
> of that I am now sure. She has done the same
> for countless others, but that does not lessen the
> miracle, but increases its wonder.

Lourdes thus marked the beginning of John's devotion to the Virgin Mary, and 25 poems would recall the event down through the years. He also encountered St Bernadette Soubirous at Lourdes. She too became close to his heart, and several poems were dedicated to her:

> The child Bernadette was a peasant,
>   As Jesus her Maker has been,
> And Lourdes is the sister of Naz'reth,
>   For both are the home of our Queen.
>   (*Lourdes*, 1949)

> O may we yet
> Like Bernadette
> Behold the Morning Star!
> (*To Beauty – an Ode*, 1949)

The two friends had planned to visit Lisieux on their journey home, but a severe toothache detained John in Paris, where he took the opportunity to visit the Chapel of the Miraculous Medal in Rue du Bac, as well as Montmartre.

Back in England they ended their holiday at North Curry, where their daily recital of the rosary together did not prevent them from visiting the pub, drinking cider and playing skittles. On the last evening, John Dove packed his bags, in preparation for leaving the family home for the novitiate. John helped him burn some old letters, some of them from ex-girlfriends. 'It would not do to take love letters to the novitiate', pointed out the young Jesuit-to-be. As he said this, a piece of paper took flight and fell at his feet. Picking it up he read out one simple word: GOD. He took this as confirmation of his decision to choose the life on which he was about to embark.

On September 7th John accompanied his friend to the novitiate at Osterly, and returned to the Hardwickes at Sidbury. It was time to pay heed to the advice of Hugh Symons, all the more so because Adrian Hardwicke, for whom John was 'a most valued friend', thought that 'both shared the same mission, to get round the world working as seamen'. They left first for Plymouth, on a vague promise of passage, which failed to materialise. They then headed for Southampton, where John discovered a ship about to depart for the Middle East. The idea of visiting the Holy Land was very attractive, but it was not to be: he did not have a union membership card, without which he could not be hired.

Undeterred, and having heard that a fleet of fishing trawlers was soon to leave for the Hebrides, the two friends hitch-hiked some 250 miles to the point of departure at Fleetwood, near Liverpool. It was already October when they arrived on the quays at Fleetwood, and got caught up in the bustle with sailors and would-be-sailors like themselves, the cries of scavenger seagulls overhead, and boats of all kinds spewing forth black smoke. Again they found out that even fishermen needed a union card to get work. They eventually got taken on, though on different trawlers, the *Coningsby* and the *Marinda* respectively. They immediately went on board, as Adrian Hardwicke recounts it, as 'stoker's apprentices', and the fleet set sail for the island of St Kilda, where John wrote a poem (and music) for his friend, who carefully treasured it. The verse was later incorporated in *Ut Unum Sint* (1956, stanza 2127):

> Northern Isle, O lone Saint Kilda's isle,
> Hilly home of gulls and nimble sheep,
> Little land of solitude and sleep,
> Let me lingering hear your voice awhile.

John was also charmed by a short stop-off at the tiny port of Tobermory ('Our Lady's Well' in Gaelic), with its seafront of brightly coloured houses which would be recalled over a dozen times in future poems. He was particularly moved by an inscription on the cliff overlooking the sea:

> Tobermory, Tobermory!
> Hebridean harbour town;
> From a trawler, Tobermory,
> I beheld the night come down.
>
> Moor and mountain, Tobermory,
> All surround your sheltered place;
> Crowned with stars and Northern light-shine,
> I could feel your silent grace.
>
> ...
>
> Tobermory, there is written:
> 'GOD IS LOVE' upon your shore;
> Thus His Name in clearest legend
> Signs your beauty evermore.
>
> (A little girl fell from a high cliff there, but was unhurt.
>
> Her parents had the words 'God is Love' set on the cliff-face)
>
> (*Tobermory*, 1949)

The landscapes were heavenly, the sea views splendid and, as Adrian Harwicke puts it, 'I often wonder how we both would have fared if we' d been able to continue our life on the ocean waves unhindered!?'

But working in the boiler house endlessly shovelling coal into a furnace was hellish work. John, who had known the hell of jungle warfare in Malaya, wrote to his mother in a letter posted from Tobermory that it was the most difficult time in his life to date: 12 hours a day shovelling coal into a fire, almost without let-up. For Adrian Hardwicke the venture came brutally to a halt. Docking in advance of John at Fleetwood at the end of the second trip he discovered that the police were looking for him: his father had died in an accident in Worcester. He returned immediately to Sidbury, forced to abandon for good his dream of a round-the-world trip. John likewise handed in his resignation on arrival, and was paid off. But he experienced some doubts: had he done enough to satisfy Hugh Symons? He resorted to a method of discerning the will of God, which he would have many occasions to use in the future: a big sign of the cross, followed by a Hail Mary, and then the toss of a coin. The answer was: go back to sea.

According to John Dove, he then set out for Lowestoft in Suffolk, birthplace of Benjamin Britten and the most easterly point of the British Isles, where he embarked on another trawler which fished off Hull. This time the work was even more punishing: still hellish in the boiler room, and the freezing cold whenever he went on deck was even worse. Yet again his amiability, his sense of humour, not to mention his mistakes, made him friends. An old Polish sailor, in poor health, confided in him, and John promised to help. Having decided to abandon life at sea for good, he handed in his resignation on arrival in Lowestoft. He immediately wrote to Jack Dunn, still training to be a forester, asking him to look after his Polish friend. The letter was full of compassion for his shipmate and mockery at his own efforts as he related the trials and tribulations of life at sea, marvelling how any ship with him on board could stay afloat.

Porter at Parkminster

John stayed a few weeks with the Hardwickes, then spent some time in Islington in London. He still felt called to the religious life, but the gates of Buckfast, open to the friend, were still closed to the postulant. Instead of seeking a less rigorous path he made up his mind to follow an even harsher one. On February 11th 1950 he set out for Horsham in Sussex, and from there made his way on foot to the Charterhouse of St Hugh of Lincoln at Parkminster.

A traveller might easily miss the modest signpost slightly back from the Henfield road indicating the route, were it not for the elegant 200-feet-high stone spire visible above the tree-tops in the near distance. Here John left the road behind and followed the path leading to the monastery. He soon found himself facing an impressive facade of cut Bath stone and red brick, more than 300 feet wide, with extended walls, flanked on the left by a guest house for visitors:

> I entered Parkminster to scan the Downs,
> The Sussex Weald and Chanctonbury Ring,
> To get as near to God and far from towns
> As possible... for an inactive fling
> On contemplation's more attractive wing:
> Heaven on earth at window of my cell
> I hoped to hold and, being goaled, to sing
> Serenely through the days and nights as well.
> (*A Ballade of an Unspoilt Vocation*, 1975)

John explained to the brother who answered his knock that he felt called to the life of a Carthusian monk. His approach was admittedly somewhat unconventional, but it worked, and even though, according to the records, his first stay at Parkminster only lasted one night, since he left next day, he was back again on the 21st. The Carthusians then got in touch with Buckfast and in due course the reply confirmed their initial impression that John was not cut out for the life of a Carthusian. But the sub-prior, Dom Andrew Gray, decided to give his young guest a four-month trial period to see whether John and the Carthusians were suited to each other. In the meantime he suggested that John take up the position of temporary porter in the building to the right of the Great Porch:

> My Sussex friend for evermore
> Who (when I was a sorry tramp)
> Welcomed me in (sans any stamp
> Credential) to keep the door...
> (*Ut Unum Sint*, 1956, stanza 1353)

John took up residence in the porter's parlour, where the walls gave off the musty odours of old masonry, and his clothes were constantly damp, with no heating. He felt the late winter cold, and suffered from severe chilblains, which swelled his fingers, causing them to burst. Nancy Maguire, who later stayed there, described the room where John lived as follows (in *An Infinity of Little Hours*, 2006):

> I found the North Parlour anything but inviting. The one small window has bars on it. My first impressions: cold, damp, dank; two antique sideboards, one with a crucifix above, the other with a clock that chimes every half-hour; lots of straight-back chairs. There is a flushing toilet but no hot water, no towel rack, no wastebasket, no wardrobes.

John did not worry about these details, and didn't make a fuss, telling himself:

> How truly sang David! these courts of the Lord
> Hold natural wealth!
> The sparrow hath found her a wonderful house,
> The swallow a nest;
> But here, I feel certain, the spider's the one
> Which cometh off best!
> (*Cobwebs*, 1950)

He received one meal a day, without meat of course, which didn't worry him, used as he was to getting by on next to nothing.

He gradually adapted to the Carthusian rhythm of life, unchanged since the eleventh-century. This was his first experience of the life of silence and solitude, devoted to the exclusive search for God, and he was thrown in at the deep end. For him, as for many young men who came to the Charterhouse, becoming a Carthusian 'symbolised a sort of emigration', as it was said in a Parkminster chapter sermon. John soon found a spiritual director in Dom Andrew Gray who, for his part, came to consider him as a son sent to him by God. But John was very different from the sub-prior's other charges, and as a result the monk had great difficulty discerning what God's will was for him. Dom Hugh Weld, the Prior, shared these doubts, but held his young guest in great regard, and later wrote that John 'was highly respected while he was here... Obviously only someone responsible can be entrusted with this post... The work is certainly exacting and means contact with a good number of people.' He added that John's modesty was edifying: on one occasion he met him recovering from the shock of being asked for his advice on something or other and wondering: 'Who would ever have thought that anyone would think it worthwhile to ask me anything.' For their part the lay brothers quickly adopted John, who, according to Gabriel Sedden, was 'very well liked by everyone.'

The presence of 'familiars' (as they were known) such as John was rare among the Carthusians, and they continued to wear their ordinary clothes, but John wanted to model his life as closely as possible on that of the Carthusians. He hoped to be admitted to the novitiate as a lay brother at the very least, and was conscious of the favour being bestowed upon him: the Carthusians do not receive visitors or organise retreats; they are simply too busy, their whole life being devoted to prayer and the search for God in the secret places of the heart. The silence of the monks struck John forcibly. They seemed to move about on a cushion of air, their cork-lined choir shoes making not the slightest sound, even though designed to protect from the cold in a church without central heating. As they made their way at night to attend the Office, each monk carrying a lantern, they radiated an air of timelessness which pervaded the entire monastery.

John was allowed to attend the Offices, and strove to follow the daily rhythm of the monks, rising at a quarter to midnight and retiring at 8 o'clock in the evening. The Offices differed in their sobriety from those he had known at Buckfast, with long intervals of silence, interrupted by Gregorian chant with no instrumental accompaniment, and stripped of all aesthetic embellishment. He had some difficulty in fitting into this rigorous Carthusian lifestyle, particularly when it came to getting up in the middle of the night to attend matins, and constantly struggled to stay awake in the piercing cold of the church. He never got used to it, nor was he the only one. He describes in a poem the dawn chorus of the birds as he rushed along the corridor in the early hours to 'bray' at the Mass:

> On deacon's side the blackbird sings,
> Cantoris chants the thrush;
> 'Tis time to wake!' a cockerel cries – 'Right, I'll to
> bed!' an owl replies:
> The jackdaws yell –
> 'There's half an hour
> By this great Clock
> On this our tower!
> We'll not to working yet awhile!'
> A Ringdove murmurs 'Hush...'
> ...
> Downwards I fly, right down the stairs!
> Then through the Cloister (where the flares
> Of morn's first fires are flinging flame
> To lighten looney whence he came) –
> And very soon (with brother mouse)
> I'm kneeling in the Chapter House,
> Where novices hear morning Mass
> With Thomas More and brother ass.
>
> Then (wandering eyes) upon the wall
> Behold the Painting in the Hall
> (Or Chapter House): and then I fall
> To sleep upon my knees...
> (*A Corollary: Carthusian Cartwheels*, 1958,
> stanzas 997–1000)

He was touched to discover the depth of Marian devotion among the Carthusians, with the result that his own, inspired by his recent visit to Lourdes, gained in depth and intensity. The Carthusians placed the stability of their profession and of their Order under the protection of Mary, and gave expression to it in Carthusian prayers. The antechamber of the room where the monks prayed and lived was in fact called the 'Ave Maria', to signify that it is through the intercession of the Mother that we encounter the Son (a theme which would remain important to John), and all the Offices were preceded by a prayer to the Patroness of the order. It was St Bruno or his immediate successors who established the Little Office of the Blessed Virgin Mary for the Carthusians, with its daily Seven Hours, duplicating those of the Divine Office itself, and John remained faithful to it all his life.

With the arrival of summer John was still missing his sleep, and spent long hours listening to the birds and writing poems, many of them about nature, and in tune with Carthusian spirituality: 'For the Carthusian, the garden is the meeting point with nature through which God speaks. A flower opening, a bird landing on a branch, even a drop of dew: through this microcosm dialogue with the Lord becomes possible' (Dom Ignazio, in Enzo Romeo, *Solitaires de Dieu*). John seems to have been fascinated by the night sky, and resumed his passion for trees, which often found expression in several of his poems, while others sing the glory of the passing seasons at the monastery. He did some gardening, and went for walks in the fields and woodlands surrounding the monastery, and became friends with Anthony Roufe, a retired naval captain who lived in the gate lodge at the end of the lane leading up to the monastery. They often conversed when the temporary porter passed by the door of the lodge.

By summer, the four months of trial were already over, but nothing changed. John did not enter the monastery as a postulant, but continued on as porter. He admired the monks and would have liked to emulate them in their spiritual strivings; and in one poem, where 'bees were buzzing in the lime', he described them as 'God's athletes':

> When they exchange their solitude
> Below, with that Beatitude
> Which is the sight of Only Him
> Who shines upon the Seraphim:
> Carthusians! O may we race
> As they amid the fields of grace,
> And sprint to see the Saviour's face.
> (*Sumer is i cumen in*, 1958)

His work as porter was by no means arduous, as visitors were rare. Those who were expected, or who spent a few days in the hostelry, hardly exceeded three or four a month. Among these were a Cistercian, a niece of one of the monks from Paris, a Carthusian procurator and an American from Kentucky. John was obliged to explain to other callers that the monastery did not admit or receive guests. His gentle manner was appreciated by visitors, rare as they were, and Brother Simon Brennan, who arrived after John had left and who replaced him as porter, reports that in the late 1990s, half a century after John's departure, elderly visitors would still ask after the friendly young porter who had opened the door for them back in the 1950s!

One day a Rolls Royce pulled up in front of the monastery door. A man got out and demanded to see Dom Gray. John explained that one could not meet him without a prior appointment, but Walter Dunkels was no ordinary visitor. This wealthy Jewish diamond merchant resided in nearby Walhurst Manor, where he had amassed an impressive art collection of old masters. His assertive personality, not to mention his irascibility, were well known, and had even led to a very public legal battle with his son-in-law Baron Stempel in 1937, in spite of family ties. John's polite but firm refusal did not prompt Dunkels to storm back to his Rolls Royce and drive off. Instead he engaged the young man in conversation, explaining to him that it was his intention to become a Catholic, and that he would like to discuss the matter with Dom Gray. For John, here was a Jew, who recognised his King, asking advice from him, who had entered the Catholic Church on the feast day of Christ the King! The conversation having become very emotional, John called Dom Andrew, who agreed to receive Walter Dunkels. For John the visit was a sign and a call to him from God. As he wrote on September 14th to John Dove: 'My enthusiasm for the Jews and desire to bring them to their King has culminated in what I firmly believe is a vocation.'

John and Walter Dunkels were to meet again soon: Dom Andrew had agreed in the exceptional circumstances to instruct his visitor in preparation for baptism. Dunkels invited John to call at the manor whenever he felt like it. John accepted, and duly arrived at the Manor one Sunday, as Walter Dunkels and his distinguished guests were concluding lunch. The unknown and unexpected visitor quickly became the focus of attention, and for two hours held the floor in the company of these City gentlemen who had come to the country to rest for the weekend, talking of religion and God. At four o'clock John suddenly got up saying 'Well, I must be getting back to my door now, the brother will want to be relieved', and was gone.

By summer 1950 Dom Andrew was pleased with the progress of his protégé, and thought he could stay on, or at least try out the Carthusian way. But John was already entertaining other ideas. He gave the reason for his departure in a letter to John Dove dated September 14th 1950, in which he referred to the baptism of Walter Dunkels, adding that he had confided in his Carthusian confessor his wish to travel to Jerusalem. Dom Gray had advised him not to worry and to wait for a sign, and John added: 'I'm waiting for a sign – some falling star.' The sign manifested itself almost immediately: a pilgrimage of local people was about to depart for Rome when a woman pilgrim cried off at the last moment, and Rome was on the way to Jerusalem. John of course was penniless, but he signed up for the pilgrimage and left the monastery, hoping for the best. Dom Gray assured him that the door at Parkminster would remain open to him should he wish to return.

But his heart was already elsewhere, and once again he was on the road, the Gladstone bag (a present from his father) and a walking stick (a gift from Captain Roufe) his only earthly possessions. After a few days in London he got a lift to Devon, where he was warmly greeted by the nuns at Ottery St Mary, and resumed attending morning Mass. He then went to Buckfast to announce his new vocation. Hugh Symons was dubious, but noticed that John's fingers still bore the marks of untreated sores; John had not been playing at being a monk, it had been for real. While there, a letter from Dom Gray informed him that Walter Dunkels had undertaken to fund his trip to Rome. It remained only to secure a passport for Jerusalem and to make some pocket money doing odd jobs. Sister Camilla supplied him with the address of some nuns in France and Italy, knowing that he was 'incapable of stopping anywhere' and that she was wasting her time. Dom Gray gave him the address of a Franciscan friend in the Holy Land. At this point John wrote to John Dove (14 September 1950) indicating that he intended spending five days in Rome, but that he would continue on to the Holy Land – with the agreement of Dom Raphael and Dom Andrew, adding:

> I am so useless and clueless and unillustrious. That makes me more truly confident in the power and guidance of the Holy Spirit. Blessed be the Lord to whom and in whom nothing is impossible. And blessed be Our Lady whose consecrated children we are. Blessed too be our friendship, divinely fashioned and cemented... Pray for the odd ones of Christ the King who fit no order, but whom He leads and uses nevertheless. We are both pilgrims seeking the same native land: you and I, Critch boy.

What was it that John had been seeking at Parkminster that he failed to find? Probably what he was to find much later: an alliance between the life of the hermit – the one to the One – and life in a community. But the imprint of those months in the monastery stayed with him, and one day he would inscribe the motto of the Carthusians on the corrugated iron wall of his African hut, at the end of his long pilgrimage. The 'most wonderful friendship and help' of Dom Gray and the time in Parkminster remained for John 'a memory of unblemished happiness'. And, several years later, John turned up at the monastery again in 'gaily coloured clothes and a violin', according to Father Gabriel writing in the 1980s – God's clown :

> I left not Parkminster because it downs
> Such aspirations as to minstrels cling
> Much and inevitably... never frowns
> The Master at his novices who sing
> Amidst their sole beatitude to bring
> Higher their hearts: I left, but not that cell
> Which holds my Treasure still, as still I fling
> Serenely through the days and nights as well.
> (*A Ballade of an Unspoilt Vocation*, 1975)

Chapter 5

The Strange Vagabond of God, 1950–1953

Pray on for my sanctification too, because it would
encourage so many souls if such a wreckage might come to
canonisation, and I do so want to by-pass Purgatory!!
(*Letter to John Dove*, 25 September 1952)

Rome, Athens, Jerusalem: return to the sources

On Tuesday September 19th 1950 John sailed from Newhaven
for the continent, carrying a few belongings in his Gladstone bag,
Captain Roufe's stick, and a few pounds in his pocket. He soon
arrived in Rome, where everything he saw astonished him, as he
tells us in his travel diary, which he called *Rome to Jerusalem* with a
subtitle in French, *Histoire d'un Âne* ('A Donkey's Story', an allusion
to St Thérèse of Lisieux's *Histoire d'une âme*):

> I saw the Holy Father thrice, once in St. Peter's
> amid a tremendous gathering of pilgrims, and
> a second time at Castel Gandolfo with a lesser
> though equally joyous gathering. The sanctity
> of our Pope is evident in his whole bearing, and
> in a demeanour full of humility and gracious
> dignity... The vast splendour of St. Peter's Basilica
> overwhelmed me, until I saw the East Window
> which henceforth dominated the scene for me in
> its beautiful simplicity: the Dove, all gold in silver
> light, sweet symbol.

He went on to describe a large group of pilgrims from Venice,
praised their 'warm, childlike devotion', and visited numerous
basilicas and churches at a hectic pace, confessing that he was
obliged to retire from the scene from time to time to recover
from his 'monumental indigestion'. He was particularly moved by

the Church of St Paul Outside-the-Walls, 'a Temple for a Golden Age, spacious, serene, and of beautiful symmetry', and above all by 'a simple little night-time procession of pilgrims singing in the Coliseum', which reminded him of 'Christ's martyrs, who once passed thence to their Native Land'.

He met a Franciscan in a Roman street, and in the course of their conversation realised he was talking to the man from Jerusalem whose name had been given to him by Dom Andrew. John told him of his plan to travel to Jerusalem, and was advised to take the boat from Naples, 'saving me the expedient of spinning a coin'. On September 27th he auctioned off his clothes to his fellow pilgrims to make some money, and that evening, as they prepared to return home to celebrate the centenary of the restoration of the Catholic hierarchy in Britain, he bade them farewell. One pilgrim took him aside and insisted on handing him an envelope, telling him not to look inside it until he was gone. Later John opened it to discover £10, and felt 'like an English lord'. At nightfall he took a bus out of Rome and then started to walk in the direction of Naples. He tried to hitch-hike, and then to sleep in a barn, only to be chased by a dog. Returning to the road he finally managed to hitch a lift to Naples on a truck. Naples in the early morning was for him 'a magic time': farmers with their mules and donkeys loaded with bales of linen, cars honking their horns, the smell of burning wood, hills which reminded him of Dehra Dun: 'saintly sadhu pilgrims by their little road-side fires in Hindustan – strangers to this world on their way to Heaven.'

On arriving in Naples he went into the first church he came across to attend Mass: 'It was a Franciscan church as I might have guessed it would be.' Having unsuccessfully searched for cheap lodgings he decided to keep going, 'St. Francis' wisdom working for me again, no doubt'. He booked a place on the first boat leaving for Piraeus (£7.10), but which wasn't sailing for another week – on the feast day of St Francis: another sign! He then set off to climb Vesuvius, hoping 'for a very very cheap existence in the more country places', even 'to find a barn or cave or some such'. Passing through a village, the villagers were fascinated by his Gladstone bag, and he gave away his pen, his pullover and a few holy pictures from his Missal in exchange for a bunch of grapes. Arriving exhausted far above Resina (today Ercolano) he booked into a hostel and dined on a plate of spaghetti. When a bottle of Lacryma Christi arrived on the table, at 350 lire, he succumbed without any guilt, and having enjoyed 'the best bottle of wine I'd ever drunk', sat back in mellow mood to watch the sun go down and the lights come up on the bay of Naples. He spent a week in this hostel, descending every day to Resina to attend Mass and Benediction, surviving on a diet of brown bread and grapes.

Then it was time to go. On the evening of October 4th the *Philip Grimian* sailed from Naples crowded with Jews returning to Haifa, with John travelling steerage. At midday the boat stopped off at Catania, where John, with another English passenger, visited several churches, and 'a huge monastery, once of the Benedictines, but now used as town offices or some such' (this was St Nicolas Arena, the second biggest monastery in Europe). Back on board, to his great delight John discovered Father Carmel, a Franciscan bound for Cyprus, only too pleased to allow John to serve Mass for him. On the 7th the *Philip Grimian* docked at Piraeus, from where John promptly set off to visit the Acropolis, which 'rises like a pale ghost above the city – albeit a most beautiful ghost', and slipped into the Parthenon by the side entrance to avoid paying. The view of the city disappointed him:

> The view made me rather sad, for I'd always pictured Athens in a green, idyllic surrounding, rather like the Thames valley at Wargrave, Henley and Marlow ... And where was the quiet wooded place near a river outside the walls where I'd always pictured Socrates praying 'O beloved Pan, and all ye other gods that haunt this place! Give me true beauty of the inward soul ...'

He decided to continue to Cyprus the same day, and arrived at Limassol the next morning at 9 a.m. He enjoyed this trip, particularly the two evenings he spent on the upper deck with a group of Jews:

> singing songs ancient and modern. It was
> wonderful to hear, in the Mediterranean night
> under the stars, songs of David and songs of today,
> all in Hebrew and mostly in harmony, very well
> sung by both men and women ... How full their
> hearts were, and how young.

He thanked God for this 'spirit of pilgrimage and the love of home', and added: 'Faithfully followed, this leads all men through much hardship home to Heaven, our true native land in the Heart of God, the joy of all desiring', before concluding, inspired by the famous sentence of Pius XI: 'We are all Hebrews, spiritually speaking – strangers and pilgrims "in via".'

Cyprus had been a British possession since 1878, but the beginning of the end was signalled some weeks before by the arrival as Archbishop of Nicosia of Makarios III, a fervent advocate of union with Greece. Father Carmel invited John to stay with the Franciscans, and he was only too glad to accept, especially as he was down to his last 500 lire and needed to get a visa for Israel. He changed his lire for 'a very few Cyprus shillings', but had to travel to Nicosia for the visa. As he set out after breakfast, Father Carmel gave him a Cypriot pound, and a letter of introduction to his confreres in the capital, where on arrival he was put up for the night. He hurried to the Greek consulate to apply for a visa, from where a telegram was dispatched to his brother Philip, now in Libya, to confirm the identity of the young vagabond. While awaiting the reply, John wasted no time, and went to the airport where he unsuccessfully tried to persuade some American pilots to fly him to Israel.

Three days later the letter of confirmation from Philip arrived, and immediately John set out for Famagusta, the port on the east side of the island. Cyprus impressed him. He was surprised that everyone seemed to own a large car or, failing that, travelled around in an enormous taxi. Arriving in Famugusta by late afternoon he made straight for the harbour master's office, managed by a kind-hearted Scot, an acquaintance of Philip, who wrote a letter of recommendation to a Greek friend, Mr Paparasilos (John wrote Parapasilon), manager of a commercial shipping company. The man turned out to be not only a Catholic but the leader of the local branch of the Third Order of St Francis. Having promised John free passage to Israel, he offered him two nights free of charge in the hotel he owned, 'a good Samaritan indeed'. The two men spoke together of St Francis, and John confided in him his wish to become a member of the Third Order. Was it at this time that John was received into the Order, by Mr Paparasilos and one of the Franciscans from the monastery at Famagusta? We will return to this question later.

Awaiting his departure, John had time to admire the local churches – 'My word, how the Crusaders built – for an eternity at least!' – and he did not hesitate to say the rosary in one of them which had been transformed into a mosque. He also met an Austrian with his Jewish wife, and 'a British doctor with a great love of Israel. He was not a Catholic, but he gave me a pamphlet he'd written on the Jews, and prophecies concerning this present time, which inspired me considerably'. On the evening of October 16th, John managed to get free passage on the *San Antonio* (another Franciscan sign, the seventh in his trip), a little wooden cargo ship, propelled by sail and steam and transporting grain. The whole crew was Italian except for one Jew who made fun of his companions, and vice versa. On the 17th, the boat sailed and John, seasick, wrote: 'The ship's motor was that of a sea-going camel, so I thought.' The following morning he arrived at Haifa.

On arrival in Israel, John had disembarked in a country already experiencing its first political crisis since the proclamation of independence of 1947 and the formation in 1949 of a government by David Ben Gurion, who had just resigned. The customs were surprised that John had arrived with no more than a few shillings in his pocket, but were satisfied that his visa was in order. He set out on foot for Nazareth, 25 miles to the east. On the outskirts of the town he asked a policeman if he was on the right road, and was offered a seat in a truck headed in the direction of Nazareth. Soon they were climbing the hills of Galilee, with John chatting to the driver, who lived on a kibbutz. He reflected:

> How wonderful it was to be driving through the
> twilight, up and up, beyond the fertile (and now

well-cultivated) plains, to Nazareth, where the
Word was made Flesh, and spent nearly 30 years
of His visible life on earth, as hidden almost as He
is now, in all the Churches which are in the world,
in thousands and thousands of tabernacles.

The Good Samaritans of Nazareth

Night was falling when they arrived at their destination, and John
took a walk in the streets, where he was immediately surrounded
by groups of Arab children (the town had been taken over two
years before by Ben Dunkelman who, defying orders, had refused
to expel the Arab population). The children followed him in the
street, 'more curious than hopeful I should say, considering my
"luggage" and un-moneyed appearance!' He continued his walk,
'aimless and unashamed', as far as the junction of the three main
streets, 'a happy orientally noisy place', with a well where dozens
of women and children were queuing up with jugs and buckets.
He suddenly became aware of what he was experiencing: he was
rediscovering the East which he loved, and above all 'I was walking
in NAZARETH, where the King of Kings so often walked, where
He ran and played as a boy'.

A large cafe ran parallel to the fountain, but John chose a more
modest one nearby, hoping he could afford to pay for a bite to eat.
The manager was a friendly Italian who spoke English:

a Franciscan Tertiary of the best kind (though
perhaps not officially one.) He had been some
years in Palestine, and had spent some time with
the Franciscans – he still wore a pair of very
ancient Franciscan sandals! – but finding that his
calling was not wholly with the First Order, he had
left – in body, though not in spirit, and now kept
this little shop in Nazareth.

John offered thanks to St Francis for leading him to this one
restaurant. Brother Amelio, for such was his name, plied John
with questions about his travels, and refused to accept payment of
any sort for the meal, pressing him to come back for breakfast the

next morning. He recommended that John spend the night at the Scottish hospital and offered to take him there.

They set out 'through Carpenters Street and a maze of alleys, twists and turns in a lovely October night, lit by moon and stars'. Amelio explained that the fountain on the square was known as Mary's Well because Mary used to come there to fetch water for the Holy Family. John was enchanted: 'Knowing this, the night became even more beautiful for me.' When he arrived at the Scottish Hospital he got a full view of Nazareth and the night sky, which reminded him of 'Omar Khayam's "bowl of night"': 'there was a wonderful sight to see. Nazareth's multitude of lights below and around, and above, the myriad stars and a bright clear moon'. The doctor in charge greeted them warmly – 'a Scot and therefore generous' – and invited him to spend the night in his house nearby. He was taken there by Amelio, and fell asleep, while 'all the dogs of Nazareth were barking their raucous serenade', and woke to the same sound, now mingled with 'all the Nazareth roosters vying with one another'.

He went to Mass at the Basilica of the Annunciation, happy to receive the body of Christ 'within a few feet of a slab whereon was written "Et Verbum caro factum est" (And the Word was made flesh)'. He then headed off to have breakfast with his new Franciscan friend, who urged him to look for work in or near Nazareth. They went together to see the police commissioner, who asked John what qualifications he had, to which he promptly replied 'Forester', but 'not adding that any tree felled by me looked as if a beaver had been on the job'. The commissioner tried without success to contact the Forestry Department, then managed to get in touch with Brother Robert, a Franciscan, who agreed to contact his superior about their forests on Mt Tabor. John learnt from the commissioner that he had fought for the Turks, for the British and for his own people, and complained of the difficulty he had controlling an overcrowded city made up of Arabs, Muslims and Christians.

The following day a negative reply arrived from the Franciscans about Tabor. John took this as a sign, and decided to leave at once for Jerusalem. He offered a part of his meagre belongings to Amelio, explaining to him that he wished to become more completely Franciscan by putting himself in the hands of Divine Providence.

Amelio was not convinced, and 'in his kindness insisted on giving me a Palestinian pound for which I was most grateful, though (for once!) I accepted with much reluctance, because Bro. Amelio was by no means a millionaire. (Happily I've been able to refund the money since).'

On the roads of the Holy Land

After an emotional farewell, John began walking east, 'feeling extraordinarily happy'. After a while a jeep overtook him and stopped. It was the police commissioner. Worried about what had become of him, he asked the young Englishman where he was going. Satisfied, he drove John to the next checkpoint and, having ordered the duty officer to find him a place on a vehicle as soon as possible, headed off back to town. Minutes later John found himself in a truck being driven at speed in the direction of Cana. Attentive as ever, he noted a build-up of clouds on the horizon, even though it was still very hot.

Having been dropped off at Cana, and anxious to arrive at the lake, he decided to keep going on foot, knowing that he was 'clueless, given that Tiberias and the lake were twenty miles away" (twelve and a half, in fact), but he was overcome with happiness to be in 'Lower Galilee at any rate, and the very word is magic with all its blessed associations'. After a few miles he asked an Arab for directions to Tiberias, received a vague gesture pointing east, and continued on his way. Describing this journey later in his diary he remembered it as difficult, the road rising and falling, the sky looking more and more threatening, and 'I connected it with the "blasted heath" of King Lear' (in fact, Macbeth). And he added:

> There was a strong feeling of exile and loneliness
> as it got darker... And the Lord, who had walked
> these very hills, did not seem nearly so close as He
> had seemed in English woods and meadows. For
> He, the King, is in exile there yet, from His own
> countrymen.

Passing by some ruins (probably Lubya), he thought of the Virgin Mary walking towards these same hills on her way to visit

Elizabeth at Ain Karem. Further on he heard voices, not of angels but of young Jews singing, 'for it was the eve of Shabat or Sabbath'. Thinking he was near Tiberias, he quickened his pace and soon found himself in a small Jewish settlement made up of bungalows, some in the course of construction. Here he encountered a man shouting at his son to come home, and asked him if Tiberias was far away. Very far, came the reply, adding that a stranger had no hope of getting a lift because of the Sabbath. John wished to keep going, but was invited to spend the night with the family, for which hospitality he offered profuse thanks, and discovered that he was in Sedgera. His hosts had recently arrived from Tripoli in Libya, and they conversed at great length.

The next day John visited the farm. There were hens, a goat, some pigeons and an acre or two of land under cultivation. John marvelled at the work accomplished, having thought that Palestine had in the course of the centuries become a 'skeleton':

> Herzl and his Zionists were heroes: how they must have said on seeing their native land 'Lord, can these bones live?' And they were helped by God because they helped themselves so manfully. How they have worked, these Israelites returned!

His host pointed out to him the scars of recent war, while John thought to himself:

> I say nothing against the Arab. May he too be greatly blessed, but his habits enrooted are those of a Nomad – (perhaps that's why Palestine agriculturally speaking became a nomad's land ... Again I say, God bless them; may He grant a happy solution to the present difficulties and estrangements.

He paid a visit to the local agricultural college, where he heard the sound of Sabbath songs coming from a nearby makeshift synagogue. He then bade farewell to his hosts and continued on his way. Remembering the two schools of thought concerning the location of the Transfiguration, he sided with the one situating it on Mount Hermon, which soon appeared on the horizon. At which point he got a lift in a large car, 'a taxi, I think', and after a long uphill drive he arrived on the crest of a ridge, from which 'I saw what I so longed to see: the Lake of Galilee, the sea of Jesus and His fishermen, spread out in a glorious expanse far below, sparkling and deep blue in the sunlight. And all about it rose the hills and mountains – a blessed sight.'

An unlikely spy

When John left the car, the driver gave him his visiting card with an invitation to overnight with him when he got to Tel Aviv. He then made his way down to the lake, past a huge refugee camp. Tiberias appealed to him, with its white flat-roofed houses, and its view of the mountains surrounding the lake, thinking, nevertheless, 'yet in David's time, and in that of Jesus, how much more beautiful they must have appeared with their forests of cedars and green slopes'. After a frugal lunch he continued his way south along the shore of the lake, spotting a bespeckled kingfisher of a type he hadn't seen since India, and whose song mingled with the din of radios and record players of groups of sightseers along the way. In spite of all the noise John enjoyed 'a great calm, and air of peace', even as he asked himself: 'What next?' Seeing some caves on the side of a nearby hillside it occurred to him: 'Why not begin being an apostolic beggar here?', thinking of a priest in Rome who had asked him: 'What are you going to do when you get to Israel? Live in a cave like St Jerome?' To which he had replied: 'Maybe.' Again he asked himself:

> So now, which should it be – stay here, or keep going towards Jerusalem? Olivet had been my objective, though I don't know which side of the grave I shall be there – it has been so ever since the summer of 1949, and still is. The Lord ascended to Heaven from Olivet, and I believe it is there that Israel will have knowledge of their King, not so long hence.

But he was worried. He had forgotten to enquire, before leaving England, where Mount Olivet was! On the boat an English Jew had told him he thought it was in Israeli territory, but in Nazareth he had been told the opposite, which meant it was out of reach, like Bethlehem and the Holy Sepulchre.

He stopped, said a prayer and tossed a coin. Jerusalem it would be. After a last look at the lake, he found a truck to take him back to Nazareth, from where he hoped to reach Tel Aviv, a mere 60 miles away, before nightfall. In the event, he arrived in Tel Aviv before midnight, too late to take up the earlier offer of a bed for the night, and headed straight for Jerusalem. It had rained all the way, so the night was cool. A soldier gave him a lift as far as Ramla (ancient Arimathia) and dropped him just outside a military camp, with another 25 miles to go. He started up a conversation with the sentry and after half an hour continued on his journey, hoping to pick up a lift, the night by now being cold.

After walking a few hundred yards singing 'It's a long way to ... Jerusalem', he noticed a convoy of military trucks lined up behind the trees. Just then it began to rain again and John, calling himself an 'unconsidering looney', having witnessed large-scale manoeuvres everywhere, approached the convoy. The driver's cabin of the first truck was empty, but the sound of a throat being cleared indicated an occupant in the next, who gave him permission to sleep in the empty cabin, and provided him with a blanket and some food. John, who hadn't eaten since morning, accepted the food, feeling slightly guilty at breaking his Sunday Eucharistic fast, but only after he had eaten. Soon he heard noises, as the rain got heavier. The duty sergeant had noticed something and came to check, 'a tendency with sergeants everywhere as you know'. He was removed from the truck and taken to the duty officer in charge, who questioned him politely, apologising for not being able to offer him a cup of tea. He was then driven in a jeep 'to find the Intelligence Officer, who was in bed, sensible fellow – the hour was roughly 2 a.m., and had to be woken up'. Half asleep, and without getting out of bed, he directed that John be taken to the police station, where he was briefly interrogated and offered a bed for the night. He was under arrest and, as he himself recognised, 'very justly, considering'.

At 7.30 he was woken up, and after breakfast interrogated, this time seriously, until midday. He sympathised with his interrogators; had he not been apprehended in the driver's cabin of a military vehicle in the middle of the night in a week of manoeuvres? And was he not an Englishman to boot? He explained that he wanted to spend the rest of his days in Israel, either in a kibbutz or working as a forester, which was true at that moment. Mature reflection had made him realise that if he went to Mount Olivet he would not be able to get back into Israel, except via Lebanon and Cyprus. At midday the interrogation was over and he was offered lunch. One can imagine the perplexity of military intelligence in dealing with such a harmless eccentric, but one couldn't be too careful. His case was referred to a higher level, and in due course to headquarters in Jerusalem. At four o'clock the message came back: John was once again a free man.

'The King had led me to Jerusalem'

He was driven, with a group of soldiers, by a military truck to Jerusalem. As the hills of the city loomed in the setting sun, he was so taken that he decided on the spot to go to Mount Sion to attend Sunday Compline in the German Benedictine monastery at Dormition. Having been deposited in front of the Knesset by his driver, and not having the faintest idea how to get to the monastery, he asked for directions to Mount Sion from the first person he met, an Israeli woman, who told him it was nearby, and offered to take him there.

They soon arrived in front of a large white building whose style suggested to John that it was Franciscan rather than Benedictine. The plaque indicated that it was in fact St Peter's House of the Jerusalem Community of Our Lady's Fathers of Sion, but he interpreted the woman's misunderstanding as the voice of Providence. Thanking her, he rang the door bell and explained to the friar who opened the door that he wished to pray with the Benedictines of Mount Sion, that he had a letter of introduction to the Franciscans, and that he would like to come back and then return to St Pierre for a room during the night. He was told that the Dormition monastery was in no-man's land between the Jewish and Arab sectors and therefore cut off. Seeing John's disappointment, the doorman advised him to go to the Franciscans at Terra Santa, a few hundred yards away, discreetly adding that if that didn't work out he could come back to St Peter's, where, perhaps, he could, for one night only, be offered hospitality. Despite the lateness of the hour John went straight to the Franciscans, presented Father Carmel's letter to the Superior, and introduced himself as 'an Israel-loving pilgrim possessing two bob or so'. The Superior explained to him that the house at Terra Santa had been largely taken over by the Jewish University of Jerusalem and, when John had confided in him his plan to convert the Jews, advised him that his best course of action, in the light of his desire for Israel, was to go back to Saint Peter's. Whereupon he gave him a Palestinian pound note and wished him luck. And so back he went to St Peter's where the friar, who had obviously spoken of John to his confreres, offered him a warm welcome, in the shape of food and a bed for the night. Exceptionally, John had missed Sunday Mass, but what a day it had been! He marvelled that:

> The King had led me to Jerusalem, and cared for me in everything all the way: Blessed be He and Amen, for He taught me to 'take no thought for the morrow'. And the Holy Spirit had answered most wonderfully the first prayer I ever wrote to Him:

> > Joy of the living and loving,
> > Fire-spirit fusing all tongues,
> > Swiftness of Mercury's wing-borne steps,
> > Light from Our Father in Heaven
> > Shine on the paths of Thy journeying ones!

'To help win the Hebrews there to Christ their King (whose jester I am)'

The following morning John inquired where the British Consulate was, anxious as he was to arrange a visit to East Jerusalem. As he was going in the same direction, the porter offered to show him the way. While he was waiting in the entrance hall, he was approached by one of the religious, a Jewish convert, originally from Alep, who said: 'I hear you are interested in the conversion of Israel. If this is so, why not stay with us for the time being, for I think we can employ you here, and your position in Jerusalem otherwise is a difficult one.' The congregation founded by the Ratisbonne brothers had at the time a double vocation: to deepen the Jewish roots of the Christian faith and to work towards the conversion of the Jews (though the latter ambition was replaced by dialogue after Vatican II). For John this was again the voice of Providence, 'although I longed to set foot on Olivet, and in the Old City of Our Lord'. The priest went immediately to consult his superior and the deal was struck.

John spent the next seven weeks in St Peter's and upgraded his skills on several fronts: collecting olives, pumping water, sweeping and gardening. Father de Condé, the Superior, made a deep impression on John, not merely because he was a 'most saintly priest', but because he had 'a wizard sense of humour and rang absolutely true'. Moreover, he was 'an aristocrat, and like all true aristocrats he moves freely among every kind of people and society, making happy those with whom he meets. Whether it was a pen-doctor at a street booth, or the Chief Rabbi – he was always welcoming and therefore welcome'. For his part, the devout new gardener somewhat intrigued his religious hosts, not only because of his love for the Jews and his ambition to convince them to recognise their King, but for his devoutness, which was for them a sure sign of a vocation. The way in which he turned up on their doorstep like a drifter was a little surprising, but did that not suggest that he had found the true way, and had been led miraculously to their community?

Father de Condé was convinced that John had been sent as a gift to the congregation, which moreover was in need of vocations, and broached him on the topic. John answered frankly that he did not feel he had a priestly vocation, having no great desire to celebrate Mass. Undeterred, Father Condé reminded him 'there was such a thing as the apostolic side of a priest's work'. John yielded to his arguments, and wrote to Dom Raphael ('I hope he'll be lenient and forget June 1949') and Dom Andrew for references, while for his part Father de Condé did the necessary to ensure that his protégé would be accepted at the novitiate at Louvain, and provided John with some basic tuition in Latin and French.

Every day John continued to climb the terrace of St Peter's to recite the rosary, from where 'the view is fixed for ever in my memory. Though bare it was full of grandeur: I shall never forget the glory of the sunrise over Moab as seen from the roof of St Peter's.' He described the panorama, dear to all lovers of Jerusalem before the great building projects which followed 1967, and spoke of his walks in West Jerusalem, 'where one does not seem to be in the Orient at all. Modern shops, European dress, very clean thoroughfares and streets, all combine to give this impression.'He didn't hide his disappointment, loving as he did 'the bazaars and most of their odours'.

He also visited Notre-Dame-de-France, from whose terrace he could contemplate the domes of the Holy Sepulchre, the El Aqsa mosque and the Old City. He noted the pious Jews of the Meah Shearim quarter, a bare 15 minutes from St Peter's, 'devout men from every nation under the heavens', but also the modern city with its 'tremendous activity, materially speaking', and its atmosphere: 'spiritually speaking, the nearest word I can find for description is "awareness"'.He also noted the speeches from the Knesset relayed by loudspeakers into the street in those days of crisis (which would not be resolved until November 1st). The silence following the call for the Sabbath sounded at four o'clock on Friday afternoon held:

> a supernatural charm – magic almost... It cannot be measured by speaking of sound or silence, one may only say that there is a great and indescribable calm. Christ the King is gathering His people to Israel and to Jerusalem out of every nation where they have been in exile.

On Sunday afternoons John went for a walk with Brother Laurent, a young Italian man with whom he often worked in the garden. On two occasions they walked to the south of the Jewish town, from where they could see the valley of Bethlehem. He regretted that he could not go there to pray, and looked forward to the day when there would be no more frontier:

> when the children of Israel may delight in Bethlehem where their King Jesus, the Son of God

was born... the Hebrews are in Israel, so perhaps
before very long the dreams of Christians the
world over concerning the Holy Land will come
true.

Two or three times he walked with Brother Laurent as far as Ain
Karem, only four miles or so from St Peter's. This was his favourite
walk, being the birthplace of his patron saint. The little town had
not yet been swallowed up by Jerusalem suburban sprawl, but its
Arab inhabitants had been expelled, though John could hardly have
known. At Ain Karem he breathed 'an air altogether supernatural',
and of course visited the churches of John the Baptist and the
Visitation, both maintained by the Franciscans. The house of the
Sisters of Sion was a veritable oasis, built by Alphonse Ratisbonne,
who was buried there, and John went to pray at his tomb. This
would become his 'most treasured memory of Israel'.

Not far from St Peter's there was a synagogue. John heard the
shofar, and discovered the different tendencies of modern Judaism:

high, broad, middle, liberal, and what not. The
Old Covenant is losing its grip, but the Lord of
the New Covenant is ready to gain His grip in
Judah when God the Father wills it. 'To be a light
to lighten the Gentiles' – that is at hand.

John also marvelled at the Jews from Yemen: 'they preserved for
all that time purity of race and religion'. And he met other Jews in
Jerusalem, whenever Father de Condé took him to meetings and
introduced him to a variety of people. Thanks to the religious, he
attended a staging of Mendelssohn's *Paulus*. On another occasion
he listened to Handel's *Judas Macchabeus* in Hebrew on the radio,
and was no less impressed. He was present in Jerusalem for the
feast of Hanukkah, which fell that year from the 4th to the 11th of
December, and listened, enchanted, late into the night to the songs
commemorating the courage of the Maccabees. In a letter to his
mother he wrote that 'the good of civilisation for the near future
and a long time to come hinges on the destiny of Israel. That is
leaving a lot unsaid, Christ being the door, and the posts and the

hinges as well.' At St Peter's he listened to the words of the learned fathers, but also of apostles of the poor like Father Joseph Stiassny, a Hungarian of Jewish origin, who organised aid for displaced refugees who had lost everything during the war.

In the meantime, letters were exchanged; the references and the Indult necessary for the son of a non-Catholic clergyman arrived. On November 27th John sent his mother his future address in Louvain – Ratisbonne House, 49 Rue des Moutons – and recounted all his experiences over the last 12 months. The novitiate, he told her, would last a year, training seven years, and mentioned that the conversion of the Jews was the special mission of the Fathers of Sion. On September 13th he left St Peter's by taxi for Mount Carmel. He spent a night with the Carmelites, feeling moved to be in the place where Elias and his 'monks' had lived 'praising the God of Israel, He who is the God of Love and the Son of Mary', and admired the view which a monk showed him at dawn of the mountains of Lebanon and Hermon, and the Bay of Haifa beyond. In the refectory, another Carmelite explained to him that the cross of the order did not include the figure of Jesus, because it was the custom since John of the Cross, who said: 'it is we ourselves who should be on the Cross'.

John described his trip in a letter to John Dove, dated December 28th. The boat sailed from Israel in the evening, and the last sight of the Holy Land that would stick in John's memory was of the receding lights of Haifa from the shore line 'all the way up to Carmel's summit, where they seemed to intermingle with the stars, as the lighthouse on the summit swept the bay with its long white beam'. A young Dutch Jew taught him the Hatikva and translated it into English for his benefit. There was a makeshift synagogue aboard ship, presided over by three Rabbis. One of them spoke good English, and he and John reminisced about Whitechapel in London's East End. He was probably a hassid, singing the psalms at great length, 'completely unselfconscious and at home in the presence of God.' John expressed the hope that this Rabbi and all the other passengers would come 'To know that God is none other than Christ their King'. He disembarked at Marseille, and took the train to Louvain via Brussels and Paris.

This pilgrimage to the Holy Land confirmed him in what he believed to be his vocation – that the Jews would come to acknowledge their true King – and that the Blessed Virgin had a key role to play: 'Emmanuel God is with us, and Our Lady, without whom there is no Incarnate God and no Salvation', has made it clear. He nevertheless felt unworthy of this:

> My soul's a desert just now, and I had today a
> fearful go of black depression and doubt. But I
> am learning to recognise these attacks not as signs
> of failure but of victory and progress.

A postulant of unusual character

When John arrived at the house of the Fathers of Sion on December 22nd 1950, the community comprised six members: two Jewish novices, two French novices, and a young Hungarian Jewish convert, Geza Vermes, who was due to be ordained the following week. Father Paul Nicolas, the superior of the community, whispered in the ear of the latter as he welcomed John: 'He seems to be a rather unusual character.' This perception would soon be shared by the others.

Louvain, a city more than 1000 years old, had been famous above all for its university, the greatest and the most venerable in the Burgundian Low Countries, dating back to 1425. The wealth of the city had been built on its trade in drapes and textiles, and later on its beer production, but in the first instance as 'the Rome of Belgium'. In a letter to John Dove (December 28th), John says he had counted no fewer than 65 religious houses, representative 'of all sorts and races', as well as the Catholic University. The city had suffered greatly in two world wars, and was far from recovered from the second. To the north, a 15-minute walk away from Rue des Moutons, was the imposing mass of the Benedictine Abbey of Mont-Cesar. Hundreds of Jews, hunted by the Nazis, had found refuge there. John became a regular visitor soon after his arrival and wrote to John Dove that he attended High Mass and Vespers there on Sundays and feast days, and he was particularly delighted by the Christmas services there. He also went to pray at the Jesuit church of St Michael, with its famous baroque facade by Hesius, where, three days after his arrival, he attended Midnight Mass, and found the Christmas canticles, sung in polyphony, very fine.

Ratisbonne House was no more than 200 yards or so from the Catholic University, whose Rector, Father Honoré van Waeyenbergh, had courageously fought to secure for his students exemption from forced labour during the Nazi occupation, and whose present task was a programme of reconstruction of war-damaged buildings. In the streets John rubbed shoulders with students from all over the world, including many priests and seminarians wearing cassocks, and nuns in habits. This international flavour, and the bilingual street signs, contributed to the pervasive sense of universality for which Louvain is renowned (John's first assignment from his superiors was to brush up his French and Latin, though Flemish was not included).

Rue des Moutons (Schapenstraat in Flemish), formerly Rue des Béguines, was named after its sheep market. Opposite Ratisbonne House was the Grand Beguinage, a veritable district in its own right, almost a small citadel, where the Beguine sisters had their convent since the thirteenth-century. It reached its moment of greatest prestige during the Counter Reformation as a community of 200 women who lived, prayed, worked, retired and died there, and continued to flourish until the French Revolution. The mixture of religious life and independence, and the memory of Adrian VI, then the last non-Italian Pope, would have appealed to John:

> If there you go on pilgrimage
> Louvain's full faith will give you hope:
> Visit ye the 'Béguinage'
> Whose vicar once became a Pope.
> (*Ut Unum Sint*, 1956, stanza 980)

Number 49 was a recent, undistinguished building, with a 'fairish garden' attached, which met with John's approval, and 'a rather hazardous tennis-court', where the residents played to 'to get warmed up and exercised'. John stuck to his recorder. The superior, Father Nicolas, was a survivor of the trenches of Verdun, where he had served as a stretcher-bearer. Ratisbonne House was far from fully occupied, which perhaps explained the eagerness to receive the young Englishman.

John soon became friends with Geza Vermes, the young Hungarian Jew, born in 1924, who had been baptised at the age of seven with all his family by the parish priest of Gyula, the future Blessed Wilmos d'Apor. A brilliant student who suffered from the prevailing anti-Semitism, Geza decided to enter the seminary in 1943. In the spring of 1944 when his parents were deported to Auschwitz, he was sheltered by the Salesians, later in Budapest and then at Gyor, where his old parish priest had become a bishop and had hidden him in his seminary. After the war Geza entered the Congregation of the Fathers of Sion, and having arrived in Louvain in the autumn of 1946 quickly revealed outstanding qualities as a scholar, publishing in mid-1949 an article on the Dead Sea Scrolls, which had been discovered two years previously. John was deeply impressed by the brilliant Geza, a Jew who had acknowledged his King!

For his part, Geza was moved by John's openness and joie-de-vivre, his love for Israel, his piety, and his beautiful singing voice (he wrote in his memoir, *Providential Accidents*, 'He was probably the most naturally musical person I have ever met'). According to him, Father Nicolas and himself were the only ones who befriended the young Englishman, whose poor grasp of French cut him off from the others (on his own admission John had great difficulty with the French 'patois' spoken at Ratisbonne House). On December 27th at Hal, near Brussels, Geza was ordained (by a bishop whose name he later couldn't recall). The next day John attended the first Mass of the new priest, who was assisted by Father Demann, another Hungarian Jewish convert. John was asked to give English lessons to his new friend, and in return he himself received lessons in French and Latin. He also got his sister Mary to send Geza a copy of *The Sphere*, a London weekly that had mistakenly published photographs of one of the Dead Sea Scrolls, thus allowing the young priest to make his name by writing about them.

John's relations with the other novices were less close. Desiré Bayart, one of the two French novices, who had also come to Louvain as a result of meeting Father de Condé, had no recollection of John, no doubt because the language barrier would have prevented him from appreciating the young Englishman's witty sense of humour. In a letter to his mother dated Easter 1951, John mentioned also a young Polish Jew, 'whose parents were both taken by the Nazis when he was about 10 or 12 – he never heard of either of them again, and it is to be supposed that they shared the fate of many others', including the parents of his friend Geza.

Most of the day was spent in silence, but John did not complain. He saw the novitiate as 'a little court – three Jews, three Frenchmen and one Englishman', held by Christ. To John Dove he wrote (28 December 1950):

> I'm only the jester buffoon and even my jests have to be mostly to Him alone because one is made somewhat solitary through not knowing much French. But I love solitude – too much, I fear. And thus, Critch, I am very happy, very certain that this is where I must be and why (without another miracle that is, as you say!). These are days of grace when Our Lady is spoon-feeding me with her gentle consolation.

He was convinced that he had arrived in the right port, and that the only 'voyaging' (a Frenglish neologism invented by John) that he would do in the future would be spiritual:

> All the odd pieces of my jig-saw are falling into place. I wonder whether I will see the full picture on earth: not that it matters – the present moment being a sacrament full of God.

He did not hesitate to write, somewhat presumptuously, to his friend: 'I am now "under orders", like yourself.' He learnt shortly afterwards that his acceptance as a postulant was provisional, but this did not dampen his ardour. He realised that study for the priesthood would take seven long years, 'if it is God's will that I live as long', but he was delighted: 'Oh to love His present, His now, I am learning bit by bit at last.'

I must follow my dreams

In February 1951 John wrote a long letter to his friend Stephen King in which he unreservedly revealed his innermost self and his loving and unrelenting search for God. It needs to be quoted in full (with my paragraphing):

> I believe in following my dreams, and never being cynical or giving way to the empty thought of 'illusions'. I have no illusions because by His mercy and grace, I follow the Holy Spirit to whose Church I belong. My course has been erratic, erotic, and zig-zag, but that has been the fault of no one but myself. I went to Jerusalem because I wanted to help win the Hebrews there to Christ their King (whose jester I am) – but that is not to be quite yet, so He sent me here having taught me much 'en route'. Here I begin to help win them.
>
> Now, women and careers (or careers with women). I love them all in that I desire the love of God and Heaven for ever for them all. I have not crept away to a negative love, mewling with self-pity and filled with disappointment and remorse. 'Qui s'excuse s'accuse' [who excuses himself, accuses himself] so I'll not enlarge on this, only deny flatly any suggestion that it may be so. As to my past with them (women) it has been a crazy course, in which I accuse myself of much sin and sadness, but in which I thank God for much blessedness and happiness. How He saved them from me and me for Himself only He knows. Certainly I am unfit for marriage (even if I'd been 'successful' as you put it). But there is a Positive way of seeing it: viz. it is God's will because I am fit for something else – His love only. And he is All and in all – bitterness and springtime, winds and mice, women, Stephen and even hornbeam. Read the Hound of Heaven.

Do I then suggest that marriage is not good and right and desirable? No, a thousand times No! If it's God's will for one it's right, if not it's wrong. He has shown me clearly that the type of adoring (make a face if you like) love that is all I have to give (because I'm a poet) is unfit for marriage, but right for the Lord. I have always wanted to be one in love with all people and all that's good and lovely in the world; do I lack, in going to the Creator of it – the Fount of life, love and beauty? Isn't it positive and logical?

What if my past seems a fantastic failure. So much the better – let it be shouted from the housetops what a chronic muddling loon I've been: the wisdom, love and mercy of God in my regard will shine all the more brightly for the broadcasting. 'What a monstrous self-centred fellow' you'll be saying Steve my old cock-sparrer... 'what a wastrel introvert – nothing but God and him, him and God, as though there were nothing and nobody else'. I reply: you talked of women and love – success and failure. I talk of the God of Love who made all women. What's the mood of a lover – is he accused because all he can see is his lover's love for him and his for his lover? Isn't that mood the essence of all love-stories, from Hollywood sobstuff even ascending to the story of the Passion of our Lord Himself? Our Lord redeemed us by the Cross because He is infinitely in love with us; with each one as though he or she were the only one. So He died for us and bought us back, and conquered death and hell. Now that was Love in action, if you like.

I have said that a lover is nuts about his beloved – any right lover. The next thing is that he does all he can to please the beloved – that too is the nature of love. But see this – first one falls in love, then one seeks to please the beloved: the other way round makes nonsense. O.K. – we both know how Our Lord likes us to please Him in this world – in two ways 1. Thou shalt love the Lord thy God with all thy heart etc etc etc. 2. Thou shalt love thy neighbour as thyself. But what I want to say, is that No 2 cannot happen without No. 1, and depends wholly on No. 1. Christianity is not just philanthropy or 'humanitarianism' – far from it: it is love in action, and love of God above all, in action.

Can you really love your enemies without the love of God as a motive to back it? What does it mean to love your enemies? It means that you desire with all your heart and ability that they will be God's forever, because you know He longs for their souls and eternal happiness: because you know it pleases Him. Then, out of the well of this supernatural love, comes genuine love of all men in Christ. So if you (or I) want to convert the world, we must first convert ourselves: to what? to the pure love of God. Because eternal life with Him is what you and everyone else were created for. As you say, convert by example – practice then preach thereby: be and attract thereby – live Christ and others will love Him and desire Him.

John then went on to tell his friend that because the latter was already practising like a 'shining light' love of his neighbour, his love for God was already great. He then concluded:

So what am I doing? I'm learning to possess the One thing necessary – the love of God. One cannot give to others what one lacks oneself. But why 'shut myself away' for the time being, why go into 'cold-storage'? Because no-one hopes to run a race and win it wearing an overcoat. Nor does that mean that overcoats are not good in themselves. Good old you! You're still Stephen King – and, by the George and Dragon, I'm still Hornbeam, but much more so than before – far livelier and far happier, with a vast ambition; and having found my vocation as the jester of Christ the King. Would that I could thank Him enough.

Studies, Father Damien and letters

John spent the whole of 1951 in Louvain happily enough, even when the foggy winter months reminded him by contrast of the bright landscapes of the Holy Land and Devon, and the gloom seemed to him reflected in the faces he met in the streets of the town. One whole year of uninterrupted stability! He noted the night song of a robin in the deserted garden of a convent, and on the feast of St Joseph he was surprised to see busloads of tourists arriving in Louvain to take part in the processions in honour of the saint, and delighted by the joyful mixture of devotion, marching and song. Shortly afterwards he attended the Easter Vigil celebrations at the Abbey of Mont Cesar, 'the most moving and beautiful I've ever seen', he wrote to his mother (3 April 1951) and lingered on Christ the Light, 'Lumen Christi – very significant in these days of dark strife among nations'.

One church in particular which attracted him was St Anthony of the Picpusians, close to Ratisbonne House, which contained the mortal remains of Father Damian de Veuster, the apostle of the lepers of Molokai. John often visited the church to pray and meditate at the tomb of the man about whom he wrote to his mother: 'He was a hero and a saint to have done what he did. I remember hearing about him ages ago first from one of your magazines.'

On July 10th 1951 the Reverend Bradburne, now in his seventy-sixth year, wrote to his son, whose future as a priest of the Catholic Church now seemed assured. John was shaken by the contents of the letter, which was discovered among his papers after his death:

> I hardly know what to say or how to thank you
> for your generosity in thanking me for anything

which I may have been the means under God, of doing for you. But alas from my side as I look back in my old age upon many things there are that I might have done for you and failed to do. And it may well be that in the white light of the Judgement day I shall be found owing a great deal more to you than you to me. So as between father and son we won't say too much about that. And do remember that whatever stresses and strains between us there may have been in the past – as were almost inevitably bound to arise in this our present state of imperfection – there cannot now or ever be any question of mutual forgiveness. Any shadow of that across our lives shall, please God, be banished for ever. Otherwise dear lad we could not approach our respective altars which would mean the outer darkness for one or other of us. So rest assured on that point son John. And if there is any debt of gratitude supposed or real that you feel you would like to discharge towards me as your father in the flesh, I'll tell you how to do it as I hope you will. Give me a real front seat in your prayers. And for your guidance I'll tell you what to concentrate upon.

The first thing I need and want before I go home and am no more seen is a good and true repentance towards God. As you may find in years to come if you ever have to deal with penitents, the greatest difficulty lies in the dismal power of self-deception inherent in our fallen Human Nature which is one of the direst results of the fall into Sin. A kind of spiritual blindness which afflicts so many of us. So much of our so-called repentance – mine anyway, has not been repentance of the Godly sort at all, but only wounded pride which has had its fall, and rising from the ditch is rubbing its bruises. It is sometimes spoken of as 'being or feeling sorry for oneself'. Wounded self respect which may give one a very bad pain indeed. That is the sorrow of the world which worketh death. Its proper name is remorse which springs really from a love of self, but not in so many cases I'm afraid from the genuine love of God.

What you say about the unities among Christians is I believe perfectly true. The differences of course are enormous and humanly speaking insuperable. Only God the Holy Spirit can resolve them in His own time and in ways we know not of as yet. However we must hang on to St Paul's words at the very end of his Epistle to the Ephesians – the great Epistle about the Church as the mystical Body of Christ. 'Grace be with all them who love our Lord Jesus Christ in sincerity.' So again as I may be a memory before we meet again, for your guidance in any prayer or Offering of the Mass you may be kind enough to make for me, I would just add this. In matters of the Faith, I think I can honestly say that in mind and will, I wholeheartedly accept and believe every word of the three Creeds. That is what unites us.

So God bless you and ora pro me. I am thrilled and almost envious to hear that you are living in an atmosphere of Ecclesiastical Latin which is the Holy Tongue. And French – the more languages the better. And what about a bit of Hebrew? But there I must frankly confess that this last stumped me completely, when once at Cambridge I tried to tackle it. But I refresh my small stock of Latin continually by taking special note of the Latin headings of the Psalms as I say my Office Morning and Evening – which still survive from the Vulgate in our Prayer Book.

The third 'Journées Bibliques' (Colloquium Biblicum Lovaniense) was held in Louvain from the 3rd to the 5th of September 1951. Geza Vermes took part, availing himself of the opportunity to make his mark in the academic world. In October John began his philosophy studies, when the novices of Sion mixed with the Jesuit scholastics, making John feel closer to John Dove. But he felt ill-at ease in the world of abstract ideas, dominated at the time by the transcendental Thomism of Joseph Maréchal, a 'metaphysical diplomacy' which attempted to reconcile St Thomas Aquinas and Immanuel Kant, against which Etienne Gilson was to fulminate at length. The main lectures were delivered in Latin, followed by 'disputations' in the same language.

John was present at an incident which nearly 30 years later inspired a poem he called *Concerning the Holy Trinity*. A student called Alec, puffed up with his own knowledge, was undergoing a viva examination conducted by Father Pierre Charles, a Jesuit pioneer of missiology and expert in Plotinus, Dante and Kant. The question he put to Alec was: 'Why do we call the first person of the Blessed Trinity father and not mother?' The bewildered student was speechless, and failed the exam. For John the answer was obvious:

> He might have said: 'Our Lord said never once
> That Pater Noster's Mater Nostra'... Dunce!

and he continued, invoking Duns Scotus, by affirming that Mary was the Queen of Love of the Triune King, his shining light. In another poem about the same incident he humorously imagined what his own reply might have been:

> Pleasure were it so, I wish,
> All the birds and beasts would boast
> With Father, Son and Holy Ghost
> The Barmaid fair who bore Mine Host!
> In Time!
> (*Summa is i-cumen in*, 1972)

Shortly before Christmas, John made it clear to Father Nicolas that he did not see himself as a priest. The latter agreed with him, not least in the light of his academic performance, and on September

28th 1951, a year after his arrival, an entrance was recorded in the archives of the congregation announcing that 'John Bradburne has decided no longer to study for the priesthood and will continue his novitiate forthwith in moving from the ranks of novices destined to the priesthood to the ranks of coadjutor novices'. In the spring of 1952 John still seemed sure of his vocation within the order of Notre Dame de Sion and that 'despite all the stones rattled against my "bathi" (hurricane-lamp)', he wrote to John Dove (16 July 1952), he stayed 'by the grace of God'. In a poem used that spring as an introduction to his *Histoire d'un Âne* sent to John Dove, he didn't hesitate to claim that he felt inspired by the Holy Spirit:

> The things which written here you see
> The Holy Ghost has told to me
> A wind-blown read – and that's a thing
> To make a riddle for the King:
> Quia quod stultum Mundi sit
> Deus Deorum Eleg-It.
> (*Rome to Jerusale*m, 1950)

No room for a vagabond, a clown, a tramp of God

The congregation at Louvain was already embarking on a more intellectual journey, in anticipation of Vatican II, leading from mission to dialogue with the Jewish world. In June 1952 Geza Vermes became the first member of the congregation to obtain a doctorate in theology, and left Louvain soon afterwards to work with Father Demann for the Cahiers Sioniens in Paris. A doctor of theology was all very well, and John was delighted for his friend, but what role was there for a clown? Suddenly everything went wrong. John was suffering from constipation, no doubt a result of his sedentary lifestyle; a trivial matter, but it was getting him down; and with the departure of Geza Vermes he had lost not only a friend but a confidant, the only one, it seemed, who understood him. He began to realise that there was no place in this community for a vagabond, a clown, a tramp of God. He admired and loved Father Nicolas, 'one of the best men I have known, and absolutely right of heart and very generous', but the goodness of this priest was no help to him in his present situation.

At the end of spring 1952 John made up his mind: he would return to the Holy Land. For his part, Father Nicolas was increasingly bewildered. Experience told him that, given John's education and evident intellectual capacities, for him to become a brother rather than a priest in a congregation struggling for vocations was a terrible waste; but he also believed John was undoubtedly called to another form of the Christian life, exceptional but by no means unprecedented. Two names came to his mind, which he discussed with Father Colson, the Superior General of the congregation, who kept a close eye on the novitiate: St Benedict-Joseph Labre and Charles de Foucauld. This was very prescient indeed.

As a seminarian, the young Benedict-Joseph turned his back on the priesthood for the monastic life. He tried the Cistercians, then the Carthusians, and later on again a Cistercian monastery, without success. Then he took up the life of a tramp. He became a member of the Franciscan family but seems not to have made profession as a tertiary. He went twice to Rome as a pilgrim and once to Compostella, and settled in Rome in 1778, living in the ruins of the Coliseum or in a hospice, and died five years later. He hid the depth of his relationship to God and love of neighbour behind the appearances of eccentricity and his life as a tramp.

The resemblances with Charles de Foucauld are also very striking: privileged family background, military career, conversion, spiritual quest, seemingly a wandering monk, attraction to the Holy Land, attempts at monastic life, the life of a hermit, and love of solitude. The two last stages of their parallel lives, when they finally found stability in the service of the most abandoned and then martyrdom, bring them together. John would later evoke 'Saint Joseph-Benoît Labre' in several poems; he admired his radical poverty, his legendary indifference to personal hygiene and, above all, his contempt for money:

> Blessed Joseph Benoit Labre
> Thought that naught was more macabre
> Than having e'en a single pence
> Because he loved God's Providence.
> (*Oculi Semper ad Dominum*, 1958)

He would also quote Charles de Foucauld in a list of saints he admired, long before the latter's beatification.

Father Nicolas and John did not therefore take long to come to the conclusion that Ratisbonne House had only been a stage in the latter's spiritual journey. After 19 months, John bade farewell to 49 Rue des Moutons, his longest stay in one place since he left Gresham's. On his file preserved in the archive at Notre Dame de Sion it is recorded: 'Renounced the religious life and left us on the 16th of July 1952'. According to Father Colson, John left to become 'a vagabond of the Good God', to Italy, near Naples, with a single bag, one recorder, one change of clothes, enough money to buy three meals: two US dollars, 50 Belgian francs and 100 French francs; a noble soul, 'of whom we have fond memories'. As proof that John departed on friendly terms, Father Nicolas asked the Superior General of the order to provide John with a letter of recommendation to the Mother Superior of the Ecce Homo House in Jerusalem, in support of 'this convert from Protestantism who aspires to the life of a perfect Christian'. The letter added that 'different attempts have led him to the conclusion that he is not suited to the sedentary religious life; rather he feels himself drawn to imitate the example of a St Benedict (Joseph) Labre or a Père de Foucauld', and concluded by stating that he had left nothing but happy memories behind at Louvain.

On the road in France and Italy

John left Louvain on foot, aiming to get to Jerusalem via Rome and southern Italy, from where he hoped to catch a boat. His sole belongings were those listed by Father Nicolas, supplemented by a sleeping bag and Anthony Roufe's walking stick. Walking and hitch-hiking, he made his way via Brussels and Mons into France, stopping from time to time to earn food or money as a farm labourer in the harvest or as a busker playing his recorder in the towns. Whenever he could he sought overnight hospitality in a monastery or slept in a barn, attending Mass wherever the occasion arose.

He arrived in Paris just as the original six founder members were signing the European Coal and Steel Community Treaty, and looked up his friend Geza Vermes. The priest of Sion had learned that John had left the community at Louvain, and was by no means surprised when he turned up penniless on his doorstep, travelling light but as cheerful as ever. He later wrote that John told him he left the novitiate because he found the atmosphere 'too stuffy', though John himself, as we have seen, was not quite so negative.

Several late poems allude to an episode during John's stay in Paris which is given humorous treatment: John seemingly had had too much to drink, nearly drowned in the Seine near Notre-Dame, and was rescued by a beautiful woman on a boat, who could only be the Virgin Mary. Was it a dream or an incident reworked by the recollection? But as soon as Father Vermes managed to procure him a visa for Israel, John was eager not to delay in Paris. He resumed his pilgrimage towards the Holy Land, with his friend's words echoing in his mind: 'This is not a goodbye. Au revoir in the Holy City.' John, 'a monk of Our Lady, and a vagabond of God', once again found himself on the roads of France, surrounded by rich golden summer landscapes, and though the early July heat wave had passed, the temperature was still intense, as he wrote in December 1952 to John Dove:

> Far from being holy and mortified, I've never once gone hungry all this picnic, and God and man have befriended me continually – blessed be God for this, blessed be He that I have no athletic feats of desert fatherdom to my credit, because I am a vessel of His mercy, His astounding mercy. Pettiness, fits of fury, intense egoism and selfishness, impatience and intemperance in my appetite for food – these are my distinguished roll of honour: but nevertheless in spite of all my frailty and because of your prayers the Lord and His Lady are with me always.

John Dove commented in his biography: 'Considering that he ate very little, and only what he begged – bread, grapes, a little wine maybe – his intemperance would put the most abstemious to shame.'

One morning, as John made his way through Provence:

> It was at breakfast-time upon the way
> From far Louvain to fair Campania,
> I'd had but little supper yesterday
> And money none I had nor walked by car;
> I thought 'I'm pretty hungry, Pater Noster...
> Libera nos a malo... fast there came
> A limousine and keenly passed and tossed a
> Whole loaf of bread from out her window-frame.
> (*Panem nostrum quotidianum*, 1974)

This event increased his blind belief in Providence, and he would return to it more than once, as he would to the memory of his pilgrim journey through France in that glorious summer of 1952: harvests, hours on end playing the *Folia* on his recorder on the roads of Provence, a night when he slept at an aerodrome, serving Mass in villages and towns, cathedrals, the Pont d'Avignon, Notre Dame de la Garde, good wine, the Mistral... Between Marseilles and Toulon he dashed off a letter to Geza Vermes: 'If I can get an "autostop" by aeroplane from Cannes, I'll be going on, by God's grace, to Assisi, Rome, Brindisi and Bari.' He spent a night in the Carmelite monastery at Monaco, whose roof tiles he admired, then went forward to Italy. He decided to walk from the frontier to Assisi. Liguria and the crossing of the Apennines doesn't seem to have left an impression on him, but he fell in love with Tuscany: vineyards, endless fields of wheat, olive orchards; nature worked by human hand spoke to him of Christ as much as chapels, hermitages and oratories.

On the eve of the feast of St Clare, on August 10th 1952, he arrived near Assisi, and spent the night sleeping in a wood overlooking the town. At dawn he entered Assisi on foot, convinced that St Francis, his favourite saint, would have disapproved if he entered his town in a bus. The medieval city cast its spell on him, as on so many others. Having begged for some bread from a local baker he attended Mass and Communion, visited several churches to pray, including those of Francis and Clare, played his recorder in the street to earn a few lire, and three days later continued on his journey.

His stay in Rome was brief. He visited the Franciscans, whom he knew already, and spent three nights there. He retraced some of the steps from his 1950s pilgrimage, and left, anxious to find a boat for his ultimate destination. He headed for Ostia, only to find there was no connecting boat from there to Israel. He would have to go to Naples, or the Adriatic ports of Bari or Brindisi. He then set off in a southerly direction and, passing near Castelgondolfo, decided to pay another visit to the Pope. After spending the night in a copse adjoining the pontifical residence, and bringing himself to the attention of the Italian police, he found himself with a group of pilgrims in the inner courtyard of the residence:

> O we entered the Yard, nor feared the guard,
>   With a throng thrice hundreds three:
> 'Twas fulfilled my hope, for I saw the Pope,
>   But I doubt if he saw me!
> (*Oculi Semper ad Dominum or Prologue,* 1958)

He had no luck in Naples, and walked and hitch-hiked his way across the peninsula to Bari. On arrival in the Apulia provincial capital, the church of St Nicolas inspired him to verse:

> In this great house of God I'd gladly die
> And join the soul of Michael Angelo
> That surely now is with the Saints on high
> Hearing the music of an organ flow...
> Lord, let me die to all the things of time,
> Bent on the destiny for which I came –
> To herald Christ and win my Native Clime.
> (*Lines written in the Church of S. Nicholas at Bari,* 1952)

He was no luckier in Bari than he had been on the west coast, and no ship was willing to give him free passage to Haifa. What then did God have in store for him: should he continue on to Brindisi or head back to Naples? At the end of this August 1952 John could not make up his mind. He felt worn out by the summer heat and by all the walking. In the event he decided to head back across the Apennines and Mount Partenio, arriving at the beginning of September in Baiano, a small industrial and commercial town between Avellino and Naples. Once there, he was arrested for vagrancy by the carabinieri, either as a precautionary measure or to provide him with somewhere to spend the night.

News travels fast in a small town, and John's plight came to the attention of Santina Tulino. The Tulinos, a wealthy family, made a habit of putting up passing vagrants, and Signora Tulino, a kind-hearted mother of eight, explained the situation to her husband: 'A pilgrim from the Holy Land. He is Christ among us, all the more so since he comes from the Holy Land.' She headed straight for the prison, went guarantor for John, and took him home. He went willingly, once again offering thanks to Providence. The Tulino house was palatial and the family large. He met the children, including Giuseppina (who would later found a missionary congregation in Africa) and Antonio, who was handicapped and loved music. John, remembers Sister Guiseppina, played some tunes for her brother, teaching him the rudiments of recorder playing. He was already asking himself whether God desired his immediate presence in the Holy Land. He settled in with the Tulinos, but wished to contribute to paying his keep, and was soon to be seen by the Tulino girls broom in hand in the local school. Every morning he attended Mass, celebrated by Don Elia Ferrone, parish priest of Baiano, who became fond of John and understood that the young Englishman could not stay indefinitely with the Tulinos, and needed somewhere permanent to lay his head. Surely this pious young Englishman could help out their cousin Francesco Picciocchi, the young priest of Mater Dei parish at Palma Campania?

The hermit in the organ gallery

Don Ferrone and the Tulinos made the necessary contacts with Father Francesco and John was invited to pay a call. He and the young parish priest, just a year older than himself, hit it off immediately. Don Francesco was indeed run off his feet by his various tasks, and in need of a helper, and offered John the job of sacristan, to clean and look after the chapel and serve Mass. Food was included, but unfortunately he could not offer John a place to stay. John had a ready solution: he would stay in the church and make his cell in a cubbyhole beside the entrance to the organ gallery, and in the gallery itself. The deal was done, and soon he was installed with his meagre belongings and his sleeping bag, like a traditional recluse, except that this recluse would not be so reclusive, and often ventured forth into the outside world.

Don Francesco had been in charge of the parish for four and a half years. From a well-to-do Baiano family, he was of intellectual bent and had studied the works of Peter Abelard. His knowing and innocent expression, his simplicity, his distrust of airs and graces, including those of the ecclesiastical kind, made a deep impression on John, who was quick to confide in him, as he wrote to John Dove (25 September 1952):

> Father Francis, my Confessor, Spiritual guide and
> Employer all at once, is wonderfully good to me.
> Here he has a parish which is no easy task – please
> God I am of use to him.

For his part Don Francesco fell under John's spell, and the Englishman's stay in Palma would in time to come be looked back on as one of the greatest graces of his life. In his eyes John's essential quality was his innate goodness, his simple lifestyle, and his poverty of spirit; he remembers how few clothes John possessed and that he didn't wish for more, but was always fresh and neatly dressed. He was impressed by John's self-discipline at table, and by his insistence that he must do penance.

Mater Dei was a quite new church, built in 1904, whose construction had been financed by Luigi Carrella, a large landowner and pawnbroker from Palma, won over to pious ways by his wife, and who had spared no expense. The sanctuary was vast, and could accommodate 500 worshippers, with a central altar of white marble, overlooked by a great painting of the Virgin Mary in the style of Bouguereau. Another altar contained relics of St Desiderio, martyr, dressed as a young soldier martyr. (St Desiderio had been a bishop of Vienne in France, and had died as a martyr aged over 60.) The ceiling also depicted the Assumption in striking colours.

It was here that John's new life began, though his duties as sacristan, cleaner and keeper of the sanctuary were hardly taxing:

> But all I did was grooming
> Of the Bride my roses wreathe.
> That broom was admirable too,
> I handled it with grace
> And swept the marble floors that knew
> Who spat upon their face.
> (*Campania*, 1977)

One of his tasks was to open the church doors at the appointed hours, a responsibility that he took very seriously. One morning some local women came knocking but he refused to open, on the grounds that it was not yet time. The women retired and soon came back with reinforcements from the ranks of the carabinieri, who knocked in their turn, to no avail. Eventually Don Francesco was obliged to intervene to restore calm.

John soon learnt that, whereas religious fervour was a feature of life in Palma, religious practice came a poor second. Before the war the parish had fewer than five per cent regular communicants, and the number had not increased in the interval. But he himself spent hours every day kneeling in front of the tabernacle, motionless, deep in prayer and adoration, which deeply impressed Don Francesco. He often climbed up to the gallery, night and day, to play the organ or to use the bench as a writing table. He wrote to his father that he slept there, and that 'it was nice if one did wake up in the night, to play the organ alone in the Church', where his principal listeners were the bats. One day a cat ventured into the church and was quickly adopted by John, who baptised him Pompey (Pompeï). He became a regular visitor. On another occasion a stray dog walked in and sat on the cool marble at the foot of the altar. He too was adopted by John, but this time Don Francesco was having none of it. It was one of the few quarrels between them.

The citizens of Palma soon got used to the sight of the eccentric but ever polite Inglese, with his broken Italian. The carabinieri kept a close eye on him: might he not be an American or Russian spy (ideological passions were near the surface in the run-up to the election of 1953)? John was free for most of the day, and was quick to use his spare time to walk around and get to know the town, with or without his recorder, often heading for Mount St Angelo, which dominated the town. He often strolled through the orchards and pine trees, but while September remained warm and dry, October and November often brought heavy rainfall.

On the heights above Palma, John discovered the picturesque village of Castello, to which he would often return. A feudal lord had built a castle there, of which only a section of wall remains. The village towers 1000 feet above Palma, and from the terrace of San Giovanni the town resembles a flock of tiled roofs grazing amid the churches. Beyond, the vista stretches right across the plain of Sarno, to the compact mass of Vesuvius and the neighbouring mountains. He ventured beyond Castello towards the mountain along Via Tribucchi, through the orchards of apples, apricots and various other fruits, and upwards through the forest. This was how one day he arrived at the chapel of Santa Maria at Miano, whose history, embellished by much local family and other lore, he would explore.

In the seventeenth-century, a man crossing the mountain was attacked by brigands, and sought refuge among the chestnut and oak groves. As his pursuers inexorably closed in, and at the end of his tether, he invoked the protection of the Madonna. Suddenly a thick bush of wild roses, gorse and orchids sprouted up in front of him, into which he plunged, beseeching heaven with his prayers, as he listened to the enraged cries of his enemies rampaging through the forest in vain pursuit. In the dead silence that followed, broken only by the beating of his heart, the man promised the Virgin to build a chapel in her honour on the spot, which he started in the ensuing days with the help of the villagers from Castello. The sanctuary was given the name Santa Maria at Miano, and a painting of the Virgin and Child was placed there. The inhabitants of Castello and Parma came together in procession on Easter Sunday afternoon, on Easter Monday morning, and on the feast of St John, a tradition that has endured down through the centuries.

A bell rings out to help lost travellers find their way. John often came to visit this chapel.

Once again he felt that he had arrived at the end of his journey, and wrote of his wonder to John Dove (25 September 1952):

> It has been a fantastic 2 1/2 months, and believe me, I've just blundered along in a most unpraiseworthy way. More and more we learn to rely upon God entirely, to love only – the life of grace, with utter contempt of our own strength... As for me, I am deeply convinced (and this half against my personal and poetic inclination) that for a time, maybe for a long time, maybe till the end, my role is here, nowhere else – and here no less than if it were in Israel.

His yearning for sanctity was increasing, and he added the following lines to his friend, not without wry humour:

> Pray on for my sanctification too, because it would encourage so many souls if such a wreckage might come to canonisation, and I do so want to by-pass Purgatory!!

The strange Inglese of Mater Dei

His love of heights began to take hold of John once more. He often climbed up inside the cupola of Mater Dei to pray, which occasionally astonished and terrified visitors, because the parapet was extremely narrow and unprotected by a handrail – according to Guiseppe Alloca, a historian from Palma, those who knew John remember, still marked by their original fear, his climbing escapades. He liked to meditate there in solitude. His walks on the roof of the church caused no less panic on the ground. To get there he climbed on all fours up the stairs of the bell tower, as onlookers wondered when he would come tumbling down. He also climbed up the bell tower itself, and wrote in the same letter to John Dove:

> All this I meditate over on the Campanile (Bell Tower) for an hour every evening, saying the 'De

Beata' Vespers and the glorious mysteries of the
rosary – all distractions, but by God's grace much
of the distraction is Heavenwards in nature.

Was it the conquest of Mount Everest by his fellow Briton Edmund
Hilary on January 11th 1953 which inspired these madcap
escapades? One day John climbed the cupola with young Gaetano
Fernandez on his shoulders, under the horrified gaze of his sister
Anna Maria. They both got back to terra firma safe and sound, and
some 50 years later Anna Maria admits to having forgiven John,
'such a good and beautiful person'.

Being obliged after all to earn some money to buy stamps and
for other modest expenses, John took on whatever part-time work
he could find, as a dustbin man or bricklayer, which he always
performed with exemplary care and attention. In time the always-
elegant English gentleman with impeccable manners became a
familiar sight to the inhabitants of Palma, emptying bins in the
streets of their town and regaling them with strange tales in broken
Italian. On May 5th, he wrote to John Dove:

So I sweep, and wash up and pray pretty
distractedly and when I have a just occasion
walk in the ways of Palma: always I'm sure to be
hailed and beckoned by sundry folk who like to
have a laugh with or at (it doesn't matter which
now by God's grace) an odd English looney-man.
Sometimes, when nothing to do here, I spend an
afternoon as dustman or cement-mixer with a
pully-rope, or some such. Dustman's my favourite
– one of my oldest ambitions. And I tell them I'm
the buffoon of Christ the King of the Hebrews, and
the herald of His strong uniting reign in from His
own special People, the People of a strong spirit.

As is often the case in Italian towns, the church facade was level with
the adjoining houses on San Felice Street, with houses and garden
walls alternating. Some facades were attractive, but others bore the
traces of bombardment, and the inner courtyards showed all the
signs of poverty. Not far from the church the Palazzo Carrera was

occupied by the Servite Fathers, who ran a cinema for young people of the street, and had a playground for children. Coming out of the church John was bound to meet some of these careering around on their bicycles and scooters, not unlike those immortalised in the neo-realist films of Vittorio De Sica. These youngsters were already picking up the siren calls of popular culture. While many of them continued to sing in the church processions, they were also tuned in to the fashionable airs of Vola Columba, which would soon triumph at the festival of San Remo.

The strange Inglese who lived in the church with his recorder intrigued many (including the Mamas of Palma, as can be seen in a photo), who readily chattered and bantered with him in the street. Antonio Simonetti, Biago and Salvatore Pristo, and Silvestro Peluso knew him and have never forgotten him. For the young Biago, who succeeded him as sacristan of Mater Dei, John was 'special, a man of God, of prayer'. He recalled him giving a helping hand to the street sweepers in Palma. His brother remembers being scolded by John when he came across him and his friends torturing baby lizards: 'Don't kill them,' cried out the Inglese, 'il buonissimo', always calm, always smiling. For Antonio Simonetti, John was 'il cordialissimo'. Fifteen years of age at that time and now a doctor, his task was to ring the church bells at Mass time. Once, when he didn't turn up, John did it for him, only to be told off by Don Francesco for not doing it properly. The young Antonio still remembers John's humble acceptance of the reprimand. Only one thing made John angry: people spitting in church.

Silvestro Peluso retains a vivid memory of meeting John for the first time:

> I was hungry, because we were short of food at home. The streets were empty because of the heat, and that's how I bumped into him. We talked together – I hadn't a word of English at the time, but he had enough Italian to carry on a conversation: I asked him 'Come ti chiami?' and he replied: 'Mi chiamo Johnny'.

He also remembered John telling him that he lived in Mater Dei church and that he had been to Mount Tribucchi 'and had seen a picture of the Madonna and decided to become a Catholic'. (This of course is mistaken. John must have spoken to him about his mystical marriage, which Silvestro Peluso must have confused with a conversion – see below.)

John continued to write home regularly, and included in one letter a picture of the Virgin of Mater Dei. His mother sent him tea and other little treats that he shared with the children of San Felice Street, so much so that the arrival of parcels from home for l'Inglese were eagerly anticipated. Don Francesco got the benefit of the tea, and over tea John often told the priest how much he appreciated his sermons. Numerous locals also enjoyed Mrs Bradburne's tea, an unfamiliar brew in Italy at the time, served by John, whenever it arrived, to the parishioners of Mater Dei after Sunday Mass.

At Christmas 1952 a letter arrived from the Reverend Bradburne, which was found alongside the one John had received at Louvain in his Tin Hut after his death:

> It was a great joy for me to get your letter today and to know of your happiness and welfare with your feet safely set upon the way which in my old age I am coming to see more and more clearly is God's way for you, dear boy. Thank you so very much. So in any of your thoughts of me or of yourself in relationship to me as your father, you must never think or feel that there is any need either to explain still less to apologise. Who am I in any case to criticise the Ways of God for any of His children! God forbid that that should ever be allowed to add to my many sins.
>
> Two days ago I came back from hospital. Pain in the hands of God can be a wonderful thing I found. It is one of God's ways of unclasping the fingers that otherwise might cling too closely to the world.

Of course one does not like to talk too much about these experiences – but you will understand, and I think I can say it to you without offence – but unless one's religion is a hollow sham and faith an empty boast, at such a time it is just a case of 'In Manu tua Domine' [in your hands, O Lord] and letting go. Even leaving Mother standing in the road – absolutely alone. Well that is all I have to say about my rotten self. What a lovely picture of Our Lady. It reminds me of a painting by the French artist Bouguereau. I like to think of you in your organ loft. But I do hope you get your proper and sufficient share of sleep and rest – for we are not out of Brother Ass the body yet.

P.S. As a link between us henceforth I will say the Creed, the Lord's Prayer and the Hail Mary in the holy tongue.

John also received a letter from Geza Vermes announcing that the boat taking him from Israel back to France was due to dock at Naples. So, on January 5th 1953 on a grey rainy day, John stepped out of the church to catch the bus to Naples. Alas, he mixed up the stops and missed the bus! He later wrote a letter of apology to his friend explaining what had happened, and expressing his regret that they didn't get the chance to polish off a few bottles of wine together.

'I married her...'

His love for the Virgin Mary continued to grow. On February 2nd 1953 he went to pray at the chapel of Santa Maria a Miano for the Feast of Candlemas, and decided to consecrate himself to her. In front of the altar in the chapel he proposed to the Virgin a mystical marriage and, feeling that she accepted the proposal, pledged a vow of fidelity to her and thus of human celibacy:

> At Candlemas, at half-past-six or so,
> I married her in Nineteen Fifty Three;
> Green between Apennines and shining Sea
> Campania lay wakened to the morn,

And, to the fact that Mary's married me,
I'll wake the world and shake it with my horn!
(*A Ballade at a Venture*, 1975)

The next day was the feast day of the patron saint of Palma, St Blaise. The statue of the saint, protector of the town, was paraded with great pomp through the streets, as also happened whenever Vesuvio erupted. The procession lasted four hours and stopped at length outside John's church, followed by a large crowd in spite of the cold (two days later a cold snap seized the town).

It was the beginning of an election year in Italy, and political passions were running high. The two local dignitaries, Giulio di Giulio, mayor since June 2nd 1952, and Biagio Sodano who replaced him in 1953, were both Christian Democrats. The Communist Party campaigned on issues of poverty and unemployment, but the region remained in the thrall of Achille Lauro, a monarchist and populist businessman famous for his distributions of new shoes – the left one before the election, and the right after. In answer to his appeal, Campania had voted in 1946, against the national majority, to retain the monarchy.

The Mafia gangrene also affected Palma, as well as the whole of Campania, and could not be ignored, given that after the assassination of the mayor of Battipaglia the finger of suspicion pointed to a son of Palma, 'Pascalone' Simonetti. Slightly younger than John and of impressive build, this Mafia Guappo had made his mark by reputedly striking Lucky Luciano on the Agnano racecourse, and he controlled the fruit and vegetable and contraband cigarette trade in Palma, Nola, and even up to Naples. He was rumoured to earn 100 lire on every hundredweight of potatoes sold in the region, and ordered the burning of the harvests of farmers who refused his 'protection'.

On March 15th 1953 Stalin died. All over Italy, including Palma, mourning processions, which doubled as anti-government protests, were organised by the Communist Party. These were not unrelated to the proposal in Belgium by Paul-Henry Spaak, president of the European Coal and Steel Community, to draft a treaty setting up a European political community, which raised hackles in Moscow. In the midst of all the emotion John wrote a poem, in neither homage nor hatred, in which 'the clown' imagines the defunct dictator putting on a smile as he meets Christ, for 'The King for all men's sake / Did die to do to death all mortal fear' (*Clown's Dilatory Supplement*, 1953).

On March 17th political tensions were interrupted for three days to celebrate Shrove Tuesday, and John discovered the dancing quadrilles of Palma, each made up of 100 to 300 singers, led by a float and dancing to the beat of an orchestra of clarinets, trombones, saxophones and drums, featuring male and female cross dressers and masked couples or groups going from door to door receiving 'migliaccie' (sweet or savoury specialities of the region) and vermouth. Since 1951 a quadrille of students had contributed novelty and a degree of licentious abandon to the occasion, in reaction no doubt to post-war austerity. This seems to have offended John's English puritan sensibility and his chaste love for the Virgin Mary.

However, the Shrove Tuesday festivities merely marked a truce on the political front. On March 29th, Alcide de Gasperi (the Christian Democrat Prime Minister) decided to implement a change in the electoral law in an attempt to preserve a stable majority, after which the election campaign took off. The Catholic Church played an active part, its fear of Communism spurred on by Church persecution in Eastern Europe. Rumour spread of a Communist plot to take over the Vatican in the event of victory, leading Cardinal Micara, Vicar General of Rome, to exhort Catholics to 'vote well, vote as Catholics, vote as Romans'. At Palma John was witness to outbursts of verbal warfare between supporters of the three major parties, which occasionally found physically violent expression in the streets. The rivalry between Christian Democrats and Monarchists, who were courting the same voters, often surpassed their mutual antagonism towards the Communists:

> The Monarchists were still as strong
> As they have ever been
> Round Lauro-town: a crowning song
> Rang to the echoes, keen!

> The Socialists were booming
> And the Communists did seethe
> But all I did was grooming
> Of the Bride my roses wreathe.
> (*Campania*, 1977)

In the circumstances John made his own modest contribution to electioneering. The three mainstays of the Christian Democrats in Palma then were Catholicism, Clientelism and anti-Communism, and all active parishioners had to take a stake in the campaign. Like everybody else the sacristan of Mater Dei contributed to the poster campaign on the walls of the town. But this didn't interrupt his long walks, and one day, on his way to visit the Tulinos, he called at the Hermitage of the Camaldolese of Visciano, which rekindled his monastic yearnings:

> In Palma of Campania I spent a year
> As sacristan and, half-way through that space of time,
> Saw wheeling o'er a spur of mountainscape sublime
> Peregrines; souls Camaldolese soared also near.
> (*Memento*, 1970)

Meanwhile he kept in touch with his friends, writing, in his usual bad French, to Father Vermes (30 March 1953), whom he imagines hunched over a Dead Sea Scroll manuscript – with a pun between *grotte* ('cave' in French, those of the Dead Sea scrolls) and *grotesque*: 'Vous serez de plus en plus grottesque, et moi de plus en plus fantastique et ridiculeux' ('You will be more and more "grottesque" and me more and more erratic and ridiculous').

Holy Week began on the same day, as colourful as it was devotional, in which John played an active part in the lead-up to the procession of Santa Maria at Miano, and also at the popular celebration of Our Lady of the Rosary at Pompeii on May 8th, celebrated at Mater Dei with High Mass and prayers to the Virgin. The day after this feast he decided to introduce his bride to the young friends who used to gather around him, having told them, to their great surprise, that he was married. The issue had arisen on Easter Tuesday. Opposite the church in via San Felice lived a young beauty called Rosa (Bruna according to some). There were several girls in the family, but Rosa in particular attracted John's attention because she was always singing. One day as John was chatting with his young friends on the steps of the church, surrounded by Vespas (the 100,000th had just come off the assembly line), his casual remark that in his country 'dark eyed beauties [like Rosa] were especially admired' was greeted with universal glee and no little teasing: 'The Inglese is in love with Rosa!' After all, this handsome young foreigner was only 32 and looked 10 years younger, and was a Catholic to boot; and even though he worked as a bin man the regular parcels from abroad suggested that he came from a 'good family'. As the days went on and the teasing became more persistent, John revealed that Rosa was not in the picture, since he was already married, and offered to introduce them to his bride.

And so they set out together in the heat of May to visit the chapel of Santa Maria at Miano, accompanied by Don Francesco, to meet the Inglese's bride. They prayed together before the painting of the Virgin and Child and he told them simply: 'She's the one!' and explained the story of his marriage with the mystical bride of his heart. Don Francesco has no recollection of the young people's reaction, except that while coming down from the mountain they hummed in unison familiar Italian love songs.

Goodbye to Palma

On the very day John and his friends visited Santa Maria at Miano, the Reverend Thomas Bradburne died at the age of 78 of a perforated gastric ulcer after lifting a heavy sack of grain while feeding his chickens. John received the news by telegram, but lack of money prevented him from attending the funeral.

A hot summer lay ahead. As the temperature soared, not a drop of rain fell between June 16th and September 10th. At the beginning of July, the procession in honour of the rosary filled the streets of Palma and – the parish of Mater Dei being a seat of the Dominican Order – the feast was celebrated there with great solemnity. On July 7th the spectre of Communism receded: Palma, and the rest of Palma, had voted 50 per cent Christian Democrat, with more than 20 per cent supporting Lauro, and a mere

18 per cent Communist. Nationwide, the Christian Democrats and their allies narrowly fell short of an overall majority.

Soon afterwards John fell out with his parish priest. It seems that the priest had spoken somewhat slightingly of 'gli Inglesi', perhaps with reference to the Union Jack that John had used to cover a notebook containing his poems, and l'Inglese took offence. Nearly 60 years later, Don Francesco remembers only this one quarrel between them (having forgotten the fall-out over the stray dog). In any case John was preparing for his return to England. He vacated his organ gallery to rent a room from Vicenzo Limatola for a few weeks, pending his departure from Palma. Philip, still in Libya, had written to tell him that their mother was alone, and that he was the only one available to keep her company; Audrey and he himself were overseas, Michael was about to go to Canada, and Mary had her family to look after. John, deeply affected by the death of his father, was convinced, and did the round of his Italian friends to say his goodbyes. Young Antonio Tulino was very emotional and John promised to send him a recorder from England. The recorder duly arrived and became for the Tulino family a precious memento of John, only to disappear in the rubble of the 1980 earthquake. On September 4th 1953 John wrote to his mother that he would leave for home as soon as the money arrived. When it did, he immediately left Palma for Naples and caught a flight back to England.

For a few years John and Don Francesco exchanged greeting cards, after which contact was lost. In 1980, Palma was hit by the earthquake which ravaged the region. Mater Dei church was damaged and had to be closed, and remained so up to the 1990s; the chapel of Santa Maria at Miano was destroyed and its Virgin and Child painting was removed to the church at Castello. In 1996, Don Francesco went to Ottery in vain, looking for news of John, unaware of his death. He discovered it from Father Claudio Rossi six years later. He had no doubts about John's sanctity and for a time ran a prayer group to ask for his intercession.

Chapter 6

A Fool, Skilled in Fiasco, 1953–1962

Strange vagabond, who knows not what to seek...
God's love within you is your Native Land!
Then seek none other, never more depart
For you are homeless save God keeps your heart.
(*To a wandering Jew,* 1958)

On October 25th 1951 the Conservatives, still led by Churchill, returned to power. The Grand Old Man had slowed down, and the Conservative government assumed a managerial role as Britain entered a period of prosperity that would continue until 1973. Household spending increased at a phenomenal rate as the consumer society took off. Religious practice, except among Catholics, showed a marked decline. These years were also marked by a social revolution of sorts, which found literary expression in William Golding's *Lord of the Flies* and the novels of Alan Sillitoe, John Braine, John Wain, Kingsley Amis, and others, and on the stage in the plays of John Osborne (from whose play *Look Back in Anger* the label Angry Young Men derived), incidentally rendering hopelessly old-fashioned the plays of John Bradburne's cousin, Terence Rattigan. Colin Wilson's *The Outsider*, a philosophical mishmash of second-hand existentialist themes, appealed to a rudderless disaffected generation at odds with a society which paradoxically seemed to glorify youth. John's guiding lights were not theirs, but echo a similar sense of drift.

The hermit on the hill and the jester of Christ the King

Back in West Hill, John's first act was to go and pray at his father's grave. He settled at Fir Grove with his mother, and seemed happy to be back, much to the relief of Philip, who was home on leave. Mist was in seventh heaven at John's return, and mother and son spoke together about the Reverend Bradburne's last days. Michael felt he could now go back to Canada, and John resumed his daily Mass-going at St Anthony's. One can imagine the delight of the nuns on seeing John again, especially Sister Camillia, who had become the community's Superior. At this time she formed a very definite opinion of John's character:

> A remarkable man, but certainly a strange man. He was a Catholic who did not hide. Yes, he pretended to be a fool, but he was not at all, it was a way for him to disguise his deep spiritual life and holiness – singing in the street or playing the recorder. Some sisters did not like him, they thought that he was doing too much, that he was too different, that this young man of good family, so good-looking and with such an Etonian accent should not have to beg in the streets or play the fool. John, being simply what he was, forced everyone to take a position, either of confidence, doubt, or opposition. He was what he appeared to be, devoid of pretence. He was not only original but exceptional. He was a saintly man, a versatile saintly man, but a very saintly man, a charming gentleman, a kind of medieval knight in our century.

John also paid a visit to Buckfast Abbey, and described in detail to Dom Raphael, Dom Placid and Hugh Symons his three years on the continent. When he yet again expressed his wish to be admitted to the Abbey, the monks made known their reservations. Obliged to consider other options, John decided to become a hermit. He confided his wish to Cecil Hardwicke, who introduced him to their friends the Curles, asking them if John could stay in a shed in their garden at East Hill, to the south-west of Ottery, and the Curles, though somewhat taken aback, agreed. So John stayed at Fir Grove for only a few weeks. Despite the strong bonds of affection between mother and son, Mist was bewildered by her son's ways, and John realised that he was causing her pain. He himself aspired more and more to a life of solitude where he could find God as he understood him, in prayer, music and song. He continued to visit her, and would often stay over, but never for long. (Mrs Bradburne did not stay long in Fir Grove, which was now too big for her, and moved into a flat upstairs in the vicarage at Ottery.)

Adam Curle, born into a family of journalists and artists, including Vaughan Williams and Virginia Woolf, worked in the secret service during the war and later taught social psychology at Exeter University, where since 1952 he had been Head of the Department of Education and Psychology. Like the guest in his garden, he played the recorder and wrote poetry. His wife Pamela was bringing up their two daughters, aged thirteen and eleven at the time. At ten years of age, she had decided to become a Catholic. But when a boarder at Bruges with the Notre-Dame de Sion Sisters, she was expelled for indiscipline, and because she had said the sisters had a superiority complex towards the Jews.

East Hill overlooked Ottery and the surrounding area, comprising Mazzard Farm and a few lanes with high hedges sheltering recently built houses. East Hill House was the largest, with a vast garden, at the bottom of which nestled a small wooden shed ten feet by ten, with a roof of ferns, built against a tree. Furniture was minimal but sufficient for John's needs. Though less than 100 yards from the house it afforded a degree of privacy, with running water and a toilet shed nearby. The view of the peaceful Devon countryside extended as far as Ottery, Wiggaton and West Hill.

John set off to Ottery at dawn every morning for Mass, often his only social contact for the day. Afterwards he would return to his hermitage to pray and meditate. The East Hill hermit nourished himself on brown bread, apples and cider. He prayed, often sang, wrote poetry and played the recorder 'to entertain the birds and the angels', as he told Geza Vermes. He also spent many an hour walking on the wooded ridge. From the steep slope and the densely planted trees, he could admire the wide valley of the Otter as far away as Dartmoor to the west, when he wasn't exploring the many pathways in the valley beneath. The countryside around Ottery is called locally 'Canaan's land where milk and honey flow' (*Exodus* 33), with rich soil suitable for both grazing and the plough. From this setting John absorbed many images, odours, tastes and thoughts which would invigorate his poetry:

> A generation, thirty years in all,
> Is long enough to learn to love a scene
> Exceedingly... I've heard a footstep fall
> Over the Otter River's valley green
> And at it I have rallied and have e'en
> Slept at Hayes Barton in the hay...
> (*A Ballade of the Mist above the Otter*, 1975)

Visitors were rare. One of these was his goddaughter Pamela, intrigued by the 'garden shed' and the strange ways of its inhabitant, but appreciating that he could do interesting things. She writes of another time, at Fir Grove:

> he was asked to look after me one afternoon when everyone else went out and we amused ourselves sitting at the dining room table writing poetry – he asked me to suggest a subject and at that age my chief interest was: 'fairies'; we both wrote a poem, but sadly I did not consider our efforts worth keeping!

Relations between John and his hosts were cordial, but their paths didn't often cross: he saw more of their dogs and cats, especially Vickie, a cross between a terrier and a pointer. When they did get together they nevertheless had a lot to talk about: music, poetry, Sion, and a shared love of the Jews, though the Curles themselves had little interest in religion. Adam Curle had treated shell-shocked soldiers after the war, and, with the detached eye of the professional, he regarded his eccentric host in his garden hut as just one more such casualty: a misfit, and incapable moreover of following anything through; and when he drank any alcohol, his pet hermit drank too much of it. Had he not confided once to Adam that he would never again touch alcohol as long as the Catholic Mass was not celebrated at the Church of St Mary of Ottery? And had he not failed to keep his promise, having found an excuse which his amused guest had described as 'Jesuitical'? And was he not given to outbursts of uncontrollable rage and anxiety?

On the plus side Adam Curle acknowledged the positive influence that his guest had exercised on him. He was fascinated by John's honesty, his innocence, and what he called – for want of a better word – his holiness, not to mention his sense of humour, and his propensity to laugh. In John's company he felt urged to become a better person, and even though he himself might be a pillar of society, he remembered moments from his youth when his mother would urge him to hate war and seek for peace. John taught him without knowing it that perhaps he had not yet discovered his way (ten years later Adam Curle became a Quaker and an international pioneer in conflict resolution studies). Finally, the master of East Hill House admired how this man with no source of income relied totally on Providence (John had told him about his year in Palma). In short he considered his guest to be 'a holy madman' (even though he continued to regard madness, holy or otherwise, as an affliction). As for Pamela Curle, despite her outward appearance of a dutiful mother, she had remained a rebel, and considered her husband's opinions to be somewhat conventional, and was not in the least discommoded by this misfit.

John occasionally filled in as sacristan at St Anthony's, where he was always on hand to help out the sisters at Dolfergan, and where he sometimes helped with lessons, all with his usual good will and awkwardness. One day when Sister Ernest allowed the chickens to escape and run wild, John's effort to catch them displayed more panic than that of the chickens themselves (she still laughed recounting the story decades later). Sometimes he looked after the handicapped children and a physically handicapped adult.

The months went by, and from the 3rd to the 28th of August the University of Cambridge hosted the 23rd International Congress of Orientalists, in which Father Vermes, having been awarded his doctorate, was a participant. John invited him to spend some time in his mother's house, and welcomed him with great joy. He had much to tell his former confessor from Louvain, whom he still regarded as a spiritual advisor. He explained that normally he lived with the Curles, to whom he had spoken much of his friend, and wished to show his hermitage to his guest. That night they slept at

John's mother's house, and in the morning headed for Ottery. After Mass they enjoyed a pint of cider in the pub and walked to East Hill, an effort which Geza found somewhat challenging.

The Curles gave him a warm reception, and Pamela made it clear that she was already prejudiced against him in spite of the enthusiasm of their friend for the Fathers of Sion, on account of the years she herself had spent with the sisters at Bruges. She told him she had always hated the 'father forgive them for they know not what they do' prayer that the nuns always recited after the consecration – a custom established by Ratisbonne. Father Vermes explained that, as far as he was concerned, Christ had not been asking for forgiveness for the Jews for all time, and that in any case the verse in question was missing from several manuscripts and therefore of doubtful authenticity (however, Raymond Brown, a recognised authority on the Passion, in *The Death of the Messiah*, considers on the contrary that 'the format of the prayer is very Lucan'). He promised Pamela to send her an article by Father Demman on this topic, published in Cahiers Sioniens – John was later delighted to hear from the Curles that the promised article had been delivered.

Teddy bears, street music and more poetry

Shortly after this visit, the Marist sisters moved from Raleigh House to a new house south of the village, near East Hill. John found himself turned into one of those dandys he had known in India, pushing a handcart loaded down by the nuns' belongings up the hill to their new home. Once again his kindness and devotion touched their hearts, and when the operation was completed the sisters had a proposal for John: 'Why don't you come and stay at Raleigh House?' And so it was that in November 1954 he bid farewell to the Curles, promising to visit them often, and took up residence beside St Anthony's, not far from the apartment where his mother was now living. Initially he moved into the ground floor, next to the laundry, then into a sparsely furnished room in the attic in conditions hardly less Spartan than his cabin at East Hill House, with headroom only when standing in the centre. But he was next door to daily Mass, and he could continue to pray, help out the nuns in the school or in their social work, and continue with his long walks. The remaining section of Raleigh House was rented out as an old people's home, where John also lent a helping hand.

The condition of St Mary, the Anglican church at Ottery, was a cause of serious concern for its vicar, the Reverend David Price, who the previous year had set up Friends of the Church of St Mary at Ottery to raise the necessary funds for restoration – in particular the two towers, which were in danger of collapsing. Though now a Catholic, John decided to do his bit for the church. Using the only talent he had for making money, he made regular busking visits to Exeter, playing the recorder in the street and handing over the takings to the Reverend Price. This was recorded in an article by Geoffrey Worrell around Christmas time in the Exeter *Express and Echo*:

> The Piper in the Close
>
> Ottery St Mary Parish Church, which needs £10,000 for its Restoration Fund, has found a champion in a young man who plays a recorder on street corners in aid of the fund.
>
> The young man, with his closely-cropped hair and cultured accent, talks with the evangelistic zeal of an early apostle, lives a frugal life in a hostel for people down on their luck, and calls himself 'the Jester of Christ the King'.
>
> I first saw him at the end of Martin's Lane, Exeter, surrounded by an admiring group, including a number of children – a sort of modern Pied Piper.
>
> From the wooden recorder, expertly played, dangled dozens of coloured ribbons. He wore a high-necked pullover, green tweed sports jacket, and corduroy trousers.
>
> I listened as old English airs floated out over the Cathedral Close and then asked him what the coloured ribbons were in aid of. He gave me a

friendly smile, and replied, 'Just to give the air of gaiety an Elizabethan jester ought to have; for we are Elizabethans, you know!'

When I asked him his name, he said 'Just call me the jester of Christ the King!' He told me he was a poet whom nobody had yet recognised. ('They probably will do in another 60 years.')

'Don't you have any permanent sort of occupation?' I asked. His eyes twinkled as he replied, 'Nothing is permanent in this life.' Surprised, I learned he is a Roman Catholic. 'But I love the church at Ottery, and it is so much in need of repair that I feel I must do something to help.'

'I long for the day when all Christians shall worship together, and for those in the Ottery area Ottery Church is obviously the right place.'

Mr R. Illing, musical director of Rolle College, Exmouth, who also heard the music, praised the young man's efforts, and the piper accepted an invitation to play his recorder to the college students.

The Vicar of Ottery said he once gave the piper permission to go into the church when it was not in use and to play his recorder there:

The acoustics in the church are excellent, and his music was delightful to hear. He is a perfectly genuine man, and I expect he wanted to come along and give me a few pounds for the Restoration Fund as a surprise. I believe he has been living the life of a hermit for some time in a little hut in an isolated spot, but is now helping to run a hostel for people who are down on their luck.

John's stay at Raleigh House was short-lived. He was often woken during the night by strange noises, which sounded to him like someone scratching at his door, leading him to believe that, like the vicarage at Tilney, the house was assuredly haunted. He baptised the ghosts 'Teddy Bears', and spent his nights praying, rosary beads in hand. He told his friends the Hardwickes about it, and they suggested he move into the loft above an old stable in the grounds of a house they had just moved into at Harpford, about three miles south of Ottery.

He moved in at the beginning of 1955, and quickly fell in love with this charming village and its twin on the far bank of the Otter, Newport Poppleford, with their church spires and thatched cottages (one of which bore the inscription *Ye Olde Tolle House 1785),* the Southern Cross Inn, and the trees which seemed to eat into the estates, straddling the sluggish river. John often returned to Ottery for Mass, to call on his mother and help out the nuns. He could often be seen in the street pushing the sisters' handcart from the Sidmouth Road convent to Dolforgan with the midday meal. He also kept in touch with Buckfast. But he found that he did not have the same independence with the Hardwickes as he had at East Hill. Cecil treated him like a son and expected him to dine with them, and John felt he could not refuse, which interfered with his ascetic eating habits. Furthermore he quickly realised that his Teddy Bears had decamped and followed him to Harpford, and in time Cecil began to believe him and share his phobia.

Whether because of the Teddy Bears or renewed wanderlust, spring 1955 saw him walking and hitch-hiking in the direction of London. He survived on what he could beg, or by playing his recorder in the towns along the route, ending up in Stanmore, a suburb to the north-west of London. In a letter to his mother thanking her, on May 19th, for a pound note she had sent him by post (and asking her not to do it again) he mentioned his current hosts, cartoonist Geoffrey Hunt and his wife Renee ('He is a Communist, and so is his wife; she is also a Jewess'). He went on to say that he was playing his recorder in various places in London, including the Tower (which was where he met the Hunts), to make some money – news hardly likely to reassure his mother – and that he had delivered a few 'funny little speeches' at Speakers' Corner at Marble Arch.

On May 19th he announced that he had played in front of St Paul's Cathedral to raise funds for its restoration. When his friend Stephen King asked why he, a Catholic, was supporting the

Anglican Church, John replied: 'They can't look after it properly without me. It used to be a Catholic church and one day it will be again, so meanwhile I need to help look after it.' (One must assume that John was referring to the St Paul's founded in 604 AD, a thousand years before the Reformation, and replaced by Wren's masterpiece after the Great Fire.) One day a pavement painter gave John half-a-crown and asked him to go and buy him a box of chalk. From that day on he felt accepted by the street people as one of their own. Another day, when Stephen King and he took the bus, whose passengers were typically immersed in their private thoughts, John struck up a conversation with the people next to him. By the time they got off the bus the other passengers were all talking animatedly among themselves.

The stay in London was also short-lived. In May John returned to Devon and went to live at Buckfastleigh. Was he still hoping to enter the Abbey or did he simply wish to live in its shadow? He was delighted to renew acquaintance with Dom Raphael and Hugh Symons, and became friendly with Darrell Blackburn, who shared his Franciscan sensibility, and who was living with a handicapped friend – soon John was also taking care of him. He resumed his old habits, and showed interest in the researches of Brother Adam, who had been travelling the world since 1950 to produce the perfect bee, a breed resistant to disease, robust, gentle and easy to manage. Dom Raphael found John work as assistant grave-digger at the Abbey (the village graveyard is famous for the Cabell affair which inspired Conan Doyle's *Hound of the Baskervilles*). He worked there six hours a day without pay, having been granted free accommodation by Dom Raphael. It seems that the arrangement fell through after a few days, when Abbot Fehrenbacher insisted on regularising social security contributions. John refused outright and left in a huff: such compliance would have been in defiance of Providence!

John took to the road again with his Gladstone bag and his recorder, hitch-hiking and begging for food. On June 11th he once again found himself at Stanmore with the Hunts, from where he wrote to his mother describing himself as the Wandering Jew. He had nothing but praise for Geoffrey Hunt, 'who thinks he is a Communist', and his wife Renee. They had nothing and shared everything, and helped John to build up his strength, because he was 'burnt up' by fatigue. But he was anxious to reassure his mother: he was doing fine, he wrote on June 11th 1955; God and men were taking good care of him. As for making a living, 'in fact I am a street musician'. It was perhaps at this time that he made contact with the Franciscans of Forest Gate and was confirmed in his Franciscan vocation.

On July 18th Britain experienced flooding on a massive scale, and shortly afterwards John returned to Buckfastleigh, staying there until November near the Abbey at 7 Higher Mill Lane – at the house of Mrs Ash, he wrote to his mother in October, 'with whom I lodged six years ago before going to Lourdes and "to sea". So life has gone full circle.' (He also wrote that he was working in the cemetery with Father Raphael, so it's possible that the clash with Abbott Fehrenbacher took place that autumn.) He explained his change of plan in another letter to his mother, in which it is possible to discern a hint of his connection with the Franciscans, but he was somewhat more explicit in a communication to Darrell Blackburn: 'St Francis is my master, and like our Master Christ he never believed in long abode.'

In the middle of all this chopping and changing, John set about putting shape on an elaborate cycle of quatrains: *Ut unum Sint: A Pastoral Fantasy for Christ the King*, 'by Hornbeam', which he completed the following year, including in it poems written at Gaveney House and Parkminster. The Introduction indicates the basis of his aesthetic creed and of what he hoped to create and write:

> There is on Earth a music that expresses at the same time both Heavenward longing and profound peace of soul; such music seems to say –'we are mortals, yes, but promised Immortality: we are pilgrims, but our Native Land's in sight, so our hearts can rejoice as we journey.' This mood may be found among works of certain great composers, especially Bach; but its most complete expression is in the Plainsong of the Church, in the chant called 'Gregorian'. Of this chant the Holy Spirit is the Composer, for all the Liturgy is work

> of His direct inspiration. And the singer is Christ's
> Church – the Mystical Body of the Son.

In the meantime his friend Geza received an invitation from the
Curles to pay a visit in September and the unthinkable happened:
Pamela Curle and he fell in love. They made no attempt to hide
their feelings from Adam, but the young priest knew 'where our
duties lay', and left East Hill for Paris via Oxford, where he spent
some time in the Bodleian. John remained in the dark about the
episode.

From Advent to Good Friday: a Benedictine interlude

The monastic yearning continued to devour John, in the shadow
of Buckfast, and since this Abbey had closed its doors to him, why
should he not try another? His Jesuit friend suggested Prinknash
Abbey, where he had recently visited a friend, an ex-commando
like John, who had just become a Benedictine. John contacted the
Benedictines, and on November 25th 1955 he entered Prinknash.
The next day, the first Sunday of Advent, he wrote to his mother:

> I begin my postulancy at 9.15 tomorrow. By God's
> grace I'll weather that and after six months, viz. at
> the end of May 1956, I shall be clothed as a novice.
> For that occasion you would be most welcome,
> and there is a nice Guest House close by where
> you could stay for a day or two.

He added that the Abbot, Dom Wilfred Upson, liked postulants to
write home every week, that he had struck up a friendship with a
black cat, and also, at the other side of a fence, with a 'papal bull, the
lord of our Guernsey stock'. The next letter, December 7th, revealed
that letters home were not allowed during Advent, but that he had
been granted special permission: 'Never before in my life have I
known such true happiness – totally estranged from elation, thank
God – as I have here... I believe this to be my Jerusalem indeed.'
He also referred to fox-hunting in the park of the monastery:

> A hunt – pink coats and all – came through the
> Park (ours) yesterday afternoon – shades of early

India time somehow; but Christ is our MFH
[Master of Fox Hounds] and we a keener pack
than theirs, God bless them, and bring them and
us to Himself on the Day of Gabriel's hunting
horn.

He wrote again on December 18th, promising to put his mother's
failing health in the care of the Blessed Virgin, and concluded:
'We are Jerusalem set on a hill and surrounded by Hills, and
Companion-looking plains below and out towards Wild Wales.'
He added that the runway at Gloucester airport, visible in the
distance, was like an estuary, but 'the only Estuary that here
concerns us is one leading off into the Heavens, rather than one
which dreams of earthly countries afar off'.

On the same day he wrote to John Dove, again invoking the
idea of the Benedictine Jerusalem, and mentioned in passing some
difficulties he was having in the Choir. But the letter sounded a note
of things to come:

> Pray for a perpetual and preposterous postulant. I
> do not look forward for clothing nor to Profession,
> nor even to become Cellarer – but only to the
> present moment, to which the Lord of Eternity
> binds us in His Love evermore. For me, to be here
> with Our Lady is to be a monk. Let come what will
> come, I ask no more.

His booming voice drew unwelcome attention in the choir, and
when chosen as thurifer he managed to tangle up the chains of the
thurible. But it was difficult to hold it against him. In the eyes of
young Aldhelm Cameron-Brown, future Abbot of Prinknash, 'he
was a charming but eccentric young man'. For him, no doubt, John
'had entered with the firm intention of becoming a choir monk'.

On January 18th John again wrote to his mother to tell her
that not only he but the whole community were praying for her
health, and continued in a visionary vein: 'The whole Monastery is
a unique Prelude to the Great Christian Era when Judah will be at
the helm, welding West with East in One Holy Hebrew Humanity.'
These early days were thus marked by enthusiasm, even if the rigour

of the liturgy continued to worry him. On January 27th he wrote to his mother: 'This morning, some of us in the Novitiate had to sing as cantors with the Head Cantor, being answered by the rest of the Choir... I didn't really get into voice till the "Benedicite" at Lauds'.

The Benedictine motto contained a double injunction: *Ora et Labora*, 'Pray and Work'. The problem for John was how to reconcile the two, especially if, when it came to the second, one had absolutely no aptitude; moreover work took up an inordinate amount of time in the postulants' day. He would have agreed with Bede Griffiths (who preceded him at Prinknash) in his *Golden String*:

> There was an atmosphere of incessant activity. The whole day was taken up in a constant round of duties, in the choir, in the house, in the garden, in the workshops, which left very little leisure for 'contemplation'. It is true that there was a half-hour every day after Vespers which was given to silent prayer, but it was difficult to see how this half-hour could be said to determine the character of the whole life.

Up to that time John had espoused the idiorythmic way of life typical of oriental monasticism. Following his own inspiration and humour, preferring as much as possible solitary prayer, he became irked by, as he saw it, the overregulated pattern of life at the Abbey. Postulants were obliged to labour at making incense, which was sold locally and far beyond, and rosary beads (which should have appealed to a devotee of the Virgin Mary). Furthermore there was plenty of manual labour to be done by postulants in the garden, under the iron rule of Brother Anthony, who had served his apprenticeship in a nursery garden. Brother Anthony never forgot John, this postulant much older than the average and so special, 'a lovable man', and became devoted to John's memory. But several tons of potatoes and an assortment of vegetables had to be produced every year to feed the community; in the autumn, apples had to be harvested to supply the cider presses, cider being a significant source of annual income; a farm and ten acres of farmland were attached to the monastery, which included pig rearing and diverse horticultural products.

As far as John was concerned, these activities left too little time for prayer, not least because it was at Prinknash that he came across (if not for the first time: he might have read it at Parkminster) *The Cloud of Unknowing*, which drew its inspiration from Pseudo-Dionysius, and fell under its spell:

> Myself was a postulant once
> In sight of the Malvern Hills,
> Unpractical, rather a dunce,
> A wight of the weakest of wills;
> Manoeuvering shirts that emerged from the wash
> I ironed them less than depressed them asquash:
> Of body inept and of soul a debosh
> I wandered in mind by the rills.
>
> But Cloud of Unknowing I begged them to let
> Me read in the times that were fit...
> (*In A Fair Field*, 1963)

This demanding mystical text, in which the dialectic of Martha and Mary loomed large, confirmed John's current misgivings. The religious regime at Prinknash, with its daily half-hour of personal prayer, smacked too much of Martha to John's way of thinking, and seemed a step backwards in comparison with his life as a hermit in Devon.

With the arrival of Lent, his ardour began to wilt even more, even if he did write on March 11th enthusiastically to his mother about the grounds of Prinknash and its views, which he described as a veritable paradise. He began talking about his health which, according to Novice Master Dom Alfred Spencer, was a bad sign in a postulant. The gloomy winter of that year no doubt played its part, but community life was also weighing heavily on John's temperament, and afforded little space or outlet for solitary prayer. The postulants were crowded into prefabs, and for John solitude was as necessary to life as air itself. And so he decided to open his heart to Dom Wilfred. But events soon took over: March 25th, Palm Sunday, marked the end of John's fourth month in Prinknash, but a week later he was gone. Dom Spencer summed it up as follows: 'In the pre-Vatican II liturgy, we prayed for "the perfidious Jews". That was too much for John and he departed suddenly.'

What exactly happened? In the course of the liturgy of the Passion the traditional prayer 'Oremus et pro perfidis Judaeis' ('Let us also pray for the perfidious Jews') was recited by the deacon. *Perfidus* bears as original meaning 'those who have wandered from the (true) faith', but also can mean 'treacherous, deceitful, disloyal'. For John it was akin to being hit by a thunderbolt, though he must have heard it on at least eight occasions since his conversion to Catholicism. By an irony of fate this prayer had just been given a modified, less offensive, form by the Vatican, and would disappear altogether under this phrasing from the liturgy three years later. When the celebration was over, John returned to the dormitory in tears, gathered his belongings in his Gladstone bag, and left the Abbey for good. His love for the Jewish people, his desire for the Church to grant them a place of eminence in its mission, his vocation towards God's chosen people as strong as ever, were such that to hear them described as 'perfidious' was more than he could bear. And so he fled, without a second thought.

Return to life as a hermit

It was a very disturbed man who knocked on Cecil Hardwicke's door at Easter 1956. That John should seek refuge with his agnostic friends at this moment speaks volumes about his mental and emotional disarray. Cecil later wrote that John told them at the time that he no longer believed in anything that he had learnt up to then. He again moved into the loft in the barn, and went to visit his mother.

He would in time recover from this latest traumatic setback. In reply to the question put to him by John Dove he simply replied that the moment of truth had occurred on that fateful Good Friday. He was more forthcoming, if somewhat cavalier, in a letter dated April 15th:

> I am very sorry indeed for the trouble and dismay
> I have caused you... 'Qui s'excuse, s'accuse' [he who
> excuses himself accuses himself] so I shall not be

wordy: I left not in a tempest, not impetuously, not in a brainstorm, but exactly as and when and how God wanted me to leave... The hour of the fool's departure was just that in which the King was made a fool of by the Gentiles. Further, best and loyalest of friends, I am by God's grace a monk till death. I do not refer to ecclesiastical litigation or terminology but to the essential, original meaning of 'monachus', viz. 'a man who is alone with The One'.

Gradually the memory of this painful and precipitate departure from Prinknash faded from his mind, and only a fond recollection of a devout and fraternal community remained.

John soon paid a visit to East Hill, having learnt that his friend Geza Vermes was staying there. During his time at Prinknash the relationship between the latter and Pamela Curle had resumed. His friend from Louvain had left Paris, his congregation and the priesthood! Soon after his arrival at East Hill Geza had taken ill and had to be hospitalised, and on his discharge he had returned to East Hill to convalesce. Adam Curle had just left, taking with him their two daughters, to take up a position in a university in South-East Asia. When John came to stay the new couple decided to keep him in the dark about their situation, having decided that in his naivety and simplicity he would suspect nothing. They were right, and on April 15th John wrote to John Dove outlining the Rule that he was following 'approved by Father Geza Vermes', unaware that the latter had already left the priesthood:

Office – that of Our Lady (I am once more a Franciscan Tertiary)
Matins – when I wake up during the night
Lauds – at first light
Prime – at sunrise
Mass daily and Communion – soon after
From Tierce till None, with a break for Sext and lunch, I am fully occupied washing up and cutting wood and what not. None at 3 p.m. From then

> on till 7 p.m. the time is with God and Our Lady.
> 7 p.m. wash up, then a few minutes visit to my
> mama, then Compline, then bed.

Leaving his friend to his devotions, Geza Vermes left for Paris at the end of May, soon to be followed by Pamela. When the penny finally dropped for John, he was devastated and blamed himself. Had it not been his invitation that had brought his friend to East Hill in the first place? He was deeply hurt by the episode.

It seems that John completed *Ut Unum Sint* about this time. In any event it was a productive period for him, almost as much as before he entered Prinknash. However, he had to make some money, and went to play his recorder in the streets of nearby Sidmouth, where he made more pals than pence. Then he decided to become, as in Palma, a dustbin man. But Ottery was not Italy, the Bradburne family was highly respected in the neighbourhood, and John's mother was mortified. His brother Philip, home on leave from Libya, got involved and made it clear to John in no uncertain terms that he should abandon this preposterous idea. John was immovable and the brothers quarrelled (things were not helped by the fact that John had disapproved of his brother's divorce the year before and had taken the side of his sister-in-law Esme). John left and returned to the Hardwickes, and the same day got a lift to London from a visitor who had been stopping over.

Homeless

In the eyes of many, this latest, seemingly headstrong, flight was an ominous sign. John was now 35, and people began referring to him as a drifter and a 'rolling stone' (these two words are Father David Harold-Barry's, at an anniversary celebration in Westminster Cathedral in 2009; they applied to another circumstance but are especially apt in John's case). Those, like John Dove, who still believed he had a vocation, and was 'simply following his unique but difficult calling at every stage', were asking themselves: 'What will he do next? Where will he go now? What's going to become of him?'

In fact John's first weeks in London were a veritable descent into hell. He was deeply upset by the family quarrel, and his future was looking grim. Even though he continued to dress neatly, and his recorder with its brightly coloured ribbons impressed passers-by (an article in *The Evening Star* in the autumn of 1956 referred to 'an Elizabethan piper' gracing the streets of London by piping Elizabethan madrigals), he was becoming something of a down-and-out, playing music in the streets or on the bridges to keep body and soul together, staying some of the time with his friends the Hunts, and sometimes sleeping rough along the Embankment, where for decades tramps, paupers and people just down on their luck had sought refuge after dark, despite legislation and the best efforts of the police to rid London of this 'plague'. In the words of one of George Orwell's acquaintances, in *Down and Out in Paris and London*, 'you got to be on your bench by eight o'clock, because dere ain't too many benches and sometimes dey're all taken. And you got to try to get to sleep at once. 'Tis too cold to sleep much after twelve o'clock an' de police turns you off at four in de mornin.' John had hovered on the brink of this world of outcasts in the preceding year, but this time he sank into it. Moreover the summer of 1956 was marked by miserable weather. August temperatures fell to 7 degrees, and it rained incessantly from July to mid-September. In such conditions few Londoners were tempted to stop and listen to airs by Thomas Tallis and William Byrd, even when played by a well-dressed wandering minstrel!

From hospital to cathedral

John must have felt he was on the slippery slope when after two months on what was effectively skid row he started to look for a job, and soon found one as a porter and factotum at St Mary Abbott's Hospital, Kensington, at £4 a week. He applied at Philip's suggestion, which hints at reconciliation between the brothers. The name of the hospital, built in the nineteenth-century as a hospice for paupers, would have appealed to John, but the work was thankless: cleaning the wards, looking after the boiler, carrying coal, and wheeling dead bodies to the morgue, quite often as night-work. He prayed every day for the deceased, which gave meaning to the work, though working conditions were not pleasant. His fellow porters, often ground down by life, were coarse and cynical, and this made him feel an outsider. His lodging, which he had found with the help of a cousin in St George's Square, was three miles away, and this meant long walks to and fro every day, making it difficult for him to attend daily Mass in Westminster Cathedral, which was his reason for choosing to live in Pimlico in the first place.

He would occasionally have cast a glance at the books on display in the shop window of Burns & Oates across from the cathedral on Ashley Place. Founded by a Catholic convert in 1847, with J. H. Newman among its authors, Burns & Oates was the most important publisher of Catholic books in England. As John's working hours at the hospital had become less and less regular, and the bags of coal heavier, he plucked up the courage on a Saturday in late October to enter the shop and ask for a job. His visit was timely in the run-up to Christmas, and he was offered work on the spot. He immediately wrote to his mother: 'I'll be selling Christmas cards and statues and things – later on books maybe.' He was to be paid £7 a week, and would start on Monday October 29th, just as winter temperatures were beginning to bite. His hours were nine to five, which gave him time to attend early morning Mass, and even 'breakfast in peace before work'. His application to join the cathedral choir was met with a polite refusal, there being apparently no vacancies. He later wrote to his mother that he had made up with 'Brother Till (money machine)'; the very same day, in accordance with the secret agreement concluded at Sevres, Tsahal (the Israeli Army) began its drive towards the Suez Canal, and John vibrated in solidarity.

He seems to have been a successful bookseller:

> I'd burnt my boats at Gloats on Backwash Booth
> And sold as many books and Christmas Cards
> As needed for the sweetness of the tooth
> Of sugared festivals, recalling bards.
> (*The Joy of Being Cloistered*, 1976)

The weeks in the run-up to Christmas were busy, and the shop was a hive of activity. John became friendly with Edward Duggan, who had also experienced the contemplative life at Prinknash a few months before John. At the beginning of December, conversation in the shop focussed on the new Archbishop of Westminster, who had just been appointed by Pius XII. At 67, William Godfrey, who had previously been Archbishop of Liverpool, was not an unknown quantity, and his reputation as a man of prayer and silence would have met with John's approval. As pious as he was talented and rigorous, and a good musician to boot, he 'never had the slightest difficulty in keeping silence' according to his successor (in Michael Walsh, *The Westminster Cardinals*).

At Christmas John stayed at Ottery with his mother. Philip had a new companion, Pamela Curtis, and intended to marry her. His brother did not approve of this 'pagan project... impenitent path' (in a letter to his mother, 29 October 1956) and didn't hesitate to speak his mind, defending Esme and above all his 12-year-old godchild Pamela – none of which deterred Philip from marrying his new partner the following year. Back in London John wrote to his mother on the morning of New Year's Day:

> Now here I am, my dear Mist, like a Lord in
> comfort, with a kettle on the gas for some tea from
> a very fine blue spoon, contemplating a benevolent
> clock that says royally twenty to eight. Last night
> at twelve o'clock all vessels of the Thames sounded
> their trumpets full blast. It was glorious.

Was John about to succumb to the lure of middle-class comfort? Hardly. After the Christmas rush there were fewer visitors to 25 Ashley Place, which John compared to a convalescent home, and he decided once again to change jobs, but this time he had not far to go, having managed to get taken on as a fifth sacristan at the cathedral.

Westminster Cathedral was a source of pride to many English Catholics, symbolising the visible return of the Church of Rome to the country of Henry VIII. Its construction had begun in 1895, on the site of an old prison. Having sought inspiration in Venice, Ravenna and Constantinople, architect Francis Bentley freely indulged his taste for the then fashionable Byzantine style (Notre Dame de Fourvière in Lyon had been completed the year the site was acquired, and work on the Sacré-Coeur in Paris had commenced nine years previously). Work on the site would continue until 1903. The interior, still unfinished when John began as sacristan, contained numerous side chapels; and from the bell tower one could see across the Thames the cream-coloured towers of MI6, the other Pimlico churches, and at the foot of the cathedral the gardens on the street named after John's favourite saint. He loved the cathedral, despite what others considered its kitsch aspect:

> Back to black Pimlico? there Christ Mine Host
> Gave to me sub-sub-sacristan for post.
> ...
> A looming gloaming of the Holy Ghost,
> A roaming to Byzantium in brick,
> A Campanile carolling Mine Host,
> A glory to the gory Catholic
> Martyrs... and a high tribute to the thick,
> Thicker than water, Precious Blood of One
> Who is The Word Incarnate, Mary's Son.
> (*The Joy of Being Cloistered*, 1976)

January 1957 was mild, dry and sunny as John started his new job. His tasks resembled those he remembered from Palma, but there were a lot more of them requiring attention in London than in a small sleepy Italian town. These included: opening and closing the doors of the cathedral, helping to prepare for weekday Masses, laying out and putting away liturgical vestments, washing the sacred vessels and cleaning the sacristy. John carried out these tasks with scrupulous devotion, for which he received high praise from chief sacristan Sam Verrall: 'One of the most lovable men I ever knew... a most conscientious worker.' But he was still as absent-minded as ever, and Edward Moberly, the first assistant, felt obliged to keep an eye on him when preparing the altar and the credence table in case, as often happened, he forgot some sacred vessel or liturgical book.

Monsignor Gordon Wheeler, the Cathedral Administrator, was himself a convert and a formidable character in his own right, and editor of the *Westminster Cathedral Chronicle*, which he had made into a journal of reference in the English-speaking Catholic world. His first meeting with John did not go very well. The administrator had a strong sense of hierarchical niceties, and when the new fifth sacristan, instead of stepping out of his way at his approach, addressed him familiarly as 'dear father and brother in Christ' and conveyed to him with a broad smile the New Year greetings of Dom Andrew from Parkminster, he was taken aback by this new 'apparition', according to Edward Moberly, who witnessed the scene. Monsignor Wheeler lost no time putting the fifth sacristan in his place, but the latter did not seem to understand. The administrator realised that this was not a case of lack of respect: the young man accepted the rebuke, even appearing to relish it, though it didn't make him change his ways. For Moberly it was because 'I guess the most important trivia just did not penetrate his empyrean'.

On the other hand John's devotion did not stop him taking in all that went on around him, as he wrote to his mother (3 February 1957):

> How I love that place with its scribes and Pharisees
> (not hypocrites however) and cranks and wise
> men, and holy women and scrupulous crackpots,
> and publicans and sinners and Saints.

Moreover he had time, in the cathedral or in his lodging, to meditate, to write his poems, or write letters; thus, when he wrote the following to his mother (25 January 1957), Mrs Bradburne must have wondered if she should take it at face value:

> I think that in previous pilgrimages in the body I
> have been both a Tibetan lama and a rogue of a
> medieval beggar and a jongleur and a mediocre
> French monk.

His first few weeks as sacristan were full of bustle, in preparation for the enthronement of the new archbishop, under the supervision of Monsignor Wheeler, Sam Verral and Monsignor Worlock, who would continue to be secretary to the new Archbishop as he had been to the old. The ceremony took place on February 11th, marking the first time that a Catholic celebration had been broadcast on British television. Thereafter things returned to normal, John's blunders causing some diversions for his fellow sacristans, while they continued to feel nervous whenever he was near the altar:

'What has he forgotten this time? What will he do next?' But they took him to their hearts, and though they became familiar with his asceticism they were also aware that he could down pints with the best of them in the local pub. Typically, he explained to Moberly that he didn't like chemically fermented modern beers but preferred good old-fashioned ale. He also became friendly with a number of priests, such as Father Harold Winstone, who was passionate about the liturgy, and Father Michael Hollings, just as eccentric as himself (he was also a boldly original theologian and he operated an open-door policy when receiving visitors, where the Duke of Norfolk, bourgeois bohemians and prostitutes might bump into each other in the corridor). John was full of praise for this 'Master of Love's art, God's heart's his gain' (*In Magno Silentio*, 1978).

At this time, before the custom of concelebrating Mass had been restored, John was kept busy by the Masses of the priests attached to the cathedral or others who came to say Mass there, and he soon discovered an unsuspected bonus. When many Masses were celebrated during the day, it was his job to wash the cruets, which were often half full of wine, with the result that by the end of it all he often felt worse for the wear:

> A roving sacristan employed
> In Westminster Cathedral
> Small perquisites at first enjoyed
> Till thirst became less frugal:
> Scant residue in cruets he
> Would drink from, say, three masses
> But when it came to seventy
> Bugled his soul Alases.
> (*Moke-song for organ-voice*, 1977)

He confessed this indulgence to Father Hollings, who soothed his conscience by quoting from Deuteronomy 25:

> 'There is a saying, Muzzle not the ox'
> Said Michael Hollings from his hollow box!
> (*In Magno Silentio*, 1978)

John was happy among the cruets and in pursuit of his other tasks, having as much time at his disposal to pray as to work. He noticed that the new archbishop spent many long periods at prayer alone on a bench in the cathedral. For his part the prelate soon became aware of the presence of the pious fifth sacristan. One day he addressed him on some point of detail and John, instead of replying briefly, as might have been expected, struck up a conversation as between peers, expressing his point of view at length. Unlike Monsignor Wheeler, the Archbishop, who was famously slow to make up his mind about a new acquaintance, but, having done so, never changed his mind, did not take offence, and was soon giving the fifth sacristan a good deal of his attention. They often joined in long conversations, during which John spoke of his quest for God, his love of the Virgin Mary, and his desire for solitude.

A mild dry spring was followed in London by a hot rainy summer, when temperatures soared to 30 degrees. John had not abandoned playing his recorder, and occasionally did so in the street for enjoyment, though he didn't refuse any offerings, promptly inserting them in the St Vincent de Paul collection box, or giving it away to a passing beggar. But one day, while playing on the steps of St Paul's, he was recognised by a Catholic passer-by who was quick to report back to Monsignor Wheeler that one of his sacristans was begging outside an Anglican cathedral! One can only guess at the reaction of the Cathedral Administrator in those pre-ecumenical times, when such behaviour could have had embarrassing consequences for the reputation of his Church. The fifth sacristan was called upon to explain himself, bewildered that he could have caused any offence. He wasn't begging, he explained, but playing exclusively Marian hymns, and any monies received had already been passed on to the poor.

He moved house several times. His lodging in Tachbrook, very near to Westminster, was reputedly so tiny that one could not stand up in it. This became a kind of legend among staff at the cathedral, recounted later by the future Bishop of Lancaster, Patrick O'Donoghue, according to whom the fifth sacristan lived in a place no bigger than a broom cabinet. However, the Bishop cautiously added: 'I never did locate the place but the story seems to have had some foundation.' It is true that in Tachbrook Street the only furniture was a table and an iron bed. John had written the word GOD on the wall and visitors reported that his diet consisted of baked beans and dry bread. He was still living there in August 1957 when his friend managed to find a place on the floor to unroll his sleeping bag. He later persuaded John to share a bigger flat with him, and they lived together for a while in Dawson Street, but John soon returned alone to St George's Square.

According to Patrick Hardwicke, John was seeing a young woman called Anne (like his former girlfriend) about this time, and became attached to her, but beyond that we know nothing. He also met during his time at the cathedral Teresa Thorp, whom he knew from Devon years, and who had busked with him previously in London at street corners. On one sunny Sunday morning, wrote Teresa,

> John had decided to wake me up for Mass with his recorder. I was staying at More House, a hostel in the Cromwell Road (now the University Catholic Chaplaincy). I woke early this Sunday morning to the sound of 'Greensleeves'. I looked out of the high window of my room to see John walking up and down by the Natural History Museum playing his favourite song.

On his days off he went for walks around Pimlico (this would be his longest period living in an urban environment), and befriended the birds and the swans in the parks, who inspired him to write:

> Yet have I seen white swans in congregations great
> Where pens and cobs and cobs and pens with
> cygnets go
> In forceful concourse over Thames from gate to gate
> Of Tower Bridge, from Waterloo at waters low
> Towards the House of Lords and broads of Pimlico.
> (*Of Swans*, 1978)

He loved to wander along footpaths, feeling the sun caressing his face. One such walk took him to a museum where he discovered a brain in a jar (possibly, at the Science Museum not far from the cathedral, the half brain belonging to Charles Babbage (1791–1871), credited as the inventor of one of the first mechanical computers):

> I saw a brainy head inside a glass
> Jar and it jars upon me even now...
> Perhaps a pauper from the bottom class
> Carried that head as high as he knew how
> And so perhaps it was not such a brain
> As Bertrand-Russell had, but just a plain.
> I begged a Priest to pray for all the folk
> Whose bygone brains stand pickled on the benches.
> (*In Magno Silentio*, 1978)

The priest gave him his word that he would.

On the feast of the Transfiguration he again wrote a letter in verse to his mother (6 August 1957). In it he invoked 'chirping' birds – in particular solitary blackbirds singing at dawn on the scaffolding of a building – and gave expression to a declaration of filial love, in a context of literary (Francis Thompson) and religious (*The Cloud of Unknowing*) allusion:

> For you are in the vanguard, you are Mist,
> For ever intertwining with the rays
> Of Jesu's Cloud that all about Him plays
> When He is hunting, peregrine on wrist
> To sight and wing and bring to Heaven all
> The little malâdas wild (which He has made)
> Into a land of light that cannot fade.

(*Malâdas* is obscure: does it refer to the inhabitants of a mythological Hindu kingdom?)

On August 24th, John Knox died. The son of an Anglican bishop, he was a famous convert to Catholicism and author of a much-respected translation of the Bible. His remains were laid in state in the cathedral. Before the Requiem Mass, presided over by Bishop Craven, the auxiliary of Westminster, John spent the whole night alone beside the catafalque playing an elegy for Knox on his recorder: (Greensleeves) 'which I piped for Ronnie Knox / Alone at night beside his only box' (*Epilogue*, 1969).

Robert Hugh Benson and Hare Street House

Towards the end of August the weather got decidedly cooler. John got to see Archbishop Godfrey on an almost daily basis, and was unexpectedly invited by him to become the caretaker of his residence at Hare Street, which had been left to the Archdiocese of Westminster by Robert Hugh Benson, the renowned priest and writer, himself a convert (and son of an Archbishop of Canterbury). Archbishop Godfrey had already asked his secretary to make enquiries about John's suitability, and Monsignor Worlock had expressed certain reservations. But the Archbishop's mind had already been made up, and on Sunday September 29th he set out with his secretary and fifth sacristan for Hare Street.

John was captivated by the historic residence and the chapel where Benson was buried. The Archbishop had decided to restore the house, which had had a chequered history, to its original function, and building plans were being drawn up. Sharing as he did the desire for solitude, silence and prayer with his young sacristan, the Archbishop considered that his country residence would suit John's needs, and that it would be looked after and maintained by the latter for his own needs, whenever he managed to escape from the hustle and bustle of London. John was to receive £5 pounds a week, and free board and lodging. In a letter John wrote to his mother he explained:

> I am to have a nice room on the ground floor. To
> be a sort of caretaker and gardener's idiot hog.
> And to look after church, sacristy, holy vessels.
> And to keep the keys like Peter.

He continued to work at the cathedral until Christmas, and then moved to Hare Street.

The village, approximately 40 miles north of London, at the intersection of the old London–Cambridge road and another from Buntingford, was in still rural Hertfordshire, where the old green England dear to John's heart stretched on all sides in rolling peaceful hills often topped by trees. It consisted of a few dozen small single-storey houses, some old and picturesque, beyond whose gardens lay fields sloping down to the River Quin. Its Methodist chapel was the only place of worship in the village, and harked back to the heyday of Nonconformism. Hare Street House, opposite the pub (The Beehive – another wink from John?) was the only building of any importance in the locality, and was hidden from view behind a high hedge and abundant lime trees, and access was through an impressive gate dating back to the time of Charles II. A vast courtyard was enclosed by two wings and a garden.

The exterior was in undistinguished red-brick Georgian style, while the interior was remarkable. Benson had not only restored the house according to his own taste, but had closely supervised the work himself, even making his own contribution, which would explain a certain awkwardness of some decorations. The house is well known for its tapestries of the *Danse Macabre – Memento Mori*, executed by Benson and his friends. Apparently the idea originated in the outrageous imagination of Baron Corvo, of sulphurous reputation, whom Benson, eclectic in his acquaintances and with a weakness for lost causes, counted among his friends. During John's stay at Hare House the tapestries were hidden, as he wrote:

> I well remember how, in Hare Street House
> Which was the happy home of Robert Benson,
> I never was disturbed by rat or mouse
> But I would give an honourable mention
> To his 'Memento Mori': in detention.
> At the top storey, grinning, it remained.
> (*I find myself not seldom being haunted*, 1978)

During John's time in Hare Street the tapestries, as he wrote to his mother (2 October 1958), 'were in detention in the upstairs attic', but this *Danse Macabre*, which he had gone there to inspect, would continue to haunt his dreams from time to time.

The oak panelling that Benson had installed in the great dining room remained in place. The walls of the office were covered in books, the majority of which had belonged to Benson. This room was nicknamed the 'Chamber of the Grail' because Benson had hung a tapestry there depicting scenes from the legend, embroidered by him and his friends. A large door opened directly onto the garden and brought a touch of green and clear sky into the room. The Oriel window was in stained glass, picturing a swan, a bear, a cardinal's hat, two coats of arms, and the chalice of the Holy Grail, from which the Infant Jesus appeared to emerge. This is where John would live, pray, write, play the recorder and the harmonium, meditate, seek God, and sleep at night. It was in this room, where everything spoke of the genius and sanctity of its former occupant, that John came to feel he had been granted a mission towards Hugh Benson; he had been appointed to stand guard over this temple of the spirit.

John shared his responsibilities with Fred Ginn the gardener, who had formerly been chauffeur to Cardinal Bourne, and who lived, now advanced in years, in an adjoining cottage. For the first months John was filled with enthusiasm, and from mid-January 1958 he wrote a stream of high-flown letters to his mother, though always remaining down to earth in spiritual matters – thus in October 1958: 'It is Heaven to be alone with God – Heaven albeit with a heavy cross – that of being alone all with oneself.' He described the house and the garden, where the mild weather of early 1958 allowed him to spend time, and imagined the shade of Benson, evoking the birds to which he had already referred in a letter-poem:

> Could You only hear the blackbird's twilight flute
> That sweetly fades to silence as the eve
> Joins hands with darkness where the angels weave.
> (*Letter to mother*, 19 January 1958)

Two days later snow fell north of London, after which daily gloom and nightly zero temperatures prevailed right up to Holy Week. John's humour varied with the weather, unlike his diet: tins of baked beans, bread and margarine. According to Sam Verrall, a regular visitor, the account set up in John's name in the local grocer's recorded tin after tin of baked beans and little else. At the same time John's poetic output was nothing short of prodigious. Early in the year he completed a long poem, *The Anathema of Melancholy*, 6471 lines long, averaging 462 lines daily written during a fortnight, even if he did recycle some previous compositions. As was often the case there was no overt unifying theme, and the 'Summary' at the beginning of his notebook was no more than a pretext. The poem featured in turn wild ducks, the Holy Grail, the wandering Jew, the god Pan, the huge tree at Gresham's, Sir Francis Drake, communists, the moon at Easter, elves, the Virgin Mary, and a hundred other topics.

When spring picked up, the Archbishop enjoyed visiting Hare Street, insisting that all restoration work should cease for the duration of his stay, which naturally caused problems for the builders. His arrival would be preceded by that of Monsignor Worlock and two Bavarian nuns, who would arrive four hours before him. John was less than enthusiastic whenever these visitors showed up during one of those weeks which he had assigned to a regime of total silence, and it was not unusual for him to cross swords with Monsignor Worlock or the nuns. For example, as an ascetic he considered himself an authority on healthy eating, and he was of the opinion that the nun was cooking too much food for the Archbishop. This was not helped when the same bossy nun insisted that he himself finish everything served on his own plate. And though he might regard the good sister as Martha and consult *The Cloud of Unknowing* for advice on how to deal with her, she by no means saw him as Mary, but rather as an idle drone!

Monsignor Worlock made it clear to John that he was expected to remain invisible during the Archbishop's visits, but John soon found himself ignoring the instruction. He seemed to seek out the Archbishop's company, engaging him in discussion about prayer, mysticism, Walter Hilton (author of *The Ladder of Perfection* and, in his opinion, of *The Cloud of Unknowing*), and was very happy to serve his Mass. The more he got to know the Archbishop, the greater became his admiration for him, regarding him as a holy man 'always up on the mountain with God', as was said of Moses (a description in his interview with *The Shield* in 1965). For his part Archbishop Godfrey developed a great affection for the young caretaker, and seemed to understand his 'madness and love of solitude'.

But John soon realised that relations between the Archbishop and his secretary were not as they seemed. Archbishop Godfrey remained above all a priest, while his secretary was also an administrator. And because the flipside of John's veneration for holy priests was a hearty contempt for administrators, relations with Monsignor Worlock (according to his biographers, the strong man of English Catholicism for half a century) were fraught. It would be difficult to imagine two more different men, though of similar age and social background. The churchman however did what was necessary to ensure that the Archbishop's protégé was looked after. He introduced John to families in the village, bought him a wireless (which John only bothered with to listen to classical music, when he found the time). He even installed a television in the house, still a novelty in Britain at the time, though it was some time before John got around to switching it on:

> Myself I lived alone inside a house
> Ancient and steeped in memories august
> For two good years, before I thought I must
> Look at that set which bids me yet carouse.
> I watched it spellbound, and I found for me
> It spoilt the place, like Eden's graceless tree.
> (*Of Television*, undated)

When the Archbishop was in London, John set off early every morning to Mass at Buntingford, two miles away; he then worked in the house all morning, and in the garden in the afternoon, time permitting, doing his best to help out Fred Ginn, for whom he had the greatest respect. In a letter to his mother he described himself digging, hoeing, weeding and painting the garden gate. Had Benson himself not dug his own garden? And did the garden not provide a healthier daily diet for John? The gardener appreciated the caretaker's dedication, but couldn't help wondering whether the work was befitting the dignity of a young gentleman. He also wondered, like 'sister Martha', whether John was a bit of an idler, especially when the latter would lock himself away for a week in a Carthusian regime of silence and meditation.

These weeks of seclusion did not however prevent John from making friends in the village, including a local woman with whom he recited the rosary, and a family he regularly visited, devoting time to their handicapped child. He also got to know the workers on the restoration building site, whose skills he admired. It was however a different matter when it came to the architect George Mathers, who was close to Monsignor Worlock, and relations between them soon took a turn for the worse. John nicknamed him 'architect archdefect' and expressed the wish: 'Would to Heaven I could live in a chicken coop and forget architexts and archdefects, past and present.' Later, in a fit of remorse, he tried to patch up matters between them.

During his stay in Hare Street House, John was given a present of a harmonium, probably by a priest at Westminster Cathedral (perhaps Father Winstone). He played this instrument in Benson's living room, and his own in the chapel. Since Palma, he had had little opportunity to sit in front of a keyboard, but here he made up for lost time and spent hours, day and night, on one or the other, playing and singing at the top of his voice. And since he had plenty of time to recite the Little Office of the Blessed Virgin Mary, he accompanied himself on the harmonium as he sang it in Latin to the slow rhythm he had learnt at Parkminster. Later he also prayed from the beautiful copy of *The Book of Common Prayer* which had once belonged to the Archbishop of Canterbury, Benson's father, and sang and meditated upon the Psalms in their sixteenth- and seventeenth-century English versions, writing later to his mother (22 September 1959): 'I like to sing them, thus so near Hugh Benson's body, and feel it is in some inexplicable way another move towards the Union of Canterbury with Rome.'

He also read widely, particularly the works of Benson himself, which were to hand. His favourites were *The Necromancers*, in which the writer described the occultist and spiritualist circles of fin-de-siècle London with insight and style, and *Come Rack, Come Rope*. He wrote to his mother after reading the former that he had been captivated by it because Benson had succeeded in turning mud into rays of sunshine, adding that the crucial scene in the book, published in 1909, took place in the room where he was now living. *Come Rack, Come Rope* recounted the persecution of English Catholics in Elizabethan Derbyshire, the cradle of the Bradburne family. The book's hero (Benson's only invention, the rest of the characters being historical) had, like John, turned his back on earthly love to consecrate himself to God alone. The caretaker of Hare Street House could not fail to be impressed by the foreword to the book, where the author describes himself sitting with a pile of 20 or 30 books in front of him at the very same table where John himself was sitting reading the book. How could he not have been nourished in his own determination to bear witness to Christ unto death, and in his disdain for the 'heresy' which led to the persecution of so many Catholics?

Most of Benson's novels are concerned with spiritual conflict, and it is not difficult to imagine them appealing to John's imagination, in particular *None Other God*, whose hero Frank Guisely, like Benson and John himself, was a young upper-middle-class Anglican who converted to Catholicism, convinced that it was the one true Church. In the novel, Frank was rejected by his father and lived the life of an outcast, experiencing one failure after another, until the final and fatal one, brought about by his attempt to come to the aid of a social outcast like himself among the poorest of the poor. But what seemed merely disastrous on the human level was rather a mystical ascension, sustained by Frank's devotion to the Virgin Mary. The parallel with John's life was striking, with the difference that John was more than a character in a book.

Such was the manner in which John's days were spent at Hare Street House: morning Mass at Buntingford, or at the house itself on days when Mass was celebrated there; the daily round of the Office, humble chores, reading, writing poems, prayers. He had become so used to this frugal existence that when Archbishop Godfrey arrived with his retinue, John had difficulty hiding the fact that their presence was an inconvenience. The Archbishop was amused, but not so his secretary. Moreover, as time went on, John was beginning to feel more and more that he was on a mission to preserve and promote the memory of Benson, seeing him as a kind of latter-day St Francis, while the restoration works directed by Monsignor Worlock appeared to him as so many betrayals. And the caretaker of Hare Street House was not for turning: the house must remain as Benson conceived, built and decorated it.

After a June marked by rainfall, the summer of 1958 was blessed with sunshine. At the end of July the great event for John was not the nomination of young Charles as Prince of Wales but the ordination to the priesthood of his friend John Dove, which took place at Old Heythrop, north of Oxford. Because the chapel was tiny, each ordinand was allowed only ten guests; John was present, as were Mrs Dove and Canon Iles. He took great pleasure in the celebration and in the meal that followed (a photo of which was found in his belongings after his death), and even greater pleasure in serving his friend's first Mass the following day.

In November he went to stay with the Kings at St Albans, 25 miles from Hare Street. In 1952 Stephen had married a Norwegian girl, Solveig. John greatly enjoyed playing with the children in the big orchard, climbing up the trees, to their great delight, and pushing them on the swing. According to Stephen, John was 'an ideal uncle', adored by the children, and he noticed that John had the knack of talking to them in a way that made them feel as important as the grown-ups, and marvelled at his friend's talent for always bringing out the best in everybody.

Francesco, panels and rafters: trench warfare

On November 17th 1958, on the same day that Archbishop Godfrey arrived on a visit to Hare Street House, news broke that he was included in the first batch of cardinals to be appointed by John XXIII, 13 days after his election as Pope. On December 15th he received the cardinal's biretta in Rome, while on the same day in Hare Street John Bradburne was writing a long poem of 1476 lines, *O Rara Avis*, a meditation on Christ the King, interspersed, as was often the case, with fragments of autobiography. The poem invoked the ghostly past of the house. Benson liked to claim that the house was haunted, although he would reassure his visitors by telling them he had never seen a ghost himself. The rumour lived on, but John seemed unperturbed. He wrote shortly afterwards to his mother that he had spent Christmas at Hare Street House, and had strongly felt the presence of Benson, stressing his hope for the future unity of all Christians.

But, unknown to John, the new cardinal had given the go-ahead to his secretary and Mathers to carry out restoration work which would in effect transform the entire house from top to bottom. The architect had managed to procure period bricks from a nearby house which was being demolished at the time, and one by one they replaced those of the house's original facade. These developments led to open confrontation between John and Monsignor Worlock, who moreover was no longer disposed to tolerate what he considered John's over-familiarity with the Cardinal. The Monsignor was now visiting Hare Street House up to three times a month to keep an eye on restoration work-in-progress, which caused further friction. According to Monsignor Worlock, in a letter to Judith Listowell (31 December 1980), their encounters depended greatly on the current humour of the caretaker. Sometimes he was perfectly charming, and all was 'idyllic'; on other occasions he was obnoxious, locked himself in his room, and refused to make an appearance.

But it wasn't entirely a matter of mood swings on John's part. He had proclaimed himself the guardian of Benson's relics, and had decided on a policy of trench warfare against the Philistines. In his eyes the house had become a mere plaything in the hands of the architect, whom he went as far as to threaten with the wrath of God. In doing so he imagined – as no doubt, in his own way, did Monsignor Worlock in his – that he was being faithful to the vision of the Cardinal (both were plausible enough, since Archbishop Godfrey was as respectful of architectural tradition as he was a great builder).

The beginning of 1959 was marked by fine but cold weather. John was a popular presence in the village. He continued to visit the young handicapped boy, the woman with whom he recited the rosary, and of course his friends the birds and the trees. On January 25th a surprising piece of news arrived from Rome: John XXIII had just announced the convocation of an Ecumenical Council. But in the following weeks John's time was taken up by his new friend Francesco, a homing pigeon he had taken under his protection:

> If ye would meet a merry bird
> Of quite fantastic measure,
> Francesco stands on pantiled lands
> As happy, beyond pleasure
> Of any other dome or rock
> In all the world: he keeps a flock
> Of starlings (and the sparrows mix
> Therein to play their knavish tricks)!
> (*Introducing Francesco*, 1959)

In April he started to write a book for the Queen's sister, 'our roaming beautiful Princess', to whom – he told his mother in a letter (20 April 1959) – he wished to send a photo of the ordination of Father Dove, in case she didn't approve of the book! In June the preparations for the Council got under way with the encyclical *Ad Petri Cathedram*, and consultation with the bishops began. Cardinal Godfrey was invited to submit a list of topics for discussion. The date for submission was fixed for the end of August, and when the Cardinal arrived in due course at Hare Street House with Monsignor Worlock for a summer of serious study, the latter made it clear to John that he should make himself scarce. As soon as the work was concluded, further instructions arrived from Rome, and John's presence became even less welcome. This prompted him to visit Ottery, where his mother was now living, still close to St Mary's collegiate church. His sister Mary's daughter Celia had come down with measles, and John sang to her songs about the birds, accompanied by convincing impressions of real birdsong. On another occasion he took her for a ride on the crossbar of a bike, gliding along the country lanes of Devon, as Celia squealed in delight and fear. She in turn dutifully listened as he read her stories from a book, or sang songs for her.

One day he unexpectedly met Geza and Pamela Vermes, who were briefly in Ottery to arrange the sale of the house at East Hill. They had married in 1958, after the Curles' divorce. The two men attempted in vain to banter in the old way: 'The atmosphere was friendly, but without the usual spirit of fun', Geza later recalled. Their paths would more and more diverge: Geza had turned his back on the Christian faith and become a lecturer at Oxford in 1965. He went on to publish a number of works on Jesus, along the lines that he was merely a dissident Jewish figure, totally at variance with his portrayal in the Christian tradition.

Autumn turned out to be pleasant, warm, dry and sunny, and the good weather continued until interrupted by December cold. The Conservative return to power with a large majority on October 8th had been interpreted as a triumph for the consumer society, and a contemporary cartoon portrayed Harold Macmillan congratulating his electoral agents: a fridge, a television set, a washing machine and a car! Withdrawing further into his ascetic lifestyle, John felt tempted to isolate himself more and more from the world around him, but he was thinking less of an island or a hideaway in the desert; rather dreaming, as once in the Holy Land, of refuge in a cave.

The months passed, and the caretaker of Hare Street House continued to work and write, praying and playing the harmonium in the chapel, while the Cardinal and his secretary came to reflect on the new demands emanating from Rome. A letter to his mother (14 February 1960) alluded discreetly to a new friendship which would soon blossom, to wit 'in the Cardinal's field's a migrant... of Nordic stock', a jackdaw which he again baptised Francesco. In April 1960, future Nobel laureate Harold Pinter's *The Caretaker* opened in London to great acclaim; its main characters, around John's age, were social outcasts torn between the temptation of the East and a love/hate relationship with the society in which they found themselves: in a strange ironic way, not so far removed from John, and the coincidence of the title might even have evoked a smile.

Meanwhile relations with Monsignor Worlock and Mathers had taken a turn for the worse. In the presence of the workers John kept his thoughts to himself, but focussed all his anger on the secretary and the architect, and bombarded them with incendiary missives. But whenever the secretary arrived at the house John invariably behaved with disarming courtesy. This involved no hypocrisy on his part; having satisfied his conscience in writing, he felt free to welcome the visitor and put aside his anger. According to Monsignor Worlock, later to become Archbishop of Liverpool, 'amidst the letters of abuse, there would sometimes be included sublime verses and on occasion pictures and illustrations of his own painting or creation, mostly of apocalyptic character, almost reminiscent of Blake'.

The chapel had become the latest source of discord. This building, with its impressive arched wooden ceiling, had once been a barn where beer was brewed, before being converted with meticulous care by Benson into a place of prayer. But it had been badly maintained and was in a state of poor repair, and a nondescript annexe had been added behind it, somewhat pompously called the R. H. Benson Memorial Chapel, where Sunday Mass was celebrated from time to time. John fought tooth and nail for the restoration of the real Benson chapel, but the Monsignor would not hear of it.

To the list of contentious issues was soon added the 'Francesco Affair'. The situation was described by John in a letter. The bird, despite its name, had laid three eggs in a disused chimney, and John fought to prevent his disturbance and/or eviction by the ongoing work. He even considered leaving the house in the event of this happening, and going to live in a cave somewhere on the Hill of Kinnoul in Scotland (he had just learnt that he was the great-great-grandchild on his mother's side of the 6th Earl of Kinnoul). On Pentecost Sunday, Pope John announced the setting-up of preparatory commissions for the Council. The Cardinal was appointed to the central commission, but took no pleasure in it. He was already experiencing the onset of the cancer which would lead to his death two-and-a-half years later, and was about to undergo a first operation. His ambitious secretary wished him to go to Rome and make himself known. That summer of 1960, John's concerns for Benson and Francesco were far removed from those of Monsignor Worlock, who didn't hesitate to tell him so, while the caretaker repeated (in a letter to his mother, 8 May 1960) that 'if it were not for the Ministry of Birds, I would not stay here'. But he still kept the confidence of the Cardinal, even though, when the latter was absent, he was always happy to find himself alone again.

During the autumn, John struggled to contain his outbreaks of anger, telling himself that after all he had the house to himself when the workers were not there for 15 hours out of 24. He spent many hours every day contemplating the birds. Monsignor Worlock was surprised, whenever he visited, to find John still about the place, but John considered he had a duty of loyalty to the Cardinal, whom he venerated, and besides, there was Benson, and then the jackdaws. From time to time the confrontation became offensive to Monsignor Worlock, by now the most powerful man in the English Catholic Church, given his increasing hold on the ailing Cardinal. John continued his enthusiastic discussions with the Cardinal on the medieval mystics, totally ignoring his secretary, or referring to him and his nuns as the 'entourage' or the 'cortege'. Meanwhile the Cardinal was torn between his duties as a 'Prince of the Church', to which his secretary constantly drew his attention, and the imminent prospect of meeting his Maker, which was pressing him to give his time to discussions with his strange caretaker, one of the few with whom he could find common ground in the topics that counted.

In December Father Dove, at that time attached to Southwell House in London, had just learnt that he was to be posted to Southern Rhodesia, and came to visit John at Hare Street. John showed his friend around the house, and they were both amused by the secret cupboards Benson had installed in his bedroom. On opening one, they discovered an edition of the *Daily Mail* of August 4th 1914, whose headline announced the declaration of the First World War. They also found the Benson coat-of-arms with its motto in old French, *Fay bien, crain rien* ('Do good, fear nothing'). When they arrived in the chapel, John sat at the harmonium, and the friends spent some time praying together. They later dined together on tinned baked beans and, as a special treat, fried eggs, honey and cheese, all served up in a soup bowl. John rounded off the evening by playing 'Greensleeves' and Bach as a lullaby for his friend on the office harmonium, and gave him a present of a Latin–English Daily Missal. As Father Dove bade farewell, he was struck by John's serenity. Three weeks later, after a freezing Christmas, it was John's turn to visit him in London, and to accompany him to Southampton on January 12th 1961.The departing Jesuit retains a vivid memory of a silhouette 'waving on the quay making great gestures of farewell', as the *Capetown Castle* sailed out to sea and into the distance. Would they ever see each other again?

Monsignor Worlock had been right to be concerned about the Cardinal's reluctance to visit Rome, especially after Cardinal Alfrink indicated that the central commission might well be more important than the Council itself! He and the Cardinal arrived in Rome in March 1961, but their principal concern was with a matter that continued to simmer back home. In his Lenten Letter, the Cardinal had taken the opportunity to suggest to Catholics that, during Lent at least, 'a plump and pampered poodle might run all the more gaily after a reduced diet, simpler fare, and perhaps after having been denied a visit to the hair stylist'. In the uproar which followed, an actor was quoted in *Time* magazine as having said that 'we have some animals who behave in a more Christian way than some Christians'. All this had a profound effect on the Cardinal, whose health was already deteriorating. Perhaps this was why John, back at Hare Street, felt that he was getting less support in his trench war than before on behalf of his friends the birds he was helping with their nests, and protecting from the cats; not to mention from Monsignor Worlock, who had convinced the Cardinal to transform Hare Street House into a place of meditation for the young priests of the diocese. Once again the 'restoration work' resumed, much to the chagrin of the caretaker.

That same Lent, four young men made their first appearance on the stage in Liverpool. The extraordinary success of the Beatles became the crowning glory of the rising 'youth culture'. Hare Street was not immune, any more than the rest of the country, and when John's young friends pressed him to play their tunes on the harmonium he duly obliged. But his fury with the architect-archdefect had not abated. Already the nightingales and the owl had fled; now it was the turn of Francesco, who had disappeared. He made up his mind to leave if the latter had not returned by Easter Sunday, which he did on April 2nd – Easter Sunday! He wrote on the following day to his mother that now he had no option but to stay on, since it was manifestly God's will, 'in the ruins of Jerusalem with Jeremiah'. He complained of being more and more disturbed by visitors: seminarians from Ware, friends, priests from Westminster, even people he didn't know, who, having heard about him, came to see him out of curiosity. His latest discovery was that the house was to be 'torn to pieces' by Mathers, meaning according to his latest whim. When the workers arrived to strip the oak panelling John was lying in wait and threatened them with a garden fork. The defence of the jackdaws continued, as a new front opened in defence of the magnificent oak rafters.

During the summer of 1961 the Cardinal's health continued to decline, with Monsignor Worlock taking increasing responsibility for the running of the diocese, while preparations for the Council forged ahead. The work of administration required for organising the event took up more and more of his time, which he spent persuading, mediating and reconciling the demands of Rome and the reservations of the bishops of England and Wales. He also needed to raise £250,000 for the completion of the cathedral, and as much again to expand Catholic schools and open new ones. In the midst of all this decision-making, how could he take time to worry about the fate of wretched jackdaws, or a few old wooden beams? In these circumstances, arriving at Hare Street House to discover that the whole village was waiting with bated breath to witness the climax of the 'battle of the house', as in a Shakespearian drama, it was small wonder that Monsignor Worlock exploded, particularly when John took it upon himself to tell him in no uncertain terms what he thought of the ongoing 'demolition' work. For Monsignor Worlock the idea that the fate of this house should rest in the hands (or the feathers) of a bird defied understanding, and having informed the caretaker of this he betook himself back to London. But near the end of October, John wrote to his mother (4 November 1961):

> two foundation beams (it took six to eight men to carry them) about 18 inches square and 12 to 15 feet long, were ripped out and burnt without ceremony on the ground outside. Solid oak, probably from ships, with a few, very few, innocent little woodworms in them. They would have lasted for centuries more.

An act of treason against Benson and his house! He decided to take action...

> when the Cardinal, whom I love, came for his convalescence. Having welcomed him I then composed a poem to tell him yet again that the pirates were upon us. He thanked me very courteously, but as usual no notice was taken of the bark of a watchdog. The Cardinal is a saint of God and not to blame, and of course likes to believe that all is for the best, but I am convinced that pirates are upon this house, that dear old ship.

It was at this point that John took his leave, on October 27th, on a bright sunny morning. He had waited for the Cardinal to arrive, so that the Blessed Sacrament would not be left unguarded, and discreetly disappeared. The event was made known to Monsignor Worlock by one of the nuns (he had himself remained in London to deal with important tasks to hand). After John's death he wrote, without rancour: 'I think we all knew that we had met a Holy Man.'

Once again John found refuge with Cecil Hardwicke, now living at Headley Down in the Hampshire hills. He took with him his Gladstone bag and his recorder, having indicated on a scrap of paper that he was leaving his books to his rosary companion, the harmonium to Father Winstone, a few cigarettes to Fred, and the dirty dishes to the sisters. He also went as soon as possible to confession, and 'the only thing' he told the priest was: 'I accuse myself of bad manners, once.' He wrote to his mother that 'the exit was exactly calculated and prepared for', and that 'I signed myself Judah, not Judas'. He then tried to put his latest flight into context with the others:

> 1. Exmouth – panic and cowardice. 2. Prinknash
> – pure exuberation. 3. Hare Street: God's cause as
> I believe... I shall no more. Chapter closed. Hail to
> a new venture, hail from a fool, skilled in fiasco.
> My soul is full of gratitude, there is no bitterness
> or shame.

A cave, no matter where!

John spent some time with the Hardwickes, then went to stay with his godmother aunt Mary Comber before returning to Ottery. But he seemed incapable of putting a plan together, other than appealing to St Francis of Assisi to intercede for him, so that he could see the path along which he had to walk. He was then struck by the idea of fulfilling an old dream of his before finding his way: to seek recognition as a poet, and maybe make a living from it. Revisiting his stock of poems, he copied out a selection and sent them to Cecil Hardwicke (November 1961) asking her to find a publisher, with the words:

> The first £300 is for you! Or if it is only 3/– have
> a drink, or if it is nothing (which is more likely)

drink to our further success next time old Patrick
brings back home.

Having read the poems she proclaimed them to be little better
than doggerel (a verdict with which posterity would not agree), but
sounding a maternal and more optimistic note added that 'maybe
the psalms of David in their day sounded pretty dotty to most
people other than himself'. John wrote in a similar vein to Geoffrey
Hunt, who had publisher friends (it is interesting to note that of the
two people to whom he entrusted the fate of his mainly religious
poems one was an agnostic, the other a Communist).

John also made up his mind to revisit Skirwith for a second time.
He took the bus to Langwathby and continued on foot to the village
where he was born, and was assailed by memories: the bridge, the
low walls, his mother's songs, the sheep, the Fells, the curlew, the
dead lamb; it seemed, to his amazement, that nothing had changed.
He searched the cemetery in vain for Ninnie's grave, but when he
saw the church and its stained-glass window he half expected to
see his father emerge from the sacristy, and he was particularly
moved by the baptismal fonts. While he was praying, John Peel,
the sacristan, entered the church to replenish the oil lamps, and
in the course of a conversation Peel suggested John visit the vicar.
Canon James Wilson, a gentle giant, gave him a friendly reception
and insisted that his visitor spend the night under his childhood
roof. They dined together and rounded off the evening with a visit
to Miss Lea, a Catholic who had attempted the Carmelite way 60
years earlier, with whom the vicar was on good terms.

John slept in Philip's old room, and remembered what his father
had told him all those years ago about the clouds. In the morning
he woke to the cooing of the pigeons, the crowing of the cocks, the
mooing of the cows, and the chirping of the curlews. Nothing had
changed, and he reminded himself that there was no more moving
place in the world except Assisi, and having once again pledged his
future to St Francis he amused himself playing with the assonances
Appenines-Pennines, Umbria-Cumbria, and saw a sign. But he
also asked himself, punning as usual: 'Whether Cross Fell and its
environs is my destiny, or whether the denial of such a destiny is
the biggest cross which has fallen to me yet, I do not know.'

Once up and about, he accompanied the vicar to the church to celebrate 'his version of the Mass', and as he recited his rosary he found the canon to be 'astonishingly canonical'. The latter then drove John to the foot of Cross Fell, which he promptly climbed, across fields and rocky ground, to be greeted there by cold winds and swirling sea gulls. Rain caught him by surprise as he made his way down to Ousby, where he arrived drenched but happy. Then the sun came back and the wind dried his clothes, and putting the lure of the Fells behind him, he took the bus from Langwathby to Carlisle. As he wrote on his return to his mother, he finished off his marvellous trip with a good meal, a large whisky and a visit to the cinema – *101 Dalmatians* – with the song of the Skirwith curlews ringing in his head.

The desire for the solitary life had by no means left him. He began to look for – and for a moment thought he had found – a suitable location, a hole in the rocks at the summit of High Willhays, looking down 2039 feet on Dartmoor and the busy bees of Brother Adam. But it was already winter, and bitterly cold, with no ravens in sight to provide food for the new Elijah, and he quickly abandoned the project. Then Cecil Hardwicke came up with the idea that he stay for the time being in her small cottage at Talaton, a few miles to the North of Ottery, which she had just put up for sale. He took up her offer and settled in to a winter of his tried and trusted diet: Heinz beans apples, and dry bread. But he continued to dream of a real cave, chastened by the memory of the icy Dartmoor cold. Why not consider a warm country? The idea took root in his mind, and it occurred to him that John Dove might know a suitable cave in Africa where he could retire from the world. Did he seriously believe what he was writing to his friend? In any event the friend did, although not literally: while there were of course plenty of caves in Southern Rhodesia he rather saw John working in a Catholic Mission (volunteer work had become popular since the founding in Great Britain of Voluntary Service Overseas (VSO) by Alec Dixon in 1958, and John F. Kennedy's American Peace Corps in 1961). John Dove wrote back and his friend agreed enthusiastically by return post. John then wrote to his mother that he was heading to Africa to join John Dove in his missionary endeavours.

The Hardwickes by this time had found a buyer for Talaton, which meant that John had to find alternative accommodation. While waiting for news from Southern Rhodesia, he stayed with his sister-in-law Esme at Cobham in Surrey, 20 miles south of London. Philip's ex-wife did not share his hunger for God. John humorously referred to her house as a 'pagan household', but both she and her daughter had great affection for him. Esme grew vegetables in the back garden to sell locally and John offered to help, to which she readily agreed in return for board and lodging. She also offered to pay him £2 a week, which he refused but later accepted, to pay off some debts.

Spring 1962 was particularly cold, and remained so into July, but John continued cheerfully to dig and weed his potato patch, singing, reciting his Office, and composing poems in his head. When his friend Geoffrey Hunt came to visit, he immediately asked him to join him in the garden, even though he had only one arm. His niece Pamela had meanwhile blossomed into a beautiful young teenager. She had left her boarding school and was studying for her exams at the local technical college, and hadn't forgotten playing with her godfather in her childhood. On this occasion she remembered John being lively and full of fun, still eager to talk to her and debate on any topic under the sun. Like many others she remembered his 'piercing blue eyes', how he dashed off poems non-stop without corrections, and one day gave her one called *Carol*, which impressed her with its multiple alliterations, and by the unfamiliar word *pavan* ('pavane'), which she couldn't understand. She felt that 'almost everything he said was a sort of prayer, but I never saw him on his knees in the open or anywhere else'.

John soon became friendly with George and especially Mary Littledale, who were also guests of Esme (originally for a few weeks, which became seven years). It was not easy to house-train John: as often as not he lived on a diet of baked beans, but his fervour took them aback, his intransigence in matters of Catholic doctrine scandalised them, and his biblical literalism (which he possibly exaggerated to provoke a reaction) seemed like a throwback to another age. They eventually realised that this was simply his nature, that he enjoyed being provocative, and that if one avoided certain topics he could be very good company, with a keen sense of humour, and easy to get on with. He often sang, both religious and traditional English airs, such as '*Sumer is i cumen in*'. With the children he composed nursery rhymes. He offered to help the Littledales to paint a room, 'blissfully unaware that there was more paint on the floor than on the ceiling. His singing while he worked though more than compensated!' He gave Mary the impression that he accepted joyously everything that happened to him, and fascinated the children by his simplicity of character and the awkwardness that often led to foolish blunders.

Pamela was quick to notice that John appealed to the opposite sex:

> it amused my mother that the ladies who came to collect their vegetables found John very attractive and they used to ask my mother who he was, to which she replied firmly 'He is my brother-in-law and he is a monk'; I doubt that John even noticed their interest!

More embarrassing for John was when he became the recipient of persistent but unwanted attention from a nearby neighbour (after he left, he sent her some rosary beads).

In the meantime John Dove had been at work. At first he had thought of the Jesuit missions. His provincial Father Corrigan, whom he had approached, had agreed to pay John's air ticket for the end of 1962, but the young Jesuit was impatient for John to come out sooner than that. Why not approach the Franciscans, who had recently arrived in the region and needed all the manpower they could get? Moreover his eccentric friend had a great devotion to St Francis, and would likely fit in much easier in a new start-up venture than in a well-oiled machine such as the Jesuit Mission, which had been in place for 75 years. The Franciscan Superior was happy to accept the offer and suggested the Mission of St Mary at Wedza, which the Franciscans had just taken over from the Jesuits.

But John's volunteer status did not mean that bureaucracy could be dispensed with. He would have to sign a three-year contract, stipulating that the Franciscans would provide him with bed, board and laundry, and monthly pocket money, plus his return flight. The work specification was deliberately vague, given that mission work involved a bit of everything: building, driving a car, administration, teaching and evangelising. In the circumstances John overcame his allergy to paperwork and signed up. To get the necessary documents he paced the corridors of Rhodesia House, the location of the Southern Rhodesia High Commission on the Strand, not far from where, homeless, he had slept rough six years before. The three days supposedly necessary to complete the formalities stretched to a week, then a month. He had to undergo a medical test, be vaccinated, produce references, certificates, letters guaranteeing good moral character, fill in endless forms. In a letter to his mother (May 1962) he wrote: 'They must be careful just now about who and what they let into the last crumbling bastions of the White Man's Burden!' But his initial eagerness for the venture had waned. On June 20th 1962 he wrote to his mother: 'Never in my life have I felt less enthusiastic about a venture than I do about this one. I am convinced that this is truly a good Sign.' He even wrote to Stephen King, who was about to emigrate to Australia with his family, asking him to look out for a desert island off the Australian coast, just in case his African project came to naught.

Although a clause in the contract stipulated that he would have to drive, John had never bothered to validate his military driver's licence after the war. He prevailed upon Adrian Hardwicke to give him driving lessons at an abandoned aerodrome in Hampshire, which enabled him to apply for a provisional licence. He also paid several visits to his mother at this time. After his last visit he wrote to her from London (7 June 1962), appropriately describing his stay as 'not a conclusion of Devon but a prelude to Heaven'. Another of his friends, Jack Dunn, had managed to track him down, having lost contact during a house move. Now married with three children and living in Taunton, he had come across a letter in a Catholic newspaper signed Hornbeam, and had recognised the inimitable style of his friend. He wrote to the newspaper and got in touch with John, who went to see him and his family before his departure for Africa. While there he entertained himself pushing the children around in their pram, and dangling them on his knees, and recounting to the young couple the ups and downs of his life at Hare Street.

He still had not given up on his desire to see his poems in print, and entered *Fons Aquarum* in a Christian poetry competition in the *Church Times*, with no success. He often spoke to Esme about his efforts in this domain, but she had scant regard for his poetic skills, though Mary Littledale conceded that they possessed certain 'mystical' qualities. He sent a selection of poems to Victor Gollancz (perhaps on Geoffrey Hunt's suggestion or with his support). He showed Mary Littledale a letter he had written to send to Victor Gollancz with a postscript attached: 'Oh, come on Gollancz / And give us a chance'. However, before he received any answer, suddenly at the end of July the administrative marathon at Rhodesia House came to an end. Everything was in order, and the plane ticket, paid for by the Franciscans, had arrived at last.

On August 5th 1962 a singular piece of news hit the headlines in the British as well as the world press: Marilyn Monroe had been discovered dead, from an overdose of barbiturates. The arrest of Nelson Mandela, the same day, passed unnoticed – as did, even more, the departure the following day of a certain John Bradburne bound for Africa.

Chapter 7

Africa, 1962–1969

From England, far, to Africa
Those minstrels go that migrants are...
We rather to Our Father's land aspire
By longing than by song, our hearts wing lightly
Up in His paces who is our desire
(*Rhythm (Owed to a Nightingale)*, 1968)

At the beginning of August, Southern Rhodesia was entering the fourth month of the dry season. The sky was blue, and even though it was winter in Southern Africa, temperatures were higher than in London. John was by no means the most important visitor in arrivals when John Dove went to collect him at the airport. At the same moment, the Catholic community in Salisbury (today, Harare) was welcoming a very important visitor in the person of Cardinal Montini, Archbishop of Milan, tipped as a future Pope. He had come to offer his support to the foundation of the hospital at Chirundi run by a group of Italian nuns – the Associazione Femminile Medico-Missionaria (AFMM), founded by Adele Pignatelli, whose patron he was. John Dove, secretary to the Archbishop of Salisbury, had organised the Cardinal's visit.

Having paid a quick visit to the Archbishop's residence, John and Father Dove set off for the Jesuit Mission of Chishawasha, 13 miles or so north-west of Salisbury. On the journey John discovered to his delight an abundance of trees hitherto unknown to him, such as mubûe and baobabs, and a veritable bird paradise – 635 species had been recorded in the zone of the Jesuit Mission, including the snake-eagle and the bateleur eagle – while listening to a crash course on the history of Southern Rhodesia and the Catholic Church there from John Dove.

The Jesuit domain occupied the entire Chishawasha valley and the hills and plateaux surrounding it. The land, once a tribal chiefdom, had been 'given' to the Jesuits by Cecil Rhodes himself. During the African uprising of 1896, the Mission had been attacked by Shona warriors, but when peace returned the Jesuits protected the Shonas against the excesses of the subsequent repression and experienced an avalanche of conversions: 300 baptisms in 1899, 1000 in 1905, 3600 in 1920. The missionaries, particularly Germans, established themselves at the head of eight kraals, which they developed as model Christian villages, and their Superior, Father Richartz, defended the Africans when they were subjected to an iniquitous tax system. The Jesuits set up schools and apprenticeships in technical skills, which over the following decades made it possible for many young people from Chishawasha to find work in Salisbury. The work of the Jesuits was appreciated by employers in Salisbury, although it had its ambiguous side, since they both defended and exploited the Africans at the same time, as is claimed by the writer Lawrence Vambe, who was born in the Mission. Father Dove frankly admitted to John that he considered this paternalism an undesirable vestige of the colonial past, and that he regarded the present task as helping the Africans to take the destiny of their country in their own hands, in accordance with Christian principles.

On arriving at the Mission, the two friends went to pray at the old church of St Ignatius, the earliest in the colony, consecrated in 1902 (a statue in the church shows the Virgin with an African slave freed from his chains), and joined the Blue Sisters (Sisters of the Little Company of Mary), mainly Irish, for tea. The old Mission was still going strong. It included a diocesan seminary, St Dominic's Girls' School, the recently opened St Ignatius' Boy's School for young Africans, and the fathers' quarters. John also paid a visit to the shaded graveyard for Jesuit missionaries who died in the colony.

A difficult start at Wedza

The next day the Archbishop of Salisbury, Francis Markall, drove John to visit the Monte Cassino Mission, 70 miles east of the capital. On his return to Salisbury, John Dove drove him south to the headquarters of the Franciscans at Waterfalls. The Franciscans, from Ireland, had only been in Southern Rhodesia for four years, though the Franciscan way had had a presence in the country for some time, albeit in atypical forms – such as those established by the Anglicans Arthur Cripps at Enkeldoorn and Francis Nyabadza at Rusape, and the Catholic Patrick Kwesha, who had founded a non-recognised branch of the Third Order in Manicaland, in the east of the country. John was welcomed by the Superior, Father Boniface Gaynor, after which the new volunteer set out with John Dove for the Mission at Wedza, 100 miles or so south-east of Salisbury.

They followed the Umtali road as far as Marandellas, passing through rich farmlands owned by Europeans, then taking a minor road which soon dwindled into a dirt track. They then entered the Tribal Trust Land of Wedza, and made out in the distance Mount Resunzwe, renamed Mount Mary. As the car approached the Mission, it began to climb the flank of the mountain, through a landscape dotted with clusters of trees, and passed over a cattle grid into the Mission. This comprised the church, the house of the Fathers, a rural hospital and two schools, set against a vast panorama of plateaux to the north, and gentle hills and wooded valleys to the south, which reminded John of the Apennines. Wild life was sparse in the region, except for a few leopards, but birds were plentiful, much to John's delight. He also noted the presence of butterflies, crickets, grasshoppers, many dudus (mosquitos and assorted insects), idle lizards running along the walls in search of flies, and a solitary baboon perched on a rock overlooking the Mission, as if keeping an eye on things. The Mission itself was remote from outside contact, the nearest shops being 40 miles away, and post was collected only twice a week.

The Wedza Mission covered an area about a quarter of the size of Ireland, reaching out to more than 40,000 Africans in the Tribal Trust Land. It had been founded by a German Trappist prior to 1914, abandoned, and then reopened in 1948 by another German, this time a Jesuit, Father Boeckenhoff. It had recently been handed over to the Franciscans, who had taken up residence six months before. The Irish missionaries had already made their presence felt in the region, meeting chiefs and elders, young men and women, rich and poor, sharing beer under the palaver tree, at funerals, and on any and all possible occasions. When John arrived they had already won many hearts, as witnessed by the words of an old African man – non-Catholic – to Father Tom Russell: 'I have something to say to you, Baba. Of course I have been observing you missionnaries for some time now and what I want to say is that "imi va Roma munokudsa vanhu": you Catholics – "Romans" in the local dialect – respect people.'

The Franciscan community at Wedza gave a warm welcome to their English volunteer, the contract signed before John's departure from England was confirmed, and Father Dove expressed his approval of the meagre pocket money his friend would be paid, as John would have handed it out to all and sundry had it been any more. The two friends then went to visit the primary school, the secondary school and the dispensary, which was run by three Irish sisters. Father Dove insisted that the sisters keep a keen eye on John, and make sure that he took his malaria pills every day.

The Mission church was a modest building, whose only original feature was a stone tower resembling a pigeon loft, except for its loopholes. But for John it was the house of the Blessed Sacrament, which was the only thing that mattered, and for this reason, as soon as he entered, he immediately sought it out and said a brief prayer of worship. His Jesuit friend, who accompanied him, once again marvelled at John's way of visiting a church: after this prayer to the Blessed Sacrament, he would straightaway look for a chapel to the Virgin, where he again prayed, then any altars or chapels to the saints, and finally the organ. On his way out he would dip his fingers in the holy water, make a slow, full sign of the cross, and emerge 'refreshed in spirit'.

The Franciscans quickly took to their young volunteer, and much appreciated his joie-de-vivre and his sense of humour. He settled into the Mission house, and dined every day with the community. There was no electricity supply, but transistor radios kept them in touch with the outside world. When darkness fell, light was by oil lamp, and all activity came to an abrupt halt. The days were pleasant, but at night in the month of August temperatures approached zero: the housing was built to keep out the heat, not the cold, and the only heat came from the sun during the day.

The missionaries were above all practical men, followers of 'Martha', and occupied from dawn to dusk in carrying out necessary, everyday tasks. In their eyes a volunteer like John was expected to lend a hand in tasks such as these, like a temporary lay brother, allowing them to devote their time to proper missionary work. Writing to his mother a few days after his arrival, he told her that his principal task was driving, but the missionaries expected him to be a general handyman, typist, builder, bricklayer and bookkeeper – skills which he totally lacked. Furthermore the Mission was just getting off the ground, and everything remained to be done. The missionaries exhausted themselves in hard work, sometimes to the detriment of prayer, and they expected the same of their volunteer, which was not the way John saw things. And since he was their first volunteer, they expected him to practise religious obedience, as they themselves did. Little did they know John. Since he did not know a word of Shona, they expected him to learn it as quickly as possible, but didn't think of offering him any tuition. Once he had picked up a few polite expressions, thanks to the children whom he supplied with sweets from nobody knew where, John felt out of his linguistic depth and quickly lost interest. Writing to his mother that 'I think I shall never achieve anything better than a barbaric kitchen kaffir', he added caustically that he wasn't the only one, referring to the efforts of the missionaries – not quite true, as it turned out. Father Sean Gildea, for example, came to speak Shona with such fluency that the Africans nicknamed him Baba Shona – high praise indeed.

The Franciscans did their best to find suitable work for him, but they had cause for serious concern: their volunteer possessed no recognisable skill, nor practical sense: he couldn't teach, he couldn't drive, they couldn't trust him in the hospital, and he couldn't even type. And what was more he claimed to know what his principal task should be: to pray, which demanded both time and removal from the scene of labour. Having expected a volunteer both skilled and full of initiative, they found themselves at a loss. A driver maybe? John had a provisional British driver's licence, but this wasn't valid in Rhodesia, so he was obliged to take the test again. In the meantime he was allowed to practise driving in the vehicles available at the Mission, even if the uneven surfaced track made for a bumpy ride. Bush schools and outposts were scattered over a vast territory, the furthest being located up to 50 miles from the Mission. One of the fathers was responsible for the whole territory, and John was assigned to accompany him on his travels. The missionary's job was to collect school fees, pay teachers, supply schoolbooks, school furniture and footballs, and supervise building work and maintenance. As well as this, he celebrated one Mass a month in every school. Getting around by Land Rover or on foot, a single missionary could cover approximately 30 outposts, in a territory stretching over thousands of square miles, at the rate of one a day for every day of the month.

Among the Franciscans John became especially friendly with Father Sean Gildea and Father Desmond O'Malley, the other missionaries having quickly tired of John's eccentricity. Father Desmond, who had arrived in Southern Rhodesia four months before John, was in charge of the Mission school. He was diminutive and frail, played the accordion, and organised the Mission choir. Later he grew his hair long and looked more like a pop singer. He was a virtuoso performer, and when he played the crocodiles would leave the rivers and the creeks to listen to him on the accordion – at least according to Father Gildea, who claims to have seen at Murambinda two saurians emerge from the Mwerihari to listen, and afterwards silently slip back into the river. John did not mention any crocodiles but he was charmed by Father Desmond:

> When I got to Wedza Mission
> What d'you think I heard?
>
> Twas played upon a gay guitar
> Not, but upon accordion
> By Father Desmond – here's his star!
> Clear Shona Lasses sang at one.
>
> 'Bobby Shafter's gone to sea,
> Silver buckles on his knee,
> He'll come back and marry me:
> Bonny Bobby Shafter!'
> (*Gone to sea*, 1978)

Did this refer to his musical affinity with the missioner? According to Father Dove, John confided to Father Desmond that he had made three wishes:

> First to serve and live with lepers; the second, to die a martyr; the third, to be buried in the Franciscan habit.

Father David Gibbs gave a different, but quite similar, version of the three wishes:

> First, to be made a member of the Franciscan Order, second to work and live among the lepers, third, to die as a martyr.

By the end of September, six weeks after John's arrival, the Franciscans were still wondering what they were going to do with their volunteer. They were fond of him, but that was not enough. Apart from his travels with the school inspector, he often accompanied other missioners on their rounds, but more as a travel companion. It wasn't as if he was work shy; on the contrary he was always anxious to lend a helping hand, but he was so absent-minded that on one occasion he emptied a can of petrol into the Mission Land Rover, which ran on diesel. Moreover he himself was plagued by doubts. He had come to Africa to find a cave where he could pray, and here he was run off his feet with petty tasks from morning till night. He was constantly forced to meet more and more people, and carry out tasks for which he was neither prepared nor capable. On top of which he had discovered the poverty of the Africans, their sufferings due to ill health, and the racial discrimination practised against them, all of which he felt helpless to alleviate, and this disturbed him deeply. He quickly realised that in African eyes he was first and foremost a *murungu*, a white man, and this increased his unease. He would not have been the first or the last European to go back to Europe after a few weeks. This he did not want. But what could he do about it?

Enkeldoorn: the discovery of the Shonas

Father Gildea came up with a solution: since he himself had received a reposting to Enkeldoorn, why not take John with him? The other Franciscans were relieved and, on October 4th 1962, less than two months after his arrival, John left Wedza for the Our Lady of Lourdes Mission at Enkeldoorn, a *dorp* (village, in Afrikaans) 90 miles south of Salisbury on the main road to South Africa, with three tasks to perform: welcome visitors to the house when Father Gildea was out, fill in baptismal registers, and help to manage the schools. As usual John did it his way, as Father Gildea recalled:

> There was a lady in a school in Badza which is near Enkeldoorn and you had to make out a report when you came back. John wrote about this particular school. He mentioned the lady teacher there who had a face like Helen of Troy and a voice like a sergeant major!

The landscape here was more monotonous than at Wedza, but whereas there was less wildlife the bird population was vast. The European settlement zone was surrounded by a huge Tribal Trust Land (TTL) Native Reserve. The European farms, owned for the most part by descendents of Boers of the Reformed Church, were of vast extent, and the Africans employed there were paid on average one Rhodesian pound a month, which was scarcely enough to send one single child of a family to school. In the eyes of the missioners their condition was hardly better than slavery. The majority of the farmers considered themselves to be highly religious, and in their paternalistic fashion paid great attention to the piety and morals of their work force. Since some of the Africans were Catholics, the missioners were authorised to enter the farms, but only once a month, which left little scope for meaningful contact.

The village of Enkeldoorn was founded at the end of the nineteenth-century by a man called Lebenberg, who arrived accompanied by 50 or so Afrikaaners, and its name (*Enkeldoorn* means 'prickly bush' in Afrikaans) was given to it, according to local legend, by Cecil Rhodes himself when he passed through in 1893. The village boasted a hotel with a vaguely Dutch facade and an ad for Castle beer, a bank, two shops, a bakery and several street stalls. The dorp had the reputation of being a very boring place to live, and a local joke concerned a raffle whose first prize was a week in Enkeldoorn, second prize two weeks, and so on.

John soon became a well-known and popular local figure in the village among Europeans and Africans alike. Among the former was Henry, the owner of the hotel. Father Gildea remembered an evening at home with him and his wife during which John entertained the guests with his mimicry, particularly of an East Anglian vicar remembered no doubt from his childhood, whose rural accent he reproduced in reciting the parable of the Good Samaritan, all without the slightest trace of malice:

> John's freedom, his good humour and welcome
> acceptance of everybody made him a reconciler.
> He didn't need to know the local language. An odd
> word thrown in with his good-humoured laughter
> got the message across.

The Franciscan Mission at Enkeldoorn extended over a territory half the size of Belgium. It had been set up two years before, without a church or fixed residence. In the beginning the missioners slept where they could, spending most days under a tree, preaching with a catechism in hand. The church and a bungalow with outhouses attached were built in 1961 on the boundary between the dorp and the township, since the faithful were all Catholics, but the missioners were almost always on the road or in the kraals. Father Gildea was indefatigable, and trekked through the bush day in day out, often accompanied by John. On one of the first nights after their arrival, they set out to bring the last rites to a bush village more than 20 miles from the Mission. The old man receiving the sacrament was greatly cheered by their visit, which made a deep impression on John. On the journey home the car hit an animal the size of a roe deer, which they brought back to the Mission.

Africans are famously hospitable, and welcome every stranger with a meal, mattress, and blankets where necessary. Father Gildea shook hands with everybody wherever he went, which was something Europeans never did, and he later learnt how much this gesture was appreciated. He took his time when visiting a kraal and never hesitated to spend hours listening to stories, drinking home-made beer, perfecting his Shona, and cracking jokes with all and sundry. The manner in which the Gospel was welcomed never ceased to amaze him. Poor people were ready to pay a lot for a copy of the Bible; so that all could afford it, he fixed the price at one chicken. Catholics were often scattered and far apart in the zone, and getting to visit them all was very time-consuming. On their travels through the bush, the missioners often had to ford rivers. Exchanging greetings with the villagers could be interminable, and when the time came to leave, crossing the river could be dangerous; currents were often treacherous, and there was always the risk of disturbing a sleeping hippopotamus. Sometimes the road would disappear into tall grass, and the driver had to take extreme care not to hit hidden rocks and become immobilised far from home.

On October 11th in Rome, John XXIII opened the Second Vatican Council on the Feast of the Divine Motherhood of Our Lady, urging the fathers of the Council 'to make use of the medicine of mercy rather than that of severity'. On the same day John Bradburne took his driving test at Enkeldoorn. He prayed to St Anthony, but consoled himself in advance by remarking in a letter to his mother that if he failed it will be 'because both his Master and he preferred walking to chariots and horses'. It is true that both had a partiality for donkeys. Sitting in the driver's seat next to his examiner, he managed to stall the car twice before narrowly missing a telegraph pole. But the examiner must have been 'clearly under the spell of Titania, queen of the fairies', and signed the precious document allowing the recipient, as John put it, 'to buy my licence to be a legalised menace to all and sundry'. From then on, Father Gildea gave him the car to do the rounds, evacuate a sick person, or deliver mail. John still seemed to nourish some ambitions to master Shona but eventually gave up and wrote to his mother (3 March 1963): 'As to the barbarous lingo, I have long since resisted the temptation to learn it. I find myself strongly in favour of pre-Babel Christianity', and a few months later: 'I refrain from speaking their language and from continually shaking hands. But I say hello and grin and so do they, and I really do hope they'll go to Heaven.'

His friendship with Father Gildea deepened over time:

John and I became great friends, because he stayed
with me in the house in Enkeldoorn. The chief
thing about him was his humanity, and the kind
of gift he had was the gift of joy. There was always
laughter there and nothing was really that serious.
He was a poet and a musician, and I became very
friendly with him. We had things in common,
apart from the Franciscan thing. We were both
in the army. We chatted about the War and all the
rest of it... He liked a drop of brandy at night; we
took a drop of brandy to make us sleep... There
was a kind of a trait of a vagabond in him – he
was a free spirit.

The Franciscan discovered in John, behind the facade of the
eccentric Englishman, a depth that reminded him of G. K.
Chesterton, who wrote in *The Everlasting Man*: 'Go round in circles,
but always come back to the centre.' He also saw something in John
that made him think of what St Francis must have been like.

John also became friendly with two Africans who lived at the
Mission. Samson the cook, the older one, was small and bald.
The other, Cornelio, was a cheeky teenager who liked to tell jokes
and did odd jobs about the place. There was also Mrs Chivusa,
who saw to the smooth running of the Mission, and lived in an
outbuilding behind the bungalow. She was a mysterious woman
who intrigued John Dove whenever he came to visit his friend, and
whom he regarded as a sort of female Melchizedech. She developed
a fondness for John, supplying him with bottled beer, to which he
by no means objected, but which greatly amused Father Gildea.

These were the first Africans with whom John had the occasion
to live: in a country where racial segregation, labelled 'separate
development', was public policy, Mission stations were oases of
conviviality where Europeans and Africans lived side by side. In a
letter to Mrs Bradburne, Father Dove, who thought that John was
destined to remain in Africa for some time, noted that her son
was very much at ease in the company of Africans, who were very
natural and ready to accept people for what they were, though it
must be admitted that Samson did not hide the fact that, hearing

John tell tales of his wanderings across Europe, he considered Europeans to be quite mad. And Father Gildea mentioned to the Jesuit that John always placed others at the centre of his stories, emphasising their finer qualities, and highlighting them without judgement.

Soon the first rains came, the landscape became greener and rapidly changed, much to John's delight, as he wrote to his mother. He also told her that he would be playing his recorder in the Christmas pageant for the missionary sisters, after he had done it for the school children, adding: 'Life is good, and eternal life will be marvellous.' Shortly afterwards (December 1962) he told her he had asked Father Gildea not to give him any more pocket money: 'I am penniless. This not a hint but a Triumphant Franciscan Affirmation.' It meant that he couldn't send any Christmas cards, but he didn't seem to feel guilty about it, and he let her know that when they went to Salisbury the fathers searched their pockets to give him some money to spend.

Prayer and contemplation always came first for him, followed by relations with his fellow men and women, and long before material tasks. He spent long hours admiring birds, especially the storks and kites as they prepared for their long migration, and this nourished his poetry at that time. His fascination for the animal world led him to collect all the pictures of animals he could find: chocolate bar wrappers, newspapers and magazines, which he sellotaped into the copybooks that he used to transcribe his poems, or on the back of a piece of cardboard, an old habit of his.

On Christmas Eve he went to join his Jesuit friend in Salisbury. Father Dove took John with him when he celebrated Midnight and Christmas Day Mass in the bush, which John served. His friend must have spoken to him about the political situation because he had written somewhat earlier to his mother (4 December) that the world was all about 'wars and rumours of war', adding, 'but the Lord of Christmas remains our peace, our hope, our salvation and our whole desire', and that 'this pilgrimage to our home is a short one, soon to resolve in everlasting joy'. The political situation was indeed serious. In the autumn a new party, the Rhodesian Front, had launched a campaign of 'not an inch' to the Africans and had won the general election on 14 December (of the 88,000 voters, only

5217 were Africans) and Winston Field became Prime Minister. At
this point the British Government had granted independence to
Nyasaland, and when Northern Rhodesia, where Africans had a
parliamentary majority, demanded a similar status, the Federation
of Rhodesia and Nyasaland, established in 1953, began to fall apart.

In January 1973 Father Dove, worried at recent developments
in the colony, invited his confrere Paul Crane, Director of Claver
House in London (an international training centre for Catholic
social doctrine) to come to Salisbury. The stakes were high: the
Jesuits felt that nationalist leaders, up to that point connected with
the churches (Abel Muzorewa was a Methodist bishop, Ndabaningi
Sithole a minister of the same church, Josuah Nkomo was the son
of Protestant missionaries, and Robert Mugabe was a teacher in
a Catholic Mission), were turning towards Marxist regimes in
search of powerful allies. Father Crane delivered lectures in the
principal townships of Salisbury – Harare, Highfield, Mabvuku
and Mufakose – making contact with nationalist leaders as well
as liberal Europeans like the Actons, at whose residence at M'Bebi
he met representatives of both sides. On his return to London,
Father Crane sent a memo to the bishops in which he explained
that the nationalist movement would win in the end, and that the
duty of the Church was to train an African elite with a high sense
of responsibility.

John did not involve himself with any of this political activity.
He was at this time developing a deep respect and affection for
the Shona people and their culture, which he was in the process
of discovering. He wished to serve them, and this would be his
concrete practical way of saying no to the racial ideology of the
Rhodesian Front. He was deeply impressed by the gentleness and
natural courtesy of this people, the time they spent in greetings and
palaver, their respect for their elders, and the important place they
gave to tradition and religion in their lives. In this way he developed
a profound understanding of the lives of the people among whom
he lived, which he was now discovering as if for the first time:

> Mashona folk would pass the time of day
> From when they meet you till the morrow comes;
> Their manners are unhurried as the sway
> Of nodding maize-cobs and of throbbing drums;

They sit not huddled over muddled sums
Prognosticating useless future care...
Their 'Take no thought' sports more than
Christendom's;
Their homes are huts, not castles in the air.
(*A Ballade of a Gladsome People*, unknown date)

While many Europeans tended to claim that Africans were incapable of emotional maturity, John believed at that time, with a mixture of empathy and condescension, that 'for the African it is essential to be loved, led and commanded'; he also maintained (in letters home) that one must approach them with compassion and firmness, rather than sentimentality about 'the lonely simple African', which served no purpose because 'saints are needed here'. He already had a precursor in this mould at Enkeldoorn in the person of Arthur Cripps, 'the Anglican St Francis of Rhodesia' (as his biographer, Douglas V. Steere described him), who had died ten years before and whose tomb had become a place of pilgrimage. Relations were good between the Franciscans and the Cripps Anglican Mission at Daradombe, 25 miles from Enkeldoorn, and in January 1963 while on a visit there John was given a present of a recorder. Cripps and John had more than one point in common, as well as their love for Il Poverello: non-conformity, poetry, serving the needy, the gift of self, love of the Eucharist, desire for solitude, and withdrawing to mountain tops.

The rounds to set up schools and missionary posts had increased in frequency. It was necessary to visit chiefs, negotiate at great length, and ensure their good will. One day Father Gildea sent John to Badza, some 20 miles from the Mission, to deliver a much needed batch of schoolbooks. At nightfall, when there was no sign of John, Father Gildea became worried. He managed to ascertain that his assistant had left Badza hours before, and next morning was getting ready to make enquiries in every direction when John reappeared. What had happened? On the way back, just before Enkeldoorn, John had come across a group of African women and had offered to give them a lift home. They pointed east, in the opposite direction from the Mission, but so what? The rainy season had just commenced and as they set off across the mountain the heavens opened. On two occasions everybody had to get out and lift the car through flood waters in the driving rain. The night was far advanced when they got to their destination, nearly 40 miles from Enkeldoorn, at Sadza, and an exhausted John was in no state to get behind the wheel again. A local shopkeeper offered him a camp bed for the night and he tried to get some sleep, his clothes suspended from saucepan shelves while rats scurried noisily around his bed. Back at Enkeldoorn the next morning he recounted his misadventure with such disarming candour that Father Gildea couldn't bring himself to be angry. But it would be the last time he sent him anywhere in the car if there were any other drivers available. John came to understand this decision in time, not without some mortification.

Under the water tank at Gandachibvuva

At the beginning of 1963, the Franciscans decided to open a new Mission, under the patronage of St Anthony of Padua, 40 miles further to the east at Gandachibvuva (soon shortened to Ganda). John was invited to participate, with the impressive title of Supervisor of Bush Schools, and in April he teamed up with Father Pascal Slevin, who was put in charge of the new Mission, and Father Ultan McCaffrey, both of whom had arrived the previous month. A small Catholic community had already been in existence here for some time, served by the Mission at Driefontein 100 miles to the south. John admired Father Slevin from the beginning, seeing him as a 'true Franciscan'. The Ganda Mission started up with two young women, Annunciata and Caroline, who looked after the kitchen and general household maintenance, and immediately were in tune with John.

The Mission included a little chapel, a dispensary, a three-room bungalow where John and the missionaries settled in, and some outhouses. It was situated on a hill bordering the river Mwerihari, whose waterfalls had given its onomatapeic name to the location, and this added to John's pleasure in his assignment. During the rainy season the swollen river hurtled down the slopes of Mount Dramombe in impressive fashion. The landscape reminded John of Italy and the heights of Palma, surrounded by hills and low-lying areas where cattle grazed. A solitary lion was said to live ten miles from the Mission, and a large crocodile had taken up residence in the nearby swamp area, not far from the pump, and baby crocodiles barked from the rocks before diving back into the river among the hippos. There was a thriving colony of baboons, and John took pleasure contemplating them as they swarmed across the river, the females with their young clinging to their breasts. John's letters and poems also contain numerous descriptions of eagles in the sky, humble lizards, crickets, grasshoppers and scorpions on the ground, and – as he wrote to his mother (19 March 1963) – 'huge furry caterpillars that bask in rows on the trunks of certain trees, enclosing them like a fur coat in a tiger-hued array'.

John was anxious this time round to demonstrate that he had more to offer than mere good will; but his task as Supervisor of Bush Schools soon proved to be too much for him, and the Franciscans didn't insist. His tasks were reduced to three: helping out at the dispensary, collecting firewood and keeping an eye on the chickens: 'Ca c'est ma vie' ('That's my life'), as he described it. It was also his job to ring the bell for Mass, the Offices and the Angelus three times a day. He was always first to arrive in Church, 'at six o'clock in the morning, midday, and six o'clock in the evening', to sing 'in praise of Him who gave us Mary as our Mother'. He was required to make himself useful in the dispensary, but was relieved of this duty after a few blunders, like when he had been assigned to drive the Mission truck.

Nevertheless the Franciscans left him in charge of the dispensary when they went off on their rounds, pending the building of a clinic which would be staffed by a team of medical sisters. In truth, his sole duty was to hand out aspirin, ointments, magnesium pills, cough mixture and castor oil, and clean and dress troublesome wounds. He gave himself heart and soul to the work, and when the onset of the rainy season saw an increase in gastric infections he resorted to medicines of his own. On asking why the dispensary was called *muti* (tree) in Shona, he discovered it was because traditional medicines essentially used fruit and leaves. He immediately made the connection with the Garden of Eden, where one tree led to all our woes, but another became the source of Life, 'giving us food for the Journey to Paradise Regained', as he wrote to his mother (18 July 1963).

He was fond of sharing his meditations with young Africans. One of them, Jerome Govere, wrote:

> I was only 8 years old. My brother Ignatius was 17... I remember well sitting on top of the hill where the convent is now, with John and my brother, and John was admiring the beauty of the countryside and describing the hills which stretch from the Mpatsi Village to Wedza mountains. He looked in detail at what most of us just glanced at. He would show one how the shape of the hills far away was shaped like a huge sleeping lion.

Relations with Father McCaffrey, who was less patient with John's ways than Father Slevin, deteriorated. This, and his love of solitude when he could turn himself completely to God, led John to vacate the bungalow, but to where? A small 'guesthouse' had been built on a rock overlooking the Mwerihari, about 200 yards from the main buildings, a somewhat grand description for a six-square-meter brick shack which served as a base for the Mission reservoir, and pumped water from the river with a diesel-powered motor. John moved in, building a floor with spare bricks, a bed consisting of a sheet of asbestos supported by four bricks, a large empty box for a table, and a small one as a seat. On the wall he hung photos from a West Country English calendar Mrs Bradburne had sent (he would receive one every year) and a picture of the Virgin Mary. He noticed that a nightingale had built its nest on the ceiling, and, there being no glass in the only window, the bird soon returned to share John's 'palace' with him.

Once he had moved in, the words that he had heard so often during his time at Parkminster seemed appropriate to describe his present way of life. He wrote to his mother (19 March 1963): 'O beata Solitudo, after a dark night of years and years, a great weight lifted from my soul. He would no longer be disturbed in his prayers, and the missionaries and the Africans understood:

> At last they know that I am 'different from all other
> animals' and must have solitude. Glory be to God,
> another miracle, in need of solitude.

He nevertheless sought to reassure his mother, telling her he was
using the bathroom of the fathers; as for the needs of nature, he was
going 'wizardly outside, somewhere in Africa' (applying the rule of
Lanza del Vasto: 'Piss wherever you please, with the shamelessness
of the innocent').

Every day he dined alone on a plate of sadza and cabbage,
washed down by sweet tea, only joining the missioners once a
week. The two Irishmen were edified by this show of frugality, and
even more so by the fact that he radiated an inner peace. Apart
from his sacristan work, John kept the kitchen supplied, including
firewood for the water heater, and collected eggs from the hen
run and elsewhere, including his living quarters, where a hen had
chosen to nest under his bed. He took pride in this responsibility,
which reminded him that his father too had lovingly watched over
his own farmyard. He made use of his Shona to call himself *fudza
huku* ('hen-shepherd'), whose flock was soon to rise to 20 hens
and two cocks, baptising the latter Count of Ganda and Duke of
Chibvuva. The Count cut a fine figure but the Duke, all skin and
bone, nevertheless usually had the better of the corpulent Count
when it came to fisticuffs to win the favour of a lucky hen. But the
resident hen underneath his bed, the most prolific of the brood,
caught fleas, and this caused John, ever the fastidious Englishman
on this subject, so much bother that he eventually evicted her. Alas
the irate hen then refused to hatch any more chicklets and so egg
production fell.

Another day an errant hen ended up among the Mission's
crockery, and an exasperated John built a 'véritable chateau'
of corrugated iron for his charges on the hill, the roof of which
doubled as a draining board and a table for writing his poems.
Later the farmyard was expanded, with the arrival of Aeschylus,
an ageing cock that had to be protected from the warlike ardour
of a younger one. At this point the hens ceased to hatch, and John
wrote to his mother telling her he was praying to his father, since he
surely must approve of his current occupation. At the same time he

was also very aware of his responsibilities towards the nightingale, and this time there was no Monsignor Worlock to worry about. He marvelled to see his nightingale laying and sitting on her eggs until they hatched, and to watch her feeding her brood when she came back from her hunting expeditions. Soon the whole family sang 'in praise of the Creator', and John was happy to join in.

Annunciata taught him how to make sadza and serve it with cabbage. As he ate only once a day and avoided meat and eggs, the young cook was surprised by this European who insisted on eating like an African. Despite Arthur Cripps' 50 years in Rhodesia, the Franciscan way, which John tried to follow, had not taken root, and his self-denial never ceased to astonish her. But the young woman could see that he was a man of God, and his example would lead her eventually to a religious vocation with the Sisters of the Children of Our Blessed Lady (LCBL), an order of nuns founded in 1932 at Salisbury by the then Bishop Aston Chichester.

One day a young African came to visit him in his hut and the conversation quickly turned to prayer and God. The unexpected disciple thereafter called every evening, and John became used to these spiritual exchanges. After a month the young man asked John to lend him 40 Rhodesian pounds. When John expressed his surprise that, seeing him living as he did in a state of poverty, his visitor hadn't understood that he didn't have any money, the young man retorted that John was a murungu and all murungu had money. John never saw him again. But other Africans admired his poverty and self-denial:

> He is still remembered in the village (Gandachibvuva) for giving one old woman his only blanket after learning that everything she owned was destroyed in a fire in her hut. John would walk barefoot for months after giving his shoes to some stranger if he felt they needed them more than he did.

Another time he went to Salisbury in an African bus, which Europeans never did, and was delighted by the experience. He was formally installed in the seat next to the driver, whose name was

Simon Peter, and they chatted together all the way to Salisbury. Once, when the bus arrived in Salisbury, the driver invited him to his house for dinner and to spend the night, and John gladly agreed. Describing the visit in a letter to his mother (March 1963) he remarked that African women were 'the last word in sheer allure', and that 'but for Our Lady I should be a lost man'. He was amused by the names the Africans gave to their children, such as 'Where did you go', 'You despise me', or 'Two Bobs' (Christian names were only conferred after baptism, which generally took place at the age eight to ten).

John Dove paid a visit from time to time. As night fell, the two friends would sit on the bank of the Mwerihari near the hut and talk, or gaze at the sumptuous profusion of stars in the southern night sky. John explained that they were his friends, and that they spoke to him of God. Their Shona names were just as symbolic as their European: for example *Nzira Ye Zoe* ('the Elephant's Path') for the Milky Way. The Jesuit was invariably struck by his friend's joie-de-vivre and serenity, and also by his progress in spiritual matters, and wrote to Mrs Bradburne in March 1963: 'We must pray that it is also Journey's End.' Father Slevin remarked also on the same progress. For him, 'John was a tower of strength at Gandachibvuva. What else could a man of prayer be? The new Mission was blessed by his presence.' When the Franciscan decided to install the Stations of the Cross in the chapel, John lent his enthusiastic support. When asked the best way to inaugurate the event, he offered to sing the Stabat Mater. Father Slevin agreed to the proposal, and at the end of the ceremony an emotional John said that it was a great privilege for him to have participated. Thereafter the priest witnessed him performing the Stations on a daily basis.

John was more and more convinced that Martha's way was not for him, and Father Slevin, knowing John's idiosyncrasies, left him to his own devices. Every day the hermit of the reservoir arrived to prepare the altar for Mass, which he served, and returned several times during the day to the chapel for the Office or a visit to the Blessed Sacrament. When alone, he prayed and chanted, and the whole Mission could hear in the distance the sound of his clear voice singing the praises of God. At nightfall he again went to the chapel to pray until the early hours before going to bed. The two women of the Mission often joined him. Annunciata and he composed a little hymn in Shona which they sang together over and over, especially when decorating the chapel with flowers, whose words were recorded by John Dove:

> Mari handina, I have no money,
> Mwari ndinoda, But I love God,
> Naye Ndiforana, I rejoice in him.

One night when they were praying together a snake approached the altar and was about to go into the sacristy. Seeing it, John grabbed a candlestick and struck it. Hearing the commotion Father Slevin arrived and discovered the snake trapped and wriggling on the end of the candlestick, and finished it off with a piece of wood.

John was writing a lot, and the desire to be published had gripped him once more, as he confided to his mother in a letter at this time (3 June 1963). But the long-awaited reply from Victor Gollancz arrived at last, after two years, and it was negative. He was disappointed, but refused to give up hope. On the contrary he was galvanised when asked to type out his manuscripts, and threatened to lay siege ('by post of course') to the doors, the heart and the soul of Gollancz. In describing his plan of attack to his mother, he predicted that 'through it the name of Bradburne will ring down future centuries, and that for the good'. In the meantime, as a neglected and obscure poet he would continue to write his poems, 'verses that rhyme and have music in their words. Untortured, untwisted, unmodish verses.' He encouraged himself that even if they were not published in his lifetime it didn't matter, for only 'posterity and immortality' counted.

Far from Ganda, the political situation in the colony continued to deteriorate. Whereas the Irish Franciscans were outraged by the ideas of the Rhodesian Front, John kept his distance from political debates. The return of Joshua Nkomo on July 15th 1963 had led to riots in the townships between his supporters and those of Sithole, and the following month Sithole, Washington Malianga and Robert Mugabe created the Zimbabwe African National Union (ZANU). (Later on, ZANU and ZAPU were mainly defined on an ethnic base, respectively Shona and Ndbele.) At the same time Winston

Field began talks with London to bring about independence. The death throes of the Federation dragged on throughout the year, and it was finally dissolved on December 30th, followed by the independence of Nyasaland (which became Malawi) on July 6th 1964, and Northern Rhodesia (which became Zambia) on October 24th. Henceforth Southern Rhodesia became simply Rhodesia.

At Ganda the wheel was beginning to turn again. Though John continued to polish the Franciscans' shoes (the two women, who noticed it, were impressed by the humility of this European), it seemed he had little else to offer the Mission. Father Slevin didn't pay too much attention, but events soon took over. With their customary energy the Franciscans had been so successful in their work that they decided at the end of 1963 to enlarge the Mission, which involved the removal of the tank under which John was housed. The work had to start as soon as possible, and on New Year's Day 1964 John woke up to discover that he was going to be homeless. As agreed, the Franciscans offered to pay his return flight, even assuring him that he could choose any destination in the world he wished. John didn't argue and set out for Salisbury to discuss matters with his Jesuit friend. He was already toying with the idea of going to Tibet (even though it had been completely closed off since the crushing in 1959 of the revolt against Chinese occupation). He had no doubt been thinking of it since his trip to the foot of Nanda Devi, and he decided to get there by way of India. Father Dove neither wished nor knew how to dissuade him from his latest venture, and John went to the Indian consulate. Here he was told he would have to get a return ticket before securing a visa; so it was back to the Franciscans, who had by this stage decided that their generosity had its limits. Then it was back to square one.

While John was looking for a solution the Jesuits came up with a proposal: he could be caretaker for a few months at the Actons' house at M'Bebi in the Mazoe Valley. The Actons had just moved to a house near Salisbury because of their children, and had offered the property to the Jesuits, who had decided to set up a novitiate there. This was to open around Easter, and in the meantime they needed a caretaker. John was happy to take up the offer, writing to his mother (March 1964):

the Actons have need of a caretaker resident here in this vast rambling one-storey castle until the Jesuit Novitiate moves in to take the place over in, maybe, April. Then a caretaker will be wanted in the places the Novices have vacated until about Easter by which time the world may end so I am deeply contented.

The hermit of M'Bebi

The property was situated to the north of Salisbury. Even after the splendours of Mwerihari, John quickly learnt to appreciate the beauty of the valley and the property, unlike Evelyn Waugh who a few years before had written: 'Insignificant country so far as I've seen it. No fine trees, no tropical birds or flowers, scrubby hills, wire fences, bungalows.' It was almost like a second Hare Street House for John, perfectly suited to a hermit's life. He was his own master, with no visits from an archbishop's secretary to trouble his days. His only task was to keep an eye on the property. The nearby presence of his neighbours, the von Niddas, kept marauders at bay, and his only unwelcome visitors were the fleas that he fought off with the help of prayers to St Antony the Great. He took up quarters in the 'Montini bedroom' and its 'gorgeous bed', with a choice of six baths, each supplied with hot water. He put up on the bedroom wall the calendar photos sent by his mother, prayed, meditated, went for walks, admired nature, wrote poems and, as he confided in a letter home (March 1964):

> Life becomes for me more and more of a definable pattern of chance and change, and I am in no way daunted by the apparent utter failure of it and waste of education as may seem – being deeply confident that I have already written at least a hundred lines for posterity.

During his stay here John was more hermit than caretaker. He spent long hours in the chapel praying in the company of two owls who had taken up residence there, and dozed off more frequently than he himself. He soon struck up the same relationship with them as he had with the nightingale in Ganda. He also became friendly with Garbage, the house cat, and when she gave birth to a litter at Easter he adopted a black-and-white kitten, which he christened M'Bebi and who, according to John, was a good example of racial cohabitation. The kitten was born in a cupboard which had belonged to Lord Acton, which gave her no doubt her aristocratic airs. Soon she was following John everywhere, even leading the way when she scented a snake and gave chase.

Through Father Dove, who escaped from Salisbury most weekends, John learnt of the inexorable drift of the colony towards rebellion, and of the nationalists towards armed revolt. Winston Field continued to insist that his government should not unilaterally declare independence, but was losing his grip on his majority. On April 13th he was replaced by Ian Smith, a farmer from Seluke, who immediately ordered the arrest of Nkomo and other nationalist leaders. On the 20th, the main Christian Churches warned the colony's new strong man to resist the temptation of a unilateral declaration, and were told by the government-controlled press to stay out of politics and 'render unto Caesar what is Caesar's'. The following month, Ian Smith declared (*Rhodesia Herald*, 11 May 1964): 'If in my lifetime we have an African nationalist government in power in Southern Rhodesia, then we will have failed in the policy that I believe in.' The Catholics were divided. The Catholic newspaper *Moto* ('fire, ardour' in Shona) began to use the name Zimbabwe instead of Rhodesia, and published articles by Robert Mugabe, ZANU secretary-general, who had been arrested in December 1963 and released on parole in March 1964. But at the other end of the Catholic spectrum, Mark Partridge explained why he had decided to enter politics wearing the colours of the Rhodesian Front, the only hope of a 'Christian Solution': 'As I saw it, the trend was to hand over the country to irresponsible people, with the end result that no people of my race would be prepared to stay, and therefore everything that I owned was at stake.'

At Easter 1964, M'Bebi was still not ready to welcome the Jesuit novitiate, and John was asked to stay on a bit longer. When John Dove came at weekends he never failed to bring along a picnic basket, so as not to die of hunger, but also to make sure that his friend would get at least one decent meal a week. On Sunday morning both joined the farm workers and their families in the chapel for Mass, with John doubling up as sacristan and altar boy, while the celebrant did his best to avoid being 'bombed' from on high by the owls, the altar boy/caretaker having insisted on their presence. Games of table tennis, long discussions with friends, including the von Niddas, took up the rest of the day, after which John found himself alone again for a week of prayer and poetry.

John Dove often turned up with a guest, to keep his friend in touch and widen his circle of acquaintances. One of these was a young woman, a great music lover and recently converted to Catholicism. Her name was Heather Benoy, who taught at the primary school in Blakiston Street in Salisbury. She came from a Scottish-Irish family who had settled in Salisbury at the beginning of the century. Her father Maurice Beaumont Benoy, an army officer turned politician, was Secretary of State for Defence and External Affairs, openly hostile to Ian Smith, and would soon be replaced, and his family ostracised. Heather had already taken note of this eccentric Englishman:

> When I first met John outside the Cathedral,
> I thought he was tremendously good looking.
> However, he appeared to not really notice me and
> stared over my shoulder. This was disconcerting
> especially as Father Dove had introduced me as a
> very good friend of his. I was left with a rather bad
> impression of him at this time. However, during
> the next few months and years we became very,
> very good friends – in fact, sadly, lifelong friends
> as it turned out.

The two were unlikely friends, she lost in her music, he in prayer and poetry, but something clicked, and the young woman soon visited again. They talked endlessly, performed duets on guitar and recorder and composed music together.

John also had another visitor around this time, a geologist called Alistair Guthrie, who dropped by to investigate the hot water springs around the house at M'Bebi. The two men hit it off, and Alistair continued to call, for the pleasure of their conversations, invited the caretaker of M'Bebi to his house, and asked him to be godfather to his son Craig. Other visitors, strangers rather than friends, began to drop by, intruding on John's prayerful solitude. His rare visits to Salisbury had not gone unnoticed, and people in Catholic circles there began to talk about the hermit of M'Bebi. Mazoe Valley was not far from Salisbury, and soon visitors in search of God, or distressed and emotionally troubled, or simply curious, began to arrive at M'Bebi. John was less than enthusiastic about this development and tried to avoid going to Salisbury unless it was strictly necessary.

One Sunday in May 1964, while he was coming out of the cathedral, not looking right or left, he was knocked down by a car. He lost consciousness, then came around to cries from all sides. Someone had bandaged his right hand, which had been injured in the collision. But he refused to go to hospital, and eventually escaped from the crowd to a nearby park where he sat dazed on a bench for hours, until it was time to go to the spot where a friend was due to pick him up and drive him home. His driver, a neighbouring farmer, took stock of the situation and insisted on taking John to his house to look after him, offering him a glass of whisky to restore his spirits. Next day John wrote to his mother (11 April 1964) telling her it was nothing serious, except that he had a sprained ankle, his left leg was hurting, and his right hand and his forehead was covered in scratches. 'Rather a lark', he added, not without acknowledging that he would have to be more careful in future. The letter finished: 'Hurrah for Guardian Angels!'

John Dove, who was still keen on his project of training an African elite, but had decided in prudence to start with a number of sessions far from Salisbury, initiated these at M'Bebi in June. The apostolic delegate for English-speaking East Africa, Bishop McGeough, an American, was interested and shortly afterwards came to participate, along with Archbishop Markall. John was dragooned by his friend into taking on the role of housemaster, and learnt how to make good tea and reheat the teapot. All went well until it was time for tea; the cups and saucers were chipped and cracked and the cakes exhaled a dreadful smell. The guests stoically ate and drank what was on offer; later John explained to John Dove that he had sprayed the pantry with insecticide to prevent insects from nibbling away at the precious cakes!

On July 4th, Pieter Oberholzer, a farmer from Melsetter, was murdered, the first time a European had been murdered in the colony since 1897. Young Peter Godwin, who accompanied his mother, a state pathologist, to the scene of the crime would never forget seeing the dead victim, with a knife protruding from his chest. It was his first encounter with racial hatred. The killers had attached a note to the body with the message: 'Crocodile Gang will soon kill all Whites! Beware!' Even though the group were quickly rounded up, the shadow of civil war was already looming. Discussions with his Jesuit friend opened John's eyes to the reality of the regime that was taking shape. By his prayers John was on the side of the Africans, but he never flinched in his rejection of Communism, towards which the nationalists were drifting more and more.

The end of July found him back in Salisbury, and one can assume that this time he was keeping his eye on the traffic while crossing the street. He was invited for an audition in the Rhodesian Television studios and accepted, despite his love of solitude. Since 1960 the station had covered news for the principal towns in the country. John queued up with many others for an interview for the post of presenter. He was the seventieth candidate to be interviewed – and got the job! With the help of books lent by John Dove, he made serious preparations for his first programme to go out on air on Sunday August 30th on 'Evolution and Genesis'. He asked his mother (23 August): 'But please say many prayers! I have never felt less certain of myself or more certain of God.' (John Dove wrote the same day to Mrs Bradburne that 'people like to hear his advice', hinting at her son's new role of spiritual advisor.) The programme went well, even though John in his nervousness was giving off so much electricity that the microphone began to vibrate, and had to be held by someone else while he spoke! He took no pleasure in the experience and would have preferred not to repeat it, but didn't tell anyone. He was promptly taken on by the station and paid two Rhodesian pounds for his monthly broadcast.

At the beginning of September he made a new friend – a lemur he had saved from being stoned by a group of young Africans:

'It was stoned by Africans in the wild for no better reason than any vandals of any race or colour have for doing such things.' John looked after it and fed it on milk and some curried beans he had to hand. He decided to call it Hugo, after the little boy of the farmer who had driven him home after his accident all the way from Salisbury. As John told his mother, the child 'has a hole in his heart and may die any time', and he prayed and solicited her prayers for him. He delighted in Hugo, the lemur beauty, which made him think of a sleek-coated baby bear, with hands that were uncannily human. Was it really a lemur, or in fact a Bush Baby, but what difference did it make? During the day Hugo dozed on the meat safe and came to life in the evening. On September 23rd John wrote to his mother that, having made a full recovery, 'the lemur has got well and returned with God to the Wild'. Two days later he was back in Salisbury to present a concert featuring the seminary choir, for which he received warm congratulations, and was now familiar to the 'Salisbury set', which led to an increase of unwelcome interruptions to his solitary life in M'Bebi.

Autumn 1964 saw Harold Wilson in power at the head of a Labour government, whose antipathy to the Rhodesian Front was well known, and Ian Smith wasted no time. He convened an Indaba (a gathering) of 600 traditional chiefs and got their approval for independence and his version of 'community development': the Europeans would continue to govern resource-rich Rhodesia, and the chiefs would govern the Africans in the Tribal Trust Lands under the control of European administrators, and provide whatever manpower the latter required. Only one chief dared to express support for the nationalists, and he was promptly deposed. A referendum had to be held to ratify a constitution based on these principles.

On November 1st, an ecumenical night of prayer was organised in the Anglican and Catholic cathedrals in Salisbury to oppose the move. John took part and prayed until dawn. He then joined Father Fortune, a Jesuit linguist and specialist in the Shona language, for two Masses in Mazoe Valley, which he served. He then went back with him to Salisbury to prepare for his broadcast that evening at the television studios. Shortly afterwards (November 3rd) he wrote to his mother that it was his earnest desire to be relieved of this responsibility, admitting that it highlighted his weakest point, his 'moral cowardice in public'. He consoled himself by thinking about Benson, who was so sick with anxiety before every sermon that his shirt was soaked in sweat, and made him stutter, coming to the conclusion that no man was stronger than his weakest point. On November 5th Ian Smith won his referendum with almost 90 per cent of the votes (the vast majority of Africans were still not allowed to vote).

Jack-of-all-trades at Silveira House

At the beginning of September, M'Bebi was ready to welcome its first novices, and John had to move out. Father Dove had arranged that Silveira House, which up to then had served as a novitiate, would be taken over by himself, and henceforth run as a Centre for training in development (with only 100 pounds, which he got from the then regional superior). He immediately invited John to join him in this venture. John eagerly accepted, and for the first time the two friends were to work together. On December 14th, they loaded up the small truck lent by Father von Kerssenbrock with the few personal belongings of the hermit of M'Bebi, including the cat, but not the owls.

Late in the hot southern summer evening they drew up outside Silveira House, where the surrounding grass had grown as high as the windows. The buildings dated back to 1958 and were located in the vast Chishawasha domain on a plateau that sloped gradually down to the capital. An avenue of recently planted pine trees led to two simple brick buildings and a few outhouses. Birds – eagles, plovers, swallows – were numerous. In the grounds one occasionally came across deer, leopards, jackals and baboons. Snakes, including forest cobras and two pythons, had taken up residence near the house. A henhouse, a garden, a cluster of trees recently planted by Father Wallace, the founder of the novitiate, made up the rest of the Centre. Beyond Chishawasha Valley, where the msasas added a dash of colour, the impressive mountain range, often covered in forest, in the north and east of the country appeared in the distance. John was immediately won over, and would spend long hours exploring the wild and grandiose landscape on all sides.

With characteristic modesty, the director of the new Centre, Father David Harold-Barry, was often heard to say of their African neighbours: 'They came knocking on our door' (in *Knocks on the door: Silveira House: the first forty years, 1964-2004*). He had understood how necessary it was to train Africans in the skills needed for the self-development of a free people, rather than force them to vegetate in the Tribal Trust Lands or on the outskirts of the towns. Here Father Dove was following in the footsteps of former confreres in Rhodesia such as Father Waddelove, who had set up a network of credit unions. Father Dove had acquired important skills since his arrival in Rhodesia, and had given lectures on the Church's social encyclicals in the township of Highfield, at the invitation of David Sterling's Capricorn Society, which promoted inter-racial cooperation. The project had been short-lived, but it had brought Father Dove into contact with key leaders in the African nationalist and trade union movements, whose 'wounded dignity' made a deep impression on him. In 1963, when Highfield became a battleground between nationalist factions, he realised the necessity of finding a neutral space for advancing his projects. Silveira House offered an ideal solution to his problem, where he could 'help people to find God and develop agriculture'.

His project was original, insofar as it emphasised training rather than aid: listening, helping to understand real situations and possibilities for action, providing equipment, and promoting confidence in God, not only in hearts and minds but also in skills, in accordance with contemporary Catholic social teachings taking shape in the 1970s, which aimed at promoting (as Paul VI wrote in *Populorum Progresio*) 'the good of every man and of the whole man'. The work developed over the years, learning from experience, and adapted for different groups: farmers, young people, women, manual workers. African farmers learnt how to manage a farm, and visited Cold Comfort Farm, run by the Englishman Guy Clutton-Brock (later arrested and deported), to see for themselves a successful experiment in multi-racial common purpose. Father Dove also set up workshops in fine art, nutrition, domestic economy, technology skills, co-operativism, credit, civics and trade unionism.

In the course of time, thousands of Africans were trained in these workshops. The Centre kept in touch with graduates and set up an informal network of groups and initiatives (there were 500 of these in 1980). For Father Dove all these activities were driven by the liberating force of Gospel teaching, and he was the first to admit his surprise at the dynamic effect faith had on the lives of the villagers. He himself had trained his first collaborators, and continued to recruit more over the years. He also knew how to promote the Centre without running up against the Smith regime, and enjoyed the protection of Mark Partridge, a Catholic who had become a government minister and believed (wrongly) that he and Father Dove shared the same ideas. He even managed to get financial support from abroad, despite Rhodesia's bad reputation. He also succeeded in maintaining relationships with Jesuit colleagues, some of whom were bewildered or even hostile to what he was trying to do, and this wasn't always easy. Nor was he even sure that John Bradburne understood, given that organised political, economic or social action was alien to the latter's temperament; but John's confidence in and support for his friend was total, though what counted most for him was the practical welfare of the ordinary poor people whom he met in his everyday life, to whom he was always ready to give the shirt off his back.

John Dove invited his friend to work for him because he needed him and, in his scheme of things, John had a very special place – at the heart of things: his essential task was to be himself, a man of God and a man of prayer. He would pray for the Centre and all those it trained and supported. But he was also allotted specific tasks, otherwise he would not have accepted the position, and while he often insisted he did nothing, he was fully occupied from morning to night. And not only 'to make tea' for Father Dove: 'sonnets for God and beds for visitors', as he wrote to his mother before the opening of the Centre (6 May 1964). He looked after the two dogs, closed the doors every evening and opened them first thing in the morning, checked the lights and the taps, performed the duties of sacristan, and served Mass for his friend every day (he felt called to a mission, and whenever anyone had the temerity to kneel in the director's place he was swiftly sent on his way by the vigilant sacristan). Though kept on the move all day, John made sure to take time off for prayer and meditation and the recital of his Office, which he chanted at the top of his voice in the church. His prayers always centred on the Blessed Virgin. As John Dove later wrote:

> He opened his heart to everyone on Mary, but if he felt some resistance, he no longer spoke about her. However, if he felt that one was receptive, he opened his heart completely on Marian devotion. He knew that many English, even Catholics, are foreigners to this devotion. For him, this sense of Mary, we have it or we do not have it.

Whenever the director was absent, which was often, John took complete charge of the Centre, sometimes over a number of days. From time to time he helped out in the kitchen, and with general housework, as well as in the garden. He also drove into town to do the shopping, but – aware of his limitations behind the wheel – he asked Heather Benoy to give him a refresher course in driving. This was a tricky business for her because John insisted on driving without looking right or left, and the lessons were short-lived. Since there was no secretary and John Dove was run off his feet, John decided to look after the typing for the Centre. He soon mastered the necessary typing skills, which had an unforeseen outcome. He began to type out his poems, and his poetic output increased (an average of ten poems a month during his time at Silveira House, as against two in the preceding years, to speak only of those that survived). He did of course continue to write his poems by hand, but the typewriter now became his normal method of composition. He also got involved in poetry evenings in Salisbury, and quickly acquired a reputation as a poet himself.

His daily life was simple. In a letter to his mother a few years later (25 January 1968), still in Silveira House, he would tell her:

> I'm as odd as ever about food: a quart of tea for breakfast; the same lunch as everyone else is having, bar potatoes or rice; in the evening a glass of wine, milk, water or orange-juice or vodka or cocoa for supper and a slice of neat cheese...

Prunes are to me the elixir of life on the material side.

Staff numbers increased rapidly after Father Dove took on a Jesuit from Uganda, Father Peter Kavumo, and some African Rhodesian collaborators. At this time John met also at the Centre other Jesuits from Chishawasha and Salisbury, and became intimate friends with some of them, including Father Wallace and Brother Peter Conway. Moreover, he joined the Samaritans, founded in London by a churchman about ten years earlier, who had set up a branch in Rhodesia. And he also made new friends in the animal kingdom: two Alsatians, called respectively Simba (the 'Strong One') and Huru (the 'Fat One'), both formidable and good-natured, who followed him everywhere. Huru was inclined to keep to himself, while Simba quickly became inseparable from his master and developed the habit of sleeping next to his room. The cat M'Bebi had adapted well to her new environment and became part of the family. The henhouse at the Centre became John's focus, where he could be heard singing as he fed the hens.

He became fascinated by the birds that flew over Chishawasha, especially eagles, and confided to John Dove that he would love to have one as a pet. His friend could not see this happening, but both began to pray for inspiration, and the miracle soon followed. John met Frank McEwen, director of the National Gallery at Salisbury, who was looking for somewhere to keep his eagle. McEwen occupied an apartment on the top floor of the gallery, where he was keeping a young bateleur he had acquired in Botswana, but the eagle was growing and the apartment was getting too small. He came to Silveira House to check that conditions were suitable, and the eagle soon arrived at the Centre in a box full of holes (John was supposed to send the bird on later to Malta). The eagle (*chapungu*, in Shona) had a special significance for John. It was a biblical and evangelical bird, but also the protective ancestral totem of several African clans, and especially the divine messenger written about by a Shona poet, Edison Zvobgo: 'Love me Chapungu, breath of the wind, / Tell me about the highest heavens'.

John welcomed the eagle with great enthusiasm, thanking God and the Virgin Mary for having granted his wish. He immediately named it Haggai, in memory of the Jewish prophet, fervent instigator of the restoration of the Temple. The African staff at the Centre called the eagle *Sekuru* ('Uncle'), and always spoke of him with respect. John built a house for his new friend, and was delighted when the eagle quickly showed his trust in him by allowing him to touch it. To feed him he solicited the help of the students at Chishawasha, who obliged by supplying mice and field rats. The bird had a keen appetite, and soon the grass was covered with the leftovers of his meals, though nobody seemed to object.

John's reputation drew more and more visitors to the Centre eager to meet him. His television appearances, his mixture of eccentricity and normality, his 'hippy-like' demeanour allied to his English 'good breeding', his religious seriousness and his ready wit, his ascetic reputation and his hilarious talent as a mimic attracted and fascinated all comers. Many commented on how this many-sided, all-round man, totally without malice, managed to combine religious conviction and humanity in equal measure. Though austere, he was always cheerful, and this seemed to be his secret. John was totally unselfconscious in his eccentricity, and though he wrote of himself (*Upon this Feast of Christ the King*, 1968), 'Surely as I am Christ's and Mary's fool', he was quick to take umbrage if anyone dared to suggest he was mad, though always apologising immediately at any offence caused. Father Dove saw clearly that those who met John accepted him for what he was: poet, mystic, man of God:

> We could say that John was a mystic but it came quite naturally in his religious life, in his case. Yes, he was a mystic, but it was so natural, so lovely for him. I would say he was a mystic, a man who readily talked about God, and had an easy conversation with Him.

And to those who asked him about his friend he answered: 'Let him be.' For many John was simply a unique holy man, even if they didn't understand him. Thus one day he and Heather Benoy were passing the little Hindu chapel on Cameron Street in Salisbury and he told her he came there from time to time to pray. He then proceeded to take off his shoes and went inside to say the rosary. Heather declined to join him, without knowing why.

He began to receive more and more invitations in Salisbury, where he was seen to dance the twist – for three hours non-stop – at a party for the Association of Catholic Women, which suggests that even though he was over 40 he was by no means an old man and could still keep up with the best of the younger set. For some time he had shown some interest in political matters, and noted that 'the paternal eye of Communist China' was turning towards Rhodesia, although this would happen later (the Russian eye was already present), remarking in a letter to his mother (December 1964) that God's eye 'makes all things gay and happy. Deo Gratias.' He continued his television broadcasts, hating it more and more. At the end of a programme, in February 1965, he managed to get himself fired ('They have sacked me in a very polite way', he told his mother), learning a lesson in the process – even congratulating himself on what he had achieved over a period of months in spite of his 'own moral cowardice', but confessing that he had rarely done anything that he detested so much.

In March, *The Shield* – a respected Catholic Review, headed by Anthony Chennels and Patrick Berthoud – published an interview (the only one John ever gave) with the 'caretaker cum general help at Silveira House', stating that 'our readers know you better as a poet'. The interview, conducted by Patrick Berthoud, began with a question about poetry, indicative of how important it was for John to be recognised in this domain. He explained that poetry was part of his calling: 'My vocation is that of any Christian – trying to get to Heaven and, in trying to do so myself, to influence others heavenward according to what talent I may have.' He was then asked to tell the story of his life, which he proceeded to do in a matter-of-fact way, explaining why he became a Catholic, attributing his poetic inspiration to his conversion. He then explained his desire to return to the Holy Land, adding that looking after a hen run with 100 chickens gave him great pleasure because it reminded him of the words of Christ over Jerusalem. 'I feel that this is as near a practical measure to the conversion of the Jews as I can get.' The interview finished with a declaration of love from John for the landscapes and hills of Rhodesia, and a hope that the Jews would read his poetry. The interview was accompanied by a photo, one of the last before he let his beard grow. He looked young, in shirt and pullover, his arms neatly folded, and with the shadow of a smile. The interview was rounded off by a poem, *Steeplejack Gallant*.

That month Harold Wilson came to Salisbury and visited some jailed African leaders. He informed Ian Smith of the five basic principles on which Britain would grant independence to the colony, including the principle of one man, one vote. But as soon as he left, the repression resumed. On May 7th, in the parliamentary elections, the Rhodesian Front, despite the opposition of the Churches, took all 50 seats in the European College, there being almost no votes cast for the handful of seats reserved for Africans. In the same month an organised guerrilla group – by now no longer an isolated pocket of resistance – discreetly slipped across the frontier and established a presence in the north-west. At the end of October Harold Wilson made it clear there was no question of Britain trying to solve the Rhodesian problem by military intervention, thereby opening the way for Ian Smith to declare the unilateral declaration of independence of Rhodesia (UDI) on November 5th 1965, which was described as 'striking a blow for the preservation of justice, civilisation, and Christianity'. The Catholic bishops immediately replied by denouncing the injustice, barbarity and the non-Christian nature of UDI, predicting that it would lead the country to disaster. Simultaneously *Moto* wrote of the great 'blow against justice, civilisation, and Christianity' which led to the article, as well as the bishops' letter, being banned, except in an English version. A state of emergency was immediately declared, which remained in force until 1980. But Silveira House was spared, on condition that it suspended all political discussion groups. And because Ian Smith continued to repeat his commitment to 'community development', Father Dove was only too willing to play along.

Friendships old and new

During his stay at Silveira House, John's personality blossomed. He liked to refer to the Centre as a *choto*, a place of welcome where everyone felt at home, free and able to work together. During

268   John Bradburne: Vagabond of God

this period he strengthened old friendships and made many new ones. His friendship with John Dove stood out among the others. Both were following different paths, and the Jesuit didn't always understand his friend's enthusiasms, his propensity for failure, nor even that poetry came to him as naturally as breathing. His own project remained somewhat strange to John, who thought he spent too much money on it, but this in no way affected their friendship, or their ability to work side by side without serious disagreement. The secret of their friendship lay in their common humility, and the fact that, as previously, 'both considered himself to be the disciple of the other and the other to be his guru', and their shared desire for God and fervent devotion to the Virgin Mary and her Son. It seemed to some a rather asymmetrical relationship: between the confessor and his disciple, the priest and the layman, the director of operations and his jack-of-all-trades. But Father Dove was conscious of the greatness of his friend and considered that, spiritually speaking, he himself 'hardly measured up to the height of his friend's ankle'.

John at this time made many African friends, among whom was Agnes Mapfumo, who taught at the Centre while raising a family, and who was a kind of spiritual daughter to Father Dove. Another friend was Sister Teresiana Muteme, six years older than John, who had entered the Sisters of the Little Children of Our Blessed Lady, becoming novice mistress at 25 years of age. This strong-willed woman, passionate about her faith and her people, was deeply impressed by the work at Silveira House. It was here that she first met John, and came to see him on numerous occasions. Some 45 years later she still recalls her friendship with 'such a good man, who often sang, whom I liked very much', and who would play such an important role in her life after his death.

Among his European friends figured Patrick Berthoud, who had interviewed him for *The Shield*. Head of the English Department at University College, he succeeded in turning it into a haven of racial non-discrimination, and asked John to be the godfather of his son Philip. John also got on well with the Italian nuns from the hospital at Churundi whom John Dove had welcomed in Rhodesia, especially Caterina Savini. He also met Doctor Luisa Guidotti, who had joined Caterina, but felt little affinity at this time with this 'heavily built Italian woman, very strong', possibly because she spoke very little English.

Heather Benoy had become very close to the two Johns. Artistic and rebellious, she was going through a difficult phase in her life, and still had not found her way. Often, her day's work over, she would set out in her car for Silveira House to give lessons to African nurses, and afterwards drop in on John. If he was working on a poem he was quite capable of making her feel unwanted, and could even be obnoxious; on one occasion he refused to talk to her for a fortnight. But she never held it against him, and needed his joie-de-vivre, his humour, his outbursts of laughter, and his infectious belief in the realities of the spirit:

> John often tended to be far away in his thoughts and was quite often aloof and distant. I think this was partly because he was intent upon his meditations and prayers. He also seemed to prefer not be too near to anyone and created a distance between himself and others which was sometimes interpreted as being remote. This was due I think to the fact that his mind was constantly searching for his vocation.

On visits to the Benoy colonial mansion at Josiah Street in Salisbury, John liked to play with the dogs, recite a poem, sing, listen to music, or banter with other family members. Heather Benoy was acutely aware of the kind of man John was:

> I always thought of John as a fastidious person. He was always neat and very clean. Although he was mostly very thoughtful and patient and kind, he could also be quite rude if he thought that a person was in any way disrespectful in the church or elsewhere.

One day he told the young woman she should join the little sisters of Charles de Foucauld, and go and live in Nazareth. She showed no interest, but he persisted for nearly one year, to no effect. Yet her admiration for him, and his influence on the spiritual journey on which he led her, counted for more than these minor irritations:

> John was terribly attractive to many people. He was eccentric, charming, witty, and incredibly gifted. People were really drawn to him. Sometimes I thought he might be a bit vain, but this was a false impression. My family loved John. They loved his visits and were always keen to keep company with him. He was very well loved by my family. As my own friendship with John deepened I realised how intent he was in his great desire to be close to God. His preoccupation was with knowing and loving Christ through our Blessed Lady. John was not a vagabond at all – he was deliberately searching to find his right place with Christ. His entire being was absorbed in this search. This is my opinion. Because of his complete absorption and commitment to being united with our Lord, I found myself to be left far behind John – in his thoughts, prayers, meditation, and intentions. He was also aware of how far behind him I was. I could not keep up with his great spirituality. I knew this very well towards the end.

Father Dove was successful in attracting volunteers from Europe and North America. One of these was Chris, a young Catholic in search of himself, who was the first to arrive in July 1965. He was bewildered by John, the handyman of the Centre, and everything he did, and the two men soon quarrelled. Eventually Chris decided to seek his fortune as a mercenary in the Congo in order to make money to train for his pilot's licence. The two Johns were horrified and tried everything to put him off the idea. When he left they prayed that nothing would happen to him, and it appears their prayers were granted. He made his fortune and became a pilot.

Then came James Rigby, at the end of 1965. 'Jim' had just completed his studies in Paris and had taken sabbatical leave. He possessed all the practical skills that John lacked, and went around fixing, improving, building; he knew how to spot a bargain at the market in Salisbury and haggle over prices. While John spent long hours praying in the chapel, Jim set about making two new pews, and giving classes in law and industrial relations at the Centre. He also took over the tasks which, for want of staff, had fallen to John, such as driving, shopping and surveillance, leading John to say: 'I'm a drone.' The two became good friends, and John was grateful for the help. One day Jim found himself confronted by a poisonous hooded cobra and cried for help. When John came, recorder in hand, Jim was furious, imagining himself in a life-threatening situation, only to be told by John: 'That is exactly why I am bringing my recorder!' In the event it worked, and the cobra slunk off. Jim left Rhodesia in mid-1966, and wrote to the Jesuit Superior that Silveira House was in need of an all-round handyman, not a sadhu, which left John Dove with some questions to answer about his strange friend John.

Among the Jesuits, John got to know Brother John Conway, who invited him to spend a few days at Murumba. This tall Irish extrovert had in common with John his laugh, his ability to make friends, his spirit of independence, and his need for solitude. Unlike John, he was multi-skilled, and everywhere he went as a missionary, at Wedza and later Musami, he performed wonders: as doctor, nurse, dentist, gardener, builder of schools and playing fields: the total Mr Fixit. He also had an extraordinary way with children, and knew how to come down to their level. Eventually all this activity began to play on the nerves of his confreres, and he left the community house to live apart in a hut – like John at Ganda – baptised Conway Castle, where the children could play and sing. He then found himself alone at Murumba, 50 miles north of the Mission, with neither school nor dispensary, cut off by mountains and forests, accessible with difficulty on poorly marked trails. The Christians in the region were mostly Vapostori, a local sect who refused medicine and whose bishops were polygamist. But Brother Conway had quickly established a small 100-strong Catholic community, composed mainly of children.

John went to visit him, and found the region desolate. He was quickly befriended by the children and the local farmers, who called him Baba John, to distinguish him from Brada John. Baba

John was flabbergasted at how Brada John could hold the children spellbound by telling them stories that he himself could make neither head nor tail of. As usual, he often disappeared for long treks in the bush. One day, accompanied by a stray dog he had adopted, he was walking on the other side of the Mazoe. The dog suddenly came to a halt outside a lair, from whose depths came a ferocious growl, at which point John and his dog took to their heels back across the river, no questions asked!

Vicissitudes of a frustrated hermit

The early months of UDI in the beginning of 1966 were euphoric for the Rhodesian regime. The economy was thriving. The oil blockade affected only the port of Beira in Mozambique and did little to prevent supplies reaching Rhodesia. The country went on to experience growth averaging 10 per cent per year, in spite of sanctions which were supposed to shut it down. Immigration surged, and soon the European population exceeded 220,000. Nevertheless April 28th saw the first clash between the Rhodesian army and a group of guerrillas near Sonoia, who were promptly crushed. Both this and the murder of two white farmers, man and wife, near Hartley on June 5th were regarded as isolated incidents, and Ian Smith was confident that he was in command of the situation.

Father Dove was dismayed by the blindness of the new regime. A discussion group chaired by Lady Daphne Acton was set up at Silveira House on his initiative to try to turn young Europeans away from the regime, and it was decided to organise a fete in the parish of Mabvuku, a nearby African township, run by Father Kavumo in tandem with his work at the Centre. John took part in preparations for the event, making new friends in the process. The fete was a success, but led to nothing. Nevertheless some young Europeans came to the Centre for discussions with John, including Peter Sanders, who later joined the Dominicans.

In spite of the political climate, the Centre continued to expand its activities. Teachers, students and visitors continued to pass John's door and, as often as not out of politeness, greeted him and tried to strike up a conversation, interrupting his meditation or his poetic inspiration. He played the recorder or sang at any hour of the day or night, but eventually the frequent comments made about this began to weigh on him. His daily visits to the hen run, and the memory of Ganda, then gave him an idea. Gathering bits of corrugated iron, bricks and barbed wire he built himself a lean-to against the wall of the hen run and moved in with his typewriter. From then on he spent long hours there writing poems, sitting on a wooden box surrounded by hens, and visiting the kitchen with Simba and M'Bebi to pick up some nourishment. Father Dove duly took note of John's new abode, and only a small group of friends knew about it, and from then on he was less likely to be disturbed by unwelcome guests.

He continued to gather eggs for the kitchen. Soon after, recalls Heather Benoy, production dramatically increased. Everybody congratulated John, until the hens began to lose their feathers. The hen run and environs was soon populated by a tribe of featherless creatures, whose egg production became as bizarre as it was prolific. Finally an agricultural expert was called in, slightly surprised to find a human resident among the hens, who readily obliged in helping him in his enquiries. The expert couldn't discover anything wrong, and was amazed and quite confused, but just as he was leaving he asked John: 'What do they eat? What do you feed them on?' To which John answered: 'Oh! plenty of layer mash', and led the visitor to the supply of sacks, which on inspection turned out to be... fertiliser pellets! The diet was discontinued and the hens soon regained their feathers.

Shortly after this, John was introduced to the Laws. John Law was the chief meteorologist in Rhodesia, but also an outdoor type who had explored the countryside surrounding the capital. One day while out walking he had discovered Silveira House, whose trees and views impressed him. His wife Kit, an Anglican like himself, was an accomplished pianist and taught music at St John's School in Borrowdale, a suburb of Salisbury. The Laws liked bees and kept some in their garden. One day a neighbour on the way to pluck her lettuce got stung by a bee. She knocked on the Laws' door and demanded the expulsion of the culprit and his fellow apians. Arthur remembered his visit to Silveira House and thought it would be the ideal location for his bees. On going there, the first person he met was a European, who, on discovering the motive for the visit, was overcome by enthusiasm: yes, Silveira House was the perfect home for his bees; the director was away but he would certainly welcome them, and John (for it was he...) told them that he had been wanting to work with bees for years. Soon the bees were granted residence near the main building, and John delighted in his new pets and their strange sense of direction:

> Truly the Lord's own marvel is the ease
> With which they so precisely can adjust
> Their microscopic radar to a change
> Of home, whither exactly they'll arrive
> From even miles away, from where they range
> Getting nectar and pollen for the hive:
> On those (their little radar-sets) no rust!
> (*Cantate Domino Canticum Novum*, 1969)

The Laws became regular visitors to Silveira House, and their circle of friends soon included Father Dove and other friends of John, who began collecting hygrometric samples for Arthur, whom John often visited in his home. He spent many hours with the Laws walking in the *bundu* ('bush') and, Kit Law later wrote, 'through his eyes one appreciated the wild life of the veld, trees, flowers, and for him the song of a bird and the flight of an eagle were the crowning joys of the day'. They found that his receptivity to everything around them on their walks never wavered for a second, the conversation never let up, and he was both full of fun and very witty. Sometimes he went off on his own through the forest with the dogs to visit the Mission at Chishawasha and pray to St Ignatius before the Blessed Sacrament. He invariably dropped in to the Jesuits for a chat about what he had seen along his way – including Father Esser, one of the first missionaries who had arrived in 1911, and founded St Patrick's school and the Embakwe Mission. The old priest, who no longer had all his wits about him, often warned John not to look at the bell tower; there were women up there, he said, no doubt with wicked intentions.

John's other great pleasure was listening to music, alone or with Heather Benoy and others, and he spent long hours listening over and over to the Brandenburg Concertos. Apart from Bach he had a predilection for Pachebel's Canon, singing the bass voice part himself with gusto. John was fundamentally an artist, and 'he expressed himself in music and poetry as naturally as he breathed'. Perhaps it was because of the hens episode, but Father Dove now insisted that John move back into the Centre. To give him more independence, he fitted out the last room in the building, which had been used as a shoe room, and had a separate entrance from the outside. John was persuaded, but made it clear that when he closed the door behind him he should in no circumstances be disturbed.

His fondness for Simba and M'Bebi was trumped by his preference for Haggai in the spring of 1966. The eagle spent the day circling the Centre, attached to his perch by a piece of strong wire about 100 yards long. John often came to play with him, and the eagle would sit on his hand, protected by a glove, or simply stay on his perch. One day, John got it into his head that Haggai was bored, and prayed for a companion to come and join him. Coincidentally, he was surprised on May 11th to see that another eagle had landed near Haggai, and the two birds engaged in courtship ritual. John called to Father Dove to come and admire their dance. But when the other eagle took off Haggai tried to follow it. Having come to the end of his line Haggai pulled so hard that it gave way and he disappeared into the sky, trailing the line behind him. For days John waited by the perch, searching the sky, trying to convince himself: 'Haggai must come back, Haggai will come back.' It never did, and John was so affected that his temper changed. Father Dove was worried, and even offered a reward for anyone who brought back the precious bird. John himself wrote to McEwen, but got no reply. At last, in August, walking in a forest a few miles from the Centre, John discovered the remains of the bird hanging from a tree. Its line had become entangled in the branches of the tree, and, having failed to escape, died of hunger and exhaustion. John brought back the remains and buried them in the middle of a forest of pines with an elaborate ceremony. As long as he lived in Silveira House, he regularly visited the grave. He asked himself why the eagle had met such a fate, before acknowledging that perhaps he had been more attentive to the bird than to God.

During the summer of 1966, John was called as a Samaritan to the suburb of Highlands to help Reuben, a young Jew who wished to commit suicide, and met Joan F (not her real name: she spoke about the matter to Judith Listowel, and wished to remain anonymous). Joan was running a family hostel, and invited both of them to stay in the hostel. For three days they shared time with the would-be suicide and persuaded him to change his mind (Reuben later returned to Britain and became a wealthy businessman). While the young man slept, the two guardian angels talked. Joan was interested in Oriental mysticism, and lent John a copy of the Bhagavad-Gita, which he read in the garden and came across the sentence: 'There is no other God but Me' (in fact: 'Nothing is higher than Me', VII, 6), which reminded him of Deuteronomy 4.34. Joan also spoke to him of the *tokoloshi*, those ape-like little devils, both cunning and wicked, from Zulu mythology, which, though alien to Shona religion, had made their way into Shona lore, and were associated with the evil eye and witchcraft. The two shared thoughts on matters spiritual and supernatural, in the intimacy of their common work of mercy. According to Joan, John opened up and spoke about his flight through the jungles of Malaya, his experience of cerebral malaria, and his vision of the Virgin. They never met again, but exchanged one or two letters.

In September, John was left alone in charge of the Centre with Francis the gardener, who was half blind. One day he suddenly saw flames on the horizon making their way towards the buildings. It was a bush fire, probably started by some young shepherds to scare off wild animals, and which had got out of control. The fire ravaged the plateau and flames 20 feet high were getting near the buildings. John struggled hopelessly against the fire, which stopped right up against the windows of the houses. But 600 newly planted trees were burnt, and John later walked disconsolately through the ravaged forest, as if in a cemetery.

The year came to an end depressingly after fruitless discussions between Harold Wilson and Ian Smith aboard HMS *Tiger*. At Silveira House Jim Rigby's letter had produced an effect. Brother Harold Francis Fitzsimons arrived. Quickly baptised Brother Fitz, this Mancunian was as handy as Jim and as devout as John, two qualities which soon endeared him to the latter. It didn't take Fitz long to realise the place of music in his new friend's life, and he set about procuring him an organ to play, with the complicity of the Laws. John was surprised one day to witness the arrival of this precious instrument, which was duly installed in the chapel. He was granted access to it day and night, and thereafter spent long hours playing to the glory of God, often accompanying himself with a canticle at the top of his voice, or declaiming one of his poems. He and Heather Benoy composed Masses together, and he adapted Gregorian excerpts into Shona, discovering that the genius of the two languages complemented each other. The sound of the organ and the singer soon caught the attention of staff and teachers, and because the Shona had often an innate sense of harmony, some of them ended up accompanying John as he sang. Among the most faithful was Agnes Mapfumo; others joined in, and soon they formed a vocal quartet. Agnes was devout and sensitive, and John used to tease her about her voice, and nicknamed her Contralto:

> While we sang, he laughed and said my voice was
> more of a man than a woman, but it was not done
> with bad intentions. He himself had a beautiful
> voice, and it was nice to hear him sing! We sang
> together for hours. It was good, they were blessed
> days. He was my friend, my great friend.

Father Dove continued to take care not to come to the attention of the authorities and maintained good relations with Mark Partridge, who was still a member of the cabinet. But even though the first guerrilla wave had failed – there would be no more murders of European settlers for seven years – the government kept a tight rein on all security aspects of the country, and it was inevitable the Special Branch would one day pay a visit to Silveira House, if only because of the training course offered on trade union organisation. John Dove recounts that John was alone on duty the day two plain-clothes policemen arrived at the Centre. When they started to ply him with questions, he cut across them and invited them in for a drink. While they sipped their beer he regaled them about the birds, the bees, the view, the flowers, the plants and the story of Haggai. They submitted him to a barrage of questions: 'What goes on at the Centre?' 'Oh, Africans come here.' 'What for?' 'They come on courses. Enough of that?' And he reverted to trees, bees and the story of his eagle: 'Look at the marvellous landscape – isn't it a beautiful view?' The two men listened but soon resumed their questioning, only to be interrupted again. 'Look, look at this beauty all around us, the birds, the mountains'. Eventually they gave up and left. He later wrote a poem in praise of the multiracial Centre in memory of the incident:

> Silveira, like a city bright
> Set on a hill that flings
> Forth graceful rays for black and white
> Whilst raceless lays she sings,
> Hath Oxford Motto midst her themes:
> 'The Lord my Light' ignites her schemes.
> (*Silveira House*, 1975)

The Christ of Borrowdale

Paul and Ann Tingay, friends of Father Dove, both taught at the Centre – he in drama, she in science. He was English, though his family came from Brittany; she was South African. In 1967 the parish of Borrowdale decided to put on a performance of Dorothy Sayers' version of the Passion of Christ, *Born to Be King* (originally a radio drama commissioned during the war by the BBC to promote Christian fervour in the face of Nazism), with over 60 actors, to be directed by Paul at Easter. But they had no one to play the part of Jesus. The director sought the advice of Father Dove, who immediately replied: 'John is your man – obviously'. When Paul met him, John had been sporting a beard for some time, which gave him a Christ-like appearance. But the appearance wasn't enough, so the director explained what he was looking for. John cut him short: 'Hold on until I consult the Blessed Virgin'. He searched his pockets, took out a coin and spun it in the air and said: 'That's fine. I'll do it'. Rehearsals continued for six weeks and they met on a daily basis. John intrigued Paul Tingay, who prided himself on his ability to judge people, and felt he could work out what sort of a person he was dealing with fairly quickly, and was seldom wrong. But he couldn't make John out: 'Fifty per cent in supernatural and fifty per cent in seriouness.' He felt that while John put his heart into the role he also seemed to suffer in it. During breaks between scenes the other actors bantered among themselves, but John never joined in. Paul Tingay became more and more bewildered. 'Who is this man? I can't make him out.' At the end of six weeks he was no wiser.

The day arrived and all went well. John, despite his upper-middle-class English diction, was convincing in the role, with a mixture of realism and interiority. On the cross he bore an astonishing resemblance to Romanesque Christs (for example the Puy Cross in Paris Cluny Museum – emaciated frame, protruding ribs, and above all a face which, though peaceful, did not hide the suffering behind it). The play was a great success, but John did not seem to participate in the general exhilaration after the performance. Watching him, Paul Tingay remarked to himself: 'It was as if he was not on the same plane as us', and once again felt that his strange actor was suffering. He still hadn't worked John out.

May 11th 1967 was the first anniversary of Haggai's disappearance, and John laid flowers on her grave, and prayed to the Blessed Virgin to give him a sign that his eagle was now free and happy in paradise. Shortly afterwards an enormous eagle, almost completely white, appeared in the sky ('not a chapungu, I think, but more beautiful and gracious', wrote John). The eagle hovered over the pine copse where Haggai was buried, and then flew off in the direction of the valley. John never again saw such a bird, but for him the sign was obvious: the eternal life brought by Christ was not reserved for 'featherless bipeds', as he wrote to his mother that day. (The reference was to Diogenes Laërtius' *Lives*, in which Plato is said to have defined man as a 'featherless biped', which prompted Diogenes the Cynic to pluck the feathers from a cock and go with the animal to Plato's school claiming 'Here is Plato's man.') John used the expression about a dozen times in his poetry. He also participated from time to time in a circle of poets who met in Salisbury, and where everyone read from their own work. Here he made the acquaintance of Peter Beverley, editor of a poetry review called *Two Tone*. In June 1967, for the second time in his life, he had work published, although his name was misspelt *Blackburne*.

In the same year, 1967, some friends offered John the key to their house on the Indian Ocean at Beira in Mozambique. Father Dove was delighted when he accepted this offer of a holiday, the first after five years in Rhodesia. In reality John was nursing a somewhat more ambitious plan; to go to Dar es Salaam where his sister Audrey and her husband William Yonge were living. But when he arrived in Beira he couldn't get a boat, diplomatic relations between Tanzania and the Portuguese colony having been broken off. He was obliged to abandon his plan and enjoy the sun, the sea, and a fight with a packet of soap powder (about which he wrote a poem, *These are the days*), playing on the assonance between *Om* (the Hindu mantra) and the name of the soap powder, *Omo*. He visited an Orthodox church to pray, wrote a few 'occasional' tourist poems, and enjoyed liquid meals (discovering that if you ordered enough wine the food was free). Back in Rhodesia he picked up his regular routine again: chores, prayer, poetry, walks, visits. People often came to him for advice, spiritual or otherwise, which always surprised him, but since it was about prayer, he did what he could to help.

My kingdom for the bees

But these too frequent visits, sometimes by people looking for novelty, did not agree with him, while the need for solitude became more pressing. He could of course hide behind closed doors in his room, but the climate militated against this, as did his moods. He lived this desire for solitude as a gift from God since, John Dove wrote, 'if you have a burning for solitude, it is not so much something in your character; it is something which is God given, a grace which is drawn in you. You can refuse if you like but it is not self-made, it is a grace which comes in to you, a wanting to have dialogue between you and God.'

John therefore turned to prayer to find a solution. Remembering the episode in the Indian railway station which had so struck him in 1945, he began to pray that a swarm of bees would be sent to him as a way of warding off nuisance visitors. His prayer was granted: on July 25th, he wrote to his mother telling her that for a number of days he was being visited by bees at breakfast time, and they were delighted that he left out about seven prune stones with a bit of juice, and didn't sting him. He explained that he had come to the conclusion that they were perfectly entitled to behave that way, and that he had decided to leave them out a little bit more, telling her that as he typed there were more than four or six dozen bees swarming around his head, and he wasn't being stung, concluding: 'I think that bees are very deep psychologists, and if one is not at all aggressive towards them, neither will they be aggressive.' On August 3rd he wrote again to his mother, telling her that they had invited themselves to dinner and kept him company for the rest of the afternoon:

> happily they all flew away before sundown, whereas on several evenings some of them missed the bus and spent a very dreary night in my room which they hated because it is not their hive – YET!

But it quickly came to pass, and John formed the habit of sitting down to type his poems in front of his box-hive where the bees had settled in, his bare legs marking the entrance and also protecting them. The first time John Dove discovered him thus seated he took fright, but John reassured him. And the director of Silveira House had to admit that the bees were very polite towards their protector, and towards himself, because he had confidence in John. He himself was never stung, and repeated after John: 'We do not speak to them, / They do not speak to us.' Heather Benoy, on the other hand, never dared enter the room, and spoke to John through the gap in the door. The bees stayed until Christmas 1967, then suddenly disappeared.

In August 1967, Ian Smith set up a commission to draft a new constitution, 'to protect and guarantee the right and freedoms of all persons and communities in Rhodesia, and ensure the harmonious development of Rhodesia's plural society, having regard to the social and cultural differences among the people of Rhodesia, to the different systems of land tenure and to the problem of economic development'. In one of his rare political letters (to his mother, 16 July 1967), John expressed his open hostility to the regime and its ideology:

> this is in order to keep the Aryan Herrenvolk of the Puppet State in splendid isolation beside their

swimming-baths (they nearly all have a private
one!). The Blacks (Africans) have always been
apart(heid) in their Townships round and about
Salisbury. I think an insistence on the nature of
Incarnate God with His decidedly coloured skin
would be a timely and sublime objection.

And he railed against an MP who had been educated by the Jesuits:

who is a 'born-Catholic' educated at Jesuit Saint
George's and exceedingly pleased both with his
body and with his soul! but even more so with
the elect shade of his skin... albeit it does not tally
with the Lord's!

His friends in Salisbury were both African and European. He
visited the latter in their mansions surrounded by vast gardens
with perfectly manicured lawns and swimming pool and, behind,
sumptuous orchards and exotic trees. He admired the tree-lined
avenues with jacaranda trees, flamboyant russet msasas, and other
trees in a variety of colours. When he visited the Africans it was in
their overcrowded townships, a grid of endless monotonous rows
of primitive shacks, their only luxury a modest *stoep* ('veranda'),
an occasional fruit tree, and an outside toilet. But he visited both
without distinction, in a country where the racial divide was
widening by the day.

Meanwhile, at Silveira House, his initial enthusiasm was
beginning to fade. Two years after its opening, the Centre had
become an institution. Organisations from overseas, Catholic
and others, had become aware of it. Father Dove no longer had
time to look out for John as much as he would have wished. And
while the bees were still there, this did not stop people knocking
on his door. Since his performance in the Dorothy Sayers play
at Borrowdale, the stream of visitors had if anything increased,
and his exasperation was at breaking point. One day he burst into
the director's office, ripped open his shirt and displayed his chest,
covered in a nervous rash shouting: 'This is what your so-and-so
friends do to me!' Father Dove was at pains to tell John that these
people were not his friends, but people who wanted to come 'to

sit at his feet'. John, it must be said, was overstating his alienation: when a group of lay people teaching in East Africa visited the Centre, including a young man called Kevin Jones, suffering from advanced malaria, it was John who nursed him back to health. He in time became friendly with Kevin, a passionate musician, and wrote him a verse letter in September 1967 which prompted David Crystal to compile the poetry database 30 years later. When he felt at the end of his tether, John would go out into the bush and wander about for hours. Someone gave him a present of the record of François Couperin's *Tenebrae Lessons*, a musical version of the *Lamentations of Jeremiah* for Holy Thursday Matins. In due course he had made them his own, and included them in his devotion to Christ the King of Israel. He had learnt them off by heart and sang them regularly, alone or with friends, telling them that this music expressed all his mind and soul. And an idea began to take shape in his mind, more or less consciously, probably at the time of the Six Day War, whose military development he was following on the radio. Nostalgia for the Holy Land was invading his soul, with a purpose yet to be decided.

The end of 1967 and the beginning of 1968 brought him little peace. He felt more and more useless and told Father Dove as much. His Jesuit friend assured him that, on the contrary, his presence was of great benefit to the community. John was not convinced and feared that he was becoming embittered. He wrote to his friend Stephen King, still in Australia, on January 18th:

> You ask me whether I am still smiling at the Africans: a very timely reminder; though I am in no way apartheid (sp) or Smith regime (I don't read the papers), my Timon of Athens bent has to be watched carefully and oiled copiously with grace from God, to prevent my face from fixing in a freeze! Not that it makes much difference to the racial deadlock either way, but every little helps, and a smile costs nothing and improves one's humour ipso facto. Also, I like being smiled at so presumably other people do.

In a further sign of his disarray, he wrote in the same letter that he had decided to leave Africa and emigrate to Cat Island in a lagoon in Tasmania, which he had found in an atlas! He asked Stephen King to help him find a little hermitage (in fact the island of 36 hectares was uninhabited). It was to be his last port of call before St Peter, he wrote. He asked his friend to help him earn enough money to buy the occasional cup of tea, milk and sundry other essentials, insisting he was serious about it. Stephen King sent him on information about the islands of Tasmania and John thanked him, but in the meantime he had come to the conclusion that his place was definitely in Africa after all.

In fact he was waiting for a sign from God, which was not slow in revealing itself. The Blue Sisters had built a rest home, which they called St Patrick's, ten minutes away from Silveira House, but the house had already been burgled eleven times, and they asked John to sleep there at night. From then on he left Silveira House every evening for St Patrick's with M'Bebi at his heels (Simba wanted to come as well, but he was needed at the Centre, and his master shared the dog's sadness). These nights of total solitude brought John the peace he was looking for. Other changes were taking place at Silveira House. Father Peter Kavumo left for a mission in the bush, and was replaced by a Rhodesian Jesuit, Father Raymond Kapito. Then a lay volunteer, Bernard, arrived, followed by Chris Shepherd-Smith, a future Jesuit with his own eccentricities, very old England, a devotee of the Blessed Virgin, who quickly became a friend of John.

Rebuilding the walls of the Temple

At the beginning of 1968 the government of Ian Smith scored some notable victories. Fifty-eight alleged insurgents were killed in the spring near Sipolio, and his government was recognised as the legitimate sovereign regime by the 'independent' Rhodesian Court of Appeal. Father Dove was recommended by his order, after seven years in Rhodesia, to take his first holiday in Europe. He advised John to do the same, and he agreed, expressing also his intention to visit the Holy Land. In April 1968 they both flew to London within days of each other and met up at Claver House with Father Crane. Before retiring to bed John climbed onto the roof of the building and sang Couperin's *Lessons* for the benefit of the sleeping population of London, as if to test the project that had been growing in his head for some time. This was followed the next morning by Lauds and the Office of the Blessed Virgin.

He then went to visit his mother at Ottery. She was now 75 years of age and recovering from an operation. John spent three weeks or so with her and all went well. Back in London on May 13th he wrote to tell her of his great joy at seeing her again, adding that her mind was younger than ever, and thanking her for her great welcome home. He also went to Tavistock to see Hugh Symons, who had retired to this town on the far side of Dartmoor. The Union Jack hung over the front door, where John sang the *Lessons* on arrival, and the wine flowed freely. The next day Hugh drove him to Buckfast via Dartmoor, which John found enchanting. At the Abbey he spoke at length with Dom Raphael, in the rain. The new chapel, which he described in a letter to his mother (16 July 1967) as 'lurid and ghastly; blaring bright' from a photograph sent by Darren Blackburn didn't look so awful now that he saw it, except for the huge Christ. The two friends were invited to stay for lunch at the Abbey, after which they adjourned to the church to listen to one of the monks playing Bach's great Fugue in G minor. John couldn't help thinking of his brother Philip, who used to play it so well, which made him anxious to see him again – but Philip was still in Libya.

He spent his last days in England with his family and friends. He used one of his last afternoons to visit his goddaughter Pamela, who kept a vivid memory of their travelling on the underground:

> He would burst into song very readily – religious songs or something like 'summer is a'cummin in'. The last time I heard him sing was when we spent a day in London together the last time he came to England, we were talking about plainsong going into the underground station, and all the way down the escalator he sang plainsong as loud as he could. The acoustics were very good and I remember people coming up the other escalator looking at him and really enjoying it!

(Probably John had sung *Lessons*, which seemed to obsess him since deciding on his grand plan.) But in a letter to Stephen King describing his trip home John confessed that he felt more out of his time than ever.

On May 24th it was time to leave for the Holy Land. Father Dove, his niece and a small group of Jesuits accompanied him to Victoria Station. It is not known who paid the fare, but we do know that he sent £5 to his mother to repay a loan. He told John Dove that they might be saying goodbye for the last time, because he would make up his mind when in Israel on whether he would go back to Africa, or try to find a cave in Israel and live there. But he kept from him any details of his grand plan, which he later described in *A Wandering* (1968):

> There are seven principles of war and although I can never remember them all I can remember one: Maintenance of Objective. So I shall state what my objective was, whilst neither you nor I but God alone shall ultimately judge if I maintained it. My objective was the wholesale conversion of Israel, and of Jerusalem in particular, to the Word-made-flesh. But another principle of war which I can remember is Secrecy, and neither the Jesuits nor my niece who saw me off from London that afternoon near the end of May knew just what my intention was, though one of them who knew me best may somewhat have guessed it and with the deepest misgivings.

After his arrival on the continent, he had to bypass France (all train services having been suspended, due to the 'events' of May 1968) and make his way to Venice. A Greek ship took him from there to Piraeus, from where he travelled to Athens on foot. On seeing the Parthenon, he sat down and wrote from memory the prayer to Pan from the end of Plato's *Phaedrus*, which was quite possibly composed in the same place. Back on the ship he gave it to a fellow passenger, who seemed to him overly preoccupied with terrestrial nourishment.

On the 31st of May, the Friday before Pentecost Sunday, he arrived in Israel, accompanied by a fellow Englishman, Charley who was utterly Anglo-Saxon, a sound and respectable norm. He had soldiered in the Holy Land towards the end of the forties, while Israel was beginning to roar distinctly for Juda and the British were still clinging to the tattered title of Palestine.

> Charley was returning partly, I think, by way of an apology: he wanted to hitch-hike up and down, equipped only with a rucksack (emblazoned with a reasonably diminutive Union Jack) for about a fortnight, and then go back to Blighty. He was a jolly decent fellow with a ready grin and very fair hair and a glowing complexion. His origins were unmistakable, even without the Union Jack. Anyone in a jam would have been ready to take his advice: he breathed out common-sense from every pore. I had chatted with Charley on board quite often, and in a weak moment of over-acquiescence I had agreed with his suggestion that once ashore on Holy Land we should both go forth together. This was quite contrary to my singular plan of solitary campaign; however, both of us having passed through the Customs, we went forward through the street from the docks in an Easterly direction, like the not very remarkable remnant of a forgotten army, a remnant of which at least half was convinced that discretion then and there was the better part. We proceeded in single file: Charley in the lead, his rucksack a close second, and myself in third place (already ungraciously lagging).

The first person they met on shore was a Jewish beggar trying to cadge something from them for resale. Having managed, with some difficulty, to shake off Charley he took the train to Tel Aviv, then the bus to Jerusalem:

During the rallentando of speed between Tel Aviv
and Ramla I had been conversing a bit with an
elderly lady sitting next to me in the bus bound
for Jerusalem. It seemed that her country of origin
had been Turkey. She was a pleasant person: from
time to time she offered me sweets from a bag and I
accepted, although they were not Turkish Delights!
She was of course a Jewess and full of joy to be going
then to Jerusalem. As we entered Ramla (I spent a
night there in prison eighteen years ago but that is
another story) I remarked to the lady, 'Nice place
Ramla!' 'Yes (she replied) but too much Christian!'
I told her that I was a Christian: that was definitely
too much! No more sweets (not that I was hungry
for these); no more conversation either (not that I
was hungry for that).

At four o'clock in the afternoon he arrived in Jerusalem, left his
luggage in the Mount Hertzl youth hostel, and headed for the Wall.
He visited some half-forgotten places he had known in 1950 and
tried singing some Couperin. He then made his way back to Mount
Herzl, 'as the July new moon rose in the sky like a sickle'. He walked
across the city, deserted on the evening of the Sabbath, except for
the stray cats and an occasional car:

The towering floodlit Wall with its huge slabs of
stone, hewn and set in the reign of David at David's
desire, to stand in defiance of every successive
vicissitude, bearing witness to an invincible
endurance: that stupendous, patient Wall, like the
inscrutable face of the God of an unconfounded
choice! There it had stood for nearly three thousand
years; and there I had stood too, for at least five
minutes, gazing astounded at the Wall and at
the praising Jews that faced it at its foot. And I
wondered to myself: dare I bray there tomorrow in
Latin amongst so much solid Hebrew? dare I stand
there seven times and bray aloud?

Finally he went back to the youth hostel on Mount Herzl to sleep. On Saturday John related in *A Wandering* what would happen (the reader may have already guessed it): the implementation of his amazing plan for the conversion of all Israel – or for Israel to recognise its King:

> I spent a morning, as many a pilgrim must, in buying picture-postcards, and writing appropriate remarks upon their backs, and addressing them to friends and relations... Having posted my cards I think I had some lunch. I had decided that my debut at The Wall should not be until after First Vespers of the Feast of Pentecost. These I heard in due course at the principal conventual church of the Franciscans, the Guardians under God Incarnate of the Land by Him made Holy.
>
> Then I went down to The Wall, no longer named The Wailing but The Western, and the time may have been between four and five. I went to the kiosk at the entrance to the sacred area and took a Jewish praying-cap and set it, as do Jews, on the back of my head. The Wall at the time was not thickly thronged and any resolute singer might be then distinctly heard by man, let alone by God whose ears record our inmost thought. With my back to the pagan West I faced The Wall and the graceful East, and I did as Juda does and kissed the Wall, and as Juda does I clutched it from time to time. And I sang the Lamentations of Jeremiah to the exact strains of Couperin, top-blast: Aleph, Beth, Ghimel, Daleth, Hé. When I had concluded with this first singing no one seemed the better and no one seemed the worse. The Western Wall had not shaken; an Eastern, a Southern and a Northern Wall to the whilom temple of Solomon had not arisen; angels invisible had not made to my singing an audible accompaniment upon

harpsichord and viol da gamba, more fully to befit the Great Couperin's Work. But a Rabbi of the Hassedim, with a beautiful countenance, who had stood by my left said, 'Won't you sing something in Hebrew? here is a book'. I replied that I knew no Hebrew and then he smiled and said, 'God will love you for what you have sung, of that I am sure'.

By the sunset of the Day of Pentecost I had sung there Couperin's Lamentations of Jeremy seven times, and things had remained as they stood. There had been some indications of pleasure by Jews, and by one a strong objection. There had also been getting together of heads, and many a curious or suspicious look; but by twilight of Whitsun the game seemed to be over. So I closed an angel-guarded play at the Old Stone Wall, and gazed up at The Plough when the twilight went. It seemed that The Plough was for pointing beyond. The stars all shone so brightly, and it was not very far to Bethlehem. Seven miles maybe? A mile for every twenty minutes which a singing of the Lamentations had taken? I took the road on foot, setting out from the Jaffa Gate of the Old City, and I went with a light enough heart.

John, in a poem written in 1971, tells us that at midnight, as he was completing his chant in front of the Wall with the *Te Deum* of the Office of the Blessed Virgin, a bird (a martin) intervened:

> One martinet flung
> His card to the bard
> And it landed fair
> And square on the book.
> (*Hassedim*, 1971)

Although he was later given a new one as a present, John kept the old one as a souvenir of the episode. But it had become clear to him that his vocation to convert the Jews of Israel had been accomplished, that God had decided the hour had not come to rebuild the Temple, and that John's chosen method was not the best:

> The moral of such a rigmarole might be this: Christ the Perfect Jew who converted eleven disciples and established twelve apostles, all Jews, to convert the world, will alone convert His People Israel to Himself.

Libyan interlude

John made up his mind to return to Africa, and tried to find a boat to take him down the coast to Mombasa or Beira, but geopolitical considerations ruled this out. He was obliged to return to Rome, where a ticket to Salisbury was waiting for him at the Jesuit house. He boarded the Greek merchant vessel *Omega* at Haifa, which dropped him off at Brindisi, after he had, for reasons unknown, a falling out with the crew, and arrived in Rome by train on June 21st. He headed straight for the Jesuit house, only to discover that his plane had already left, and that the next one was in August. Unphased, John decided to visit his brother in Libya. A Jesuit was kind enough to offer him some money, and he immediately left Rome for Naples, intending to board the *Tunisi* the same evening for Tripoli via Malta. But he had no visa and so couldn't buy a ticket. He bought one for Malta instead and set out for Valetta, travelling steerage. After a stop-off in Syracuse, and a poem on Sicily, he arrived in Malta on the 23rd. He succumbed to the magic of the island, and the piety of the men impressed itself on him: they 'have their being in a way / That shows their lives are as they pray' (*Incognizant*, 1968).

After this the *Malcom Pace*, a cargo ship built in the shipyards of Newcastle in 1947, took him to Tripoli, surrounded on deck by a large herd of goats. Philip was now an executive at Mobil Oil, and hadn't seen his brother for a dozen or so years. He was struck by how thin and tired John looked, and his long beard, when he knocked on the door. John told him about his stay in Malta, his long night on his feet waiting for his boat, and the voyage itself, but soon headed for bed. Next day a friend called, and Philip introduced him to his brother; 'Oh, but he looks like an El Greco picture', said the friend. Philip knew that John had disapproved of his marital affairs but, as with others who disappointed him, John had long ago forgiven him, and the two brothers quickly rekindled their childhood camaraderie. They listened to classical music from Philip's extensive collection on an expensive record player. John enjoyed the view of the port from the terrace and felt the resurgence within him of his poetic inspiration.

In the excitement of seeing his brother again, Philip had forgotten to inform the police of his arrival. When he thought about it after a few days, he discovered that John's passport had not been stamped at the port of entry. John explained innocently that he had arrived in the freight section of the port and had passed through without going through the usual formalities while the sanitary inspectors were inspecting the sheep. Philip immediately sent him down to the port, where John's disarming charm soon rectified matters.

On July 3rd, John sent his mother an idyllic report of Philip's life: a motorcycle accident the previous year (some children had stretched an iron cable across the road to see what would happen) was by now a distant memory, and his brother, working hard, fluent in Arabic, a perfect host, was loved by all, Europeans and Arabs alike ('I would not like to use a weaker word than loved'). As for Philip, he was visibly proud of his brother, as original as he was pious, and soon they were showered with invitations. John was happy to turn up in his usual motley, but Philip insisted on buying him a pair of jeans, of which John was so proud that he wore them every day for the rest of his stay. He had the same effect on the people he met as he had on the audience of the Dorothy Sayers play in Salisbury the year before, as if they were in the presence of a new Jesus Christ. One evening at a party a secretary from the company asked Philip if his brother could dance, to which he replied: 'Ask him yourself', which she did, and John accepted. Later she told Philip: 'He can dance, but it was like dancing with Jesus Christ.' Another evening a young American began to mock the Christian faith by quoting from Ambrose Bierce's *Devil's Dictionary*. John rose to the challenge and unravelled the witty arguments of his fellow guest. Those present on the occasion compared his attitude to that of a wise schoolmaster gently but firmly putting a wayward pupil in his place. The American soon made his excuses and left.

John soon tired of the social occasions, especially on reflecting that: 'I like alcohol but it does not like me and wars against my spirit' (as he wrote in August to his mother). Every morning, even after a late-night party, he attended the first Mass of the Franciscans at Tripoli Cathedral (Colonel Gaddafi took it over and turned it into a mosque two years later), and spent a part of his day in the company of the friars.

As always, he was a keen observer of everything around him. To this we owe a poem about the ghibli, the dry wind from the desert, another about the street urchins of the port, several about the muezzins, and one about Ishmael, who also had to turn to the King of Israel – in total about 60 poems written during his stay in Libya. But while Philip who, as vice-consul in Iraq, had followed closely the archeological excavations of Max Mallowan (Agatha Christie's husband), and was interested by the Roman dig in Ghirza, John did not share his interest. On the other hand, he wrote to his mother about his love for the old Arabs he came across in the street, adding: 'How Ishmael needs his brother Israel' and putting him in God's trust. In *A Wandering* he looked forward to the time 'when Israel and Ishmael cease their colliding and come to a glad coalition'.

Once he felt rested, John decided to return to Israel, and had worked out a plan. He would cross the frontiers clandestinely, and once in Israel throw away his passport and work illegally. This led to long arguments with Philip, to whom he had somewhat naively revealed his plans. Philip was understandably hostile to the whole thing, which he saw as a threat to his own career. John had already decided on a date for his departure, even though he had no money. But two days before this he received two unexpected proposals to travel for free across Africa. He regarded this as a providential sign and decided to delay his departure to Israel. In the meantime a letter arrived from his mother and another from John Dove, both of whom, alerted by Philip, urged him to return to Salisbury. The two proposals fell by the wayside, but John abandoned his Israel plan, and soon another sign arrived in the shape of a plane ticket from Father Hall, a confrere of John Dove, to Salisbury via Rome.

Eagles, friendships, and how John came to hear about the lepers of Mtemwa

After one more memorable evening on the terrace, this time listening to Richard Burton reciting Coleridge's *Ancient Mariner* and *Kubla Khan*, John set out for Rome, on September 6th. Smartly shaved, for his long beard had got out of hand, he had resolved that his days of long journeys must come to an end. From now on he would get by on one journey a week, in the pickup truck from Silveira House to Salisbury and back.

When he got to Rome, he discovered he was due to travel to Rhodesia on the same day, just in time to go into town for Mass at St Andrea delle Fratre, drop into St Peter's to say a prayer, go to Borgo Spirito for his plane ticket, and have an experience which is difficult to interpret:

> I wed Maria in Campania
> But did not see her clearly till I came
> From Tripoli in Northern Africa
> And saw her near The Tunnel in a frame
> That was a cover featuring a Belle.
> (*Roma, Italia, Il Mundo*, 1975 – the
> identification of 'The Tunnel' is unclear)

This episode seemed to indicate a new stage in his relationship with the Virgin Mary. She was no longer the Mother, but had become (as Pierre Teilhard de Chardin puts it) the Eternal Feminine, in whom all women are joined, including the most desirable.

His plane flew to Salisbury via Brussels, Nairobi and Johannesburg (the sanctions were beginning to bite: no direct flights to Rhodesia were allowed). During the stop-off at Nairobi, Colin Carr, then a teacher at St Ignatius School, Chishawasha, later to become a Dominican, met John for the first time:

> I saw the back of this – at that time short-haired –
> man with a jacket on; I somehow expected to meet
> a rather hard-faced and not particularly likeable
> man, but when he turned round and I saw this
> beaming, welcoming face, I was immediately
> attracted and delighted.

Colin would later come to visit him, and got into the habit of going to Silveira House to share ideas, where he found John 'making everyone feel welcome, and introducing us to the two enormous Alsatian dogs whom he declared to be Buddhists, they were so peace-loving'. The next day, September 7th, John was happily back in Silveira House, and renewed his resolution no longer to wander on the face of the earth:

> I left Mashonaland for twenty weeks
> And during five whole months my soul asked, Why?
> (*Return to Mashonaland*, 1968)

Father Dove was not yet back, so John was burdened with extra tasks, but he soon resumed his walks, and marvelled at the mysteries of the night sky. He wrote several poems which were exercises in admiration, when for example he discerned and celebrated the Virgin and Child in the full moon. A mongoose had killed a dozen pullets in the hen run, which made John grieve. He redoubled his prayers that the bees would come back. On October 3rd, while walking in the woods around the Centre, he left a cattle trail and suddenly saw an eagle at the summit of a tall tree, probably a Montagu's harrier. He had just spent the day meditating on the Communion Antiphon of the feast of St Teresa of the Child Jesus ('Like an eagle he stretched his wings and seized her and carried her on his shoulders', cf. Deuteronomy 32.10), and told himself that the bird was watching over its lair, which must have been close by. He searched for three days before finding it, as well as a second bird. He often went back, and little by little he gained the trust of the eagles, whom he baptised Tierce and Teresa.

For several weeks he kept a veritable diary of daily observations in verse, noting, a few months after the Encyclical *Humanae Vitae*, which ruffled so many feathers in the Western world:

> I never saw Theresa take the Pill
> And yet am fairly certain that they mate
> Daily because their joie-de-vivre is still
> Fresh as a daisy, and to celebrate

> The fact that proof of fruitful act is now
> Safe in the nest, upon the eyrie hatched
> Amidst the greenwood African.
> (*During this Merry Month*, 1968)

He dated the birthday of the young eagle from the feast of St Luke on October 18th, and recorded daily the development of the family. But he hadn't forgotten his other friends from the animal kingdom. On October 20th he wrote to his mother that Huru had to be tied down:

> Poor Huru has succumbed to fashion
> Of local lady-dogs – is slave of passion
> And now must be enchained nigh all the time.

Also, M'Bebi had just given birth to a litter:

> M'Bebi has produced a further three,
> Of kittens soon she'll make her century!

Chapter 8

Baba John, Father of the Lepers, 1969–1973

I had a horror about leprosy and when I first heard about
the Mtemwa leper colony, I felt unwilling to come here. But
my conscience would not rest and I decided I had to do
something to help. Now I am very happy here. This is my
journey's end.
(*Rhodesia Herald*, 6 September 1979)

Heather Benoy was less than enthusiastic at the idea of setting out
for Mtemwa in her battered Volkswagen, but her friend had insisted
as only he knew how, and so we find them, in mid-March 1969
'on a terrible road headed for a terrible place'. It was John's first
trip to north-eastern Rhodesia. The narrow tarmac road to Mtoko
crosses three rivers – Nyagui, Musami and Nyadiri – through a
rocky landscape of kopjes, which loom ever larger as the miles pass.
It was the end of the rainy season, and green predominated; signs
of European commercial development were everywhere visible,
as well as the fields of maize of the Tribal Trust Lands dotted with
kraals, often hidden from view by the flourishing crops. Halfway
to their destination they passed through Mrewa, the only village of
any size en route, which was the administrative centre of the region
of the same name, from where they caught their first glimpse of
the mountains.

Having crossed the Nyadiri, they entered the Budga country
and soon arrived at its capital Mtoko, 90 miles from Salisbury.
In 1969 it was little more than a village, home to a few hundred
inhabitants, the local administrative centre, a post office, a small
hotel for Whites, a handful of shops, including the drugstore run
by the Kassim brothers, a bus stop for Africans, a hotel for Africans,
a beerhall where aficionados of *chibuku* (a thick strong beer made
from maize) hung out, and a small government hospital.

'I have to stay here!'

The car took a right turn at the hospital along a track which after two miles brought them to Mtemwa. The name itself seemed predestined, meaning as it did in Shona, 'separated, isolated, cut off, sliced off' (it might refer to the shape of Mount Mtemwa, whose plateau seems to have been 'sliced off'). The buildings of the Centre were hidden behind a more modest kopje (500 feet high). The car arrived along an avenue of magnificent jacarandas, and pulled up in front of an unassuming house, from which point could be seen the huts of the lepers standing out in the lush greenery of the rainy season. Though the landscape in the background might have seemed idyllic, what John and Heather discovered there was truly horrendous. The wretched creatures they encountered were repulsive, their faces and limbs deformed by a terrible disease. The lepers were covered in filth and untreated running sores. As John and Heather approached, the sight of the curled up dislocated fingernails of the lepers added to the horror that seized them. More than 30 years later, Heather Benoy was still lost for words to describe the sight that greeted them that day: 'It was just terrible, terrible'.

Worse was to come. Surprised by the arrival of strangers, the lepers retreated to their huts and re-emerged with a sack or a blanket covering their heads. John and Heather witnessed a leper with a sack crawling through mud along the ground on all fours. Stupefied, John demanded to know what was going on, to discover that the lepers were forced to cover up their faces, because they were too ugly to be seen – as ordered by Chaka, the Director of the Centre, a former policeman, and his assistants. Overcome, John's only words were: 'My God! My God.' However, his compassion swiftly turned to anger. Seeing an elderly woman creeping in the mud and licking a bowl on bended knee, he exclaimed that no human being should ever be reduced to such a state and vented his fury on the assistants in charge. Heather Benoy was no less shocked: all those old lepers, as they appeared to her, were being treated as subhuman, and she made a mental note to file a report to the authorities back in Salisbury.

But she was in for another shock. John decided to resort to his usual method of discovering God's will. Taking a coin from his pocket he said a prayer, and tossed the coin in the air: he would stay in Mtemwa. He announced to his companion that he was not leaving. To the young woman, who had been thinking of doing just that, and at the earliest opportunity, he seemed to have suddenly completely lost his reason and, amazed and horrified, she begged him to pull himself together. What was she going to say to Father Dove if she returned alone? Not to mention all the others. She admits that her mind was filled with 'idiotic notions': she was even thinking she would lose a friend! She tried to reason with her companion, using all the arguments that came into her head. It was unthinkable, he just couldn't do this. But he said to her: 'OK, Benoy, damn you for taking me here. You know I have to stay here. I have to stay here. I'm staying.' She could just about persuade John to return with her to Salisbury, where he could gather some belongings, then return to Mtemwa as soon as he wished.

The return journey was difficult. John seemed to be in emotional turmoil: on the one hand he felt called to this work. But at the same time he was afraid, wishing that he had never seen what he had just seen. Back in Silveira House, he immediately sought out John Dove to tell him what he had seen, and of his determination to go back to Mtemwa. His friend recalled his words:

> You know, I don't think that I could be very useful at Mtemwa because I've never been a boy-scout. I don't know anything about medicine, and they are in a very, very poor and serious state. They are dying of neglect. They have been treated appallingly. At any rate, I'm a reject, they are rejects, so I think we will understand each other... And so I go down on that ticket.

His conflicted emotions found expression in a short poem he wrote very soon after his return to Silveira House, on March 17th:

> In that I've always loved to be alone
> I've treated human beings much as lepers,
> For this poetic justice may atone

My way with God's, whose ways are always helpers;
    I did not ever dream that I might go
And dwell amidst a flock of eighty such
    Nor did I scheme towards it ever, No the prospect
        looms not to my liking much;
    Lepers warmly to treat as human beings
        Is easy to the theorist afar,
    Near to my heart from bondage be their freeings,
        May it be flesh not stone, O Morning Star!
    Miriam, shine, sweet Mistress, in thy name
    Salvation wake, lepers make leap, unlame!

This poem (which seems at odds with the 'first wish' – see p. 238) forces us to abandon the oversimplified image of a man taking a decision on the spur of the moment to devote himself to the care of the lepers. The 'theorist' mentioned in the poem, who looks on the lepers from afar and indulges in noble sentiments about helping them, was obviously a self-portrait of John himself – if not of the young boy who listened all those years ago in Skirwith to J. A. Douglas' story of the man who met a leper, then at least of the young man who prayed and dreamt at the grave of Father Damien in Louvain, and read the well-known episode in the life of St Francis. He was now faced with the moment of truth, and his determination acquired greater significance, now strengthened by the belief that it was a call from Christ himself, and the Blessed Virgin herself, who had brought him to Mtemwa.

Father Dove took his friend's decision very seriously and decided to contact Father Ennis. By coincidence, the latter arrived at Silveira House just then to actually ask John if he would like to become the manager of Mtemwa. John saw this as a confirmation of the call he felt he had received, but the notion of managerial responsibility held no appeal for him. He flatly refused it, on the grounds that he had no talent for administration of any kind: his experience as battalion Adjutant at Dehra Dun had already convinced him of this, and he had no desire to repeat it. Many discussions were to follow before he was persuaded to accept.

Father Ennis spoke to Philip Dighton, Chairman of the Friends of Mtemwa, who immediately wrote to Shirley James that she must meet John Bradburne, a 'remarkable man'. He himself paid a visit to John, and outlined for him all the tasks involved in his new job: managing accounts, supervising the assistants, site administration, overseeing medical care, keeping track of food donations, and all other matters pertaining to the efficient running of the Centre. On hearing his job description, John was more than reticent but, feeling that he had received a call, he accepted. Dighton spelt out the terms of his employment contract: a monthly salary of £20, to be lodged in a bank account in John's name, and one of the assistants as his personal helper to be paid by the Lions Club of Mtoko. John insisted that he intended to live in a hut like the lepers, but Dighton would not hear of it and forbade it, writing to Shirley James to the effect that it was unbecoming for a gentleman, who ought to enjoy a minimum of comfort that the committee should provide. A decision was then taken that the old butchery beside the ration shop would be fitted out with a bathroom, hot water, toilet and shower.

While preparing his departure for Mtemwa, John continued to fret about his poems. He had become a regular contributor to *Two Tone*, who published two poems in its first number of 1969 (this time misspelling his name as Bradburn). On April 28th, he received a rejection slip for a sheaf of poems he had submitted, but asking for more because 'Dear John, We enjoy your vigour and hope you will send us more recent work.' John immediately replied with a letter in verse, slyly hinting at the misspelling of his name, describing himself as 'scarcely modern but a bard'. But *Two Tone* struck a more politic note, and chose only one poem, which was finally published in 1972.

Whether it was the prospect of his departure for Mtemwa, or the discovery that Pep Muspratt-Williams, the brother-in-law of John Dove and the same age as both of them, was dying of cancer, John seemed to sense suddenly his own mortality. In April, he copied out a prayer from Teilhard de Chardin's *The Divine Milieu* on growing old and sent it to Pep (who died two months later). He included a poem about the bees, who had returned to his room (he had prayed for their return, to which he had contributed somewhat by leaving a bowl of syrup on the table):

> A swarm of bees has come
> Into my cell; I feel the time is ripe
> For proving faith myself amidst this hum!
> There must be fifty thousand bees at hand
> And they are settling down inside a hive
> Two feet from where I'm typing this.

During May, the bees continued to invade and buzz around his room in a benevolent fashion, creating a smell of honey everywhere, which made him write to his mother that 'it seems my mission is to bees only, to tell them that we men want to forget their stings and our own fear and avarice (which gives us guilty consciences) and to bee friends with bees and the rest of creation', with no mention of his own private 'bee mission' in Mtemwa. On the 4th, he was pleasantly surprised by the visit of a former colleague at Burns & Oates in London:

> His name is Ted Duggan, vocation he tried
> At Prinknash not long before me,
> Apart from the Church he's made search for no bride.
> (*Cantate Domino canticum novum*)

Ted brought with him the gift of a recorder, and they drank and sang together late into the night.

The same month saw the publication of the regime's White Paper institutionalising racial discrimination in Rhodesia, in which the demarcation lines between European and African zones became more rigid. The implications for the Churches were all the more serious in that Christianity was spreading mainly through the bush schools, which were now under threat. On June 5th, they launched *An Appeal to Christians,* stating that 'it will be extremely difficult for us effectively to counsel moderation to a people who have been so patient for so long under discriminatory laws and are now presented with such extreme provocation' (see *The Tablet,* 21 June 1969). But the majority of Europeans supported the regime and distanced themselves from the missionaries. This was the beginning of expulsions and non-renewals of visas for missionaries, and opinion was divided in the Catholic Church itself, marked by sharp disagreements.

The new constitution was ratified in June by 72 per cent of the electorate, all Europeans. It stipulated that the number of seats allotted to Africans in Parliament could never exceed 50 per cent, thus guaranteeing White power in perpetuity. On October 14th total arable lands were divided in half between Africans and Europeans (respectively approximately 95 per cent and 5 per cent of the population). The Europeans held on to the best lands and indeed increased their holdings. Land which up to then could be bought by Africans disappeared. Furthermore the legislation forbade them to reside in European zones, unless they were employed there. Rhodesia became a Republic and severed its remaining ties with Britain. Even though only Portugal and South Africa recognised this new status, Ian Smith could congratulate himself on having gambled and won: his paradise for Whites had survived decolonisation.

At the beginning of June, one of John's links with Silveira House was coming to an end: Simba was dying. An undetected parasite in his tail had spread, leading him to contract the mange. One day he disappeared into the bush to die. His master buried him beside Haggai:

> So the odd dog died and the long long grass
> Sighed, 'Lay him away by the pine
> Where eagle lies buried while over her pass
> Her peers that her presence divine'.
> There lies like a lion at rest in the shade
> Of the pines as they sigh like the sea
> Old Simba the strong: there's a song in the glade,
> 'Je ne meurs pas, j'entre dans la vie'.
> (*The Passing of Simba*. The last line is a quote from St
> Thérèse of Liseux: 'I do not die, I enter into life')

As if to compensate for this loss, the bees became even more numerous in his room. One day in July, Colin Carr was alone at St Ignatius' when a swarm of bees ventured into the dormitories of the college, and with the help of a colleague he cautiously set about expelling them.

A few days later he went to say goodbye to John, who was preparing to leave for Mtemwa, while he himself was heading home to Britain. He knocked on the door and entered, to be greeted with a grunt by his friend, busy writing at his table. Having sat down on the bench he suddenly became aware that there were other inhabitants in the room! His host explained to him that the bees were his guests, adding, good disciple that he was of Brother Adam of Buckfast, that they would be nice to him if he was nice to them. Carr noticed an upturned shoebrush on the windowsill, and was calmly told that it was 'for them to wipe their feet on as they went in and out through the window'. Asked if he had ever been stung John replied that 'when they were killing off the drones they got a bit excited, and he got the odd sting, but he didn't seem to think that was a big deal'. His friend said goodbye, and it later occurred to him that he had experienced a sort of miracle: he had not felt the least fear in the presence of the bees: 'I had been at least temporarily a resident in the peaceable kingdom where the wolf lies down'.

Director of Mtemwa Centre

The renovation work on the old butchery was completed on July 31st, and the next day, in the middle of a Southern African winter, Fathers Ennis and Dove drove John to Mtemwa, his belongings, such as they were, contained in his Gladstone bag: a few clothes, a sleeping bag, his recorder, a record player, and some records. On arrival they headed straight for the chapel, consecrated by Bishop Chichester many years before. Little more than a hut, and in a pitiful state, Mass had not been celebrated there for many years. The windows and their frames were broken, birds had taken over, and their abundant traces were everywhere in evidence. John decided on the spot to clean it up, noticing that wisps of straw were decorating the picture of the Sacred Heart nailed to the wall. Lifting it up he discovered a yard-long snake in hibernation, which he proceeded to kill with the broomstick he happened to be carrying. A few weeks later he came across another snake there, and in a letter to his mother (25 September) he remarked that he felt confident, as 'Our Lady keeps the snake beneath her feet'. He would later develop the habit of coming here to pray, with the Missal given to him by John Dove eight years before when he was leaving England, but the chapel was in too bad a state for Mass to be celebrated at that point.

John settled in with his luggage in the renovated butchery. As in Silveira House, the furnishings were sparse: a bed with a mosquito net, a table for his typewriter, a chair, and a basket for carrying things to and from the Centre. To put his own mark on the place, he hung a few photos on the wall. After a quick tour of the Centre, the two Jesuits set out on their return journey to Salisbury, leaving John to his own devices. He had been granted the grand title of Director of the Centre (Warden of the Leper Settlement, according to John Dove; Camp Superintendent according to John's letter written end of August to his mother) with full responsibility for its running, except for strictly medical matters. He was also charged with overseeing both administrative and disciplinary duties, with the back-up of three assistants: Phineas and Solomon, two Shonas, and Amos from Malawi.

He soon became aware of the extent of the fraud carried out by Chaka, the former Director of the Centre. The assistants were hardly innocent of negligence or embezzlement, but John decided to establish good relations with them, which hardly presented a problem, given that he would be doing most of the work himself from the word go. A quick overview revealed the extent of the neglect and decay into which the Centre had fallen. The whole site was reliant on only six taps for its water supply, the huts were covered in dried straw, and when the temperature dropped the lepers lit fires to keep warm despite being forbidden to do so, and accidents were frequent and sometimes fatal. They were often hungry, dependent on a small ration of corn flour to make sadza. The sanitary facilities were deplorable. Apart from various illnesses aggravated by the negligence of Chaka and his assistants, and malnutrition brought on by pilfering of food supplies, disease was endemic: malaria, bilharzia and hook-worm, all leading to anaemia and gastroenteritis. It was necessary to start from scratch, though most of the medical files had gone missing, and medical care was hit and miss, which would lead to problems down the line.

On the first day, he introduced himself to the 78 lepers who made up the colony, and explained to them that he would be sharing their lives. He asked them not to put a bag or a blanket over their heads when talking to him or the assistants, but realised from their reactions that they would have to be gradually encouraged. Over the years they had become used to being treated as animals, and were fearful and withdrawn. As he later wrote in *Concerning Mtemwa* (1975), he realised the degree to which they had been dehumanised, 'both dragooned and despised'. But his obvious joy to be with them sparked a glimmer of hope in more than one heart. One of these was Coleta Mapfuta, the daughter of two lepers, who had herself contracted the disease at ten years of age and had lost her fingers and was suffering from eye problems. A widow, she had married at a young age; her husband had contracted the disease and died leaving her with seven children, who themselves were not lepers. She remembered the day when John arrived at Mtemwa: 'He was greeting us, he was very happy. He had come to look after us and he hugged us like a brother.' But others were sceptical: 'What does this white man want?' And a few, like Luka Takawira, wondered whether the *chirungu* ('white man') had 'gone out of his head'.

The weekend after John's arrival, John Dove paid a return visit, and celebrated Mass for the lepers who wished to attend, near the former butchery. John had still not written to his mother since starting work at the Centre, afraid no doubt of causing her anxiety. After a second visit to the Centre, John Dove took it upon himself to write to Mrs Bradburne, telling her how moved he had been by the fervour of the lepers and by the flame he had felt in John: 'He now has a flock of his own', with real responsibilities, and he no longer had to be told what to do. He already knew by heart the names of his 78 charges (soon to increase), and could recognise each one after two weeks. To reassure Mrs Bradburne, John Dove added that there were two hospitals nearby, and pointed out that his Superior held ultimate responsibility for Mtemwa, adding that her son had felt a 'greater call', and that he himself was missing John.

In his first letter to his mother from Mtemwa, written two days later, John outlined his tasks at the Centre: keeping an eye on food supplies and the number of rations, bandaging the lepers, healing their bruises, handing out pills. He was careful to point out that medical matters were outside his remit, because

> Italian Sisters three and also one
> Doctor Italian (sent by the Pope
> All four) visit twice weekly.

He was referring of course to Caterina Savini and her companions. John soon paid them a return visit. All Souls Mission, located about 12 miles from Mtoko, and the same distance from Mtemwa, was overlooked by a craggy, jagged rock 500 feet high. The climate there was harsh: hot, dry summers, and infested with mosquitoes. The large Mission church was striking, with its mural frescos painted by Italian prisoners-of-war – already, alas, damaged by rainwater infiltration. The Mission included living quarters, a hospital, an orphanage, a primary school and a small secondary school. Between 1956 and 1959 it had received a boost from the presence of Father Rubio, a Spaniard, and the number of adult baptisms had risen. However, Father Rubio's tolerance of polygamy led to his being moved on. He was replaced by one of the first Shona priests, Father Simon Tsuro, and then another African, Father Patrick Chakaipa, helped by an English Jesuit.

Wondrous as Heaven

For John, his early days at Mtemwa were one of the happiest periods of his life. He experienced great joy on his first ascent of Chigona (the kopje that overlooked Mtemwa) with its panorama of the surrounding hills: Chiwore, Chidamwoyo, Murenje and – the highest – Mtemwa, with its green tree-dotted plateau; the dam, the kraals; and far in the background to the south, the tall range of Iyangani. Here his love of vast horizons, seen from the tree-tops, the spires and the fells of his childhood, and later at Silveira House, found their counterpart. Here he could give himself over to contemplation, as noticed by Father Webster, one of his visitors:

> He had a great ability to marvel at beauty wherever
> he saw it in people, in the young, the old, in
> animals... a capacity to be 'still' and admire that

beauty. This is very important today when the
emphasis is on thrills, not to marvel at beauty.

His days at Mtemwa kept John busy. In a verse letter to his mother,
dated August 29th, he speaks of 'five full hours' being left to sleep,
eat, pray, and if possible some contemplation or leisure. Apart from
that...

> Work's hours for most of men are fully eight
> And many, when their day is at an end,
> Are met by kids agog at garden-gate
> Whence, willy-nilly, with their joys they blend;
> But this neurotic ass, this nervous wreck,
> This having-idled-eight-and-forty-years
> Goes home to utter peace from call and beck
> Of gentle failing folk in vale of tears
> Whereto I needs must add: wondrous as Heaven.
> (*Nocturne*, 1969)

From September on he gradually won the heart of the lepers, and
a new sense of joie-de-vivre struck visitors to the Centre. The signs
were many: the photo with Father Ennis, with a boyish John looking
ten years younger; the Laws, who recollect hearing him singing all
the time; or in John's own words, often repeated, that at Mtemwa,
'I'm very happy here. This is my journey's end.' He was very aware
that his happiness shone on the lepers, that he had become, as he
wrote to John Dove, 'eyes for the blind, ears for the deaf, fingers and
feet for the maimed', adding, 'Gosh! It is good for them to have me,
it is bad enough having leprosy without having John.'
    That September, he began a cycle of poems entitled *A Jumbly
Alphabet*, in which each leper is invoked by name in a poem
containing personal details. But suffering and death were never far
from the Centre. On August 16th Jacob Foro, the only Matabele,
always cheerful and beloved of all, died. John was deeply moved, but
at a loss as to what to do. On the 22nd he received an urgent call:
Solomon, a Methodist nicknamed Panzeh ('Outside!') was dying.
John immediately went to see him, and spoke to him about God.
Suddenly Solomon asked to be baptised into the Catholic faith. John
didn't think it was necessary, but granted the dying man's request:

... Solomon was [a Methodist]
Until he roamed to Catholic that day because
He asked to enter where he scented then to be
Truth at the height O mighty Pan! (baptised by me).
(*At Lauds,* 1971)

Solomon had only ten hours to live, and John stayed with him to
the end, witnessing a strange and profound peace on the face of
the dying leper. He decided to bury him himself in the graveyard
of the Centre, in the presence of his fellow lepers, according to the
Christian rite (he was never interested in the traditional Shona
kurova gura rites, which were later officially incorporated into
Catholic liturgy).

One Friday towards the end of August, John, in Mtoko to do
some shopping, ventured into a bar, where he met a white farmer,
who was intrigued by this stranger in a town where everybody
knew everybody else. Although coming from two families of old
Southern African colonial stock, Don Purdon had started out with
nothing, and made himself into a prosperous farmer by sheer hard
work. The two men spoke and discovered a shared passion for
animals, especially birds. John continued to come to Mtoko on
Friday evenings to meet up with his new friend, who introduced
him to other farmers. Whether or not the latter approved of the
presence in their midst of a European dedicated to the service of
the lepers (in obvious contradiction with the ideology of the UDI
regime, and in the name of the same Christianity which the regime
claimed to be upholding), they were impressed by the dedication
of the new director of the Mtemwa Centre.

Don Purdon and others soon visited him. At the beginning most
of them were repelled by the sight of the lepers, and betrayed their
discomfort throughout the visit. Some however got used to it and
came back. John's closeness to the lepers effectively ignored the
racial gap that was widening in the country at the time. Moreover
since arriving in Africa he had always lived in mixed communities,
in effect the only ones that existed: the Mission centres. The racism
euphemistically called 'separate development' was repugnant to
him. In a satirical poem in 1970 called *Of Dignity*, inspired by
the title of a prose poem by Baudelaire which had stuck in his

mind – 'Assommons les pauvres' ('Let's kill off the poor') – he openly criticised the insistence of the European Rhodesians that the Africans call them Boss, as an assault on their human dignity. Most Europeans, starting with administrators or policemen, felt obliged, consciously or otherwise, to 'behave as Europeans' towards Africans, and hide behind this facade. John refused to do this, and consequently created unease among those who despised and feared the African. The fact that he was a true-blue Englishman would have made them even more uneasy.

Philip Dighton visited Mtemwa almost every week. The two men shared their ideas and plans for the future of the Centre, and John found in Dighton a willing listener. He later wrote (in *Concerning Mtemwa*, 1975):

> Our relations were harmonious, our ideas on the running of the place tallied, and he congratulated me, almost weekly and ad nauseam, well-meant though it was, on having transformed Mtemwa into a happy village. This was all of course relative: after the regime of the five years preceding, any ass might have stood for a halo.

The medical team from All Souls also attended the Centre on a weekly basis, tending to the needs of the lepers, and giving instructions on bandaging and daily medication. John was supposed to share the workload with the assistants, but in effect carried out most of the tasks himself. Illnesses as such, whether leprous or not, did not interest him, only the man or woman who suffered. Furthermore, he had little understanding of the strictly medical side of things, and his attitude towards the distribution of medication was a hit-and-miss affair. He often increased the prescribed dose with the best intentions in the world, which created its own problems later on. Fortunately Luisa Guidotti, the newly appointed doctor to All Souls Misssion, soon became aware of his shortcomings in this area, and established essential procedures and protocols for him to follow.

John had already been installed at Mtemwa for four months when a car arrived from the Mission with a new passenger, a short stocky young woman with tied-back hair and severe features. She was the new doctor from the Mission whom he had already glimpsed at Silveira House, and from now on she would attend at Mtemwa twice weekly, even when the Mission hospital became overcrowded during the rainy season with up to 150 patients a day. Luisa Guidotti, for it was she, was accompanied by Caterina Savini and Maria Greco, and they supplied medical care free of charge, the Centre paying only for bandages and medical supplies. She started investigating the pathologies related to leprosy, in order to deal with them better: she identified at least 42, and set about systematically tracking them down.

This time she and John struck up a bond, and became as if they had always been friends; she was as heavily built as he was emaciated, but they shared a keen sense of humour, the same horror of pretence, always at the disposal of their charges as if time didn't exist, the same stubborn streak, and above all the same love of God and compassion for the afflicted, in line with the motto of the AFMM (Associazione Feminima Medicale Missionaria): 'To serve man and especially the poor and the sick'. In this case it meant working for the sake of the lepers themselves and not for the sake of protecting the European population from the spread of infectious diseases, which was the policy of the health authorities in place at the time. John developed total confidence in Luisa, and from that time on preferred to await her arrival at the Centre to deal with serious cases, rather than refer them to the government hospital in Mtoko, where lepers were less than welcome, and where the nurses would feed them scraps and keep them isolated from other patients.

Busy days

We can get an idea of John's daily routine from a letter he wrote to his mother on July 29th, which can be filled out from other correspondence and poems, and which will remain constant over the years (as he was writing to his mother, he was maybe somewhat idealising his diet and lengthening his sleeping hours) :

> For a day or so I will keep for you a little diary and you shall see a bit about the life of this 'Camp Superintendent'.

1.30 a.m. Waked (by my angel personally) for the singing of Our Lady's Mattins and Lauds. Sing these and go to back again and sleep from 2.30 a.m. until 5.45 a.m. Get up and wash and sing Prime of Our Lady. Then boil kettle on excellent, Calor Gas cooker and make pot of tea and drink my morning quart. (Lots of sugar, lots of tea leaves, plenty of Skimmed Milk Powder milk.) Sweep room and make bed.

By 7.30 a.m. I have sung Sext of Our Lady too – the day will be quite long and so one gets ahead with the Office. Then open the Ration Store (quite near my room – there are three narrow rooms detached from my house, erstwhile butchery, and they were built and long used as lock-ups for transgressors in the way! I prepare for issuing fourteen days rations of Mealie Meal, beans, nuts, salt, soap, skimmed milk powder) for 76 people. (The 77th died last Sunday evening and was buried on Monday afternoon. Jacob Foto, known as Dick, our only Matabele – blind absolutely – a lovely cheerful soul and everyone here loved him.)

8 a.m. My troops of three Orderlies – Phineas, Solomon and Amos – (two Shona, one from Malawi) arrive and report for duty as usual. We load the rations on two wheel-barrows and a wheel-chair, and they are taken to the Compound and the people – about 100 yards away from chez-moi, down the long jacaranda Avenue. A glorious leper called Joshua has already blown his bugle to call folk together to the Ration Assembly Place (those who can walk). Joshua is valiant and keeps Muscovy ducks. His legs come only so far as his knees.

8.30 a.m. 'Camp Superintendent' goes to the medicine hut in middle of the 80 huts (little square huts with glassless window and tin roof). He greets each person he may pass then or thereabouts until mid-day. He gives out special pills to special cases as directed by the Doctor (Italian Luisa Guidotti) on her last visit three days ago. (The Italian medical missionaries come twice a week – Dr Guidotti, Sister Caterina Savini and two others. They are absolutely dedicated souls, and a great help to me.) He does also dressings and bandagings of various wounds and sores. Gives pills also for coughs and headaches to those who come to the medicine hut. The people have their morning-meal between 10 and 11 a.m. 56 can cook for themselves. 20 are cooked for by two Shona ladies in a near-by kitchen of severest simplicity.

12.15 a.m. 'The Camp Superintendent' opens his thermos flask for a pint and a half of sweet tea and heats up and eats a whole one pound tin of braised steak and vegetables with much satisfaction. So do not worry about vitamins or diet any more. Upon this Gargantuan repast a goodly measure of raisins follows. Wherefore, be Raisinable and do not worry. Needless to say it was The Dove (Thurston) who supplied these delicacies when he visited here first, and my stock is still in grand fettle. As the Raven brought food to Elias, so The Dove brings food to me. Benedicamus Domine. Never felt better in my life.

12.45 a.m. I shall now try to mend the rosary of a chap with one wooden leg called Stephano.

1.15 p.m. Stephano's rosary is mended to the best of my ability. Now (since here one never knows what may happen next) I will sing Vespers, and be ahead with Our Lady. For instance, last Friday at midnight one of our holiest old men died, and was buried on Saturday last. A staunch Methodist but, at 2.30 p.m. on the Friday, I baptised him into Rome at his own request. A long agony of ten hours then for him, but he wore the deepest, strangest expression of peace on his face, which was witnessed after his passing. The name is Solomon Panze.

1.45 p.m. Now I am going to our rather ruined little church to do a sweep for Sunday. The little church, built for the R.C.s here, (they represent about one-third of the village) built I should say fifteen or even twenty years ago – has a sound roof of corrugated iron and timber, good walls of local home-made mellow brick, windows from which the glass has been stolen or broken, some statues, an altar with a simple little open tabernacle, Stations of the Cross, some Holy Pictures in poor condition. Birds roost in the church and leave their cards in abundance. The floor is good and of smooth concrete. The door is on its hinges still. Mass has not been said here for ages. The monthly Mass and the Mass of Thurston, are said in the hall near the butchery, but I want to see our little church in use again: the Blessed Sacrament in it. There is talk of making me a deacon so that I can administer Holy Communion. No one remembers to whom the little church is dedicated. When I first swept it out a month ago I noticed straw and sticks obtruding from the cardboard backing of a picture of the Sacred Heart. I took the picture down to dust it and to remove the bric-a-brac – a snake about three feet long came out of it – it was hibernating there! It was easy for me to kill it with the broom handle. Earlier that afternoon I had killed a puff adder with someone's crutch and had broken the crutch in the process! That was quickly replaced, however.

2 p.m. Phone District Commissioner about Orderlies' monthly pay. Dragoon my platoon of three for Afternoon duties.

2.15 p.m. Saunter down to Compound with a wheelbarrow and pick up bits of broken glass and odd jagged tins and pots from along the side of the Jacaranda Avenue which borders the Compound. Absence of these, when they have all been cleared up by degrees, should reduce our leg and foot stump wounds greatly. A leper called Simon sees me doing this and hastens gaily to help me.

3 p.m. Open medicine-hut again and do dressings, pills, etc. until 4 p.m. or so. Soon the kitchen cart (two wheels and pushed by Gertrude) comes with food for the evening meal of those who cannot cook for themselves. Of these 20 there is an old lady (called Marchareeda or Matilda) who has no eyes and no hands, and has until this month been feeding herself with her face in her plate much as an animal might. She cannot use a spoon. Of the food she was given, dogs and hens used to steal at least half, and a quarter further would be either spilled or smeared over her face and dress. So now I either feed her myself with a spoon, slowly, or if I am too busy with medical matters, I get one of the orderlies to do it. It is great fun feeding her and she thoroughly enjoys it. When she had been fed this evening (3.30 p.m.) she said she was worried that a thief might steal her belongings from her card-board box in the night! I calmed her fears (I hope) by telling her to ask her Guardian Angel to keep a special watch upon the box. I feel sure that he will do that and that she has asked him to. She never begins her meals without saying grace. Who else would have remembered in her circumstances down the years till now?

316 John Bradburne: Vagabond of God

5 p.m. About that time I returned home pushing the Wheel Chair which I chain up on my little verandah at night in case it runs away. Then Compline, and a Rosary. Then supper and then this continuation of this terrible scrawl by the light of two candles. By 8 p.m. I shall be in bed and probably asleep! A very happy day. Shalom!

(Next day was Sunday, which brought some differences.)

7 a.m. John picks flowers which he places in the church.

7. 45 a.m. John meets Solomon, tells him to take Francesca (a very Franciscan lady with no feet) to the church in the wheel-chair (Solomon is truly wise and I like him best of my Army of Three).

8 a.m. Go to the Compound (the church is 150 yards due East of it) and am told by Joshua (the half-legged bugler) that Emilia Duo Darwin (who has been having special pills lately) is extra ill this morning. I find her on the floor of her hut very resigned, but very disconsolate, and I give her pills and re-make her bed and and put her to bed and tuck her up and tell Solomon (who has just arrived on the scene) to keep an eye on her today. (He is on duty this Sunday until 4 p.m.)

8.15 a.m. Return to church for Sunday Service which includes lots of hymns and lots of prayers from the Canon of the Mass and from the Prayer of the Day. Also the Epistle and Gospel ('Seek ye first...'), and a sermon, all read and done by another Stephano – a very holy man with no fingers; One wooden leg, a wasted other leg, no toes and an angelic countenance — he radiates the peace and still joy of God. The Sunday morning service lasted an hour and a half at least! The countryside and the weather are absolutely beautiful. I love this place. 'I would not change my place and situation For any range of any clime or nation'.

10.45 a.m. Return to Compound, open Medicine store, go round with essential special medicines.

11.30 a.m. Return to my Cell – grasp the Bread Basket; and the mosquito pills (Chloroquine to everyone, twice weekly) and go with bread and pills to Joshua's house and he sounds his bugle for everyone to come and take a piece of bread and a mosquito pill. Then I am told that a totally blind man called Charley is extra-ill today and I go to his hut and find him groping his way out of the door. So I give him two aspirins, put him to bed and instruct a neighbour of his called Mattheo Barone to keep an eye on him and ask his (Mattheo's) wife, Elizabetha, to cook Charles some food of a warm kind if he wants it and to warm him up some powdered milk.

Prayer, service, welcome

John continued to follow this programme, enriching it over the years. He soon got into the habit of climbing Chigona at dawn to pray. During the rainy season this could be hazardous and slippery, and he discovered from experience that 'Thy granite it is hard' (*Jocundly for Joachim,* 1973). Two of the important places in his life were at the top of the kopje: one of his oratories, and his 'swimming pool'. The former, decorated by brown, red and green lichens, hardly noticeable, served as his 'path of prayer', where he would walk around saying the rosary; the other, though shallow, filled with water during the rainy season and for a time afterwards, where he swam, sometimes with friends.

During his rounds John would change bandages and dress wounds wherever necessary, and distribute medication to those in need. He washed those unable to care for themselves, with a smile, a pleasantry, a kind word. This is not to suggest that he took it all in his stride. According to Father John Gough, a Jesuit from Salisbury who for a while visited Mtemwa once a month:

> I've sat with him and talked with him when he
> has been with the people who were suffering from
> leprosy. And he was just as unwilling as the rest
> of us. It is not a nice disease and yet John totally
> gave himself to these people. I stayed at the side of
> a bath where he was washing an old man. I don't
> think you would like that sort of thing but it has
> to be done, and John had to do it.

Neither could Father Dove hide his revulsion the first time he discovered Mai Francisca drenched in a bed that she had been soiling for two days. But he too got used to it.

John thus followed in the footsteps of Francis of Assisi, who reminds us in the first line of his Testament that he felt bitter at the sight of lepers but that 'when the Lord brought me among them my heart went out to them'. John's desire to identify with the lepers, which he had felt from the beginning of his time at Mtemwa, deepened, so much so that he often prayed that he would contract their disease, like Father Damien. He became closer to them, with no thought of hygiene. However, when his friends became aware of this they persuaded him of its folly, reminding him that if he caught leprosy he would immediately be removed to the European hospital and would be obliged to abandon Mtemwa. John accepted the wisdom of this, but continued to be in contact with his charges with minimum precautions. His personal enemy was less leprosy than the mosquito, that miniscule vampire that plagued him at night:

> A loathsome floating whining thing of blood
> Which never is its own, a vile banshee.
> (*Mosquito*, 1970)

It was the only creature from the animal kingdom, apart from snakes, with whom friendship was not possible.

From the beginning of his time at the Centre, John received unexpected gifts. One day he was delightfully surprised to see visitors arrive with a harmonium, a gift from the parishioners of Braeside in Salisbury, who had just acquired an organ. He stored it in the old butchery, pending a solution for the chapel, and invited the lepers to come and see it, telling them it was a present for them more than him. From now on he was able to give choir lessons, and soon decided to form a choir. Music continued to play an important role in John's life, whether in the Offices and communal prayer, or on his own playing the recorder (or later the organ); or yet again when he joined his friends the Laws for a picnic at the dam; or when he sang out loud the office in Latin while Kit painted. His tastes never changed: above all Bach, Pachelbel and the old English masters.

On October 26th he was surprised by the arrival of another present, more utilitarian this time, a refrigerator, which inspired a poem. Meanwhile the pupils from the school at Blakiston decided to collect money to buy a donkey and cart for the Centre. The idea came from their teacher Heather Benoy, who was upset to see her friend struggling to push overloaded wheelbarrows around the Centre, or returning from Mtoko to the Centre pushing a wheelbarrow with fresh supplies after shopping trips. Enough money was collected to buy the cart, but the donkey never materialised. John took its place, thus enabling him at last to claim membership of that exalted species.

As Christmas 1969 approached, friends began to wonder about suitable presents to buy for the lepers. The Laws sent 83 cardboard picnic boxes wrapped in brightly coloured paper, and got the pupils of Kit and her colleague Mary Scrase to write Christmas cards. In each picnic box they put a pound of nuts, biscuits, sweets, toys offered by pupils when there were children, snuff and a Christmas candle. John Dove was also on hand to make his contribution. From the beginning of November the nuns at Silveira House and other convents in Salisbury recycled and repaired old clothes for the lepers.

Shortly before Christmas, John Dove arrived at Mtemwa driving a truck loaded with presents. He had been due at eleven in the morning, but because of heavy rains arrived five hours late, to be greeted by eagerly awaiting lepers, soaked to the skin. Presents were distributed, and received with cries of delight, even though the picnic boxes had been damaged by the rain. Father Dove celebrated Christmas Mass, after which the two friends did the rounds of the Centre. Alone finally in the butchery, the Jesuit produced a few presents which he had kept in reserve: wine, chicken, Christmas pudding and half a box of chocolates. John hungrily partook of the fare.

His friend had also brought along a bottle of brandy (a local Rhodesian confection distilled from imported South African wine). The old banter started up: 'Like a vodka?' 'Yes, I'd love one.' 'Haven't got any.' 'Did you bring any brandy?' 'Yes I did!' 'Don't tell Stephano. No doubt he'll sniff it out. I'll give him some anyway.' The brandy was produced, and a glass or two drunk, but John would give most of it to Stephano, because a gurgling throat had already announced his arrival at the door, jumping excitedly up and down and demanding his brandy according to a well-established rite. That evening John left with his friend to spend Christmas at Silveira House. As he was in the habit of doing, on his rare trips to Salisbury, he visited the Laws, where he enjoyed a good meal and a hot shower. He was their prodigal son, and their different religious persuasions cast no shadow between them. When he got back to Mtemwa he organised a grand party, which continued long into the night.

John had little by little constructed himself an 'Ark', which was hitherto to play an important role in his life. It is not clear where his inspiration came from: perhaps from the dilapidated condition of the chapel, or his desire to give a place of honour to God's Word, or to manifest his devotion to the Virgin Mary? He put together an installation consisting of a low table and a wooden chest covered by a cloth, on which he pinned pictures, and variously coloured ribbons of the kind he tied on his recorder, and a place in the centre for a copy of the Bible. The symbolism was obvious: the Ark of the First Covenant, and the Virgin Mary, the new one who gave birth to the Word of God. Over the years John never ceased to work on his Ark; adding, taking away, modifying volumes, ribbons, pictures and images. He placed on it new pictures, postcards and any objects which would turn his attention to God and the Virgin Mary.

Like many poets he was a 'seer' for whom sight was a source of inspiration both religious and poetic. For him everything was a symbol in the strong sense of the term, both a support and a concrete expression of his relationship to God and the Virgin Mary – even if sometimes the symbolic force which he gave to an image or an object allowed him to lose sight of its original meaning (as in the picture of a flamenco dancer pinned to the wall of his hut which he called Our Lady of Spain, or a pin-up girl baptised Notre Dame de Paris, which shocked more than one visitor). John liked to show off his Ark, to talk about it, and invite people to say a prayer in front of it. He was also its fierce defender: in the course of a visit, 'Père Peachon' (the French Jesuit Roland Pichon) made the mistake of casually leaning against the Ark, and was roundly reprimanded by his host. The Jesuit retorted: 'What's wrong? C'est une idole [It's an idol].' John said nothing in reply, but his silence made his displeasure apparent.

At the beginning of 1970 the UDI regime was still holding its own, although a ZAPU commando attacked a South African police camp near Victoria Falls, and in March another launched a rocket attack on Kariba airport. In April the Rhodesian Front yet again won all the seats in parliament. The return to power in Britain of the Conservatives under Edward Heath led to the reopening of negotiations with the former colonial power on the basis of the Constitution of 1969, ending in victory for Ian Smith. But the Catholic Church did not remain silent. The Irish bishop of Umtali, Donal Lamont, publicly denounced the regime, declaring that 'the real terrorists in this court are the people who framed the new Constitution', alluding at the same time to the struggle of Titus Brandsma against the Nazi regime (see *The Tablet*, 14 March 1970). On March 31st John gave poetic expression to what he considered the role of Mtemwa:

> Politically here our part is least,
> Clearly Mutemwa is at heart a priest
> That, being freed from prejudice and pride
> May plead against Rhodesian suicide.
> Our local preachers, upright on their stumps
> (Solomon wise and Joshua who trumps
> To victuals with his bugle) thump and say
> Just what they do: how good it is to pray.
> (*Status Quo*, 1970)

By this time John was settled in the old butchery, and in March he was delighted to see that 'This day bees landed on the moon', referring to the photo of the moon he had pinned to a box. He noted (in *Heyday beedom*) that they were everywhere in Mtemwa, especially in the eucalyptus trees.

At the end of April / beginning of May 1970 John paid a rare visit to Jasper and Gertrude Savanhu on the banks of the Mazoe. Jasper, a trade union leader, had become in 1959 one of the first Africans appointed to a position of political responsibility as parliamentary secretary to the Federal Government, from which position he had resigned in 1962. John was a close friend of this African couple, and shortly before his arrival he had addressed a sonnet to them, entitled *Nemo*, with the acrostic GERTRUDE JASPER. While out walking he came upon a cave on the south bank of the river. Always attracted to caves, he couldn't resist looking inside. On this occasion his visit was short-lived; the cave was occupied by a lion, whose growl quickly made known his displeasure at this intrusion. John recorded the incident in a poem, which he sent to the Savanhus:

> Methinks I see afresh the stream
> Mazoe flowing like a dream,
> Meseems I hear the lion's roar
> As I enter his hideout's door!

In May a worrying development occurred at Mtemwa: cattle belonging to the local farmers began to graze on the land belonging to the Centre, and proceeded to ravage the lepers' gardens. In the first poem referring to this intrusion, *Mootamewa*, the tone was still 'charmingly unmorose', even though financial compensation had been sought. But when the problem persisted, the tone gradually changed.

Visits to Mtemwa continued throughout 1970. John was particular about his attire when receiving guests. Usually wearing shorts and an old pullover, he hastily donned trousers and shirt when visitors appeared (he later abandoned this practice, born of a desire to appear the gentleman to those who took the trouble to drop by the Centre). When the rainy season came, it led to difficulties of access to the Centre. Since the new tarmacadamed road to Mtoko had still not been completed, it was necessary to take the old route, and when the Nyadiri was in flood the ford crossing could not be relied on.

John was always happy to see John Dove arrive, often accompanied by Heather Benoy, and carrying a large picnic basket which the three friends would share as they caught up on news. The young woman kept an eye on John, conscious that if anything happened to him it would be the end for the lepers. On one occasion she brought a bottle of expensive South African wine which she had received as a present, and had decided to give to John, for which he thanked her profusely. On her next visit she couldn't help asking John if he had enjoyed the wine, and he replied: 'It was marvellous ... We filled a barrel of chibuku and brandy and mixed in the bottle of South African wine, and had a fantastic party.' She was horrified at the idea of mixing a superior wine with cheap liquor, but resigned herself to the fact that, whether it was fine wine, a chicken, or his own shirt, John could not be relied upon to keep it for himself. The three friends set out to climb Chigona, and the day ended with Mass at the Centre, always the highlight of a visit from John Dove. Even though Heather felt the departure of her friend from Silveira House as a form of 'exile', which she struggled to understand, his joy and his high spirits always impressed those who visited him.

Shirley James came to Mtemwa almost every month as a representative of the Committee, while visits by Philip Dighton became rarer. At the beginning of September 1970, when she paid a visit, John had already rebaptised the row of jacarandas, planted a generation earlier, 'Greensleeves Avenue'. When Shirley arrived, she saw John approaching, a basket dancing in his right hand, with 'his blue luminous eyes'. She even saw a halo around his head. It was not, as she discovered when she got nearer, a mirage: swarms of bees were buzzing around John's head. According to John the bees helped him in his round of chores.

Another day she came to visit with a friend, Violet Stewart. Immediately John said: 'Shirley, I know you will solve my problem', without specifying what the problem was. They continued talking when Violet, impressed by what she saw, told him 'I do admire the work you are doing – and I want therefore to make a small contribution', took out her chequebook and wrote a cheque for £25, whereupon John turned to Shirley and said: 'You see, Shirley, I knew it. I needed £24.50. Your friend has given me £25.' But their discussions were often long and stormy, especially concerning medical matters. Shirley Jones, who mixed in medical circles, realised that John was not for turning when it came to doing things his way.

One day he greeted the arrival of his friend Alec Israel, accompanied by Wilfred Mbanga, later to become a distinguished journalist, and Dr Wayne Perry, a surgeon from London. Wayne later wrote:

> Sometimes we would shin up a baobab tree and sing hymns much to the astonished delight of the lepers. Being agnostic at that time we had long discussions on evolution, God, and Uncle Tom Cobbley, but though fun we resolved little. The Jacaranda trees were in bloom giving the whole atmosphere a Galilean ambience: the landscape of rock, sand and scrub evoked the Holy Land and the appearance of an angel would have settled the argument. The lepers and John were as one and he was totally immersed in their well-being. Of course materially they had nothing and neither did John. This also made a unique bond for I realised later that their only possession was their feeling and suffering i.e. their souls. John was there for them.

In the evening, as Alec Israel wrote some 25 years later, a strange event happened:

> The room was lit by a candle or two. And then at one point, John fell asleep. And it seemed to me, as I watched his eyes closed, that the light in the room diminished: the candle(s) burned less brightly, as if something had gone out of the air the moment he lost consciousness. I don't suppose this meant anything but I have never forgotten it.

> And it occurred at a time when I was not on the
> lookout for anything unusual.

John changed the life of Alec,

> simply through the power of his presence and
> example... Anyone who knew me as I was would
> say that's something of a miracle I suppose... It is
> clear to me that my awareness, such as it is, of the
> workings of Providence may be attributed largely
> to him.

The visitors included various farmers and other Europeans from the neighbourhood who had adopted the hermit of Mtemwa, among whom was Elaine Barkess, wife of the man in charge of the district mechanical equipment depot (who was later murdered, in 1981). From 1970 on she had made a habit of visiting Mtemwa from time to time, with or without her husband Bill. She would settle in the shade of the jaracandas of Greensleeves Avenue and paint the sumptuous splendour of the overarching trees. She enjoyed conversations with John, climbing Chigona with him or sharing a bottle of Cinzano. She described John as having a 'kaleidoscopic personality', meaning that, depending on the day or indeed the hour, he displayed an astonishing array of attitudes, all of which she believed to reflect icons of an unchanging inner reality. Neither did she fail to notice his fondness for alcohol, which, by the way, she herself shared: John often served her a coffee fortified with brandy which he preserved in a jar of large beans. One day, she noticed he appeared to have sunburn, and he asked her: 'Elaine, do you think that this is due to sunburn, Cinzano or skin cancer?'

Other visitors included what Elaine Barkess referred to as the local 'young blades' – members of the Mtoko Lions Club, who gave financial support to the Centre. She witnessed occasions of overindulgence in the old butchery, followed by excursions to Chigona led by John, expressing surprise that no one ever fell off the top – in particular one night when the revellers were too drunk to go home, and slept in John's room on the bed or on the floor or in the stoep. John himself disappeared, and no one ever found out where he spent the remainder of the night.

In October 1970 Mona Smith appeared at Mtemwa for the first time. Born in 1901 in Enkeldoorn, daughter and wife of companions of Cecil Rhodes himself, her history was inseparably entwined with that of the ruling elite of Rhodesia. When her husband died, she went off in 1954 to live in the ashram of Aurobindo Ghose at Pondicherry, where she worked with lepers, having had no medical training. She returned to Rhodesia in 1968, and two years later, having heard of the existence of Mtemwa, decided to go there and offer her services. She rented rooms with a local farming couple, the Palmers, about 15 miles from the Centre, from where she commuted to Mtemwa twice a week to supervise dressings and to bathe the women lepers. She soon took on the task of making underwear from the scraps of material donated by Whitehead Textiles. Luisa Guidotti and John were delighted, and from that moment on Mona Smith became an integral member of the team. Every Sunday she arrived at All Souls Mission with a pre-cooked lunch from Mrs Palmer and a bottle of fine wine (John was invited but he rarely turned up). Relations between Mona and John were highly charged: she was temperamental and John was stubborn. They quarrelled often, but were good friends. He wrote to Shirley James (11 October 1971): 'Mrs Mona Smith is doing marvels as Mistress of the Wardrobe of Mtemwa. She is the salt of the earth, heaping coals of fire on my head in the most charming and unwounding way!' Their main source of discord was the lepers. Mona didn't hesitate to address them harshly, which was unacceptable to John. When she scolded them, he leapt to their defence. In his eyes they could do no wrong. One day he surprised some young Africans in the jacarandas and, assuming that they were stealing grains which the lepers used to light their fires, he shouted at them. It was Mona's turn to intervene and vent her anger on John: the young Africans had been sent by the District Commissioner. John accepted the rebuke. Mona also noticed that women were attracted to John, and that it bothered him. One day she brought him some garlic, saying that it would chase them away!

A chapel for Mtemwa

Mona Smith made her appearance at Mtemwa just in time to join in the celebrations inaugurating the new chapel, which in due course became the heart of the Centre. The dream which John had cherished since he first arrived had at last become a reality, thanks to the Laws, his Anglican friends. Arthur had drawn up the plans for a great rondavel to hold about 50 people. A total of 1124 Rhodesian dollars (in February 1970 the Rhodesian dollar had replaced the Rhodesian pound, at a par level) raised from several sources paid for the wooden roof beams, the thatch and the window frames. John had recovered bricks from the ruins of the old abandoned section of the Centre, and transported them to the new site. When Arthur arrived at Mtemwa to begin construction, he found he had enough material to meet demand. Father Ennis contributed a metal safe that would serve as a tabernacle, Shirley James provided the cash to buy the altar and a chalice, and the Laws provided a large crucifix, a generous ecumenical donation from the Anglican Mission of Cyrene near Bulawayo, celebrated for its mural paintings of African martyrs. John fashioned a makeshift bell by hanging a metal bar from the branch of a tree, which one of the lepers would strike to summon to Mass and Office. The harmonium was installed beside the altar, and choir practice began forthwith. As at Silveira House, John's energetic playing was more like an assault on the keyboards as he conducted his choir of lepers while they chanted in Latin or Shona.

The consecration was set for Saturday October 31st 1970, and Archbishop Markall came to preside. John had spent days rehearsing his chosen repertory, a mixture of Gregorian chant and hymns in Shona, solemn, stately and majestic, in line with the liturgy that he admired. Only a few friends were invited, the place of honour being intended for the lepers, and seats in the chapel were scarce. But just as the celebration was about to begin, who should arrive unannounced but 'Pear Peachon' with a lorry-load of young enthusiasts from his Chikwiso Mission, beating drums and twirling rattles, eager to contribute to the festive occasion, much to John's displeasure. Before he had time to react, the motley crew had invaded the church as he watched on helplessly. The poor lepers had to scurry to find a place as John elbowed his way through the throng to guide Kit Law to the harmonium. Meanwhile the guests from Salisbury and the local farmers who had funded the building of the church were obliged to wait outside, while the imperturbable Archbishop led the celebration amid the general mayhem. Father Pichon's young charges danced so energetically that they damaged John's cherished statue of St Joseph. When they finally vacated the chapel at the end of the Mass, they made a beeline for the buffet table and devoured the sandwiches and cakes so lovingly prepared by Shirley James and the other women, while the lepers were lucky to get a glass of lemonade. John was furious, and accused Père Peachon of being a 'gate crasher' and a party wrecker. Later in the day, when everybody had left, John, still fuming, opened the Bible at a passage on forgiveness. He immediately wrote a verse letter to Father Pichon apologising for his outburst, making fun of his own anger.

From then on the chapel became the heart of Mtemwa. Shortly afterwards John paid a visit to Chikwsoto to cement the peace accord with Father Pichon, and was astonished at the vastness of the Church of St Martin's which the Jesuit had built at his tiny Mission. Without consulting the Archbishop, he had planted this 'miniature Gothic cathedral' (in the words of Paul Tingay) right in the middle of the bush with stones from the nearby river. The architecture was decidedly not to John's taste, and on returning to Mtemwa declared: 'It was good to get back to Israel out of Egypt.' Two years later, Father Pichon, while on leave in France, was forbidden to return to Rhodesia (in 1975 he had published *Le drame rhodésien*, in support of the liberation struggle of the African population).

Tensions between Church and the Rhodesian state continued, but the bishops prepared to accept a compromise, which they signed up to in February 1971. They agreed to accept the government decision on segregated schools, with an assurance that their exception clause (in practice, the admission into a 'white' school of one or several black pupils) would be met. In this way the Catholic bishops saved their schools, but in the eyes of some of their members they had sold their souls. In the meantime Father Dove continued his programme in favour of Africans, and kept up his contacts with the nationalists. At this time John got to know

Sabina Mugabe, sister of the imprisoned ZANU leader: she had been engaged as nutrition advisor at Silveira House, later taking over the sector. Outbreaks of violence were still rare in the country (although three soldiers died in a mine explosion in April), but the coordination within the two branches of the armed struggle did not augur well for the regime.

'Lepers – they make a mighty mystery'

Meanwhile the honeymoon at Mtemwa continued, and seemed destined to go on for ever. John had made serious efforts to master Shona, acording to Heather Benoy, with the result that his relationship with the lepers deepened, even if he would always speak the language with a pronounced English accent. He was very aware of his debt to his friends:

> I feel like a usurper in this place,
> A person having little more to give
> Than foreign manners and a foreign face
> And knowledge bare of how they fare and live;
> Vast fields of earthly hope are far behind
> And wide is their experience of woe.
>
> ...
>
> Lepers – they make a mighty mystery
> Excruciating mainly for themselves,
> Perhaps a matter for my poetry
> Easily writ by him nor digs nor delves;
> Rose-coloured glasses better are for them
> That never had a cataract nor went
> Totally blind, though I would not condemn
> An optimistic mien where it's meant;
> So much of thought that leads to naught subsists
> In wishing well to fellows in distress,
> Yet, you may enter into heaven's lists
> By sending hither just one simple dress:
> If in my place you stood with these at hand
> By God's good grace you'd better understand.
>
> ...

I've visited, and frequently, some hut
Wherein a mortal draws towards a death
Whilst by him lies, as if in wonted rut,
Some bed-foresaking friend to blend his breath;
Nor is this matter only masculine
For half of these are women that are here,
Friends, they will come at sunset to assign
The night to floordom, boredom never near:
Orientate I will, fakirs are these
Whose gears change softly oft, their peers to please.
(*Mootamewa*, 1971 – the spelling of this name is
not consistent in the poems)

He continued to write personalised poems to each leper, which
reveals how attentive he was to who they were, how they lived their
individual lives, and to their desires and aspirations – not just from
a general point of view but acknowledging the unique personality
of each. He observed their actions, thoughts, feelings and wishes,
sensitive to the depths within them, exploring what hidden depths
they might reveal, through them and by them. *The Vision of the
Blind* (1971) is dedicated to the ten or so blind lepers in the Centre,
whom he held in special affection:

All ye who see with eyes
That earthly sights apprise,
Give ear a little while to this my song;
There are near where I dwell
Ten lepers, blind as well,
And, out of four score people in our throng
Of motley lepers here,
They shine with secret cheer,
Their vision of our hidden God is strong.

Quaint Peter, take the lead,
You are a saint indeed
Unless there are no saints to grace our time;
Not headlong down you fell
To the dead abyss of hell
From seeing no more earthly sights sublime:

You, with your blind-man's stick
And a faith full Catholic,
Went roaming slowly up to heaven's clime.

And that is where you are
In spirit, like a star
That shines amidst the darkness of the void;
Empty of eyes, your face
Is all a smile of grace,
A sight that gives a brightness unalloyed:
Your soul it is that shows
And outwardly it glows
Declaring even blindness is enjoyed!

He listened attentively to the intimate confidences of these men and women, whose sensibility and interior lives had evolved in parallel with the gradual loss of their exterior sensitive faculties. One in particular, Bofu, the simpleton of the Centre, blind, whose legs stopped at his knees, as did his arms at his elbows, made his way from his hut to the toilet propelling himself as best he could by his shoulders, head held high, with a smile on his face. One day when John asked him why he was so happy, he replied that he had just seen a fellow leper, who had recently died, bathed in a pool of light.

John continued to receive visitors from Salisbury. On July 11th, it was the turn of Gordon Read, a young doctor who was considering the priesthood, to pay a call. John Dove, also present, later wrote to Mrs Bradburne remarking how well John looked, and how at ease he was with his lepers, who revered him so much that they nicknamed him Ndi Mwari ('It's God') in recognition of how he had 'divinely' transformed their lives. During his visit Gordon performed a minor operation on one of the lepers, which was much appreciated by his host. The young doctor was impressed by the Mass celebrated by John Dove, and the accompanying music played by John, who always began on the harmonium with a piece by Bach, while the lepers sang the *Kyrie* in Shona, using Gregorian melodies. In conclusion John directed a *Gloria Patri* in Shona for four voices.

Sunday Mass, celebrated by a priest from All Souls in the absence of a visitor from Salisbury, was far from being the only Sunday service at the Centre, as we can see from a poem written on September 22nd that year:

> A 'sank-I-not', a light unmoody song
> Our Methodists are singing in array;
> 'Thy kingdom come, O God' becomes the throng
> Of Anglicans as wakes Mootamewa's day;
> I think, I know, and I could almost swear
> None of our Roman ones lie still abed,
> I'm latest up (from combing long my hair
> Moreover I've delayed who might have led);
> The Father from the Mission of All Souls
> Is fairly fast upon his way nor far, –
> The cripples hobble, chair on wheels there rolls
> And Mona comes a-sudden in her car:
> A little while to wait, our style is then
> The Kyrie de Angelis, Amen.
> (*Rechitatu*, 1971)

After Mass, John rolled out a carpet and sat with his guests of the day under a mango tree (it would be some time before he acquired a table and chairs). A battered jerrycan served as a jug to pour the water into old cracked cups. John himself ate little, but often drank a glass of wine, with the usual joke not to tell Stephano, because he would sniff out the smell on his own, and that anyway he would give him some later. He then read out his latest poems, ever increasing in volume (369 are recorded from 1971 alone), and banter and song would ensue.

When alone with John Dove, the conversation often turned to religion and poetry; when guests were numerous it would fly off in every direction. Nobody took himself seriously, conversation ranged from the frivolous to the solemn, while John recounted everything that he had learnt or gained from his friends from the Centre, their joys as well as their sorrows. He always took his visitors on a guided tour of the Centre, stopping at the door of every leper to say hello, distributing any offerings received, such as Mazoe oranges, cigarettes, loose tobacco, radio batteries. This would be followed by a climb up Chigona, at the summit of which John liked to ask John Dove to hear his confession, particularly when they were alone.

His friend Alistair Guthrie called to Mtemwa from time to time with his son Frank and young friends of his. One of these, Anthony Trethowan, retains a vivid memory of such a visit, when the two teenagers brought along food rations and some clothes:

> The year was probably 1971 or '72 and at the time John was living in a crude brick and cement hut. The thing I remember about his accommodation is that there was very little in it save a crucifix and a picture of Jesus. Also the smell of freshly baked bread. While we were there Frank, John, and I climbed to the top of Mtemwa hill which was more of a large granite boulder, and we swam in the pools that had been formed by rainfall.

Often on Sundays John welcomed strangers at Mtemwa, from Salisbury or elsewhere, who had heard of him and were curious to meet him. Not only Europeans but also Africans from the Mtoko district came to visit him, and sometimes soldiers, both European and African. Many went away in wonder, as if returning from a visit to John's patron saint, John the Baptist, in the desert. What were they searching for? Did they themselves know? Maybe, according to Heather Benoy, a glimpse of God, or, more simply, a touch of humour, or eccentricity. As for Heather herself, she knew that she often came with her problems, sometimes in times of distress, and that John invariably managed to make her laugh at herself – perhaps one of the explanations why people were attracted to him.

One day John decided to take the Laws and Brother Fitz on a search for hamerkop nests. This large bird, akin to the swan, has a fearsome reputation in Africa, and builds its habitat along waterways. Having made their way upstream through the mud and bramble of the nearby river, the group found, to their great delight, a nest full of eggs. On other occasions he took them to see the fishing eagle on the dam, or to the pools on top of Chigona.

Sometimes they just sat down to sing, or allow Kit time to paint. John never tired of seeking out new kinds of birds, or other animals.

In August 1971 the problem of stray cattle from the nearby kraal reappeared in his poems. Theresa, in charge of the kitchen and the laundry, came to him to complain that two cows had ravaged her garden. John held Theresa in high esteem, she being the only member of the staff who gave him unqualified loyalty, which did not endear her to the other assistants. He tried to deal with the problem, but more encroachments were to follow, as the kraal owned plentiful cattle, who were irresistably drawn to the green pastures of Mtemwa during the dry season. In a poem, *Mombe!* (*Cry Cattle!*), John sang the praises of the kraal for its prosperity, while wishing that Mtemwa itself were spared the intrusion of its bovine predators. He instructed Phineas to build a strong wire fence around the gardens, a victory which he celebrated in *So What* (1971) with the words: 'Let a Bos [Latin, 'ox'] attempt to Boss.' Another problem soon followed: convinced that another cook, Gertrude, was stealing from the Centre, and thus from the lepers, he sacked her. The latter appealed to Mona Smith, who stood up for her; John relented and took her back.

From time to time he visited the administration at Mtoko, with whom relations were good. On July 12th he wrote a poem to the District Commissioner, Ron Taylor, to thank him for flowers and a crate of oranges he had sent. Politics rarely got discussed during these visits, but John learnt that Ian Smith had signed an agreement with London advantageous to the regime, following a visit by a British commission of enquiry. The nationalist groupings rejected the agreement, and proceeded to set up, on December 16th, the African National Congress (ANC). Meanwhile the Catholic Church established a Commission for Peace and Justice to enquire into human rights violations. In the meantime expulsions of Africans to so-called Tribal Trust Lands continued, including over a thousand Africans uprooted from their ancestral lands at Chishawasha.

The Committee of Friends of Mtemwa reaped the fruits of John's work: visitors to the Centre familiar with it before John's arrival went away in admiration and wonder. As a result, Secretary of State for Health Mark Webster requested the committee to extend its work to Rhodesia as a whole, which they agreed to do without consulting

John, and four new recruits were co-opted to the Committee. These, however, did not share the spirit of the founders, and having visited Mtemwa dispatched a lukewarm report: the Director was hard-working but spent too much time lavishing care on minor tasks with the lepers. They recommended that administration of the Centre be rationalised and extended to include stricter and more transparent control of expenditure on food supplies, fumigation and maintenance of the lepers' huts. Their proposals were discussed and approved by the Committee, with only Father Ennis supporting John. In August 1971 the Committee was renamed the Rhodesian Leprosy Association. Father Ennis, no longer the Superior of the Jesuits, was replaced by Father Patrick McNamara, who was none too pleased at recent developments on the Committee, and whose opinion was shared by John himself.

At this juncture, Dr Louise Westwater, with overall responsibility for medical affairs in Shona country, appeared on the scene. She had come to Mtemwa to meet John and had been impressed; they shared the same love for birds and whisky, and the same sense of humour. But they soon clashed. For her the lepers were primarily carriers of a disease – leprosy – to be cured; but for John they were first and foremost a group of remarkable men and women, whose humanity must be acknowledged for what it was. For Dr Westwater women lepers should not have children (even though leprosy is not hereditary, if precautions are taken at birth) and should as a matter of course be provided with the contraceptive pill. When John disagreed, their relations deteriorated. Moreover she wished to operate on elderly lepers with cataracts, which he found cruel, pointless and contrary to the divine will. Dr Westwater became furious and accused him of being 'a religious hippy', and 'perhaps a little mad with an innate fear of responsibility', even though she continued to respect his 'spiritual dimension', or even his 'special vocation'. Caterina Savini, having arrived on one occasion to tend to a leper suffering from an eye ailment, was told by John not to bother, that holy water would suffice. Even Luisa Guidotti disagreed with John in these matters, and operated on cataracts when he was not around. One day he explained that he didn't wear glasses because neither did Moses.

Another bone of contention with Dr Westwater was even more serious. During winter, temperatures could fall close to zero, and there was no heating in the huts, which caused considerable hardship to the lepers, especially when they were close to death. John allowed them to light fires, as had always been the case, despite this being forbidden. Accidents – including one fatal – happened, but the Director of the Centre could not be everywhere at the same time. The matter was brought to the attention of Dr Eric Burnett Smith, chief medical officer at the Ministry for Health and future Secretary of Health of the Rhodesian Government. As if these problems were not enough, Dr Westwater took it into her head to demand access to the Mtemwa registers, and up-to-date accounts of all expenditure. On this point she agreed with the most recent complaint from the Committee: John thought money fell like manna from heaven. When he supplied the accounts, she was surprised to discover that they were in perfect order. Furthermore it turned out that the four dollars allotted to each leper every month were judiciously used. But suspicions remained.

Clouds on the horizon

On January 11th 1972 the British Commission led by Lord Pearson arrived in Salisbury. This was the first time in the history of Rhodesia that London set out to discover the opinions of the African population. When the Commission left Rhodesia in March, their verdict was unanimous: that while the vast majority of Europeans approved the agreement of 1971, it was rejected by the vast majority of Africans. Edward Heath and Ian Smith had thus unwittingly conferred the legitimacy on the nationalist cause that had been denied it by the Rhodesian Front; and when Ian Smith dismissed the conclusions of the Commission as 'unrealistic', the nationalist leaders, invited to address the United Nations, announced that the only way forward was by armed struggle. On June 6th an explosion in a mine at Wankie killing 426 African miners united the nation for a time in an outpouring of grief, but this was soon followed by the beginning of open armed conflict.

Relations between the regime and the Catholic Church continued to deteriorate. Len Idensohn declared in the *Rhodesian Herald* that

'To give money in the collection' was 'contributing to the knife that will cut your throat.' Divisions deepened in the ranks of the Church itself, where African priests and seminarians became more and more susceptible to the nationalist siren call. The Justice and Peace Commission began its work in spite of the hostility of the regime, and Bishop Lamont continued to criticise the government, while Silveira House continued its training programmes, and became, in the new space opened up by the release of the Peace Commission, a centre of robust debate. In his relations with the government, John Dove maintained a degree of ambiguity, so much so that the Centre even received praise in a report in 1972, despite its declared aim, which was in direct contradiction to the policies of the powers that be: 'The primary goal was arousing black consciousness in a truly Christian sense... so attempting to mobilise oppressed people into realising their own potential power.'

The Peace Commission also had its effect at Mtoko, and the ANC, which brought together rival nationalist groups in the interior, gained a foothold. At the end of January one of its leaders, Arthur Chadzingwa, was arrested, charged with having spent a night in the Tribal Trust Lands. The following month, military manoeuvres were carried out to deter incipient sedition, even though the region itself was free of guerrilla activity. But John seemed remote from this gathering storm, and appeared worn out to John Dove, who felt that he needed a holiday after two years of unremitting dedication. He confided as much to Sister Nora Broderick, an Irish nun from the Presentation Sisters, who knew John and agreed to replace him for three weeks in January 1972. In due course Sister Nora moved with Sister Catherine Cousins into the old butchery, and John took off for a well-deserved break, we do not know where. The two nuns operated a stricter regime than John, and followed to the letter the instructions of Luisa Guidotti and Caterina Savini, while recognising that 'the important thing was that John loved the lepers, and did everything he could for them, even though they could be difficult and we have occasionally seen them fighting among each other'.

Caught up in his search for God, prayer, looking after his lepers, poetry and welcoming his friends, John was kept busy throughout 1972. Visitors from Silveira House, European and African alike, continued to call, including Agnes Contralto, who often arrived with John Dove. On March 26th John had a visit from journalist Lady Judith Listowel, a remarkable woman in her own right, and her 16-year-old grandson, the future Lord Grantley. She planned to write about John, and her grandson was convinced he had met a saint. She later started to write a biography, unfinished when she died, aged 100 years and 3 days – leaving behind much precious documentation. Other callers included Mark Hanley, who lived in Mtoko before travelling abroad to study to be a doctor. He made several visits to Mtemwa, and John later wrote letters to him which he has carefully preserved. David Savage was another, who in November brought snuff for the lepers. He recalled John as 'different', adding: 'The love of the Lord shone through', and that he was grateful to have met him. John also impressed young Jewish convert Cheryl Methven: 'He was an amazingly quiet and humble individual, very easy on the nerves and considering his remarkable gifts, most self-effacing.' She added: 'I consider it one of my life's greatest privileges to have met him.'

When Dr Sheffield, one of the new members of the Committee, invited Lt Colonel (retired) William Ellis onto the board, no one was aware that this man had scores to settle with the Church he had left behind. According to John, in *Concerning Mtemwa* (1975):

> he was, as he avowed proudly to journalists at a private meeting on a later occasion, a lapsed Catholic... He once told a journalist that 'he knew all about the scoundrels of the Roman Church: we were typical!'

In March he arrived unannounced at Mtemwa Centre with his wife. The Committee had decided to construct a new wing, comprising toilet and washing facilities, and the new member had taken it upon himself to supervise the work on site, including the installation of solar panels paid for from his own pocket. Nothing in these new developments was displeasing to John, apart maybe from the haughty attitude displayed by the new arrival towards himself as Director of the Centre. At the start Mrs Ellis' kindness smoothed contact between the two men, who ate and drank brandy together, but had nothing in common. Ellis had served in the RAF, and after the War served as part of the guard at the Nazi Bergen-Belsen camp, and later in a prison in Jamaica, before coming to Rhodesia. He strode up and down the Centre and saw nothing he liked, starting with the Director, fiddled with the plumbing here and there, muttering ideas for the future. Then after a few days he upped sticks and left, with a few gruff words for John, leaving Mtemwa 'with a clatter of nuts and bolts' in his head, according to John. Peace returned to Mtemwa, but they hadn't seen the last of Ellis, who soon became vice-president of the Committee and its *de facto* patron, which led to the resignation of Father McNamara.

From then on John had few friends on the Committee whose support he could rely on. But these worries were soon displaced by others. Incursions of stray cattle, the recurrent scourge of the Centre, resumed, which led to veritable trench warfare with local farmers. As usual this found expression in John's verse. In May 1972 he wrote about the damages in a short sketch, *Estote fortes in bello*. The tone remained good humoured, but anger occasionally flared up. Other poems followed on the same theme, and on others, during these years of intense creative activity. The spring had become a torrent: since his arrival up to the middle of 1973, John had written a poem a day on average, to speak only of those that have survived. In all of these the lepers occupy a privileged place, as do the Virgin Mary and the divine mystery. This intense creative output, night after night, did not get in the way of John's work at the Centre. The team from AFMM continued to come twice a week in a Land Rover donated by the Amici dei Lebrossi in Italy. He himself often went, on foot when necessary, to All Souls. Moreover Luisa Guidotti herself drove those requiring special care to Salisbury, where their arrival, singing and clapping their hands (those who had hands to clap), caused a minor sensation.

All Souls had recently acquired a new recruit, the young Elizabeth Tarira, a niece of Father Chakaipa, whom John had met when she was a pupil at the Mission School. Touched by the devotion of Luisa Guidotti and her fellow sisters she had asked to join the AFMM, and was now working side by side with them. She had been originally reluctant to visit the Centre, being afraid like many Shonas of catching the disease from contact with the lepers.

She wept while seeing them, and was also afraid of John, with his beard and unruly mop of hair. For six months she refused to go back. When she eventually did, her heart suddenly opened up to the lepers and, sensing their humanity, she experienced a great inner peace, and began caring for them without hesitation or fear. She got to know John that day; he asked her to help him dress the wounds of some lepers, and as he sang, joked and laughed, her heart was won over. Her vocation was strengthened, and she realised she wanted to be a doctor. Her new friend warned her about going to Zambia to pursue her studies, telling her the boys were handsome there (although he had never been to Zambia) – 'you might mistake one for Divine' – but that it was the same in Italy. He then proceeded to write a poem, putting into her mouth the reply she must make to any boy who made advances to her:

> 'No, I will not marry you, you handsome thing,
> Because I'm getting married to THE KING' –
> And HE'll join in, with an immortal laugh,
> 'Well done, you've won, take up your pilgrim-staff!
> (*Nocturne*, 1972)

William Ellis had not forgotten Mtemwa. On May 15th 1972 he wrote a belligerent letter to John accusing him of making nonsense of the Committee's attempts at administration by wasteful expenditure. He cited as an example the purchase of white bread instead of brown, exceeding the monthly meat ration of 500 grams per leper, spending too much money on soap, and unspecified amounts on sweet things and snuff. He went on to conclude that the Director of the Centre had created a group of people whose standard of living was much higher than that of those living around them. To crown his boorishness he asked John what he intended buying the lepers at Christmas and other festive occasions, given that they were already living in the lap of luxury. In conclusion he decided that apart from salt, paraffin and brown bread, all supplies would be bought in future in Salisbury and sent to Mtemwa. John refused to accept these decisions, and war was declared between the two men.

In September John wrote to Shirley James, who remained faithful to him on the Committee, saying that the time had come to confront Ellis directly, on the grounds that 81 human lives depended on it. An initial battle was fought on the question of blankets. The residents of Mtemwa were issued with four every year, and were allowed to resell them at the end of winter to make some pocket money. Ellis was demanding that the number of blankets issued be reduced and that the right to resell be abolished, and John refused point blank. Did he feel that he, and his friends the lepers, were under threat? His feelings can be gauged from one of the most moving of his poems, written that year:

> This people, this exotic clan
> Of lepers in array
> Of being less yet more than man
> As man is worn today:
> This is a people born to be
> Burnt upward to eternity!
>
> This strange ecstatic moody folk
> Of joy with sorrow merged
> Destined to shuffle off the yoke
> Of all the world has urged:
> This oddity, this Godward school
> Sublimely wise, whence, I'm its fool!
>
> ...
> Hazy are not
> These folk, nor forgotten
> By Father not far but full near
> With His Love for His Only-Begotten...
> 'You are cut off' (Mutemwa signifies)
> But not from One and all in Him who share His size.
> (*Mtemwa (Mutemwa)*, 1972)

In October Father Chakaipa was nominated Auxiliary Bishop of Salisbury, the first African in the country to be raised to the episcopacy, and the appointment was celebrated with great joy at All Souls. Before leaving, the future bishop asked Luisa Guidotti not to visit any outlying posts (there were 44 in the zone), because the guerrillas, even though they had not yet shown themselves, were certainly on the way. In fact after autumn 1972 insurgents were already infiltrating the district of Mtoko from the north, led by John Gwitira and his political commissar and former seminarian Josiah Tungamirai, and settled in the territory of Charewa to the north. In the beginning the insurgents – *vakomana* (the word means 'boys' in Shona, and designated the guerrillas) as they were called by the villagers – went underground; but from November on, the Rhodesian security forces realised that something was going on to the north of the Mtoko zone. On December 21st Ian Smith declared: 'I have been taken to task in certain quarters for describing our Africans as the happiest Africans in the world. But nobody has as yet been able to tell me where there are Africans who are happier or better off than Rhodesia.' The same day Altena farm, in the west of the region, was attacked by the guerrillas.

John continued to live for the moment. A few days before Christmas in 1972 Caterina Savini, passing through Silveira House, had a telephone call from him: 'Hurry back to Mtemwa. It's very serious, Andrew needs to be evacuated urgently.' She told him she still had some shopping to do, but he insisted so strongly that she set out in her car immediately. To her surprise, when she arrived in Mtemwa John was nowhere to be seen, nor was the sick man. She searched everywhere and finally tracked him down: 'Where were you?' 'Me? I was praying.' 'Where is Andrew, the sick man?' 'Andrew? I haven't a clue!' They set off to look for him, and eventually found him; he had felt much better and gone searching for wood! Caterina Savini was furious, but recounting the episode nearly 40 years later she still laughs: 'That was John!'

Soon afterwards John went to spend Christmas at Silveira House. On New Year's Eve, Father David Harold-Barry, an Irish Jesuit who would the following year become John Dove's second-in-command at Silveira House, arrived, accompanied by a Rhodesian Jesuit sociologist, Roger Riddell. On a visit to Mtemwa the previous October, he had come upon John 'crouched on the floor of a hut reading a passage from St Paul in Shona to a person whose leprosy had not yet dried out'. While a Jesuit scholastic, Father Harold-Barry had spent two years, 1966–68, at St Ignatius' School in Salisbury. At that time he met John once or twice at Silveira House, but did not have a vivid memory of him, other than John sitting on the ground, surrounded by bees. This time their relationship would be closer.

On arriving at the Centre, the two Jesuits had brought a bottle of brandy and presents for the residents, donated by the parish of Mount Pleasant. John poured the brandy into the cocoa rations, saying that if he kept it for himself he would end up an alcoholic and that, in any event, it would give good cheer to the lepers for the New Year. They sang together, and Father Harold-Barry celebrated Midnight Mass in the chapel with Gregorian chant and Elizabethan songs in Shona, and agreed that *Greensleeves* sounded good too. On New Year's morning the three of them climbed Chigona and bathed in the 'swimming pool', returning for morning Mass. Then they did the rounds of the Centre, and John introduced them to the lepers: Peter, Joseph, Veronica, Hanzu. They then said the rosary together, John's slow dignified recital making an impression on the young priest, as he recalled:

> When I returned from visiting John in Mutemwa I decided I would not put sugar in my tea and coffee from then on... and I have never done so since! At the time it was not a decision I connected with the visit, but it was certainly his influence that prompted me. He impressed me as being very ascetic, and this marked me. Was he an eccentric? He was not an eccentric in the sense of being odd or crazy. But he was eccentric in the sense that he was unusual, quite different from others in his way of life. His simplicity, joy, openness, and friendliness made us reflect on our attitudes and way of life. His most remarkable trait was that he was truly human, immensely human. There was something very beautiful in this quality of humanity that he had. He laughed at himself, refused to take himself seriously, but at the same time I felt he must have struggled long to become what he truly was: himself. His great quality, which I have also felt in the presence of other holy

> people, was that in his company you felt good. He
> was neither frivolous nor hail-fellow-well-met,
> but quite simply positive, affirmative, interested
> in you for what you were, what you had to say,
> what you did.

At the beginning of 1973, the government was preparing its
response to the mounting power of the insurgency. On January
18th the frontier with Zambia was closed, and the Rhodesian
security services proceeded to arrest 300 leaders of the ANC. This
did not, however, put a stop to guerrilla incursions: on January
24th, I. Kleynhans and, on February 4th, L. M. Jellico were killed by
insurgents at Centenary, in the north of the country. These were the
first killings of European farmers since 1965. More would follow:
six between January and June 1973. The situation in the north-east,
and particularly in the Mtoko district, was particularly worrying
to the Rhodesian army, given the vastness of the territory, and it
was decided to create two new administrative districts, Mtoko and
Mudzi, the better to police the area.

The visits to Mtemwa continued. Silveira House, with support
from Oxfam, had launched a micro-credit programme in the
Mangwende region, to the south of Mtoko, and this gave Father
Dove more opportunity to call on his friend. In February the
Centre received a visit from Rhodesia's top journalist Philippa
Berlyn, a supporter – though devoid of any racist prejudice – of
Ian Smith, whose biography she went on to write. (She was later
dropped into the guerrilla zone for all-night talks with a group of
African women, and the ten guerrillas keeping an eye on her from
the shadows were so taken by her courage that they didn't fire at
the helicopter that came to pick her up at dawn.) She published an
enthusiastic article in the *Rhodesia Herald* (23 February 1973) on the
Centre. Struck by 'the radiance of their smile', she wrote that 'when
talking to the lepers their eyes, if they had eyes, lighted up'. When
embedded with the Rhodesian security forces, she often visited the
military bases in the Mtoko zone, and called on Mtemwa whenever
the opportunity arose.

One of John's greatest friendships, with Pauline Hutchings, dates
from this time. Mother of four children, she and her husband Tony

owned a farm near the Nyadiri; she had felt the desire to become a Catholic since the age of six. This desire was rekindled one day on hearing John Dove on the radio, after which she wrote to him. But Silveira House was far away, and Father Dove immediately thought of his friend, who lived about 12 miles away from the Hutchings' farm (from where you can see Mount Mtemwa). Pauline called on John, and agreed to receive instruction, on condition that it would not be in the form of catechetical question and answer, but in a living dialogue between the two. They agreed to meet every Wednesday, when the priest from All Souls came to say Mass.

As with many others, Pauline Hutchings was deeply affected by attendance at these Masses. Before Mass began, the priest stood behind the altar to hear confessions, while John pounded on the harmonium to ensure privacy. As a result the priest did not always hear what was being said to him, but nevertheless granted absolution with a few words of encouragement. Then John also confessed, and the sung Mass began, in Shona, accompanied by the harmonium. John led the queue for communion, and the celebrant was obliged to scramble over the front rows to reach those behind. The blind lepers were seated along the walls of the chapel, and John would give each one an affectionate tap under the chin when his turn came, punctuated by a sonorous Amen. John then returned to the harmonium until Mass was over. After being received into the Church, Pauline Hutchings herself joined the communion queue:

> Somehow, kneeling before the priest among all those physically wretched people, taking one's turn in the line-up for Confession at the side of the altar, with John 'ad libbing' on the harmonium, lifted one right away from the daily problems. John's whole bearing in that little church made one know that the King was in the tabernacle and could one but move the veil, one would see Him face to face. John knelt right down when he genuflected, something one felt drawn to imitate.

John prayed, moreover, not just with the lepers, in the chapel or in their huts, but also for them, and sometimes beseeched God at great length for one or other of them, like Moses in the desert.

After the Mass or service, John received his visitors in the old butchery, which seemed to Pauline like a 'concrete box house'. Breakfast consisted of bread and butter with marmalade, and coffee from the Hutchings' farm, which became the staple Wednesday meal. John regularly commented: 'You make them in the nicest way, with more butter and marmalade than bread. That's the way I should make them myself.' The rest of the time he continued his diet of powdered milk, oranges or orange juice, even though he occasionally suffered pangs of conscience: was he not depriving children of what they needed more than he? He gave away anything he got, which worried his friends who saw him losing weight, but he defended himself, protesting that he prayed better on an empty stomach. In the event, said Pauline Hutchings, he appeared to be immune to the ageing process.

John and Pauline usually climbed Chigona together after breakfast for instruction. John spoke to her of the abundance of the heart, with neither book nor preparation, and the young woman felt her own heart filling up. She understood that he was instructing her through prayer, by his devotion to the Blessed Sacrament, by his attentiveness during Mass, by his simple humble life, and by his cheerful attention to the lepers. Through him, words became flesh. She discovered also the universe of Mtemwa, and began to see it differently:

> One of the things which happens in a leper colony
> is that the people all begin to look entirely normal.
> One ceases to notice that lips or noses or hands or
> feet are missing. I used to feel a sense of surprise
> when visitors who sometimes came with us were
> so upset by what they saw. These people had
> charming dispositions and great humour. They
> unceasingly helped each other and were close
> – sharing each other's troubles and pains and
> laughter.

John continued to visit Silveira House three or four times a year; sometimes getting a lift with a visitor back to the capital; sometimes taking an African bus, more than once renewing his Ganda experience; sometimes hitch-hiking and arriving, as he put it, 'by flying bedstead'. He took with him his stencilled poems, seeking out an obliging friend to run them off for him. He also visited the Laws, or the Berthouds to see his godchild. One evening while visiting the latter, he heard the sound of recorder-playing coming from the house of their neighbours the Northwoods. Unable to resist, recorder under his arm, he dragged his host next door, where they came upon a group of amateur musicians, and asked if they could join in. The neighbours, Christopher and Anne Wortham, never forgot the occasion, seeing in John a man 'refined and well educated', visibly at peace with himself and happy, which made all the more surprising to them his decision to bury himself in the middle of the bush in the company of lepers. John visited them again some years later, with his recorder, and they were again struck by the purity of his playing, and by 'his aura of being and doing within the moment'. When he bade a musical farewell to them and left, recorder in mouth, Anne whispered in her husband's ear, 'It's blessed John Bradburne', and Christopher, convinced that she was merely anticipating a judgement of the Church, remembers 'one of the most remarkable people of our time'.

Father, friend, brother

The honeymoon in the community of lepers seemed never-ending. As Arthur Law remarked, John's love for his companions went far beyond the bounds of conventional charity; he loved them 'as Jesus loved'. Peter, Joshua and Hanzu, to name but a few, were his family. Sometimes when he was absent from the Centre for any length of time he would fret. One day, while visiting the Laws, he exclaimed: 'What if someone has taken ill and needs me?' He looked after them in every sense of the word, and they in turn gave him their love and friendship. In the words of Arthur Law:

> When we visited John at Mutemwa, we also visited his 'family' and were introduced to them all. One never came away from there without feeling

spiritually refreshed. There was always something
special to remember about our visits. On two
occasions, on our arrival, we were met by John in
great distress – a sick leper had to be taken to the
hospital at All Souls Mission immediately; so our
car became an ambulance.

Whenever a resident of the Centre fell ill, John spared himself no
pain. If necessary he walked all the way to All Souls to get Luisa
Guidotti to come back with him to Mtemwa. He was once even seen
carrying a leper on his back to Mtoko, thus re-enacting an incident
he had read about as a child in *The Young Christian's Progress*. Such
actions made a deep impression on Africans who witnessed them.
It is even said that on one occasion he walked the 90 miles from
Mtemwa to Salisbury in the hope of touching the hearts of those
from whom he was seeking help. He stopped on the way at the
seminary at Chisawasha to encourage the seminarians, though
didn't stay long, despite their desire to talk with him.

The death of a resident was always a source of sorrow to him.
He would keep vigil with the dying person in the company of other
lepers, praying and chanting with them, reading words of comfort
from the Bible. He would struggle to fight off nausea in the hut
where the stench of putrid flesh, of a leper literally rotting to death,
threatened to overpower him, staying on until the bitter end. He
never forced the dying to accept baptism, but gently urged it. In
September 1971 in his *Inventory of God's Goods* he drew up a list of
those of the dead with their baptismal names Panzeh (Solomon),
Kamujona (Peter), Mutenya (Herbert), Martha, Naomi (Mary).
Others followed. But he didn't stop at healing and nourishing,
chanting, playing, praying and accompanying the dying on their
last journey. He encouraged those who could to work to cultivate
the ground around their huts with the wooden badza, both hoe
and stick. Joshua the bugle player raised Muscovy ducks; others
kept chickens.

It was not just by his dedication, but by his love, his respect,
evident in his speech, his smile, his every gesture, that John gained
the love of the lepers. Veronica Karugu's face was so horribly
disfigured, and her distress so great, that no one had ever seen her

smile. One day John said to her in front of all the others: 'O, Mai Veronica, when you get to Heaven, you will look so beautiful, really beautiful', in such a confident and matter-of-fact tone of voice that she smiled for the first time, and everyone began to see her as she would then be. He said something similar to Stephano Kamyana: 'O, Stephano, you will be such a handsome young man and you've only got a little while to wait.' Through such simple expressions of encouragement, the lepers came to feel that their person, and their life, had a meaning: that they counted for something in the eyes of this white man who had come from far away to share their lives, and that they counted in the eyes of God. As John said to them: 'Other people in the world: what do they do, what use is their life? Yours is the number one vocation: patience, suffering in the likeness of Christ.' They in return revealed to him that 'This strange ecstatic moody folk' was a 'mighty mystery', that they are the signs and the mystery of God, the images of the presence of Christ and of his mission, models of joy in the bottomless pit of their pain, profound philosophers, for 'They seem to cogitate for hours / On what surpasses thought' (*Denizens of the Deep*, undated).

It is essential to grasp this reciprocity in order to understand what was happening at that time in Mtemwa. John might never have come, never have put himself at their service, never have loved them; but the residents of the Centre might not have welcomed him, never understood him, nor loved him in return. And if these years reveal the greatness and beauty of John, they also reveal in no less measure the greatness and the beauty of the lepers. The richness of his relationship with each and every one of the lepers was boundless, as is testified by many witnesses and by his own poems. He was a father to each particular individual and to all at the same time, and was quickly known as Baba John – a brother, a friend, a confidant, a consoler, a master, a servant.

He had the good fortune to be understood and supported by Luisa Guidotti in his relationship with the lepers of Mtemwa. Like him, she was to discover that the lepers needed not only care and compassion, but also friendship, and even deep friendship. She wrote in one letter:

> At first, these poor people appear disgusting with their sores, their stumps, their deformed faces. Later on, one enters into God's light, achieving real friendship with them. They become loving people and one notices their patient resignation. No longer do you love them for God's sake, nor because they help one to give in charity, but because they become one's own dear friends. I hope you can understand what I mean. It is a wonderful experience.

This love intensified her desire to help them, as is revealed in John's description of her and her fellow workers written in *Concerning Mtemwa* (1975):

> Their prodigious efficiency was equalled by their warm-hearted humanity and abounding good-humour. Very soon the lepers loved them and trusted them and felt entirely at home in their presence. They came to Mtemwa and worked there like Trojans twice a week, doing dressings, diagnosing, and giving remedies.

But while he trusted and defended his leper friends, John was not blinded by sentimentality when he felt that they had behaved in unacceptable ways. He reprimanded them severely when they got drunk, or cut branches off the trees, while defending them against others. He fought against alcoholism, sexual promiscuity, violent disputes and lack of religious fervour, and though often disappointed he never lost heart (there is only one poem expressing strong irritation with the lepers, out of some 4000 John wrote in Mutemwa). Above all he was saddened and suffered with them in their affliction, their humiliation, their living death. He remained convinced that they contributed in a special way to the salvation of the world, and often advised his friends: 'If you want to storm Heaven, ask the lepers to pray; their prayers go straight there.'

He had his favourites, such as Peter Katsandanga, mentioned above: blind, deaf, without a nose, or fingers, or toes, almost a walking skeleton, except when he smiled, and then his face lit up, serene, beatific:

> His peaceful look has booked celestial fields
> Yet have his features paid horrific bills:
> Nearly no nose, no eyes, deaf to the trills
> Of chanticleer, but cheerful as his laugh.
> (*A Triple Ballade Royal of a Singular Habitation*, 1978)

John used to bathe Peter, who was ticklish, and loved to make bubbles in his bath. Another was Mai (mother) Hanzu – a tiny, frail 80-year-old:

> Preoccupied with people she is God's
> Preoccupation: toddling goes and nods!
> (*Hanzu: God's oddity*, 1969)

Always smiling, she seemed ageless and accepted everything 'nodding like a Godward gnome'. For John she was a saint, and he dreamt that in the brightness of spiritual sunbeams shone 'That quaintest of the saints, that Hanzu blest'.

Mai Coleta Mapfuta, the young widow who became sacristan and assisted John conducting the choir, was remarkable for her dignified bearing. According to him:

> This lady is by nature like a queen
> And no infirmity can mar her poise,
> She is the dignity amidst our scene,
> Filled with integrity, empty of noise;
> Most musical of all the women here
> From pitch she'll sometimes fall and switch to flat
> But while her concentration is in gear
> Her voice rejoices God's own habitat;
> Through her I know what beauty truly means
> She bears Maria, wears the Queen of Queens.
> (*Coleta*, 1973)

Mai Francesca was in John's eyes another saint. She stood at the foot of the Cross, always quiet. Even when the woman from the next hut switched partner every fortnight, she never got angry, being herself too pure to pay attention to such things. Mai Veronica Karugu, was another saint, according to John, since she began to smile. 'A toeless ballerina', she would run to help whenever a resident became distressed. She was present at all deaths, always finding the words to comfort, and John compared her to Veronica's veil. He and this sensitive woman shared the same sense of humour, as 'she makes some joke well-known to both of us' wrote John (in *Veronica Karugu*, 1971). Elizabeth and Matthew were his Philemon and Baucis. Though Matthew was blind, love – as John remarked – was not, and the two of them made a perfect couple.

By mid-1973, in spite of the difficulties with the Committee and the stray cattle, John had found peace of mind in this fourth year following his discovery of Mtemwa. He was in possession of what he had been looking for all his life, and had imagined to be unattainable: solitude and community. He had time to talk to God and pay homage to the Blessed Virgin Mary; time to marvel at everything that surrounded him; time for his most afflicted and needy neighbour; and time to turn it all into poetry. He was both Martha and Mary for a people as insignificant in the eyes of the world as himself. He could still write of Mtemwa what he had written to his mother on his arrival (29 August 1969): 'Wondrous as Heaven'.

Chapter 9

War and Storms over Mtemwa, 1973–1979

But would they waste a bullet on a clown?
(*Letter to Stephen King*, 14 March 1977)

Suddenly everything seemed to go wrong. A new bone of contention had arisen between John and the Committee. Dr Molesworth, living in Malawi, was advocating closing down the leper colonies and training African carers to visit lepers in their homes. William Ellis was impressed by his ideas and wished to apply them in Rhodesia, having being promised finance by LEPRA, a British organisation for fighting leprosy. He saw here an alternative to Mtemwa, which he now wanted to close down, but John knew that the residents of his Centre had nowhere else to go.

Ellis had found an ally in the person of his namesake Paul Ellis, former medical officer at Mtemwa, who did not see eye to eye with John on how the Centre had evolved during his time there. Dr Ellis was still working on the leprosy issue at the Ministry for Health. As far as he was concerned, John had no training, knew nothing about leprosy, and had no respect for the professionals. In other words he was a dangerous man. Dr Ellis was no doubt thinking of his own experience of Mtemwa, when he called by to pick up medical samples for articles in learned journals. John, who had been present during these visits, disapproved of the brutal manner in which the doctor interacted with the lepers, showing little respect for their human dignity, and hadn't hesitated to say so. Yet he had nothing against medical research as such, and he fully appreciated the necessity for the scientific, epidemiological and therapeutic work of Luisa Guidotti; and Professor Michael Gelfand, highly respected in Rhodesian circles, in turn appreciated John, to whom he gave his full support at Mtemwa, even going as far as to say that John should be recommended for the Nobel Peace Prize, like Dr Schweitzer at Lambaréné.

For William Ellis and the Committee, the chief concern was the way the Centre was being administered – or rather, wasn't. To them the situation was clearly unacceptable. John later wrote (quoted in the *Rhodesia Herald*, 6 September 1979): 'I was sacked because they [RLA] claimed I was careless with supplies and did not keep proper books.' He had no difficulty accepting the last point, but he felt no guilt. He knew he was neither a thief nor was he negligent with the rations, and that was all that counted for him. Whenever a member of the Committee raised the subject, he brushed it aside. He was only interested in the real needs of the lepers, not in figures drawn out of some hat. And when Ellis claimed that the rations were too extravagant and would have to be reduced, he was incensed. On the contrary, John considered them inadequate: a bowl of sadza twice a day, a few fistfuls of beans, one cup of tea with milk and sugar, and at best two oranges and one piece of meat per month. While he himself was ascetic, with the appetite of a bird, he nevertheless insisted that the lepers should eat their fill.

But Ellis was determined to have his decisions respected, and went even further: he instructed John to put a badge around the neck of each leper to prevent queue-jumping, and to make it easier to recognise each leper (the ex-prison warden had come to the surface). This was too much for John, and he lost his temper. The lepers were not so many cattle to be branded; they were human beings. Just like Ellis and the other committee members, they had their own name, face and personal life with which John was familiar, as he told Philippa Berlyn when she came to see him.

Ellis then discovered that Shirley James had invited John for a meal at the Mtemwa hotel, during which the hotel owner served wine freely, and that the local European farmers came up and saluted John as the Director of the Centre. He interpreted this as a provocation, and at the next Committee meeting, on April 12th 1973, he demanded John's instant dismissal, throwing in other complaints for good measure: the Director gave over-long holidays to his assistants, didn't pay sufficient attention to the petrol expenses of the team from All Souls (which they took advantage of), and so on. The Committee backed his proposals, and John was summoned by Ellis to Salisbury. Philip Dighton was present at the meeting, but Ellis took charge of the debate. A year-long build-up of resentment boiled to the surface and was directed at John. In the end Ellis agreed to give John one last chance, but insisted that rations be cut, that nothing be given to spouses or family members, and that the lepers must carry an identifying badge. John indignantly refused. Ellis shouted at John, insulting him, and the two men almost came to blows, at which Ellis again insisted that John be sacked, and leave Mtemwa before May 1st.

As he walked out, John slammed the door behind him. It was the end of Mtemwa. It had lasted for three years and nine months, as long as his stay at Hare Street House, but no longer. This time however was different, because it wasn't about him, or a jackdaw, or the memory of some dead writer. It was about his friends the lepers, and that changed everything. He was determined to fight for them.

The news of his sacking astonished his friends. Father Dove actually felt ill, and in his prayers complained to God, and wrote to John:

> I was quite sick at heart about the whole business yesterday. I complained to the Lord in my prayer. When you came to the lepers they had no heart, no spirit. They had been down-trodden and neglected. You came and you put a new heart, a new spirit into them. You did this by loving them, and bringing them by love back to God. Before, they had no love; they died in squalor. Now they have love through your love, and they are a happy community. This is why there have been fewer deaths. The Committee wants these people to die so that they may close the camp and claim there are no more lepers. To remove love is a good way to bring along death, for it is the meaning of death. They will bind up their limbs, limbs which are destined only for eternal life. They preserve the useless material body in their eagerness to prove to mankind (not to God) what good humanitarians they are, while all the while denying the spirit, the

love for which it is made. May God have mercy
upon the Committee, whose sin is very great.

And he added for John:

This all means that it is imperative for you to
remain near to continue to show forth love and
to nourish these poor folk on the Bread of Love.

He then went on to say that he had already taken steps to ensure
that an official letter from the Archdiocese officially appointed him
to distribute the Eucharist every day at the Centre.

Other friends refused to accept John's sacking, and those who
were giving financial support to Mtemwa wanted to cut off funding
immediately. Even Dr Westwater took John's side, as did Luisa
Guidotti, who did not hesitate to make her anger known. The
Committee then demanded that she hand over the Land Rover
donated by the Amici dei Lebbrosi, even though it was being used
for sanitary evacuations at All Souls. Luisa refused point blank,
having herself got funding for the vehicle in the first place. At this
point Ellis despatched somebody to All Souls to effectively steal
the Land Rover.

At Mtemwa the news greatly upset the lepers: they were going
to take away their Baba John, and they called a meeting to express
their anger. Ellis had very astutely appointed Philo Runganga, one
of the assistants, as new Director. This brawny ex-truck driver was
illiterate, and totally incapable of administering Mtemwa along the
lines being proposed by the Committee; even less was he capable
of keeping accounts or other records up-to-date; but the choice
was a clever one, because the lepers knew and liked him. Moreover
he would be pliable, and grateful for a promotion that he could
never have looked forward to. But Philo was not Baba John, and
the agitation continued. Furthermore, on the Wednesday following
John's dismissal, the Committee members came to Mtemwa to
make sure that Philo reduced the rations of flour and maize. John,
still on the premises, took one of the rations and weighed it: 5 ¾ lbs
instead of the 7 lbs which he was in the habit of serving (in other
words 1270 calories instead of 1600 calories a day). He immediately

informed the Lions Club of Mtemwa, who were financing the Centre, and succeeded in having the old ration of 7 lbs reinstated.

Exile and the Kingdom

April was coming to a close. At daybreak on May 1st, John sang the Office of the Virgin Mary, took his Gladstone bag, Mr Roufe's cane, his sleeping bag and his recorder – the Ark, which had grown considerably in size, and the poems, had already been stored with the Kassim brothers – and left the old butchery, with most of the lepers who could walk accompanying him. Some of them carried his sleeping bag, others the kettle or the Gladstone bag, while the women carried tea, milk powder, bread, a few jars of fruit jam, powdered soup, two saucepans for cooking, and two cups. John himself carried nothing but his recorder. To complete the picture, two policemen were sent from Mtoko to make sure that the ex-Director left the premises, and to prevent any disorder.

From the old butchery it was but a few steps to the exit from the Centre. The procession turned right and arrived at the foot of Chigona, which was John's destination, and the climb began for those who were capable of it. John walked in front, and the column stretched out behind him. After the trees, the group arrived at a less strenuous point, with a sheer cliff face to the right. The climb left many people out of breath, but John was well used to it. Finally they arrived at the summit, where John stopped beside the pond, which was not yet dry, and made an attempt at a joke: 'Look, here is my splendid bathroom – I can use it free of charge.' But nobody laughed, and everybody put down what they had been carrying, and an air of embarrassment set in. One at a time the lepers went back down the mountain and John was finally alone.

He spent the whole day sitting in that position without moving. When evening fell, he collected some dry wood and built a fire, while at the bottom of the hill the lepers heating their rations noticed the glow of the fire on top of Chigona and felt sad. They couldn't understand: they had certainly heard the Europeans saying that John was mad, but they knew it wasn't true. Baba John had saved them from the hell where they were rotting in their own bodies. Day after day he had washed them, dressed their wounds, and given them their medication, towels and enough to eat and make a fire. He had prayed with them to this God that he had told them about with such love, and to the Virgin Mary who protected them. He had sung for them and had stayed with them at the moment of their final journey. And, just as important, he had taught them how to laugh again; he had given them love and had put love back into their lives. He was their friend and continued to love them, otherwise he would have gone away and not camped on Chigona. And they loved him back.

John dined frugally on top of the mountain, prayed, and meditated on his Aventine. Then he got into his sleeping bag and went to sleep (without imagining for a second that one day thousands would come to do the same on the same summit every September in his memory). At dawn he washed in the pond and said the Office. But at this point he became aware of shadowy figures climbing up Chigona, both Europeans and Africans. When they got nearer, John recognised Alistair Guthrie, with young Frank his son, and his friend Bill Watt, three Africans, and Peter Donnelly, who had bought a tent, a good sleeping bag (autumn was on the way) and a little stove. After exchanging greetings they set about putting up the tent – not at the summit, which was too windy, but two thirds of the way up. Since it was impossible to drive the pegs into the hard ground, they secured the tent with big stones. In the meantime Pauline Hutchings had arrived with a pillow, some food, two blankets and some matches. A *braai* ('barbecue', in Afrikaans) was quickly prepared, and a party got under way at which large quantities of wine were consumed. In the afternoon a few lepers arrived in their turn: they had cleared the track with their badza, and promised to come back. In fact the track which John used to climb the mountain was now a real path, accessible to anybody who could walk. For Frank and Bill the day was one of exaltation, and decades later Bill would boast proudly:

> At the ripe old age of 16 a very good friend of mine, Frank Guthrie, and I, at Frank's father's request, went out to the colony and assisted him to set up camp outside the colony after his fallout

with the leper association. All I can say is WHAT
an experience.

His friends left and John found himself alone again. Was it really so
bad after all? But down below the lepers were afraid for him: they
had heard that a leopard lived on Chigona, although nobody had
ever actually seen it. What if it attacked Baba John?

On May 4th John sent his mother a lively piece of verse
describing his new life:

> They would call my people 'inmates',
> Institute a living morgue,
> Pinion them within their gates
> And Number them: by God, by George,
> I've objected to the dragon
> Till they've cried 'Away with John!'

> But I have of friends a legion,
> I am tented on a hill
> Just above my people's region,
> Thrice content at heaven's will:
> This is Ararat – here set
> Is the Ark and mighty yet.

He then went on to tell her: 'I distribute the Eucharist': every
morning after his exercises or a bit of jogging and the recitation
of the Office, John came down from the mountain to visit his
friends the lepers. Archbishop Markall, to Ellis's great annoyance,
had approved John's appointment as minister of the Eucharist, as
requested by Father Dove and Father Ennis. The lepers came to
meet him as he arrived, and he went with them to the chapel, where
he sat down at the organ before distributing the sacrament. Pauline
Hutchings joined them every Wednesday, and they prayed together
for a long time.

His love for the Eucharist increased during this difficult period.
He still considered himself the herald of Christ the King of Israel,
whose paladin he had considered himself for the past 25 years, but
it was the host of the tabernacle and of the soul who sustained him
every day. Later a 'photo' of Christ given to him by Father Rossi,

which he treasured and put in a place of honour on the tabernacle, comforted him in the certitude that the host and the Man of Galilee were one and the same – and, according to Ferdinand Spit, he was convinced it was a photograph of Christ.

Having distributed communion, he immediately returned to Chigona so as not to disobey the order barring him from the Centre. He continued to respect the order except when told that one of the lepers was ill or dying. Then he came down during the night and slipped noiselessly between the huts until he arrived where the person was waiting for him, and spent the rest of the night praying before the Last Journey. His relations with Philo, who for John was the least bad solution after his own expulsion, were amicable. They often talked together, and the exile of Chigona became the advocate of the lepers whenever they wished to complain of a problem. Philo seemed willing to listen, and anxious to do his best.

Up on the kopje, his very own kingdom, John continued to pray, to play the recorder, and to search for his God, and gradually began to write poems again, either out in the open air or in his tent. In July he was delighted to see the bees had come to find him, and he offered them his box of poems, but they didn't stay (*Ave, Saint Anne*, 1973). He missed his Ark, and built himself a minor version of it in his tent. Solitude brought him nearer to God; and his meditation on the Trinity, which he had long practised, arrived at a decisive point during his time on the mountain, becoming a major theme in his poetry and his spiritual life. One might say that it became the basis of his devotion. As always with him it was rooted in everyday reality, not a pretext for stylistic virtuosity in his poetry. As John pointed out in a post-scriptum to the poem *No Other God*, which he wrote on August 31st:

> Meditation upon the Blessed Trinity is as restful
> as singing a canon and as restless as running after
> a ball: which is why the British, who are better
> than anyone at ball-games and rules, must have
> been God's Chosen Race (Syllogistic tautology by
> an untaught silly ass).

For 25 years (see *Sanctus Spiritus*, 1949) he had been nourishing the obsession of St Augustine, among others: to find the words for that which reveals itself to the soul and in the soul of him who contemplates the Trinitarian mystery. And like his predecessors he often resorted to analogies from nature (heat, light and sound, for example), but above all human analogies For ten years he had been using the analogies made popular by his illustrious predecessor: memory, intellect and will, to which he returned again and again. But from 1973 onwards, he developed his own logic: Father/ thought / Son/word / Spirit/voice. This image is not entirely without precedent. Among those whom John may have known were: St Augustine (*De Trinitate* and, more directly, *Sermon 288)*, St Thomas Aquinas (*Opusculum XIII, de differentia divini Verbi, et humani*), and Ludolph of Saxony (*Vita Christi - Great Life of Christ*), much valued in Charterhouses. This Trinitarian analogy became so familiar to him that its expression often became interchangeable with the Trinity itself. We arguably have here an original contribution to the theology of the Trinity, and that it arose from prayer and poetry will not surprise those who are aware of certain trends in contemporary theology. But we will leave the last word to John, written on Chigona at the end of August:

> I grappled with The Trinity
> Till Saint Augustine said,
> 'You'd better stop, God's Mystery
> Is bigger than man's head!':
> Hugging the Doctor's good advice
> With a mug of tea was very nice.
> (*Discretion*, 1973)

But down below, the lepers continued to suffer

The team from All Souls continued to come to Mtemwa, but they couldn't fail to notice a sharp decline in the health and living conditions of the residents. Some lepers were passing blood in their urine, being left untreated, and were no longer getting their medication. Whenever Luisa Guidotti dropped by, the lepers would run up to her saying, 'See, doctor, I'm sick. Don't you have a medicine for me?', because the pharmacy was effectively without supplies. She could only advise them to go to the hospital at Mtoko, which was just what they didn't want to hear. In June, when she came to Mtemwa for a wedding, she was struck to see the lepers cuddling up to her friend like chickens with their mother. Many of them were in tears and told the two Italian women that Baba John must come back.

The situation at Mtemwa was now going rapidly downhill: Philo was decidedly not the man for the job. The complaints of the lepers increased daily, and in spite of John's suggestions nothing was done. Philo had soon realised that the Englishman no longer had any status in the Centre, made John aware of this, and after a few drinks became overbearing. John wrote at this time, in *Concerning Mtemwa*:

> Philo loved and loves to be accounted a very
> kindly and compassionate man by all outsiders. He
> is a very able driver and an efficient administrator.
> He is physically gross but exceedingly powerful.
> He is obsequiously polite to nearly all Europeans:
> I am proud to be one of the notable exceptions.

Moreover his successor went everywhere by car, even within the Centre, and the Committee said nothing, though they had accused Louisa of wasting petrol. But there was worse to come.

Ten days after his appointment, Philo had made explicit and crude advances to Maria Greco. The Italian nun had given him short shrift, in great indignation, and the matter came up before the Committee. Philo denied everything and the matter rested there, because Maria Greco in her goodness had no wish to complain to the police (an African male making indecent proposals to a European woman who was also a nun was liable to receive a long prison sentence, and could expect no mercy from judges, who were all white Europeans). But Ellis, blinded by his anti-Catholic rage, defended Philo and accused Maria Greco. Luisa furiously opened her heart about the matter in a letter to Adele Pignatelli, whose job it was to protect the missionaries, and who immediately forbade them from setting foot in Mtemwa as long as Philo remained in charge. An official protest was sent to Salisbury, but the attitude of the Committee was such that they counter-attacked in a letter signed June 4th, informing Dr Guidotti that the contract with her team was now at an end, and that Mtemwa no longer had any need of their services. Ellis could now claim victory on all fronts. He had got rid of John, and there was no longer any Catholic presence at Mtemwa except for the chapel, and no longer any medical care: the way was open to get rid of the lepers. For the lepers, the consequences were catastrophic. Not only did all provision for them come to an end, but funding and the supplies of medication from Italy also came to an end. Mona Smith was now the only visitor and did what little she could.

John learned that Philo had also tried to abuse a leper woman, Ida, and all the residents of the Centre now complained that they were not getting enough to eat. This was not because of the rationing system, which had been abandoned after John's intervention: Philo was obviously operating a scam with the rations and the fruit. John could see that the lepers were again starting to develop sores, which had been eliminated under his charge, and other pathological symptoms. Even worse, on one occasion when a leper was dying, Philo had sent him to Mtemwa unaccompanied. He later returned in a coffin, and nobody ever knew what his end had been like. John was deeply upset by these developments, and went from time to time on foot to the Mission at All Souls to share his distress with Luisa. She had the utmost admiration for her English friend, who never complained about his own situation on Chigona but only about the lot of his friends the lepers.

What was to be done? John was more upset than he was prepared to admit. He experienced bouts of depression from time to time, which did not escape the attention of Pauline Hutchings, and even talked of destroying all his poems. He confided to Father Harold-Barry: 'They think I'm mad', adding in his self-deprecatory fashion: 'Perhaps I am!' He was deeply traumatised even if he didn't complain openly, and remained highly indignant about the consequences of his sacking for the lepers. Weeks and then months passed, followed by a very cold winter on Chigona. In a letter to his mother on October 10th he once again complained about Philo, and wondered whether he himself should remain at Mtemwa.

Had he not spent five months on his mountain, powerless? But he immediately answered his own questions:

> Am I desirous of a fresh employ
> As Captain of this static ship aground?
> Say Nay, say Yes, if be it to their joy
> I'll drink to it right now and blight confound.

Elsewhere in Rhodesia life went on, as did the war. On July 5th 1973 a Catholic Mission – St Albert's in the north of the country – was attacked for the first time and 295 students were taken away by force (all except eight were rescued by Rhodesian forces). Old Father Rea himself was assaulted, and extremely angry. He was already hostile to the nationalists and later become their implacable enemy. At this point rumours of war were coming nearer and nearer to Mtemwa. In September a report by the security services indicated that the guerrillas were infiltrating the district of Mtemwa from the north (they had in fact been a presence there for a year). The same month the government passed a law whereby any refusal or omission to signal the presence of guerrillas could lead to the death penalty. This in itself was a sign of the growing powerlessness of the government to put down the insurgency.

Piper's Vale

The dry season was coming to an end, and the lepers were becoming more and more anxious about the leopard, which had recently been sighted. John's European friends took the initiative on his behalf. They discovered a ruined hut where John could shelter near the western entrance. John showed no interest, but the rains were now coming, though somewhat late, and the winds were blowing stronger on the mountain and soon carried his tent away in tatters. He finally decided it was time to abandon the mountain, gathered his few possesions and moved into the ruined hut. In reality it was hardly an improvement: the roof was leaking badly, there were no windows, and the rain was seeping through on all sides, and even from below, because the ground had not been drained and the hut was quickly flooded. He then dug a trench and covered up the entrance with corrugated iron, but to no avail. When his friends came upon him paddling in water, Don Purdon went back to his house and returned shortly afterwards with more corrugated iron, a hammer and nails, and secured the roof with thatch.

Now closer to the Centre, John was tempted to visit more often, especially since the lepers came to see him in his hut with an endless stream of complaints. He continued to visit secretly the huts of the dying. Philo steered clear of the dying, sharing as he did the fear of the Shonas of coming into contact with a corpse. He nevertheless complained to the Committee about John's visits, who then lodged a complaint to Mtoko. An injunction was issued forbidding Mr Bradburne from setting foot in the Centre on pain of imprisonment or payment of a fine. The District Commissioner and the Chief of Police went to Mtemwa to notify John of the ban. He could visit the chapel and the central walkway which formed part of the public domain, but if he stepped right or left of this area he would be prosecuted. Their duty completed, they assured him of their sympathy and apologised, explaining that their hands were tied.

But Don Purdon, as president of the rural council of Southern Mtoko, intervened on his friend's behalf. The Committee had important contacts in Salisbury and John was very popular with a lot of local European farmers. He moreover had the support of Archbishop Markall, a moderate in a Catholic Church which was becoming radicalised against the government, and it was clear that it would be inadvisable to make a fuss over such a minor affair. A compromise was found: John was officially authorised to settle within 300 paces outside the Centre and come inside in the performance of his duties at the chapel, and to bring religious consolation to dying lepers, but to them only.

Don Purdon decided to find John a habitation worthy of the name, bought a building site prefab, and loaded it onto his vehicle (Father Dove insisted that the Jesuits reimburse him to the tune of 200 Rhodesian dollars). With the help of some friends the hut was quickly erected. The eighteen pieces, each about two yards high and one yard wide, were secured together by screws, and other triangular pieces served as a roof. John attached to the summit an upturned whisky bottle and a hat that he had brought back from the Holy Land. The whole was quite large, almost six yards in diameter, and afforded real protection from the rain. A low table, a few boxes and a camp bed were supplied to serve as basic comforts.

John was happy enough to have a place of his own again after six months at the mercy of nature, and especially at being able to recover his Ark from the Kassim brothers and rebuild it. His new abode was a perfect expression of his personality. The Ark and the Bible were given a place of honour, and his poems were arranged in proper order. The photos from the West Country his mother sent him every year were hung on the wall, recalling his attachment to Devon. He wasted no time in finding a name for his new residence: Piper's Vale, a far-off echo of his ancestor Randal of Pipe Hill. At night he continued to write his poems by the light of candle stubs which he recovered from the chapel for the purpose.

As soon as the warm season came, the hut became a veritable oven, and when the wind blew the walls would creak and wail. There were no toilet facilities: as John said to Elaine Barkess: 'Just think, the world is my lavatory.' Later he was able to build two traditional-style huts topped with thatch beside his own. One became his kitchen; the other was for lepers waiting to be accepted into the Centre or who had been thrown out by Philo. Sometimes he went there himself to sleep when the wind was too strong and his own hut became too noisy or the heat made it intolerable. John of course never complained, and told John Dove that of all places on the face of the earth it was here that he felt most at home. Pauline Hutchings came every Wednesday bringing food, most of which he gave to the lepers. Don Purdon and other farmers visited him regularly, as did his friends from Salisbury. Philippa Berlyn also called, and published an article recounting the stand-off between John and the Committee. Visits became more numerous, since to see him it was no longer necessary to climb Chigona. The situation of the lepers, however, gradually worsened. In a letter to Shirley James on November 19th, John mentioned that they had eaten nothing for three days, and that when they had warned Philo, 'he just shrugged his shoulders and smiled and said that it had not come from Salisbury in time. Unless with the help of friends I had procured a couple of big sacks or so, the lepers would have gone very hungry.'

On New Year's Day 1974, some farmers and other Europeans from Mtoko came to organise an alcohol-fuelled Hogmanay first-footing at Piper's Vale. The Anglican Bishop of Matabeleland, Robert Mercer, also attended with some friends. The visitors announced themselves in advance, which was just as well, as John was inclined to display bad humour when disturbed without warning. He was sitting under a tree when they arrived by car, and gave them a gracious reception. He was attentive to everybody, and on this occasion got to know Anne Lander, a young Anglican who was accompanying the Bishop. Having come from England to the colony in 1953, she married Roy Lander, who was of original white Rhodesian stock and worked in Water and Forests, eight years later. She had discovered she had a gift as a healer, and devoted herself as much as she could to sick people (which resulted later in her meeting Jean Vanier and participating in the foundation of the first L'Arche community in Zimbabwe). John pointed out to Anne a very beautiful eagle hovering in the sky above. The two of them looked for some time at the bird and something seemed to happen between them unnoticed by the others. She later described their friendship as triangular, based on the Trinity, to whom they both shared a special devotion.

During the meal John hardly ate anything, but enjoyed sharing a bottle of Portuguese rosé brought by one of the guests in the shade of a *ndondo* ('spirits') tree. John served coffee all round, listened attentively to everyone, told some jokes, and introduced them to Veronica, who was also an Anglican. Bishop Mercer noted how much John wished his guests to feel relaxed. He seemed to understand the paradox of this man who, though he sought out solitude, was at the same time naturally sociable, telling himself that John, far from being a misfit, as he had heard, was simply a man whose sole aspiration was to live close to God. For her part Anne was deeply impressed by John's sincerity. She later became a frequent visitor to Mtemwa and Silveira House, and ultimately sought admission to the Catholic Church.

In this beginning of the year 1974, John was not in great health. He didn't yet have a mosquito net, and spent most of the night warding off insects. He didn't have a penny to his name: when the annual Christmas box arrived from his mother with the precious calendar, he didn't even have enough money to claim it from the post office at Mtemwa, and had to wait until John Dove arrived. But his real concerns were elsewhere. The lepers were starting to die again because of neglect, four of them during the first two months of the year. Philo had no interest in them, and when they were dying John was obliged to stay with them right up to the end and bury them himself in the cemetery of the Centre. At Piper's Vale day and night the lepers occupied all his attention, outside the enclosure. And when those members of the Committee who continued to support him came to visit, he wanted them to worry about the lepers and not himself. He had moreover found an ingenious way of helping those who were sick, which didn't escape the attention of Caterina Savini: he would fill a hollowed-out book with medication and then enter the Centre as if he was carrying it for devotional purposes, and distributed its contents to the lepers. In the 1970s, Hansen bacillus became more resistant to sulfones and stronger medicine was necessary, which the Committee refused to finance.

The Committee continued with its plan to disengage from Mtemwa, with a view to eventually closing the Centre. John Ingram, representative in Rhodesia of the Beit Trust, which made an annual subscription of 4000 Rhodesian dollars, had proposed a supplementary grant of the same amount. The secretary-treasurer, Mrs P. Beecroft, who was closely linked to Ellis, turned it down on the grounds that there was no need for it at Mtemwa, even though the Committee was proclaiming elsewhere that there wasn't enough money for rations and medication. In February, John sent a memorandum in verse to the Lions Club of Mtemwa on the situation at the Centre, which the club was financing. He told them that the lepers in the hospital at Mtoko were given no right either to a bed or a mattress. Three of them actually died lying on the ground, and the Centre had not been informed about the third death until a week later. At Mtemwa bandages were only changed once a week, and when new symptoms appeared they were ignored by Philo. Rations were being distributed irregularly or not at all, and the same went for petrol and medication. In conclusion John defended Philip Dighton, 'a friend of the lepers', but once again criticised Ellis, suggesting an evil spell by the 'Cockatrice' (a mythical beast), and told the Lions that their Christmas present was represented as having coming from Dighton. He apologised for appearing disrespectful of the eighth Commandment and the Gospel injunction to turn the other cheek, but it was not a matter of himself but of THEM, who suffered so much.

The letter infuriated Ellis and his supporters, who next tried to suggest to Salisbury that John was mad, in an attempt to have him committed to an asylum and be rid of him once for all. John then discovered yet another reason to worry:

> The weekly beer-drinks, which through the long tradition of Mtemwa had always been from Saturday until Sunday evening only, were allowed to begin on Friday and drag on to soporific tedium ending on Wednesday. This spoilt one of the happy contrasts of Mtemwa's life and blunted the edge of a beer-drink's healthy joy.
>
> (*Concerning Mtemwa*, 1975)

Alcoholism was beginning to take hold at the Centre, and John was appalled by the turn that events had taken and by his own helplessness. His daily visits to the Centre became an ordeal for him, exacerbated by the fact that he was obliged to remain outside for most of the day, but in this time of trial he continued to pursue his life of prayer. He sang his Office in his hut, which had become more and more suffocating, the tree which he had planted being still too small to offer much shade. His poetic inspiration had reawakened: he wrote a dozen poems in a single day on March 1st and as many again six days later.

The same month, Jocku, the leper with the Scottish accent – 'there's Scottish intonation / In every word of English he'll assay' (*Joku*, 1969) – and who had only stumps for legs, died without even a mattress or a bed after a long agony, during which John read him the Bible and prayed for him with other lepers (he had baptised him and given him the name of Joseph a month previously). This death and other worries took a great deal out of him, and he went through another period of depression.

The majesty of the law

Still, in March 1974, the affair of Ida the leper became known. Philo's easy going ways in allowing anybody who wished into the Centre had attracted a lot of hangers on, and the presence of no longer infectious female lepers was not the least reason for this influx. These women in search of affection as much as protection were easy prey. Among these was Ida, who had offended Philo by rejecting his advances and had welcomed into her hut a certain Tom, who claimed to be a sailor. The latter soon disappeared, taking with him the meagre belongings of the unfortunate woman. She tried to make a formal complaint, but Philo had no desire to have the police prying into the affairs of the Centre, and threatened to expel her if she persisted in her plan.

On March 12th (or the 15th, according to another source) Philip Dighton was visiting Mtemwa. Philo, calling Ida a slut, accused her also of manufacturing kachasu, a beer high in alcohol, which was forbidden, and demanded her expulsion. When she heard this, Ida ran to John to ask for his help. He jumped on his bicycle and peddled straight to Mtoko to inform the District Commissioner of this latest injustice. At the administration offices he met Rob Boell (which he spells Bell), an Assistant Commissioner with whom he had occasionally shared a gin and tonic. He told him the story of Ida, which Boell noted, and they went for a meal together, during which John was unable to swallow anything. The administrator told him not to worry about recent events, that he would file a report to the District Commissioner, and that the matter would be dealt with.

As they left, John saw Dighton's car heading for the administration offices. Bell told him to wait in his office and went to see Saunders, the District Commissioner, and John waited for his return the whole afternoon. As evening fell, Boell and his wife returned, both carrying a firearm: there had been a Terr (terrorist) alert. The Commissioner had only been able to listen to Dighton very briefly, and the conversation did not get around to Ida and Philo, but was confined to John. Dighton had handed on to the Commissioner a letter from the Committee. Moreover, at Philo's request, Dighton had accused three lepers of manufacturing kachasu.

When John got back to Piper's Vale, the lepers were waiting for him. Philo had insisted to Dighton that Ida should be expelled from the Centre, but they had intervened in her favour and Dighton had suspended the order (which was why he hadn't spoken about it to Saunders). The next day John went back to Mtoko and learnt from the Commissioner, who did his best to give the impression of 'looking as stern as such a good-humoured and reasonable person could manage to look, for the reading to me of what turned out to be another big Bluff' (*Concerning Mtemwa*, 1975). The contents of the letter about himself were as follows: the Committee was threatening to withdraw totally from Mtemwa if the administration did not agree to ban John completely from the Centre.

John felt that Saunders was laughing behind his back, and went for lunch with a farmer friend without too much concern. But on Saturday the 16th, things took a turn for the worse. Following Philo's complaint, two police officers came to Mtemwa to enquire into the illicit manufacture of kachasu, of which Simon, Lazaro Chimatashu and Timu were suspected, and which they vehemently denied. When the police left, a fight broke out between Philo and the lepers. Philo attacked the leper who had defended Ida, Lazaro, blind and without hands, knocking him on the ground three times. John arrived at this point and reacted as an ex-Chindit, punching Philo, though causing little harm to his burly successor. He then went to file a complaint against Philo for attacking the lepers. Lazaro was shocked and shaking, but furious, and managed to walk as far as the administrative office near Mtemwa, which was within the district of Mudzi. He was refused a hearing because the Centre was attached to Mtoko, and a policeman drove him back to Mtemwa. On the way they met Philo's car. Denying that he had beaten Lazaro who, Philo claimed, could not walk straight because he was drunk, he managed to convince the escort. To make matters worse, the doctor at Mtemwa, Dr Croce, examined the lepers on whose behalf John had filed his complaint on the 20th, and concluded that there were no signs of an assault. In his certificate he cleared Philo of the charge and the latter was pronounced not guilty, to the great distress of his accusers. Both Ida and Lazaro were then forced to leave the Centre.

In the meantime, during Sunday Mass on the 17th, Father Martin Charira, a cousin of Philo who had replaced Father Chakaipa as chaplain to the All Souls Mission, announced to the lepers and their assistants that his cousin Philo had admitted his wrongdoing and asked for forgiveness. The lepers were edified by such Christian behaviour, but John remained sceptical. Three days later, when Father Martin left the chapel, Philo arrived and asked his cousin to forget everything he had said because another cousin had taken charge of the affair and so he had nothing to fear. Moreover he claimed to have discovered wooden troughs, needed to manufacture kachasu or nepa (a very potent alcohol), including one under a banana tree beside Ida's hut, and he had taken them to the police as evidence. He then went off for a two weeks holiday, but not before pushing Timu and shouting: 'Before I leave here, I will kill one leper!'

John was horrified. The police came to serve the summonses on the three lepers in whose hut the wooden troughs had allegedly been found: Ida, John Kawirawira and Stephano Sianona. John was adamant: these old wooden troughs had not been used for donkey's years. Before the accused were due to appear in front of the magistrate, John went to him to defend the lepers, and the judge agreed to say that, even if the charge was true, the life of the lepers was already hard enough. John spoke to him of Philo's vengeance, and the magistrate advised him to come in advance of the trial on the following Monday to defend his friends in the presence of the prosecutor. John did as directed, and all three were set free after a little lecture on the dangers of nepa. Philo, who had had to drive them to the courthouse, was furious, but all this legal wrangling was reflecting badly on the Centre.

John learned later that the Committee had contacted Father Dove to arrange an amicable departure for him, which his friend of course refused to sanction. But the members of the Committee went to the ministry and made their position clear: it is either him or us. After this, John experienced some days of deep depression, particularly as some lepers were beginning to turn against him. In effect they had lost everything: medical provisions, love, and John himself, but they had to get on with their lives. Some of them were terrorised by Philo and others totally dependent on him. So while they continued to welcome John to their hut at night, they started to give their backing to Philo during the day whenever he badmouthed John. The loyalties of the Centre became divided. John discovered that the lepers who had been taken to the hospital at Mtemwa were left in the sun for hours on the back of Philo's truck and came back even more ill.

John saw his life's work being destroyed and realised that he was gradually being sidelined. In a letter to Shirley James he asked himself if he would always be a failure? The Africans themselves sometimes regarded him as mad. On top of this everybody called him John, even the children, and he began to ask himself if they were laughing at him behind his back. He also spoke about it to John Dove when they met: 'Everybody calls you Baba but me, John, even though I am older than you and I am 53 years of age.' This was in fact not true: the lepers called him Baba John, and John then realised what he had just said and burst out laughing. His ability to laugh at himself indicated that he had not yet reached rock bottom, but he was beginning to wonder whether he should go back to Jerusalem.

In the meantime he left for Silveira House to take a break. The Jesuit house was under surveillance, and voices within the Rhodesian Front had been heard to describe it as a Communist safe-house. It was the case that two of Mugabe's sisters worked there (Bridget had joined Sabina), but the protection of the immovable Mark Partridge still carried some weight and the matter went no further.

At the end of February 1974, Harold Wilson won the British General Election, which was a setback for Ian Smith, who had always enjoyed the backing of the Conservative Party. In the meantime the guerrilla threat was becoming stronger: five white farmers had been murdered in the Centenary and Mount Darwin regions between February and October. But an event in a faraway country was about to play a determining role in the future of this rebel colony. On April 25th the 'Carnation Revolution' broke out in Portugal, leading to the withdrawal of the Portuguese from its colonies in Africa (including nearby Mozambique). In an election in Rhodesia at the end of July, 50 seats out of 50 went to the Rhodesian Front (2980 Africans had been allowed to elect eight deputies, and eight others were designated by the chiefs). At Mtoko the Rhodesian Front hardliner Rodney Simmonds got two-thirds of the votes of the farmers and other European voters. Meanwhile guerrilla infiltrations were stepped up.

John continued to defend and help his friends the lepers. At the beginning of August he went to Salisbury to meet Louise Westmaster, who promised yet again to help all she could. He took advantage of his visit to see his doctor. He had caught bilharziasis, but apart from that he was fine. At 53 years of age he went jogging daily and continued to climb Chigona like a young man, though he slipped from time to time on the way up or down and came back one day of August with his face 'transfigured' with blood (as he wrote in *Cribsongs*)! He struck his visitors as being in good health, even though he himself was a little frightened by what he saw as his old man's face, his wrinkles and his horrible teeth, and his greying hair held in place by a headband. He only saw himself in the mirror on his visits to Salisbury – he had no mirror at Mtemwa and tended to forget what he looked like, and when someone tried to sell him a moped his first reaction was: 'It doesn't have a rear-view mirror. I couldn't even use it to look at myself.'

One question continued to torment him: how far must he go in loving his enemies?

> However, 'Love thine enemy' is such
> A leap beyond the best in lesser creeds
> That we may not assess its meaning much
> Till some fell enemy impels its needs:
> But God The Holy Ghost compels us never.
> (*Love thine enemy*, 1974)

He came back to Mtemwa on August 9th with a piece of advice from John Dove: make peace with Philo. On top of his other vices, Philo was also bone lazy, and when he saw John coming humbly in his direction without asking for anything other than to serve the lepers, he was only too glad that John seemed to want to do the work for him and readily agreed. John gradually recovered his *de facto* position at Mtemwa, under the eagle eye of his former assistant. But he still had great difficulty in forgiving Philo's treatment of lepers. Thus in his *Ode to an Odious Committee* on September 24th he cynically congratulated the Committee on the number of lepers who had died since the beginning of the year, adding for good effect that 'with luck / By Christmas-time the score will climb to ten' – in other words, a mortality rate of nearly 15 per cent, even though it had fallen sharply in preceding years. And this was not forgetting those who had been expelled, Ida and Lazaro, who were now living near his own hut.

The war intensifies

A new threat had now appeared on the horizon: the spectre of total war. For the first time, machine-gun fire could be heard in the distance, and was getting nearer all the time. On August 29th John wrote to Shirley James: 'Can hear machine guns firing quite nearby now. Helicopters hover all day long. But shall probably die of hiccups only.' The same applied to All Souls, and in a letter addressed to Adele Pignatelli, Luisa Guidotti alerted her that the vakomana were already dug in in the Mount Darwin region, 60 miles to the north-west of Mtoko, and were now making incursions into their zone, some of them quite near the Mission. This awareness of the dangers inspired in John on September 22nd an astonishing poem:

> To those who, loving little, live life not
> I make for death no deep apology;
> To those who look upon it as the cot
> Of rest in Christ till rising, I reply
> Duly with Alleluia; but, to die,
> Wait not till death: die to the deadly seven,
> Put on in time sublime eternity,
> Think immortality, link up with heaven.
>
> Anticipate, undissipate and plot
> To overthrow the sloth, the jealousy,
> The lust, the pride, the avarice, the lot
> O steep your greed in abstinence and fly!
> Be angry but injustice to defy,
> Relish God's grace and not the hellish leaven

And, lifting heart and mind aligned on high,
Think immortality, link up with heaven.
(A Ballade of a Blithe Anticipation, 1974)

All of a sudden a détente seemed for a while possible. Ian Smith had understood that the inevitable independence of Mozambique would favour the guerrillas, and had begun discreet negotiations with the nationalists. He had Sithole and Nkomo released from prison, and declared a ceasefire on December 11th.

At Mtemwa, despite the threat from the guerrillas, the roads were still safe and visitors were still as numerous, including Sister Kathleen Keane, an Irish nun of the congregation of the Blue Sisters, whose house John had once kept an eye on, and who was now working at St Anne's Hospital in Salisbury. A trip to Mtemwa to spend a day with 'this aristocratic Englishman, mystic and wandering poet' was for her something to look forward to. One day in September she arrived with Father George Carry SJ and some African sisters. Sister Kathleen had put a hamper in the boot of the car for the picnic, and everybody sat down under the mango tree while the food was passed around. News and jokes were exchanged. According to Sister Kathleen, John was the most 'gracious and entertaining host', although this wasn't always the case for others. She felt that he was teaching them not by delivering sermons, which was never his style, but through anecdotes, poems, philosophical reflections and song.

The Irish nun did not fail to notice that new lepers continued to arrive at Mtemwa, and that for John each one of them, and especially the most deformed, was 'a loved and cherished friend – never "a case"'. All the services he provided for them, whether material or spiritual, health care, or acting the peacemaker in an argument, were always given with love. She watched him dressing a septic wound, never stopping joking or offering a word of encouragement, or whatever the situation demanded. The nun noticed how these diminutive creatures, who came to John sometimes on all fours, seemed to be reassured by him. He never demonstrated any superiority, he was only their servant – as on the day when he took the wheelbarrow from Jam-Johnson, who wanted to build himself a new kitchen, and used it to fetch the bricks the leper needed for the job, which demanded five wheelbarrow trips. Sister Kathleen was also highly impressed by the religious life of the Centre. John knew how to communicate to the lepers his love for the Holy Sacrament:

> He loved to bring them Holy Communion, and his own transparent love-relationship with God seemed to permeate the whole sorry encampment of pathetic shacks.

John himself also retained a happy memory of Sister Kathleen's visit, and on October 1st sent her a poem of thanks to Father Carry, something he often did for his visitors.

At Christmas Father Dove arrived and celebrated the feast with John and the lepers. After Mass, John gave out the Christmas boxes which had been prepared this year by his friend Sister Jeanine Frank and the pupils of the Dominican convent in 4th Street in Salisbury. The next day he left for Silveira House, where he would most certainly have met one very special guest: Robert Mugabe who, on his release from prison, was given an office and telephone in Silveira House. Father Dove asked him to give some classes on Christianity and socialism and, according to Doris Lessing, on trade unionism. He also introduced him to Luisa Guidotti, who told Mugabe of the catastrophic sanitary situation in the north-east. Mugabe's sisters were still working at Silveira House (they were also involved in underground activities, in particular collecting money for ZANU). After ten years in prison, Mugabe was still relatively unknown (unlike the head of ZANU, Herbert Chipeto, who lived in Lusaka). This former Mission schoolteacher called himself a Catholic Communist, which was not an exceptional label at the time. Prison life had hardened Mugabe's vague socialism and he had become Marxist-Leninist, even though he was hiding it at Silveira House, especially as the Centre was being watched by members of the security services. Whenever Father Dove came across one of these he would say to his team: 'Today, we are sailing close to the wind.'

Back in Mtemwa John received a visitor at the beginning of 1975 which revived his interest in the Franciscans. Bruce Wilkinson was a young Englishman who had won a trip to Rhodesia in a raffle for the Jesuit Missions, and he intended to take full advantage of it in spite of the war. Father Mangan took him to Mtemwa, and John soon discovered that they were both of the Franciscan Third Order. Bruce gave him a picture by Giotto of St Francis preaching to the birds, which his host kept as a precious souvenir, and received from him in return a picture of the saint walking through a forest. When he got back to England he wrote to John to thank him and sent him a tape recorder, which never arrived. John wrote back to him in March in the form of a poem which he called *A walk through two hemispheres*. He saw in Bruce a kindred spirit in search of the Golden Fleece. Each verse of the poem ends with the refrain: 'And freedom in the Truth, Franciscan brother'. A friendship had been born.

Luisa Guidotti came back from Italy, where she had taken her final vows. This time she found herself in a region where war had definitely taken control, and she heard three times in one week outbursts of machine-gun fire close to the Mission, despite the ceasefire. Like Caterina Savini, she refused to allow herself to be recruited into the military medical corps. Both women wanted to keep their freedom and not to appear as agents of the government. She started to visit Mtemwa Centre again, but this time without a contract.

In February a new priest arrived at All Souls mission: Father David Gibbs. This son of English teachers who had emigrated to Rhodesia had discovered a vocation while working as a farm manager. Fresh from his theological studies in South Africa, where he had been ordained and had taken a course to perfect his Shona, his first post was to All Souls. This tall, lean and bearded young man was also consumed with devotion to God and the Eucharist: 'A confrere calling upon him one day found him in his simple church, staring at the Tabernacle as if he wished to pierce its metal with his gaze' ('Tribute to a Zimbabwean priest', *Independant Catholic News*, 9 November 2001). He quickly got to know Mtemwa, and shared John's great compassion for the lepers. He picked up the habit of dropping by every Wednesday to celebrate Mass at the Centre, and he admired John's eccentricities without ignoring his human frailties. He became a special support for John. Pauline Hutchings and her children were the most faithful attenders at his Masses, and John was always at the organ to make sure that the sanctity of the place was respected. One day a couple of African strangers arrived in the chapel before Mass began and started to chat and took out a packet of peanuts and began eating them. John arrived and scolded them for their lack of respect.

A year before, Anthony Wilkinson had written an article in the *Observer* concluding that Ian Smith had already lost the war:

> White rule was unlikely to survive a protracted guerrilla war... White Rhodesia was founded by force and for eighty years has been successfully maintained by economic and military superiority. It is not altogether surprising that many black people in Rhodesia have taken from this experience the precept that 'might is right'.

The Mtoko zone bore out this diagnosis while, on a national level, the hanging of rebels was continuing at the beginning of the new year, despite the ceasefire – which in any case was less and less respected on both sides. Robert Mugabe succeeded on April 1st in leaving Rhodesia undercover for Mozambique, with the help of a priest and some nuns. He rapidly imposed himself as the new head of ZANU (Herbert Chitepo having been assassinated in March). Ian Smith launched a campaign to bring a million new settlers into the country. He failed, and the migration was reversed. On June 25th, Mozambique gained independence and allied itself to the Front Line countries. The Marxist government at Maputo began closing down Catholic schools, expelling missionaries, and indoctrinating the population in the principles of the new regime.

Ian Smith used these events to reinforce his claim to be defending Christian civilisation, while moves towards negotiations in August, then at the end of the year, were cut short, as the war intensified. From the beginning of the year skirmishes and mine explosions became more numerous, as did the roar of helicopters overhead in pursuit of the Terrs. In Mtemwa, John could see almost every day Dakotas and Alouettes flying overhead, coming and going from anti-terrorist operations, which he described in a poem on January 25th:

> To watch a river-crossing by a troop
> Of gray baboons is gay in the extreme;
> To see a helicopter loop-the-loop
> Is fitter far for nightmare than for dream.
> (*A Ballade of a Crossing Crowned*, 1975)

Once they had moved into the Tribal Trust Lands at Charewa, ZANLA in effect settled into the Chimoyo zone nearer still to Mtemwa, and with the end of the war in Mozambique the region had become of vital strategic importance. The frontier was long and often mountainous, the valleys formed a corridor through which the guerrillas could pass, and the kopjes and their caves provided hiding places.

Philo was still nominally Director of the Centre, but John had resumed his work, which was scarcely different from how he had operated before his expulsion. He tried to help those with special problems. Thus he wrote on March 13th 1975 to Sister Fidelis in Salisbury to thank her for a gift that he had used to buy groundnuts for the lepers, and asked her to arrange for the baptism of young Chamanorwa Shumba, Ida's son, who wished to embrace the Catholic faith, and send him to Mtemwa at the Easter break. But his goodness still found it difficult to include his enemies. He described William Ellis as a 'blighted swine' in *Concerning Mtemwa*. Pharisaism, even when anti-clerical, was for him the one unforgivable sin.

Father Gibbs, with the curiosity and the wonder of a new arrival, leaves an account of John's life at Mtemwa at this time:

> John's day began in a sense at dusk with the chanting of the evening Office in his hut. The night hours were his, unless there was a death or a very sick leper in the compound, to be spent in prayer and meditation and – 'when the Muse came' – in writing poetry. In the early hours of the morning he would run a mile, 'just to keep fit', have a quick wash in the plastic basin outside his

front door, and then set off for the compound to open the church in preparation for the morning communion service. A priest would visit Mutemwa each week for Mass, and on the other days John would hold the morning service, reading from the Bible, reciting the morning prayers, administering the Blessed Sacrament, and playing the organ.

The voices die away, the organ stops, the doors are opened and the lepers file out led by Baba (father) John carrying a basket. As the lepers come out of the chapel, having just received the Body of Christ, they stop to chat to Baba John. Some say 'hello', others ask for medicine for a headache, a cough, a cold, malaria, itching body, or sore eyes. Baba delves into his basket and produces a bottle, a tube, a few capsules, an ointment, a cream, or just a few sweets for those who need cheering up. There is something for everybody. Spiritually fulfilled, materially helped, the lepers move off to their huts happy, cared for, and at peace with God and with each other. Some walk, others crawl and still others are wheeled away in wheelchairs.

After the last leper has gone to his hut, 'Baba' John puts away his basket, closes the harmonium, shuts the church and makes his way slowly down the avenue towards his hut to have breakfast. John lived on bread, cheese, coffee, lactogen (powdered milk), orange juice, and the occasional egg, giving away most of what he was given to the lepers. 'After all', he said, 'the lepers need these things more than I do'. He didn't believe in saving anything. The lepers were always needing something and John was always receiving just what they needed at the time they needed it, or else money would find its way to Mutemwa in time to buy what was wanted in the compound. 'Help', John was fond of saying, 'always comes from somebody.' He received clothing, food, medicines, and numerous other gifts which he used to make the lives of the lepers more bearable – snuff, pipes, sweets, sacks of nuts, powdered milk, and fresh meat. All sorts of gifts came from all sorts of people – all were passed on to the lepers and all were used to help them.

Once breakfast was over, John went back to the compound for his 'rounds'. He visited every leper every day just to make sure that all was well. If anybody needed any help, John was there to give it. He would bath those who needed bathing, build fires, make beds, change dressings, and give out whatever he had received or bought for his people. At the beginning of the 'round' his wheelbarrow was always full – full of sugar, tea, sweets, onions, vegetables, nuts, tomatoes, bread, meat – anything he had to give out. By the time he reached the chapel for the midday Angelus, the barrow was empty and each leper had been helped in some way. After a period of quiet in the presence of the Lord, the afternoon would be spent in much the same way – cutting firewood, cleaning out the cattle grid, collecting reeds for making hats, making tea or coffee for the sick, or just popping in to chat and cheer up the people. Once or twice a week, John would go up to the village to do the shopping for the lepers. For those really ill or dying, John would buy something special at the village – perhaps fresh oranges, an egg or two, an extra portion of milk, or a pint of 'real' milk. On his return from the shopping he would visit his special patients – those seriously ill at the time – and help them to get their fire lit, bed made, pipe filled, coffee boiled, or whatever other small tasks needed to be done. Sometimes he would simply crouch on his haunches and chatter away, trying to help and encourage.

At a death John was always present to give comfort to the dying and to all the lepers who were losing a dear friend. In a small community like Mutemwa a death affects everybody very deeply, and John helped the lepers, even those who had no beliefs, to see that death was, in most cases, a blessed relief from many years of suffering and the opening of the door to joy, peace and happiness.

At about four o'clock the bell rang for the saying of the rosary and evening prayers in the church – held early so as not to coincide with the lepers' evening meal at five o'clock. After the last leper had left the church, John would lock up, pop in to see anybody who might need help to settle down for the night, and then make his way down the avenue back to his hut to spend the night alone with his God, singing, praying, writing, or just sitting quietly in the presence of his Maker.

On top of these activities John continued to read. He received several books in 1975, even if he never got around to reading them (apart from the Bible and *The Cloud of Unknowing*) in spite of encouragement from Father Harold-Barry. In reply to *A Ballad of the Valentine*, which he had sent her on February 13th, Shirley James sent him *Jonathan Livingston Seagull* by Richard Bach. He didn't have time to read it until August, then wrote to thank her for this story in which he recognised a parable of his own journey. Later he would read Gavin Maxwell's *Ring of Bright Water*, a story about sea otters which gave him much pleasure, and *The Cruel Sea* by Nicholas Montsarrat, which he didn't enjoy.

Visits remained uninterrupted by the war. Michael Gelfand had brought Professor Stuart Saunders to visit his Department of Medicine at the University. Saunders, head of a similar department in Cape Town, was an adversary of apartheid. When he expressed a wish to visit a Mission hospital, Gelfand sent him with one of his young confreres to Dr Guidotti. The gravity of the pathologies which he discovered there shocked the South African doctor. The war and its depredations were wreaking havoc on food supplies. An enquiry set up revealed that a third of children in African hospitals suffered from malnutrition, and field research indicated zones where this was affecting up to 80 per cent of the population, while the commercial farms were flourishing.

The war was in full swing, and skirmishes continued to occur in the vicinity of the Mission. When Stuart Saunders asked Luisa whether she was afraid, she replied that yes, she was very afraid. He then asked her what she feared the most, to which she replied: 'making the wrong diagnosis'. Luisa then took her visitor to Mtemwa, where Saunders was also shocked by the gravity of the condition of the lepers 'crawling' on the stumps of their elbows and knees barely covered by a piece of cloth. When he arrived at John's hut, which he described as an 'aluminium wigwam set in the blazing central African sun', he was struck by the simplicity of the interior: a mosquito net and a hammock occupied one part of the room, and there was one chair. John offered Saunders the chair, and the other three sat down on the ground around him. (Saunders, at the time in his 40s, spoke of John, who was 10 years older than him, as 'a young man'.) Somewhat taken aback by the religious symbolism of 'an altar with a cross and also the star of David, the crest of Islam and a Buddha' (John's Ark), he was no less struck by John's 'devout' Catholicism. John spoke to him about his leper friends and of their suffering in a tone that 'deeply impressed' Saunders. (In his memoir, *Vice-Chancellor on a Tight Rope* (2000), he referred like many others to John's possible beatification, and associated Luisa and John as 'two extraordinary persons who made a deep impression on me'.) But while John gave a courteous welcome to doctors like Michael Gelfand or Stuart Saunders, he never hid his disagreement with those who seemed to treat his friends as laboratory guinea pigs, like Dr Paul Ellis, who had just arrived again to take tests for medical purposes from 77 lepers.

On April 12th 1975 the *Rhodesia Herald* published another article on Mtemwa which was favourable to John. He wrote to thank the newspaper with the following clarification:

> But, what with 'a tiny tin hut' and 'the tiny
> makeshift church', I might almost write to *The
> Times* and tell them I'm Tiny Tim! We are very
> proud of the church and of its excellent Architect;
> I want to stress this.

Ellis was infuriated by the article and even Dighton was irritated. On the 17th a certain Rob Mascetti with an address in Union Avenue, Salisbury, wrote a letter to the *Herald* claiming that all was going for the better in Mtemwa. When John heard about this, he wrote an angry but obscure poem to the newspaper, which refused to publish it. A few weeks later Philip Dighton came alone to Mtemwa. John had never stopped respecting and liking him, and had always regretted seeing him under Ellis's thumb. The two men had a frank conversation, and Dighton returned to the Centre on two other occasions during the year. By Christmas their reconciliation was complete – at least for the time being.

Intensification of the war

John learnt from Luisa Guidotti that on the evening of May 17th some vakomana had arrived at All Souls Mission. They had entered her room and their chief saluted her with a raised fist. Astutely she had clapped her hands, which was the traditional Shona greeting, offering a sonorous *Manheru* ('Greetings'). She told him that she had left Europe and its sign language behind and that she preferred Shona. The man had seen the joke and laughed. The guerrillas then took her and Caterina Savini to attend a *morari*, where a hundred or so villagers had gathered together. The chief had made the villagers welcome 'Comrade Luisa' with chants and slogans, and when she sat down the meeting resumed with slogans and revolutionary songs whose melodies were often those of ancient Christian ceremonies repeated again and again. The chief asked the two women to stay at the hospital, saying that 'their services were greatly needed.' John left reinforced in his conviction that the 'Russian Bear', as he wrote in several poems and letters, was behind the vakomana (John never spoke of the USSR and the Soviets, always of Russia and Russians).

On July 25th a curfew was declared by the Rhodesian government in the east of the country, and the Mtoko zone was given the war name of *Takawira*. A Joint Operations Commandment (JOC) was installed at Mtoko airport, from where airborne troops would scramble whenever a group of Terrs were identified, backed up by ground troops mainly composed of African auxiliaries, directed by European officers and conducting patrols. The comings and goings of planes and helicopters passing over John's hut became more and more oppressive, while the villagers of the district found themselves caught between two fires. But it was the army who terrorised them most, as is indicated by a witness, Rukariro, at the time five years old and the son of an African farmer:

> My memory at this time of White rule in then Rhodesia was lying in the sun naked on the rocks after a swim and seeing the army convoy trucks crossing the bridge by the dam. One day they stopped on the bridge and by the motions that were being made by the soldiers, the orders were to get us to them for questioning. Although I was below the age of six and had not had any preschool education, my instinct was to run. To run wildly into the bush and find cover, camouflage yourself with the bush and hide from these, terrorists? I didn't know who was what.

John himself was most of all concerned with the housing problems of his friends at the Centre. He continually tried to find alternatives to the ridiculous suggestions of the Committee concerning medication, constantly pressing his correspondents (especially his brother Michael in Canada, and Stephen King, who was enjoying a very successful career in Tasmania) to send him more supplies. During a visit to Canada, Father Harold-Barry paid a visit to Michael; but the Jesuit actually asked John's brother not to send too much because John gave it all away to the lepers. (However, according to David, Michael's son, Father Dove was less reticent on a visit to the family on the occasion of this trip to Canada.)

John kept in touch with Father Ennis, now parish priest of Salisbury Cathedral, who from time to time sent him visitors, no doubt thinking that they could serve Mtemwa in some way, or who were themselves on a spiritual search of some kind. Such was the case with Margaret de Haast, who found herself one day on the road to Mtemwa. She announced herself on arrival, but found nobody at the tin hut. After an hour's wait she was preparing to leave, thinking that she had mixed up the day, when a tall and thin bearded man appeared running out of the bush, which irresistibly made her think of what John the Baptist must have looked like. When she greeted him saying: 'You must be Robin Hood,' he replied: 'And you must be Maid Marian.' From then on they used these same nicknames for each other. John apologised for being late: he had been playing his recorder beside the river. Margaret expressed regret that she had forgotten to bring her harp. He immediately invited her to pray and the two of them got down on their knees. He felt that he had found a new friend (Margaret and her husband later contributed DTT and mosquito nets to the Centre).

On the occasion of a visit to Silveira House John made another friend, Sister Angelina Katsukunya, an African nun who was working there as a secretary, and she agreed to run off stencils of his poems after he had shyly suggested it to her. (He sent other stencils to his brother Philip, and his niece Pamela, who spent many evenings producing numerous copies in the basement of her workplace, bringing them later to her father, who preserved them, waiting instructions from John to send them to various destinations.) Sister Angelina wrote:

> He would arrive at Silveira House from Mutemwa by public transport in the afternoon bringing a box of stencils which he wanted run off that afternoon in order for him to return to Mutemwa the following morning. I used to run off stencils (one copy per stencil) in which he had typed all the poems he would have composed during that week or month until late in the evening, sometimes failing to finish them that day. Whenever I finished them he would then say: 'Thank you very much, I will take you to watch a film at a cinema tonight.' He would then go to Father Dove and say: 'John, would you like to go to a cinema tonight, I have

invited Sister to come with us, but remember to take enough money to pay for us all.' Once at the cinema he would order the things he loved most and then ask Father Dove to pay. He would say: 'John, you know Sister loves ice cream and chocolate, can you buy her that.'

He was so happy about Sister Angelina that he wrote the *Ballad of an African Sister* to her on September 20th, not failing to pun on her 'angelical' name and comparing her joyful and winged laugh to the choir at King's College in Cambridge and the spirituality of *The Ladder of Perfection* by Walter Hilton: 'Sister Angelina's joy / Is joy angelical.' (He later asked John Dove if it was appropriate to offer a box of chocolates to a nun to thank her.)

John often used his trip to the capital as an opportunity to go to the cinema with his friend. The two would act out little comedy sketches together, such as this one, as related by John Dove:

> On entering the cinema, he said: 'I'll buy you a box of chocolates'. I replied that that would be fine. I knew he had no money. He then said: 'Could you lend me a dollar or two?' I did that. By this time, people in the cinema foyer were beginning to stare, as people do. The cinema was modern and at that time rather elite and White. He wore his habit, gym shoes with holes in them, no socks, and a red head band like tennis players. We took our seats. I could hear the rustle of chocolate papers during the first half of the film, but took no notice since it was such a good show. The lights went on during the interval and I discovered a sea of chocolate papers all around our feet and into the aisle. People stared even harder. I told him that I just could not sit with him any more. He laughed, saying that he had not had such a good meal for a long time.

On another occasion at Silveira House, John Dove, who had become aware of Anne Lander's gift of healing, had asked her to come to the chapel and lay hands on Sister Mary Hildeberta, the bookkeeper at the Centre who for years had been losing her voice. John, who was there at the time, followed them but remained shyly in the rear until his name was called out. Then Anne Lander, the nun, and John crossed hands and he said a prayer, after which Anne put her hands on the nun's head. Father Dove kept discreetly to the back of the chapel. The three Europeans met up again in the dining room with John dozing off when suddenly a group of African nuns, led by Sister Mary Hildeberta, who shortly before could hardly speak, burst into the room singing at the top of their voices the praises of God. Anne and John fell on their knees to give thanks to the Holy Spirit who produced the healing.

Back in Mtemwa, John met up again with Lazaro and Ida, who were still living with him, and with whom he shared everything he received. In a poem dated October 11th, *The Lamentation of the Racist*, he plays on colours to mock racial discrimination. He picked up this theme again in 1979 in *Consider the Birds*, opposing human racism to the racial harmony of birds of different coloured feathers: 'Consider these two kinds, combined their shades / Make nonsense of the racialistic blades'. But in October he was obliged to fight on a new front, this time on behalf of the trees which were regularly cut down or which had their branches lopped off by intruders precisely at the time that the lepers needed them most. Moreover the trees were his friends: he wrote a poem, *Vox Clamantis contra inclementes*, in their defence, and one can see how for him the trees were living and friendly creatures:

> Hewers of wood, drawers of water, that
> Cleaves to you, cleaver, like a heaving curse!
> You'd make a desert of God's habitat
> Mashonaland, you'd have it sand and worse!
> Pleasure it is to hear the birds enchanting,
> The measure of their leisure is their song,
> Why must masasa-trees of breezy planting
> Go slanting down so fast to fall flatlong?
> Were you not ever struck at sun's first rays
> By bright idea of striking off your stroke?
> Nor bard nor bird shall wander where your ways

Will have made desert which your blade bespoke:
Bantu barbaric, vandal in the green,
Acute's your axe as you obtuse have been!

1976: Civil war in Mtoko, private war at Mtemwa

The guerrillas had by now infiltrated all the Tribal Trust Lands of the Mtoko zone, which was now considered to be 'semi-liberated'. The guerrilla chiefs were in general well educated and polite (they were often products of the Mission schools). They wished to gain the confidence of the rural populations by a demonstration of gentle force, and presented themselves as freedom fighters who were fighting to recover the land stolen by the Europeans. But they had no mercy on 'traitors', informers or agents of the government, whom they forbade anybody to bury after their execution (which was worse than death for the Shonas). The Rhodesian army and its African auxiliaries no longer dared to venture by day into the African zone when an outrage had been committed, and often perpetrated acts of unjustifiable violence. In a report, the Justice and Peace Commission declared: 'There is a widespread belief in the Mtoko area that the Security Forces are liable to open fire on people found near the place where a landmine has just exploded.'

On a national level, escalation continued throughout the year. Sabotage of railway lines became more and more frequent. Cars were obliged to circulate in convoys, at first on the central axis of the country but then gradually on all major roads. Ian Smith was himself aware that the war was a lost cause and was looking for a compromise which he could control. In September, he announced that power would be transferred to the African majority within two years. From 9th October to 14th December 1976, Henry Kissinger orchestrated the Geneva negotiations between the UDI regime and the Patriotic Front, which now brought together ZANU and ZAPU. The negotiations failed, and Ian Smith decided to put in place a plan for an internal solution.

At Mtoko, on March 19th, 12 young Methodists were arrested returning home after a prayer meeting. They were accused of coming from a meeting of the guerrillas and they were badly beaten, even though they were carrying Bibles and prayer books.

The auxiliary troops were not averse to inflicting abuse on their fellow countrymen: for example Saul Bhebe, chief of a section of the Guard Force, a special unit composed of white officers and African men created to keep an eye on the keeps ('protected villages' – see below), regularly got drunk with his men in the beerhall of the keep at Mtoko and once opened fire on customers, killing two women and one man. He was later brought to justice, but other and similar actions were often hushed up. The war also raised other demons from the dead. Rumours of witchcraft increased, and led to a veritable collective hysteria in the region, and a resurgence of the Mchape witchcraft movement of the 1930s.

Mtemwa was no longer safe, but John went back there after celebrating Christmas at Silveira House. A few days later, when Hanzu, the doyenne of Mtemwa, died aged 93, John observed that, in spite of his reconciliation with Dighton, the lepers were still at the mercy of Philo. He continued to look after them discreetly with the medication that Stephen King sent him, but Luisa Guidotti was sceptical, knowing as she did the somewhat unsatisfactory methods of John in medical matters.

As the war continued, the serious problem of cattle damage in the gardens of the lepers became a big issue. The villagers from the neighbouring kraals had never accepted the confiscation of their land at the beginning of the century, and continued to consider themselves the legitimate owners, because these were the lands of the ancestors who continued to direct their lives, seasons and rains, as well as abundance and famine. Moreover the lepers were often foreigners from Malawi and Mozambique, or Shonas from other regions. The land of the villagers could no longer be expanded, pressures on it were becoming stronger, and cattle herds more numerous. In the circumstances, the temptation to seize the lands of the Centre, intensified by the propaganda of the guerrillas, was all the greater because the lepers, unlike the Europeans, could not defend themselves. John did his best to protect them, even though his expulsion from the Centre, followed by the acquittal of Philo, had undermined his authority. In the eyes of the villagers he was no more than a powerless white man at a moment when his fellow Whites were displaying, by ever-increasing violence, the real meaning of power.

Confrontations over cattle were becoming more numerous, and crystallised around Mudzinganyama, whom John had nicknamed 'Black Croesus'. This rich African farmer, named after the short-lived last king of Rozvi Shonaland during the 1896 insurrection, and who owned the butchery named after him, was dealing directly with the District Commissioner, but from time to time gave out positive signs to the guerrillas. The lepers of Mtemwa were but a grain of sand, from his point of view. Following a somewhat shady deal, he bought a piece of land bordering on the cemetery, which he anticipated would belong to him one day when Mtemwa closed down and all burial ended, and he could allow his cattle to graze on the graves unhindered. But John was determined to defend the lepers, dead or alive, and did his utmost to thwart this plan.

Despite the armistice with Philo and Dighton, his problems with the Committee had seen no let-up. To hasten the closure of the Centre, Ellis set about demolishing the huts of dead lepers. In March the *Rhodesia Herald* published a letter from Pauline Hutchings defending John. Dighton immediately demanded to meet her at Mtemwa. He arrived at the Centre with a female member of the Committee 'all dressed up as for a garden-party', according to Pauline, including a fashionable hat. They spoke to the young woman: 'Their message was that I was mistaken in trying to champion John's cause, that in fact he was unstable, not fit to look after the lepers.' But she stood her ground and continued to give John her full backing.

These difficulties didn't prevent John from writing more poems, nor from looking for aid for Mtemwa. On April 6th he thanked Mrs Carey, a benefactor of the Centre who had come to visit, in a poem full of humour. At the end of June he thought he had discovered a new way to make money: his friend Bruce Wilkinson had asked him to forward poems that he would try to publish. John wrote back immediately saying that he would soon send him some poems (although nothing ever came of this project).

Little by little the discussions with Dighton bore fruit. Philo was to remain Director of the Centre, but the appointment of another African was under discussion. Ellis resigned in a rage, and the faithful Alistair Guthrie was co-opted by the Committee. John was overjoyed, but his joy was short-lived as, on June 28th, on the eve of the arrival of Alistair Guthrie and Father Dove at Mtemwa to inaugurate the new era for the Centre, Luisa Guidotti was arrested for non-denunciation of terrorists and threatened with the death penalty.

Luisa Guidotti, terrorist

In April the All Souls Mission was affected by the curfew. Luisa Guidotti and Caterina Savini decided to sleep at the hospital so as to be permanently available to the patients. Father Alois Nyanhete was now in charge of the Mission – this priest was involved in the founding of the popular *Maria Hosi Yedenga* (Mary Queen of Heaven) prayer movement, whose members wear a typical white and blue uniform. He told Luisa Guidotti that two parishioners had been killed by the security forces for having broken the ceasefire by coming to early Mass, as they had always done. Both she and John were devastated. On May 5th two African agents from a community development centre, W. Mawire and W. Muchenje, were subsequently killed in the zone by the guerrillas. Still in May, confrontations between the Rhodesian army and the rebels were getting closer to All Souls – a little more than a mile, according to Luisa. On a number of occasions vehicles on the main road were blown up by landmines. By the middle of 1976 All Souls Mission had become a keep.

To contain the advance of the guerrillas, the government had decided to create 'protected villages', called *keeps* ('fortified sections'): a high enclosure was erected behind which villagers were confined and obliged to wear a bracelet with an identification number. Those not wearing one of these were declared Terrs, and the soldiers were allowed to shoot them on sight if their badge was not visible. The keep was obliged to receive hundreds of villagers, sometimes as many as several thousand, with a garrison of African auxiliaries camped nearby to 'protect' them against guerrilla attack. On the day arranged for the opening of a keep, when troops arrived in the kraals, sometimes the villagers had no more than ten minutes to prepare their departure, and for a people so attached to their land this was a terrible wrench. Sometimes huts were burned to the ground to prevent them from returning. In the keep they were forced to build their huts on a tiny parcel of land. There were no fields in the keep, so they had to travel to their own fields during the day, at the risk of being fired upon after the curfew hour, even though they didn't have a watch to check the time. They were not even authorised to bring along anything in the way of food, for fear that they would hand it over to the Terrs. Women had to go down on their knees in front of the soldiers guarding the entrance to the camp to show that they had nothing but water in their jugs, whereas the Shona tradition was that no woman would go down on her knees in front of any man but her husband. The gates of the keep were kept closed for 12 hours a day, and those who found themselves outside were summarily executed. Sometimes the gates stayed closed for one or two days at a time for no given reason.

The beerhalls encouraged heavy drinking, and those who succumbed to alcohol became human wrecks, while others came to loathe even more the system which was degrading their brothers and sisters. Prostitution, up to then unknown in the countryside, became rife; and many women fled to Salisbury, or at least to Mtoko, with their children. The administration also obliged the internees in the keep to build latrines on the tiny parcel of land that had been granted to them. All this affronted the natural modesty of the Shonas, and disease, spread by the large flies and mosquitos, broke out there as a result. Luisa Guidotti became alarmed, and complained also that amoebiasis was undermining the health of families. To be able to serve them night and day, she thereafter slept in a hut in the keep, which was just as suffocating as John's. She kept track of the alarming mortality rate, which was mostly a result of malnutrition. She and Caterina Savini prepared litres of *mahewu* (an African beer) to improve the nutritional balance of the children, but the authorities were quick to forbid her from doing this.

ZANLA, who made things worse by forbidding the villagers of the keep to accept any aid donated to them by Silveira House, soon attacked All Souls. The vakomana made their way into the keep and opened fire on the garrison scattered among the huts, which provoked a rapid response, and the keep itself was caught between two fires. Luisa Guidotti and Caterina Savini hid under their beds as the bullets flew. Before disappearing into the night, the vakomana set fire to the huts. One night, wounded vakomana arrived at the hospital, and Luisa Guidotti cared for them as for the others, a crime punishable by the death penalty – a dilemma faced not only by her but by all Missions who had a hospital or a dispensary.

Early in the morning of June 24th, a young man from a village of Manyanga, Anthony Kodo, arrived at the hospital with a bullet wound in his arm. She suggested two solutions: that she herself amputate it or that he go to a hospital in the capital and try and save his arm. The young man chose to go to Salisbury, but was stopped at a barricade and arrested as a member of the guerrillas (which he probably was not). The police immediately accused Luisa Guidotti of non-denunciation. She replied that it was the young man's choice to go to Salisbury, knowing that Terrs were automatically hanged there, which was proof for her that he wasn't one. The police left, but not before threatening her.

On the 28th the police returned to All Souls and arrested her for having violated Section 51 (a) and (c) of the Law and Order (Maintenance) Act, chapter 65, according to which:

> any person who (a) gives shelter, hides or assists
> in any way a fellow who may be considered or is
> known as 'terrorist' or as a helper of terrorists;
> (b) knows a person who is a terrorist or assists
> terrorists in Rhodesia and does not report to the
> police these facts as soon as possible and at any
> rate not later than 72 hours is guilty of a crime
> liable to death or life-term punishment.

Luisa Guidotti was immediately brought before a judge at Mtoko and transferred to the women's high-security prison in Salisbury. She was allowed three books and three pills and she spent a freezing night in her cell. The next day she had breakfast with African detainees and was visited by a lawyer and the prison chaplain. Then, due to regulations governing racial segregation, she was transferred to the European sector. The following day Alistair Guthrie came to see her, and Luisa was very moved by his visit, as she later wrote:

> He was European Rhodesian Front one hundred
> per cent but he came to visit me in jail... One
> would never have expected him to visit me, a
> political prisoner; he was a true Christian, son
> of the Father, and when he came to visit me he
> behaved with wonderful delicacy, kindness and
> unselfishness.

Alistair Guthrie took action, and on July 2nd Luisa was released
and assigned to a named residence in Salisbury to await her trial.
She paid a visit to the Archbishop, who asked her, according to
Luisa's Diary:

> Do you remember in the Acts of the Apostles when
> Peter was in prison he was freed by an Angel. Tell
> me what the Church was doing? I replied 'I don't
> remember' – 'Praying. We prayed all of us, a lot
> for you. I never prayed so earnestly.'

Afterwards she went to stay at Silveira House. John arrived
immediately from Mtemwa and greeted her with a vibrant welcome
as 'the proto martyr of Zimbabwe'. He told her that the lepers were
all praying for her, and that the friends of the All Souls doctor were
planning her defence – Professor Gelfand and Dr Joan Lamplugh,
president of Catholic Doctors, who was funding her foundation
Glendora for poor Africans, thanks to revenues received from her
European clientele.

On July 4th, Ambuya Luisa (*Ambuya* is a Shona greeting to a
mother-in-law, a grandmother or an elderly woman) went to
Mtemwa, where the lepers gave her an unforgettable welcome:
songs, dances and abundant tears: 'they knew that I could be
condemned to death ... I was risking expulsion from Rhodesia but
I would have preferred to be hanged.' The threat was by no means
illusory: more than 60 hangings had already been carried out, and
the regime had its back to the wall. In the Mtoko zone, the excesses
of the Rhodesian army were increasing daily (for example, soldiers
took control of a kraal at Mtize Chikata, and the young Athanasio
Mutikiti died during interrogation). On August 2nd, Caterina
Savini was allowed to visit her friend at Silveira House. Luisa

accompanied her as far as Lot, near All Souls, where all the staff of the Mission were waiting for her. On her arrival she introduced herself as the 'European Terrorist': everybody burst out laughing, before bursting into tears.

On August 7th, Patrick Chakaipa was appointed Archbishop of Salisbury. The celebration took place at Rufaro stadium in the presence of 9 bishops, 100 priests and 20,000 faithful. Ambuya Luisa was present and received a standing ovation from everybody in the stadium ('I really felt like a Shona among the Shona', she wrote later). The following day at the Archbishop's house she met the Papal Nuncio, who read her a letter from Paul VI: 'The Pope sends his blessing and is taking a personal interest in her case.' The following day the Rhodesian air force bombed the ZANU camp at Nyadzonia in Mozambique, killing 1000 people, including many women and children. On the 18th the *Rand Daily Mail* in Johannesburg spoke of the 'first white to be charged under Rhodesian law and Order Maintenance Act ... an offence which can carry the death penalty or life imprisonment'. Two days later in the Rhodesian parliament, Rodney Simmonds (who was also a sales representative for an Italian arms trafficking organisation) denounced her without mentioning her name (the preceding month, he had attacked her in the *Rhodesia Herald* (29 July): 'Many churches were now communist infiltrated... and some Missions were actively aiding terrorists').

Two days later the trial took place, but to everybody's astonishment the judge stood up and declared: 'The case is withdrawn. Dr Guidotti is free, free even to return to All Souls Mission Hospital' – but she was obliged to forfeit her salary paid by the Ministry for the two months she spent in prison and house arrest, these being treated as 'holiday periods'. She made a triumphal return and had to stop off at every kraal to be feted by dances and chants. The same thing of course happened when she arrived at Mtemwa. But at Mtoko many people were already plotting revenge.

The following month, Bishop Lamont, convicted for declarations which were seen to support rebellion, was condemned to 10 years forced labour (the sentence was subsequently provisionally suspended). During the last months of 1976, attacks against Catholic Missions, either by the forces of the regime or those of the guerrillas, stepped up. Father Mutume and Father Mhonda were arrested at Avila Mission and tortured, while the Africans of the Mission heard a soldier shouting: 'One dead missionary is worth one hundred dead terrorists' (Bishop Lamont also heard the same words being spoken). On November 25th, Father George Joerger, a Swiss missionary, was abducted while on his bike in the Mshawasha zone, then murdered. He had protested against the theft of cattle of the Mission. Bishop Adolph Schmitt, emeritus Bishop of Bulawayo, had just declared in Germany: 'The African majority is today convinced that no other choice remains open to them but violence.' On his return to Rhodesia he quickly and tragically proved that his words had been prophetic: he was assassinated by the guerrillas along with Father Weggartner and Sister Maria van der Berg on a road near Lupane, to cries of 'Missionnaries are enemies of the people!' The Justice and Peace Commission met Robert Mugabe in Switzerland and told him that atrocities were also committed by the guerrillas and that he should impose some authority on them. Mugabe became angry and threatened the Church with reprisal if they published any suggestions of this kind, and they were no longer to report on crimes by the guerrillas.

Hardly had Luisa returned to All Souls when a new drama occurred: on September 19th Wayanne Palmer, Mona Smith's lodger, was murdered by the guerrillas and her husband gravely wounded. Yet the European zone of Mtoko district received special protection from the security forces because tobacco farming was one of the most important resources of the country, and geography made it possible for patrols to move about freely in the zone. Furthermore, the Rhodesian Farmers Union, generously funded by the government, was helping the farmers to equip themselves with radio Agric-alert and to recruit armed staff to defend themselves. Mona Smith was so traumatised that she decided to leave for Salisbury. When she left Mtemwa with a heavy heart, leaving behind her clothes for the lepers, the last image she had was of John helping a dying woman leper, cradling her head on his knees. He held onto her hand as she breathed her last breath: 'Death is never a pleasant sight, but the death of a dirty, smelly, deformed creature is repellent. That is when John's saintliness was really apparent.' John deeply regretted the departure of his friend but remained in contact with her. The death of Mrs Palmer confirmed him in his certitude that the 'Russians' would win out in Rhodesia, by means of the guerrillas.

But would they waste a bullet on a clown?

At the beginning of 1977 Mtemwa, lying sheltered in the shade of its mountain, was also at the centre of one of the most intense military concentrations in the whole country, being ferociously contested by the two main parties to the conflict. The backbone of the Rhodesian army, its air force, was concentrated at Mtoko airport, as well as ground troops, special forces and mercenaries (African troops from Internal Affairs, in particular the ARU (Administration Reinforcement Units) and the keep guards). A camp of ARU District Assistants had been deployed in the Mtemwa zone, not far from the Centre. Commanded by Sergeant Major Svondo, they took part in anti-guerrilla operations. As the tide began to turn in favour of the insurgents, African elements in the Rhodesian army started to get anxious and much less inclined to show sympathy towards those rare Europeans like Luisa Guidotti, who in their eyes were accomplices of the Terrs, or who like John were disinclined to speak out in favour of the government. Moreover the vakomana were also keeping track of them and had promised them swift punishment after victory, while the villagers looked on them as the watchdogs of the keeps on behalf of the Europeans.

Racketeering became widespread; particularly the abduction of women and young girls. Vakomana and mujibhas also took part in those abductions. (The *mujibhas* – 'youths' in Shona – were young men from the kraals and villages, traditionally given the job of looking after the herds, unless they were still at school. The term became synonymous with guerrilla auxiliaries in rural zones.) In the wake of one such abduction in the district next to Mtemwa, a group of African auxiliaries had to face the fury of the local menfolk and lost three of their own men. A village was burnt in reprisal, even though it had no connection with the guerrillas. This particular event became well known because a nearby Mission drew attention to it, but there must have been others. At the Centre itself, Philo was dealing illegally with the men of the local ARU in rations and clothing destined for the lepers.

Rhodesian army patrols often skirted the perimeter of Mtemwa, and John received regular visits from them. He could overhear the openly racist language of the soldiers, which he deplored, but he couldn't help sharing their anti-Communism. Even if many considered him to be mad, his fame had travelled far beyond Mtoko. Dr Sandy Kirk, a medical officer, had heard about him and decided to pay a visit. This was arranged by Mike Glenshaw, a local intelligence officer, who gathered a platoon and escorted the doctor to the Centre. Glenshaw was indifferent to religion, though somewhat anti-Catholic, and outraged by the apparent attitude of the Church in favour of the Terrs. When he arrived at the centre Dr Kirk examined the lepers while Glenshaw observed from afar, having no desire for contact with 'these people'. The visit continued, and the group met John, whom they originally took to be 'a vagrant and down and out', but John soon struck him as a man who 'did not have the aura of a "yahoo", but somehow gave the feeling of dignity'. Having conversed together for a while, Glenshaw made his way off with the group (he later on became a fervent Catholic, and became active in the cause of John Bradburne's beatification).

The guerrillas were by now all around Mtoko, and the army was getting edgier all the time. A tit-for-tat of summary executions had become the norm, and massacres increased. While massacres of Africans at the hands of government troops or by guerrillas were regarded as mere figures in official statistics, European deaths created a much greater stir. On February 3rd, Alexander Hamilton and ten Africans were abducted at Kye mine to the north of Mtoko. The Africans were later released but Hamilton was shot. On February 7th, John learnt with horror of the death of two Jesuit friends, Brother John Conway and Father Christopher Shepherd-Smith of the Jesuit Mission at Musami, as well as another priest and four nuns. The Mission, about 60 miles from Mtemwa, was a source of great pride to the Jesuits. Its enormous church could hold up to 3000 faithful, and it also comprised two convents, a novitiate and a complex of schools. But soon rumours began to circulate at Mtemwa (which Father Dove was inclined to believe), that it was not the guerrillas but commandos of Selous Scouts connected to the Smith regime, disguised as vakomana, who had perpetrated the massacre, either in revenge against the Catholic Church, or simply to add to the confusion. However, the sole survivor, Father Duncan Myerscough, was adamant that they were the guerrillas.

John couldn't bring himself to believe that the government was capable of such savagery, and wrote several poems about the massacre in mourning for his dead friends:

> John Conway was the Jesuit
> Whom children loved to follow;
> The saint's allure, the minstrel's wit:
> Gone... like a migrant swallow.
>
> ...
>
> And are you ready now to go?
> Ready to go am I?
> We all are migrants, even so
> But for these lost we sigh.
>
> John Conway gone, the shining friend
> Of every Shona child;
> The Land is weeping, end to end,
> Shall it be reconciled?
>
> Christopher Shepherd-Smith... his smile
> Was like an angel's joy:
> All innocence, no hint of guile,
> An everlasting boy.
> (*Seven to Heaven, or, Musemi ku Musami*, 1977)

In another poem he evoked the sheer hell that had enveloped the Shona country:

> And well I understand that Hell has crept
> Into Mashonaland with woes and strife.

And in the same poem he writes of the Russian manipulation of vakomana for its own political ends:

> What human heart has got no time for such
> As fight for freedom of their native land?
> Not yours, not mine, we are inclined so much
> To freedom that we truly understand;

'The Boys', though, are not leaders of the band
Of Backroom-Brains; who stains with red the dust
Of Africa but Russia's greed run must?
(*Aware on the Ides of March,* 1977)

However, probably shaken by the arguments of Father Dove, he did
not totally exclude the possibility Whites could have ordered the
massacre at Musami, not 'the Russians'.

John was not the only one to worry about the Soviet influence
on the guerrillas. On May 17th and 19th the leaders of the Catholic
Church met in Driefontein in the south of the country to debate
the Communist question and consider the looming scenario of a
Marxist regime after the war, which everybody already considered
as lost by the Rhodesian Front. Concrete proposals were considered
in a situation where anti-religious measures might come into force
in a new regime, including the distribution of the Eucharist in rural
communities, something which John had already established at
Mtemwa. But in a poem written on March 21st John seemed to
regain heart, and this found expression in another poem written at
this time. He distributed stencilled copies of the poem to his friends,
and its message of love should be read against the background of
the murderous mayhem in which it was written:

Now let me tell you this, you pilgrims all,
Love is a long desire, a short disease,
An everlasting healing and a call
To highest things that do most greatly please;
Love is an elixir to drink down fast
And love is like a fool who hails a Queen,
None of those strolling players in the cast
Of vast humanity has missed its sheen;
You'll see it on the leaves that stir and dance,
You'll feel it in the breezes as they blow,
Its deep appeal is on the seas that glance
Up at the skyscape... canst escape it?
No: Love is the very substance of the Lord
And merrily He moves and proves accord.
(*Eirenicon,* 1977)

Following the Musami massacre, and in the same month, another missionary, Father José Manuel Rubio Diaz, was murdered. In March, Bishop Donal Lamont was stripped of his Rhodesian nationality and deported. This was followed on the 10th by another massacre: a group of drunken guerrillas entered the hospital at the Mission of St Paul and killed Dr Decker, who had served in Rhodesia for 20 years, and Sister Ploner, an Austrian nun who had arrived only six months previously. Four days later, the 14th, John wrote in a letter to Stephen King:

> The terrorists have not yet shot me down,
> But would they waste a bullet on a clown?
> I find that feeling brave's a 'piece of cake'
> When there is nothing near to make me shake;
> All fear I do believe is cast right out
> Where Perfect Love expels the final doubt,
> And all those things we think we'd fear to face
> Are banished not by Oddbod but God's grace.

Apart from the black humour referring to the wasted bullet, the letter-poem contains a truth of which John was all too aware: his life was in the hands of the vakomana, like that of the Musami missionaries and all other missionaries in the country. It was no less in the hands of the mujibhas or of their relatives in the neighbouring kraals, who could denounce him to the vakomana any time, as was happening in all the Missions. In the words of one missionary, Joseph Amstutz:

> The daily life and safety of rural Missions increasingly depended on the good-will of the population to the point where traditional dependence relationships had been turned on their heads. Missionaries survived by the grace of God and by the grace of their parishioners who recommended them to the guerrillas, or condemned them.

This might have encouraged John to be prudent and to compromise in his relations with his neighbours; but what concerned him was less his own life than that of his leper friends, and he continued to complain about the damage done by stray cattle or other infringements by intruders into the Centre. His friend Alex Israel wrote:

> Everyone who visited him was struck by his enormous courage and phenomenal spirit. It was the end of the road for him. And he knew it. And it oppressed him. But he found the strength to overcome with joy. From the start he had a premonition that he would be killed.

The kraals and the villages around Mtemwa were in fact in the control of the guerrillas, who now seemed to be everywhere. Had John around this time a visit from the vakomana, drawn there by the rations stocked in the Centre? Judith Listowel thought so, without quoting her source, and it was very possible. Perhaps he managed to convince his night-time visitors that the lepers would die of hunger if he were to give away their rations. In any event he said nothing to the authorities, in spite of the law, nor did he refer to it in either his letters or his poems.

John worried about the safety of his friends at All Souls Mission more than his own. It was true that All Souls was particularly vulnerable at this time. Father Aloys Nyanhete was visited in March by the Selous Scouts, who accused him of supporting and abetting the guerrillas, and tortured the old priest. On May 13th the Mission came under mortar fire from the guerrillas. Like everyone else, Luisa Guidotti hid under the bed. The guerrillas later came to apologise to her and the priest for their mistake, explaining that they had been aiming at the keep. Four days later, soldiers from the keep burned down all the villages in the vicinity as a reprisal. The mother of one of the nurses there was killed, along with the child she had been carrying on her back. The medical team at the Mission also had to contend with the soldiers of the garrison who were raping the women of the keep and spreading sexually transmitted diseases. At the keep 'a traitor' had been executed by the guerrillas and his body allowed to rot for two weeks on top of a rock. This was calculated to intimidate the villagers, traditionally so attentive to the afterlife of the dead.

The Franciscan habit

The Franciscan way had been close to John's heart for many years, even though, apart from his fidelity to the Office of the Blessed Virgin, his practice of the Way had been intermittent. His encounter with Bruce Wilkinson marked a new phase in his Franciscan devotion, which was soon to find its apotheosis and become formalised. Father Sean Gildea, now the new Franciscan Superior, came one day to Silveira House bringing his own Franciscan habit, and asked Father Dove to tell John to wear it on his next visit to Salisbury. In his own words:

> John was more Franciscan than the rest of us put together... I gave John the Franciscan habit because he was living a Franciscan life, was committed to St Francis and made the values of St Francis present; prayer, love, poverty, generosity, joy, deep faith... I could go on...

On July 24th at midday, in the chapel of Silveira House, Father Dove robed his friend in the Franciscan habit. Not knowing the Franciscan ritual, he improvised a prayer asking for St Francis' intercession in the spiritual struggle in which John was engaged. John was overjoyed and the same day wrote to his mother:

> A postulant since five & twenty years
> In certain Orders, equally uncertain
> Of whether he is mad as he appears,
> On postulancy now rings down the curtain;
> More daisylike than anything at Gerton
> Emerges a new mannikin in habit
> Fully Franciscan – stetit, stet et stabit!
> I even preached a sermon on Saint Francis
> This very morn amidst admiring glances,
> And now I am delighted as can be!

He would often have occasion to wear this habit. Father David Harold-Barry noticed that he even wore it to go to the cinema in Salisbury. Father Dove summed it up when he wrote at the beginning of October to John, who later used it in a poem: 'Your new Franciscan habit is your cell', to which John replied with this enigmatic verse (*Magnificat*, 1977): 'I'll move in it with wit will prove my Belle.'

During 1977 John visited Silveira House several times, aware that John Dove's position was becoming increasingly vulnerable. Father Dove had no illusions about what the future held, but continued in the work of the Centre for the future of the Jesuits in his adopted country. In his report for 1976 he pointed out that 15,000 Africans were being trained every year, especially in leadership, to prepare the transition towards the new Zimbabwe, and that 'in this context, Silveira House has endeavoured and intends to continue its work of helping the oppressed, spiritually, economically and politically. This was effected by 77 courses, seminars and retreats; plus field days, congresses, and above all education in the field.' He continued in his efforts to adapt to the ever-changing circumstances around him. Courses at the Centre and reports and pamphlets such as those from the Justice and Peace Commission and the series *From Rhodesia to Zimbabwe*, systematically avoided confrontation with Marxist doctrine, and almost never referred to it in the socialism that they advocated. It was not a matter of disguising a crypto-Marxism, nor of ignorance, but was a tactic to work around the problem. Father Dove believed that when the new regime arrived there would still be a role for the Church, and that it was better to continue to promote the true Christian message than to cross swords with what had then become the official ideology of the ascendant political powers.

John now learnt of the death of Peter Donnelly, who had brought him a tent to help him survive on Chigona in 1973, and who since had more than once accompanied him walking on the mountain. He wrote a long ballad in honour of this big-hearted Scot (*The Ballad of Peter Donnelly*), referring to his struggle with alcohol, the Lauds that they sang together at dawn, and his simple and unaffected piety. He was particularly moved by the murder – even as the news became an almost daily recital of violence, murder and massacre and attacks on the Missions – of Pastor Sabuku in July at a Mission in many ways similar to All Souls and his own centre at Mtemwa. All the Missions tried to stay neutral towards the guerrillas and to avoid being identified with the security forces, and to defend the villagers. Mtemwa had become just as vulnerable as any other rural zone, protected neither by the JOC (Joint Operations Command) nor the ARU (Administration Reinforcement Units), and the vakomana roamed freely and unimpeded. John was the only European in the whole Mtoko zone without protection, since even All Souls was under the umbrella of a resident garrison. The campaign of terror by the guerrillas could at any moment find him an easy prey, especially since the articles about him and Mtemwa had appeared in the *Rhodesia Herald.*

Sunny spells over Mtemwa...

All of a sudden, the Committee, acknowledging John's impossible situation since his return to the Centre two years previously, decided to appoint a Director, thanks to Alistair Guthrie. Since the war had come to Mtoko, Alistair had been the only member of the Committee who continued to come to the Centre, which he visited once a month despite the risks, often with Father Dove, because petrol was now being rationed. He informed the Committee of what was happening at the Centre, and John was finally in a position to make known to them the real plight of the lepers – rations going missing, neglect in medical care, and so on. He was successful in regularising John's return to the Centre, thus recognising what had been the status quo for two years.

Later, during a visit by John and Luisa Guidotti to Silveira House, the Committee finally understood the true character of Philo Ruganga, and decided to sack him. But John no longer wished to resume his administrative position, which was given to Phineas Mwende, one of the assistants, whose father had planted the jaracandas of the Centre, and who came from Mtemwa village, at the foot of the mountain. This was a risky appointment, given that several families from the village were at loggerheads with John for allowing their cattle to trespass in the Centre. Moreover, members of Phineas' own family regularly came to the Centre and cut branches from the trees without permission.

John fought back incessantly: not only was there no longer any shade, or small branches to cut, or grain to collect for the lepers' fires, but the soft grass which used to grow in the shade had now become dry stubble which scratched and cut the lepers who had to crawl through it. Even the fruit from the trees planted by Shirley James was stolen. Like a mother protecting her children, John flew into a rage whenever he came across the results of the endless pillaging and vandalism. Nevertheless he was delighted with the new appointment, thinking Phineas could only be an improvement on Philo. He helped him to pass his driver's licence test – or more to the point, they helped each other. On Tuesdays and Fridays on trips to Mtoko to buy meat and bread, John explained the road signs to Phineas, while the latter made sure John changed gear.

Beyond the Centre, on the other hand, there was no glimmer of hope on the political landscape. The Rhodesian Front won another landslide in the election on August 31st; but on the following day Britain and the United States made a joint declaration that the future African majority government should be led by ZANU and ZAPU. In November Ian Smith declared his commitment to the principle of majority rule on the basis of universal suffrage, but he was determined to remain master of the electoral process. ZANU and ZAPU again rejected his proposals, but the Reverend Sithole and Bishop Muzorewa accepted, hoping for an internal agreement. On September 29th the murder and mutilation of 6-month-old Natasha Glenny on a farm in the Chipinga region horrified the European community. The continuing attacks on Missions and the possibility that he himself might be the next casualty gave John food for thought:

> dying... is it so
> Terribly heavy? say, if it is made
> Early as even now and in a raid
> Arrive five terrorists, who can fly more
> Lightly than Mary up? up, to adore
> With Portia Coeli!
> (*A True Assumption*, 1977)

On October 4th, the feast day of St Francis, Father Paschal Slevin, with whom John had kept in touch since happy days at Gandachibvuva, received his expulsion order. He had criticised in an interview the indifference of the European majority to the injustices regularly inflicted on the Africans, citing examples, and drew attention to the dilemma facing missionaries, 'denounced by the Security forces if we do not report the presence of guerrillas and faced with certain death if we do'. John heard the news on a visit to Silveira House, where he had been talking with Father David Harold-Barry about the Gospel. (Back in Mtemwa, John sent some reflections of his own to Father Harold-Barry, which prefigure some recent biblical scholarship: he defends, from stylistic considerations, the single authorship of each Gospel, using the analogy of great musical composers.)

The Catholic Church was forced to shut down vulnerable Missions, while the murder of the Reverend Andries Brand and his wife Sabina, parents of six children, by insurgents at Gokwe in the same month, demonstrated clearly that other missionaries were not safe either, despite the fact that the nationalists continued to deny any involvement in these outrages. In November an airliner was shot down by the guerrillas, and a Rhodesian army raid on a ZANU training camp at Chimoio in Mozambique inflicted 1200 casualties, including many women and children. The next day Ian Smith opened talks with Bishop Abel Muzorewa, leader of the moderate UANC, the Reverend Sithole, and Chief Chirau, to try and bring about an internal settlement.

Meanwhile the Committee at Mtemwa had recruited a new member, Boniface Foya, who went on to become its chairman after independence. John got on well with him, and impressed him by his dedication and his love for the lepers. But the situation was becoming more and more difficult because of lack of means. In a letter to Father Dove on All Saints Day, John informed him that since the sacking of Philo he had cut off the supply of rations and clothes that the latter had been passing on to the local African assistants, and that the ex-beneficiaries were less than pleased. On a visit to Mtemwa, he wrote:

> Boniface Foya was told by Mrs Sithole on
> Saturday that the D.A.s [District Assistants] are
> heartbroken, and presumably out of extra rations
> and clothes over the wire, at Philo's firing? She
> says that it is their intention to polish me off. That
> would be small loss to anyone, but please in the
> event try to publish at least six lines of my verse!
> You have already published four on your dear
> father's memorial stone.

Relations with some of the Europeans were hardly better, apart
from those who knew him well. How was it, they asked, that while
the Terrs were murdering Europeans and taking great risks while
attacking their farms, they left untouched such easy prey as the
eccentric at Mtemwa, who was unarmed and didn't even have a
radio to call for help in an emergency? Those who didn't like John
or thought he gave a bad image of Europeans, whose role it was to
command Africans rather than to serve their needs like John at the
Centre, had a ready explanation: the reason he hadn't been killed
was that he had come to an agreement with the Terrs, or was even
in cahoots with them like his friend Guidotti. John must have been
aware of the innuendo, because his feeling of being abandoned and
rejected had found stronger expression in several recent poems. In
fact the insurgents were likewise troubled by 'the Bradburne case',
as explained with insight by Rory Kilalea, who has written a play
about John:

> Never underestimate the impact of a 'white'
> person voluntarily (he was not even a priest, a
> nurse or a doctor!) devoting his life to help lepers
> in a terrorist area. Social opprobrium and pressure
> were immense. And not only for the dying embers
> of a whites-only society. The black guerrillas were
> often as confused. A white man offering himself
> on the altar of danger was suspicious. Was he an
> informer? He was not a priest. He was not a nurse
> or a doctor.

In 1977 violence intensified all over the country: deaths included 68 Europeans, among them 52 farmers, 1365 African civilians, and an unknown number of guerrillas. In the Mtoko zone, the worst massacre took place at the end of the year. With five other Grey Scouts, Sergeant Bruce Moore-King was three miles away from the position that they had been guarding for five days, including Christmas Eve, to 'protect' a large keep of 5000 huts being built below them. The villages all around had been evacuated and burnt to the ground, and a small earthen fort had been built in the middle, but the safety wiring fence was not yet in place. When the guerrillas attacked under a clear sky, Moore King and his men went down and discovered that the guerrillas had set fire to the entire keep, lined up the villagers and forced them to sing the glory of the Chimurenga. The guerrillas then bayoneted to death a man working for the government. The Grey Scouts opened fire with grenades and machine guns, while the villagers were caught in the crossfire; 134 died in the ensuing carnage, not to mention those who escaped and died later in the bush.

The Horsemen of the Apocalypse

At the end of 1977 John had the pleasure of seeing his friend Margaret de Haast entering the Catholic Church, and he wrote to congratulate her (30 December). He couldn't help resorting to a play on words, calling her the 'Roman Unroaming Catholic'. In his Christmas greetings for 1978 to his friend Stephen King he thanked him again for sending provisions, and made little of the dangers besetting him in the backwoods of Mtemwa (an oasis of Shangri-La, he wrote, referring to the novel by James Hilton), expressing his hope that 1978 would finally bring peace after a terrible year. But in fact the opposite happened, and like the Horsemen of the Apocalypse evils continued to rain down over the region. It was the same in the rest of the country: on January 9th young Bruce Forrester was murdered, with his father, his grandmother and a family friend at Rainbow's End Farm west of Salisbury. For Laureen St John, 11 years of age, and Bruce's classmate, the war which the white children had thought of as a bogey man to scare themselves had suddenly become her reality, 'It wasn't a game any more. It wasn't a game at all', she wrote in *Rainbow's End*.

A few days later the Superior of the Jesuit Missions at Makumbe, Gus O'Donovan, was abducted and his body never found. Like John at Mtemwa, Father O'Donovan had been at loggerheads with the African farmers of the kraals next to the Mission, over the incursions of their livestock, and it was these who almost certainly delivered him to the vakomana. As he listened to the tragedy of this confrere of Father Dove, John must have been reminded of his problems with his own neighbours, though he had never killed any cattle who had entered the Centre. Meanwhile, levels of violence had not fallen in the Mtoko zone. On April 4th, for example, the guerrillas staged a daring ambush on Rhodesian forces, killing three African soldiers. The next day they blew up the bridge at Nyabini, and on the 19th attacked a Rhodesian commando, killing Richard Cecil, son of the Marquis of Salisbury. The curfew now operated for 18 hours a day, and 24 hours a day for all young men, an indication of the powerlessness of the Rhodesian army, which, as was reported in the *New York Times*, no longer had any control outside the European zone, and only to a small extent the zone of African farmers, and was reduced to controlling the road to Mozambique and the keeps.

John was writing a lot at the beginning of 1978. In a letter to his mother on January 19th, he returned to the death of his cousin Terrence Rattigan on November 30th the previous year. He reminded her that he had been friendly with Rattigan's invalid brother, and in *In Memoriam: T.R.*, written on February 9th, he refused to join the 'jackals' who tried to publicise the writer's homosexuality. He wrote to Shirley James on the 20th, complaining bitterly about the Committee, 'the most ineffective body that ever jerked itself to the assumption of a title'. On January 25th he replied to a letter from Bruce Wilkinson recounting the latter's conversion. Having punned on the risen sun and the risen Son, John continued in the same playful vein:

> Our Lady is a dashing Blonde,
> Our Lord is her delight
> And nobody can get too fond

Of playing in their sight:
The song of heaven's Queen and King
Is plainly sung by monks who sing.

Among his Jesuit friends was Father Fidelis Mukonori who, though
John was unlikely to have known it, was close to Robert Mugabe.
This African priest made his way around the country without
attracting too much attention, and three or four times a year he
visited John at Mtemwa 'to give him a bit of company', bringing
on each occasion parcels for the lepers. Father Fidelis liked the
way John seemed to be always happy and jovial, and he was in no
doubt as to his saintliness. One day when he was passing through
Mtemwa with Father Harold-Barry, John invited the two priests
to go for a walk. The Jesuits were very worried because there were
mines everywhere, and their host seemed just as anxious as they
were, but for totally different reasons: he was thinking about the
bees with nothing to drink.

Another Jesuit visitor was Father John Gough, who had been in
Rhodesia for 25 years, and for some time had dropped by Mtemwa
once a month. At the beginning he would bring along a bottle of
brandy, but 'after a few weeks he asked me not to bring him any
more as he liked it too much'. One visit in particular struck the
Jesuit:

> I called at the store on the left hand side of the
> road and, as I had been instructed, I asked for
> packets of oranges for Mutemwa. Although the
> store was loaded with these bags of oranges, they
> said they hadn't anything to take to John and could
> I come back in a couple of weeks time when it
> will be all right. A couple of weeks later, I went
> back and the store loaded my pick-up truck with
> many sacks of oranges. I turned off to the lepers
> just down the road and John was waiting there and
> he asked me how had I got through. I said, 'very
> bumpily!' We then off-loaded the oranges. We had
> been stopped once or twice on the road by armed
> men who waved us on as soon as they recognised

us. There were enough oranges that day for all the patients, some 91 of them, the nursing staff and the little children.

John played the harmonium while Father Gough said Mass, consecrating enough hosts to fill the ciborium for subsequent daily communion. Then he joined John as he went to bathe the lepers.

Caterina Savini remembers another meeting with John, when he was pushing his loaded wheelbarrow on the road to Mtoko. Having transferred the contents of the wheelbarrow to her car, she continued on to the Centre. When John eventually arrived, the wheelbarrow was again full of provisions provided by people along the road, as well as having two children on board.

John's attitude in chapel and elsewhere struck 7-year-old Perpetua Robert, whose aunt Ruby helped out at the Centre:

> I remember attending daily Mass with Baba John, as we used to call him. He was a very kind and loving person... He had an infectious laugh, and yes the hair band! How good a person he was, also that he seemed happy and contented with his life, although from an observer of my age he was very poor compared to the average white person in the then Rhodesia.

Around this time John paid a visit to the keep at Kaunye, which was very close to Mtemwa. On his return to the Centre he wrote a poem in which he pointed out the absurdity of the keep system, which 'Is a conglomeration to forget / So soon as boon of peace is here once more'. The poem went on: after a day's work in the fields the villagers resort to alcohol to keep the horror of the war at bay, and this in turn leads to sexual promiscuity, which brings John to this conclusion:

> Prince, the erotic force of life in store
> Plays marbles with mere mortals: clear's the Star
> As Ninghi chases Nancy, door to door,
> Makes an erratic course from bar to bar.
> (*A Ballade of a Distant Prospect of Kaunye Keep*, 1978)

Sometime later this keep was attacked by ZANLA. It was described in a ZANU propaganda tract as 'an operation that was prosecuted in close collaboration with the Zimbabwean people imprisoned in the Nazi-type concentration camp, and so liberated from the forces of Smith-Muzorewa-Sithole, were allowed to grow their crops wherever they pleased'.

On March 3rd an accord was finally signed in Salisbury between Ian Smith, Bishop Muzorewa, the Reverend Sithole and Chief Chirau, opening the way for an election on the basis of one person one vote. The Europeans were to maintain control of the army, the police, the economy, the administration of law, and the civil service. But when this was immediately rejected by the Patriotic Front, the war stepped up in intensity and Muzorewa let loose his own militia across the country. Meanwhile,

> At Mtemwa old Kimbini was on the verge of dying.
> His body grew more fat, his soul more lean;
> Blind as a bat he thought that none played Cricket
> As cricket should be played but he himself.
> (*Posthornbeaming*, 1978)

He claimed to have played cricket better than anybody else. John baptised him, giving him the name Thomas on March 4th, just before he died. On the 5th he buried him at dawn, in the same poem noting that

> The most depressing leper I have known
> Has had the gayest burial I have seen.

Under clear blue sky, facing the granite outcrop of Chigona, John and his helpers dug the earth of the cemetery, but had to stop at a depth of three feet because they had hit on a spring. Kimbini-Thomas was stretched out rolled up in his blanket:

> Six feet of forty years of woe
> Which had been called Kimbini
> Lay in a blanket wrapped to go
> Down but for five feet, cleanly.

John rejoiced at the sound of the spring, which sang of the resurrected one, and reflected that the same chant of the water would remind the recently baptised Kimbini of the resurrection to come.

Shortly before this, John had received from John Dove's mother a book with photographs of Father Damien, at whose grave John had often prayed in Louvain. On New Year's Eve, John wrote to his friend: 'What a wonderful man and what tremendous work of dedication. It is of no use to shudder at the contrast of his life and mine, but only to say and to mean Gloria in Excelsis Deo.' He wrote of his admiration for this priest, who struggled from morning to evening for his lepers, when he had only bathed

> Blind Peter and blind Simon in succession
> And then this afternoon when all were yawning
> I paced the compound in a sole procession...

He added about Father Damien and himself:

> I've hardly glanced this evening at a booklet
> Which tells how Father Damien behaved,
> How from the island-sunrise till its sunset
> He toiled and toiled and never respite craved;
> Excuses are bad reasons for wrong-doing
> But he was made of sterner stuff than this
> Bottom of all the class!
> (*Brandy in The Whisky Den*, 1978)

In fact we could write, as Plutarch did for famous men of antiquity, a kind of Parallel Lives of St Damien and John Bradburne:

- Both spent many years of their life with the lepers (sixteen for St Damien, ten for John).
- Both treated the lepers, fed them, assisted them, built houses for them, played and sang with them (St Damien created a band, John a choir), and even made coffins to bury the dead ones.
- Both defended the lepers against discrimination or violence.

- Both quickly restored joy and hope to the poor lepers who were living a hell on earth before their arrival. Both Molokai and Mtemwa became with them oases of peace and love after being places of despair.
- Both were deeply happy, in spite of many daily problems, challenges, opposition, threats and setbacks.
- Both gave the lepers Christ (Father Damien celebrating the Eucharist, John distributing it), and both promoted adoration of Christ in the Blessed Sacrament.
- Both served Catholics and non-Catholics without discrimination.
- Both promoted cooperation for medical and other needs – with an ecumenical dimension (an Anglican Parish supported St Damien, Anglican friends supported John).
- Both worked with dedicated consecrated women who also served and gave their life for the lepers and the poor: St Marianne Cope on one side, Luisa Guidotti and other members of AFMM on the other.
- Both had to bear their cross, and both were misunderstood, not only by hostile persons, but also by those who might have supported them: St Damien had to endure defamation by jealous Protestant missionaries who insinuated he had caught syphilis when he became a leper himself (Robert Louis Stevenson wrote a magnificent open letter to *The Times*, defending his memory), and was misunderstood by his superiors most of his life in Molokai. John also suffered calumny from both sides in the Rhodesian civil war and was expelled from Mutemwa Centre by the Leprosy Association.
- While St Damien died from leprosy, and John was murdered, we know the latter prayed to catch the disease.
- Finally, both gave their lives for the poor lepers.

The Catholic Church has already recognised in Father Damien of Molokai one of the saints of compassion. St Teresa of Calcutta was instrumental in Father Damien's cause. On May 7th 1984, she wrote to John Paul II about the lepers her sisters were nursing (quoted in Glynn MacNiven-Johnston, *Father Damien*, 2009):

> We need a saint to lead and protect us. Father
> Damien can be this saint. Holy Father, our lepers
> and everyone on earth beg you to give us a saint,
> a martyr to love, an example of obedience to our
> religion.

She added that the miracle for the beatification so needed was
already there, in the heart of the lepers. What for John?

African civilians continued to bear the brunt of this terrible war.
One of these deaths had a particularly strong effect on John. Among
the faithful who regularly attended Mass at Mtemwa was a certain
old man of whom he was very fond, an ex-member of the British
South African Police in the 1930s, who continued to wear his old
military shorts. One morning he was assassinated by the guerrillas
or by mujibhas. John was saddened, but most of all outraged by the
cowardice of it: to kill such a harmless old man was just too much
in his eyes. Luisa Guidotti had to calm him by reminding him that
the mujibhas were everywhere, and it was useless to bring attention
to it more than was strictly necessary.

On June 9th, in a political poem on 'the Russian bear', John
had no hesitation in seeing behind the guerrillas the hand of
Satan perverting a genuine thirst for justice, freedom and truth.
In another poem, *Maria's Ready Answer to The Reds*, written out in
the blue by the reeds, he spoke of 'Christ barefoot in Siberia', and
mentions again the 'Freedom Fighters' as following 'the practices
which Satan preaches'. On June 29th his disgust was evident in a
poem where he refers to children who had been bayoneted, the
diphtheria which was rife in the keeps and, in the Centre, a leper
who had cancer of the liver and for whom medication could do
nothing, but who might be cured by the force of prayer. The same
day in a letter to his sister Mary, he rails yet again against the
'Reds' whose propaganda worked even in England. In his eyes the
Russians coveted the farms which had been built by 'Guests / That
uninvited came'. His disarray in the face of the situation where evil
answers evil was obvious.

John was more alone than ever. Visits had almost ceased except
for those close friends who were willing to take the risk of coming

to see him. All that remained was the post, and the generous gifts which it often brought, like the one he acknowledged on May 3rd:

Generosity
Of fifty pounds makes lepers bound for glee
Of being free from lack of nourishment
For three full months.
(*A Solitary's Lament*, 1978)

In the same month he renewed correspondence with Pamela and Geza Vermes, almost 25 years after their last contact. Geza, having left the Catholic Church, became in 1965 Professor of Jewish Studies at Oxford. His book *Jesus the Jew* (1973) made him famous. In this book, he insisted on the Jewishness of Jesus, and revealed it to numerous Christians. Later, he attacked head-on all that Christians believe about Jesus Christ, starting with the Resurrection. He considered that the historical Jesus belonged only to Jewish history, and that Christians should revisit the basic tenets of their faith. That year, Geza and Pamela had met Alec Burkill, who had come from Salisbury, in Oxford, and they discovered that all three of them knew a certain Bradburne. Burkill was quick to send Vermes' address to John.

On May 15th, John wrote a letter-poem to the couple in which he expressed his delight at renewing contact with them, and spoke to them of the Trinity as Thought, Word, Voice. He seemed to have forgotten that Vermes, once his spiritual director, had moved away from Christianity. The poem expressed a vibrant love for the Jewish people and ended briefly: 'Forgive me if I was ever unkind.' The Vermes wrote back, Pamela in verse, complaining about his silence and his vision of the Trinity, Geza in a few pages denying the Incarnation. John took him up point by point in prose and then in verse, a good example of the dialogue of the deaf between historical-critical erudition and spiritual interpretation (there is no record of later correspondence).

At the end of June, John was once again at Silveira House. The Franciscan Tom Russell, at the time posted to Marandellas, had come to Silveira House to attend a meeting of the local clergy. While he was parking his car he noticed Sabina Mugabe and, 'across to my right, John Bradburne, talking to Luisa Guidotti near another car'. When he arrived at the meeting, he learned that Father Gerhard Lisson and Brother Gregor Rickett had just been assassinated at the Sinoia Mission. 'Pasi panodya zvakakomba', he said in Shona: 'death is insatiable'. Praying later beside the remains of Brother Rickett, who had been his friend, he could not help noticing the 'almost exultant look on Brother Rickett's face', adding: 'My intuition told me that he had seen beyond, as St Thérèse did, at the very moment of death'.

John was no less moved by these new murders, which concluded a particularly bloody series of episodes: three members of the Red Cross, including two Swiss, were killed near Regina Coeli Mission on May 9th; Brothers Geyermann and von Arx were murdered at Embakwe Mission on June 2nd; two young female English teachers of the Salvation Army on the 7th; 27 civilians massacred by the army near the St Augustine Mission run by the Mirfield Fathers; the Baptist mission of Sanyati attacked; Archie Dunaway murdered on the 15th; and, on the 23rd, the carnage at the Pentecostal Mission at Elim: 13 victims, including three children and an infant, after most of the women had been raped, responsibility for which could only be attributed to the guerrillas – during the burial of victims, a survivor prayed for the killers, which led to an argument with the Rhodesian Front. (The head of the Elim murder commandos met the people in charge of the Mission some years later, and gave them his reason for the massacre: the need to terrorise the Whites and close down the Mission. Six members of the commandos were later converted to the Christian faith and became Pentecostal preachers.)

Back at Mtemwa, John's friendship with Father Gibbs had deepened. The latter had been forbidden to go into the villages with his truck to bring Red Cross first aid to people who were succumbing more and more to malnutrition, because such supplies could also have served the guerrillas. But he could still come to Mtoko, and from there to Mtemwa, where he helped John to transport provisions for the Centre. The poetry of the wheelbarrow lost out, but his friend was happy. Like Father Gibbs, those who still came to Mtemwa, such as Pauline Hutchings and Father Dove, noticed a gradual transformation in John. He had learned to live with the war and the possibility that he could be abducted or murdered from one day to the next. People noticed the resilience which he had developed, even though the cattle which continued to stray into the Centre often made him very angry.

His spiritual development also struck them. John often spoke to them of the only two books which, with the Office and the Bible, he still read: stories of *The Russian Way of a Pilgrim* and *The Cloud of Unknowing*. The first of these had been given him by Father Michel Ivens, a Jesuit passing through, and John recited for hours on end under the mango tree near his hut the 'Prayer of Jesus'. He had changed the title of the classic text to 'Jesus of Nazareth, King of the Jews, triumph through Judas', as he wrote to Father Ennis on January 16th 1979. He had made it his prayer of intercession for his leper friends, for those whom he loved, for peace in Rhodesia, and for the Jewish people. He introduced Anne Lander as well as several lepers to this prayer.

But it was above all the meditation inspired by *The Cloud of Unknowing* which structured his spiritual life, and his poems were deeply impregnated with the spirit of this work. He knew it probably since his time at Parkminster, and down the years it had become a companion of his life and thought (in 1968 he asked for it as a Christmas present in a modern English translation by Justin McCann published four years before). As with the plays of Shakespeare, the paternity of this work fascinated John, and he claimed loud and clear that it was Walter Hilton – even though he was not entirely convinced, as is indicated on the first page of his copy 'Water (sic) Hilton, who knows?' Although he had a certain Marian interpretation of the work, even going so far as to impose his own meaning, seeing in Mary the Cloud of which the work speaks, he remained faithful to its general thrust which had nourished the mystical life and guided many generations of contemplatives, English and others, towards a fruitful meeting with God.

What did he find in it? On the level of form, a kindred spirit and a culture which spanned centuries: humour, paradox (for example that Martha was right to complain about her sister Mary, but that Mary was also right to remain at the feet of Christ), good sense, a place of honour given to silence, and the rejection of exaggerated ascetic practices. It is surprising to see John, so anxious to reach invisible realities through the visible ones, embracing an apophatic spirituality which, without condemning visible and material things, situates them at a lower level of the spiritual life (maybe he found there a necessary counterweight to his imagination). But he held on to its essential principle: the rejection of the way of knowledge in favour of the way of love, and a simple method: to throw, with all one's loving heart, to God his name: 'God'. Father Crane, who knew John, expresses this dimension to his life revealed by *The Cloud of Unknowing*:

> This is the story of one for whom the final reality was all. That is the difference between John Bradburne and most of the rest of us. In Bradburne there was no false dichotomy; his love was not split between created being and Creator. How could it be? He saw in all the imprint, in beauty, of Him Who is Beauty itself.

But for John there was no escape from the more mundane realities. In addition to the threats from the war, the problems of the straying cattle had resurfaced. At the beginning of July he recounts in a poem:

> No wrathful theme
> We'll meet with in the herd:
> Cattle in line, one hundred kine
> And ne'er a battling word.
>
> If you wish for peace prepare for war
> For the cattle-boys have cut
> Our wire three nights ago or four.
> (*Pilgrimage*, 1978)

Once again he tried to explain to the 'cattle boys' that their behaviour was unacceptable. But he remarked in the same poem that they were becoming more and more arrogant because the African farmers, above all the voracious Mudzinganyama, were behind them against the white man.

Alcoholism was gradually taking a stronger hold on Mtemwa, despite John's efforts to bring back the 'beer-drink's healthy joy' (as he had written three years before in *Concerning Mtemwa*), and it was at this time that he decided to deal, once and for all and with the grace of God, with his own personal difficulties in this domain. The strength that he derived from this resolution can be felt in his struggle against the beer suppliers, which some of the lepers had difficulty in understanding. Alcoholism, vandalism, insolence, incivility, and the feeling that everything was permitted, because the Europeans were on the run, increased at the Centre. One morning John discovered that the mango trees had been pillaged. Then the farmer-butcher drove his cattle into the graveyard of the Centre and demanded this as a right. And as if that wasn't enough, thieves arrived in a truck, took away what remained of the mangos, and sold them at the nearest keep. John tried once more to solve the matter in an amicable fashion. He knew that a number of African farmers were in close contact with the European farmers, and he asked one of the latter, Tony Turner, to intervene, in particular in the matter of the cemetery. As usual he did so while preparing a dozen memoranda in verse which he sent to Tony and Janet Turner, signing off with typical humour: 'Sniper's Hill'.

'I got onto nodding-terms with Sister Death'

A few days later in 1978, Luisa Guidotti drove John urgently to Salisbury, his face and jaw half paralysed, his voice scarcely audible, and in a state of exhaustion. Shortly before, he had had a tooth removed after a persistent sore throat. But this had no effect, and the paralysis had now spread to his face. Luisa happened to be passing through the Centre, and immediately took him with her to Silveira House. Father Harold-Barry saw them arriving, with John unsteady on his feet. The next morning Luisa took him to see Professor Gelfand, who diagnosed encephalitis, needing urgent treatment, and arranged for him to be transferred immediately to St Anne's Hospital, but the disease had already spread to his lungs. The doctor did his best, but feared that John would not survive. All his friends had been alerted and were praying. Two days later, John was experiencing difficulty breathing, the medullary centres having been affected, and Gelfand thought it was the end for John. He was transferred to the intensive care unit in the new Andrew Fleming Hospital, where he was given respiratory assistance.

He recovered, to the surprise of Professor Gelfand, after three days hovering between life and death. A week later he was able to return to St Anne's, and little by little recovered the use of his facial muscles and jaw. Professor Gelfand spoke of a miracle. When John heard what had happened he simply said: 'the little beggar stopped'. But Gelfand insisted that in no circumstances should he return to Mtemwa, where there was nothing for him but permanent danger.

When visits were allowed, friends, friends of friends, and the simply curious, knocked on his door. To Anne Lander, who thought he looked emaciated, he complained about the food. 'I am putting on weight', and added 'but that won't stop me from flying away'. Father O'Halloran, who had become headmaster the previous year at St George's College and who hardly knew John, came to see him, and remarked: 'So there he was, a free spirit for once in captivity, and friends poured to see him. Effortlessly, patiently, and with great charm he held court for all comers.' Another visitor was Father Claudio Rossi, an Italian Jesuit: 'He was in hospital and I visited him. He said to me "Father give me your blessing", and I remember so clearly that moment, thinking: "You're so good, so holy, so humble, it's you who should be blessing me." But of course, I gave him my priestly blessing.' A severely handicapped young girl came to see him one day when Father Harold-Barry was at his bedside, and talked to him about poetry. John asked her if she had ever written poetry, and she told him that she couldn't write. He replied, 'but this shouldn't be a problem because Jesus only wrote once and it was in the sand'. All three of them burst out laughing, and the young girl departed looking radiant. But John, exhausted by all these comings and goings around his bed, asked John Dove to put a notice on the door of his room with the inscription: 'Dead'.

Finally Professor Gelfand gave the green light for John to leave the hospital and begin his convalescence at Silveira House. He borrowed a pair of binoculars and a map from Father Kennedy to try and see Mtemwa in the distance. He had every intention of going back, even though Professor Gelfand doubted whether he would ever make a complete recovery, and tried unsuccessfully to convince him to stay in Salisbury. However, at the beginning of

September he set out for Mtemwa with only a bag, a toothbrush, his Office of Our Lady, a pair of trousers, and his freshly laundered Franciscan habit. Luisa came to fetch him and drove both him and another young patient back to Mtemwa. She was annoyed because the young man was a mujibha, and she was afraid that John might bring up the subject of the old man who had been murdered and give vent to his anger. Throughout the journey she talked endlessly to John to prevent him from turning around to talk to the passenger, who might subsequently denounce him. (According to another source it was Father Mukonori who drove him back to Mtemwa. In which case the episode with Luisa Guidotti relates to another journey.)

On October 3rd John wrote to thank Mrs Dove for the book about Father Damien, and mentioned his illness and his return to Mtemwa. In a postscript Father Dove added that his friend's eyes were weak but that he hated wearing glasses, that everybody came to see him at the hospital, and that he was already famous for his work in the service of the lepers. Back in Mtemwa, John wrote a letter-poem to the sisters at All Souls:

> God bless you, Catherina and Louisa,
> You helped a white who might be black as coal
> Except for Absolution!

In the same letter, he jokingly referred to the new Polish Pope: 'It is a relief that John Dove is not Pope, though a disappointment to me in a way: it is better for us to have him in our midst these days, don't you think?' On November 24th he wrote to Bruce Wilkinson about his illness: 'I am almost persuaded to refer to Sister Virus, but not quite! But I got onto nodding-terms with Sister Death.'

In Mtemwa John resumed his old life: service to the lepers, prayer, climbing Chigona, contemplation and poems. He continued his struggle with the local farmers to protect the graveyard. He learned as well of the illness of his friend Alistair Guthrie, who was suffering from cancer and going downhill rapidly, and he promised himself to go and visit him in Salisbury. The welfare of the lepers also continued to preoccupy him. Because of lack of medication

426   John Bradburne: Vagabond of God

and insufficient rations, 11 lepers died in 1978, the highest figure for 10 years.

The military and political situation of the country and of the Mtoko zone worsened during autumn 1978. On September 13th an airliner had been shot down near Kariba, and 10 of the 18 survivors were massacred by Nkomo's men. The Proclamation of Martial Law on the 23rd of the same month did nothing to contain the guerrillas, who continued to destroy the crops and harvest of those villagers who remained recalcitrant to the new order, in Mtoko and elsewhere. The European farmers began to negotiate for protection with the local commandants of ZANLA, while at the same time reinforcing their own systems of security. In fact no killings of Europeans were recorded in the rural zone after the death of Mrs Palmer, even though, on October 12th, Chris Stobart was seriously injured in an ambush, and owed his survival to the arrival of the Guard. (He subsequently spent six months in hospital, while his wife Marjorie continued to supply humanitarian help to the Africans.)

A new source of tension arose at Mtoko: partisans of Bishop Muzorewa's UANC, now supporting Ian Smith, effectively controlled the town and claimed to represent all Africans in the zone. In reply to this challenge, the guerrillas stepped up their violence against 'traitors', a category which from now on included anybody who spoke favourably of the UANC. Mujibhas continued to carry out assassinations: ten villagers were liquidated in one village (by the end of the war the mujibhas had killed more villagers than the Rhodesian forces, in spite of the many massacres perpetuated by the latter). By the end of 1978 the military situation was so confused that the high command of the guerrillas for the zone decided to reorganise its troops, fearing they were losing the support of the population.

In his letter and his poems John gave expression to his feelings about the situation at this time. On November 24th, he wrote to Bruce Wilkinson that the Antichrist was on the march, and that his Christmas celebrations were tinged with sadness. The murder of another Jesuit, on St Stephen's Day, added to his grief. Father Gerhard Pieper, 38 years of age, was killed when he refused to abjure his faith at the demand of the vakomana. This confirmed

John in his apocalyptic interpretation of the conflict as being anti-religious.

'I can't leave them'

The war continued to rage around the Centre. The reservoir dam at the foot of Chigona was attacked by the vakomana, who on numerous occasions made an appearance in the vicinity of the Centre, but remained invisible for the most part. In spite of the danger, Father David Harold-Barry came to Mtemwa to celebrate the New Year, accompanied by Father O'Halloran. Early in the morning John rang the bell for Mass and, so Father O'Halloran tells us:

> On so high and holy a day he was wearing the habit of a Franciscan Tertiary (in fact it was a habit of the First Order which had been given to John by Father Gildea), something very dear to him. I marvelled at how John has taught his congregation to sing the ordinary parts of the Mass to the lively melody we know as Greensleeves while he accompanied them on the harmonium, which was a gift from the parish of Braeside.

The next day the District Commissioner of Mrewa, David Mirans, was killed when he stepped on a mine near his house – John's guests also took the same road through this large village. The situation of European farms in the Mtoko zone was getting worse: about 20 white farmers out of 66 had left the zone between 1975 and 1978, but almost the same number again left in 1979, and their herds dropped from 35,000 to 7000 heads. Nevertheless most of John's friends among the farmers hung on to the bitter end. Europeans also left the village of Mtoko, except for those who had no choice: at this stage they were effectively under 'house arrest' under the protection of the patrols, while the African population of the town increased tenfold because of the general insecurity in the rural zone.

The war continued, but it was becoming more and more – apart from the shock troops of the UDI regime and their airborne operations – a war between Africans. Many mujibhas would have liked to go to Mozambique and come back as vakomana, but they were prevented from doing so by the commanders in the zone because they were needed on the ground. Some mujibhas were waging a war of terror among themselves: right beside Mtemwa the bodies of a young boy and girl killed by their companions were exposed for a number of days on a rock very visible from the neighbouring kraals.

At the beginning of January, Bonaventura Mugabe, Robert's mother, who was a devout Catholic, was examined by Luisa Guidotti on her way through Salisbury. Luisa diagnosed a serious illness requiring hospitalisation. As it was forbidden for Africans to be admitted to a hospital for Europeans, Mrs Mugabe had to be admitted to St Anne's under disguise, with the complicity of Sister Margaret Murphy and Professor Gelfand. Shortly afterwards it was Alistair Guthrie's turn to be admitted. When John found out, he rushed to Mtoko and boarded an African bus for Salisbury. He arrived after the curfew, but walked to Silveira House, risking summary execution if stopped. Early next day, he went with John Dove to St Anne's hospital and arrived in the room of the dying man, who was surrounded by family and the Blue Sisters. He joined in their prayers and shortly afterwards Alistair Guthrie died in 'great peace'.

In Silveira House, Ferdinand ('Ferrie') Spit, a Belgian layman who was working there as accountant, and who was also a Third Order Franciscan, was impressed by how the two Johns had made Silveira House a 'house of prayer'. John Bradburne's 'warm personality', which inspired confidence, his headband, and his total absence of vanity, was a mystery to him, and he saw 'a light in his eyes one could not define'.

John and Luisa Guidotti soon returned to Salisbury with Caterina Savini, who was flying to Italy for a surgical operation to her spine. Just as she was about to leave she handed her keys to Luisa Guidotti, who said to her simply 'we will not meet again'. John went back to Mtemwa with Luisa, from now on the only non-African, apart from himself and Father Gibbs, in the whole rural zone of Mtoko. Because there was no matron to replace Caterina, the young priest took over her job. At night more and more guerrillas came to All Souls. One day two seriously wounded men arrived. Luisa disguised them as a grandmother and her daughter, and Father Gibbs, risking his own life, drove them from the Mission as far as Salisbury, where they could receive discreet care. Luisa looked after everybody who came to the hospital, even though the guerrilla chiefs had forbidden her to look after 'traitors'. One day a seriously injured woman arrived, chased by guerrillas, who insisted that Luisa hand her over to them. Luisa refused and they threatened to blow up the hospital. The woman, who witnessed the scene, decided to give herself up. Luisa, devastated, never saw her again.

In February another plane was shot down by the guerrillas above Karoi. The murder of European farmers continued, along with massacres in the villages and keeps. Rhodesia was becoming more and more a pariah nation. When, at the beginning of 1979, Ian Smith was refused an entry visa to Norway for the marriage of his son Alec, he finally understood that in the eyes of the West he was not the defender of Christian civilisation, as he had considered himself, but an outcast. (His son, far from sharing his father's ideas, was a militant in Moral Rearmament, and took part in efforts to facilitate the transition from his father's White rule to Mugabe in 1980.) Smith dissolved parliament and set about organising, on April 17th, a general election on the principle of 'one man one vote', with 28 seats out of 100 reserved for Europeans. As David Caute put it at the time:

> 90 years ago the white man appeared on the scene with guns and sjambok (heavy leather whip): he made the rules and killed anyone who seriously disagreed. Nothing has changed. Now his gunships come snarling low over the thatched kraals, his loudspeakers informing the people that they must vote and be free: they obey.

But the guerrillas made it known that they would consider anybody that voted as a traitor, at which point many of the villagers preferred to seek refuge in the bush. Officially 64 per cent of Africans cast their vote, and Muzorewa's UANC won 51 seats, but the war became even more violent.

The Catholic Church persisted in its efforts to find a settlement. A delegation of two bishops and a member of the Justice and Peace Commission met with John Paul II and tried to persuade him of the necessity to alert world opinion. The Pope decided to act promptly. Even before the delegation had arrived back in Rhodesia, he had contacted the ambassadors to the Holy See of all the great Western powers to press upon their attention the Rhodesian problem, and spoke directly with the British Ambassador asking for immediate intervention from his country.

The Superior of the Jesuit Order had refused to grant authorisation to Father Dove to go to Mtemwa on the grounds that 'it had become too dangerous, and my Superior, who had lost seven Jesuits to the gun, was not keen for us to take risks'. John and Luisa Guidotti came to Silveira House to celebrate Easter on April 15th. In earshot of her friends she spoke to Adele Pignatelli on the phone of the joy of the Resurrection, and added that 'if by chance she was hit by a stray bullet it would be so wonderful to find oneself in the hands of the Risen Christ'. But she became angry when the founder of AFMM refused to send anybody to back her up, considering that the risk was too high.

Father Dove insisted that this time under no circumstances should John return to Mtemwa. But John was adamant: 'When the last leper has left Mtemwa, then, and only then, would he leave.' He was however all too aware of the risk he was taking. The Mtemwa zone was still on the line of contact between the guerrillas, who were everywhere, and the Rhodesian forces who had dug in to their positions. The war was stepping up and at any moment the worst could happen. At which point John wrote, before passing his childhood in review – the key to his life – envisaging his possible coming death:

> In case those 'Vakomana' bright
> This very night come here,
> Slowly O slowly let me write
> Why never shed a tear.
> (*Prologue to the next possible exit*, 1979)

At Silveira House at this time he met and became friendly with two German women, Frau Pätz and her daughter. They spoke together about Bach. Later John was driven back to Mtemwa by Father Fidelis Mukonori, of whom John was very fond, even though they differed in political matters. During the trip back (or on some other occasion – the date is somewhat vague) John told him 'I know you want to talk, but let me play the flute, good for you', and John played his recorder for the duration of the journey. Father Mukonori nevertheless took time to tell him that Mtoko and Mtemwa were no longer safe, and that he should go back to Salisbury. But John wouldn't hear of it.

On April 26th John thanked his mother for sending him a print of Christ by Leonardo da Vinci. He confided in her that 'The New Rule (Muzorewa) is now in, and I do not put much trust in it', repeating also his conviction that in Africa 'the Continent is earmarked by Russia for the Abominable Bear-Showman Marxist Heresy'. He believed that for every Christian the conversion of Russia should be an objective of their prayers. Minimising the dangers of his own situation, he referred to 'a lull', but didn't hide his fears that Christianity was about to be put to the test. And above all the most important thing for him would be the spiritual struggle for the Kingdom. The next day he wrote a similar letter to the Bourdillons, other friends in Salisbury, where he referred to his reservations about 'political bishops' and asked them to pray for the conversion of Russia.

On May 3rd, he thanked the Pätz's for their gift of 100 deutschmarks, remembering their conversation about that 'master musician Johann Sebastien Bach' and accepting their offer to send him some Bach records. He finished off his letter with a quotation from Cantate BWV 80, *Ein Feste Perge* (sic: John was citing from memory as usual). On the 23rd, he wrote to Mona Smith, telling her that since the death of eleven lepers in 1978 the Centre had not recorded one single death, and thanked her for the picture of Padre Pio, which he quickly placed on his Ark. He also shared with her a victory, about which he was now sufficiently confident to speak, over alcohol:

The blandishment of the Bottle no longer bothers me, but I am never averse to having a bottle in stock, in case an angel comes or a King or a Queen or, more likely, a beggar like myself. This is not a hint for a case of Brandy!

On Ascension Thursday, towards the end of May, John went to see Luisa Guidotti, who was going on a spiritual retreat of several days in Silveira House, but he left immediately to go back to Mtemwa. Upset by her falling out with Adele Pignatelli, and by the death that was hovering over her, Luisa Guidotti asked Father Dove to speak to her only of the Kingdom of Heaven and not of the Passion, 'since I live this day in day out'. Her friend replied: 'Luisa, I have never been to heaven and may not get there.' They both laughed and shared their meditation on the Resurrection of Christ, and of their last end.

At the beginning of June there was no let-up in John's epistolary activities. He thanked his correspondents for gifts and asked them to be prudent about the political situation in Rhodesia and rather turn their attention more towards heavenly Jerusalem. He wrote to Pauline Hutchings: 'The battle for real detachment finds in me a rather frail soldier', adding: 'But maybe it is better to know what an infant one is than to count oneself the pick of God's Own Infantry!' He compared himself to a reed at the mercy of the wind, unlike his patron saint dressed in camel skin. He wrote to John Dove thanking him for his card and birthday presents (milk powder and a bottle of wine) and spoke of storms in all senses of the word: 'The blustery weather is rather like the situation.' On the 30th, in a letter to his mother, he joked tenderly about Luisa Guidotti putting on weight: 'our dear Italian lady Doctor, still in exile from her medical practice here, Louisa (sic) Guidotti. She is a great lady weighing 250 lbs!' He continued to often sign his letter 'John the Bee' or 'Drone', a discreet way of indicating that his attachment to this winged species was still part of his everyday life, as we can also see from his poems.

The death of Luisa

A week later, on July 6th, Luisa Guidotti was killed close to All Souls on the way back from a medical evacuation. She had just

written: 'Papa Dio, grant me to be inwardly ready to die... Padre
mio, dammi une bella morte, My Father, give me a beautiful death.
A beautiful death is to die from love.' On June 19th she had arrived
at Silveira House so exhausted that Father Dove had put a drop of
brandy in her coca-cola. She told him about her working day, which
often lasted 21 hours, with a team that was getting smaller every
day. She reproached herself for having scolded an elderly African
sister, and confessed. The Jesuit told her that she must take time
off. But she answered: 'You know very well that I can't go away', and
before going back to the Mission she confided that she was lonely,
but also that 'she really felt that she was His child'. On her return,
she noticed a police van arriving at All Souls. She was threatened
by shots fired in the air, and accused of aiding the Terrs, and being
one of them. She replied that she was only obeying the Geneva
Convention by caring for everybody who came to the hospital, and
would continue to do so as long as it was necessary.

On July 6th she drove a sick villager in the Mission Land
Rover for an operation at the Methodist hospital in Nyadiri. She
refused to take anybody else with her, not wanting to risk the life
of a passenger. She dropped off the sick man and on the way back
stopped in Mtoko to buy some things in the Kassim brothers' shop,
then went to the offices of the District Commissioner, where she
got a frosty reception. A certain Munyaradzi who worked there
later said that he overheard two soldiers of the Guard saying: 'That's
the one.' She then set off on the main road to Lot, where the track
for All Souls begins. The village had suffered greatly from the war,
and an entire kraal had been massacred by the security forces in
a nearby quarry, and there were mines everywhere. That morning
the soldiers had combed the zone, after discovering the body of one
of their own men 300 yards from the village, with a note attached:
'a traitor who served with the Guard Force'. The African soldiers
were anxious that the death of a comrade perhaps pointed to their
own fate and opened fire blindly on the supposed positions of the
guerrillas.

Luisa Guidotti's vehicle was stopped and searched, and she was
told to drive on as far as the turn off for All Souls. She did so,
took the turning, and started along the track. At that moment,
a hail of rifle fire struck her vehicle. She was hit in the knee and

the leg and fainted at the steering wheel, losing a lot of blood, and the Land Rover skidded to a halt. The soldiers approached the vehicle, and seeing only a white woman whose blood was flowing rapidly they opened the door. Luisa murmured: 'I am a doctor. Why are you shooting me?' What happened then is unclear. An officer recognised her, and a mercenary officer who knew her family asked him to look after her. Apparently the officer applied a tourniquet to stem the blood, but the wounded Luisa, before losing consciousness, reportedly tried to remove it (according to another source there was never any tourniquet and the soldiers allowed her to bleed to death). She was finally taken in the vehicle to the hospital at Mtoko, but died shortly before arriving. When the vehicle stopped in front of the hospital, a soldier cried out to those coming towards him: 'Unochengeta magandanga, nhasi wafa' ('You who look after terrorists, today you die'). A later official enquiry came to the conclusion that it was an unfortunate accident. Orificero, the commandant of the guard, apparently did not hear the order to Luisa to proceed and had told his men to stop the vehicle. But for the friends of Luisa there was no doubt that it was a case of cold-blooded murder, which did not prevent some ultras from the Rhodesian Front describing her as a Terr who had been carrying Chinese mines in her vehicle.

On July 12th a Requiem Mass took place in Salisbury Cathedral. (Her remains were later repatriated and buried in her native Italy, and transferred to Modena Cathedral in 1988.) In spite of the risks, John travelled for the occasion in an African bus with some villagers from his zone, wearing his Franciscan habit. He was one of the carriers of the coffin. Visibly overwhelmed, he seemed to have aged ten years, but he prayed on his knees, bolt upright beside the coffin for most of the liturgy. Sister Theresiana Muteme was beside him, and at the end of the celebration he asked her, visibly devastated: 'What can we say about this? What can we say about this?' To which she replied: 'John this is sad, what else can we say.' As John carried the coffin of his friend out of the cathedral, Father Dove, who was beside him, heard him muttering to himself: 'I told her that I should go first.' He was in a hurry to get back to Mtemwa, as if afraid that he would be forcibly prevented from doing so, but he took the time to send a telegram to Caterina Savini, at that moment a patient in the Gemelli hospital in Rome, and to go to the hospital to see Margaret de Haast, who was about to undergo an operation. As he entered her room he quoted the Arabic proverb: 'If Muhammad cannot come to the mountain, the mountain will come to Muhammad.' And they prayed together for the departed Luisa.

To the bitter end

There now remained only two Europeans in the African zone of Mtoko, Father Gibbs and John. On August 1st, ten years to the day after his arrival in Mtemwa, John set out again for Silveira House because John Dove was flying to Europe on the 6th for a holiday, and John wanted to say goodbye. Heather Benoy was there also. John drove the young woman to pray at the Lourdes grotto, and contemplated the view of Chishawasha at sunset:

> The last time I saw John was at Silveira House. He had come in briefly from Mutemwa. I told him that I was very afraid for his life and begged him to remain in Salisbury. He replied that he could not leave the lepers at Mutemwa and that he was definitely going to return there shortly. This was the last time I saw him alive.

And she added: 'He knew there was a good possibility that he should be killed, and it was the culmination of his offering.' Before leaving her, he repeated several times: 'I will pray for you.' As far as Heather's father Maurice Benoy was concerned, 'He was going somewhere, he knew where he was going, and he was not worried about what happened to him at all.' During his stay in Salisbury he also visited the Dominican nuns who were helping the lepers by sending them Christmas parcels. Sister Philomena later said that 'he was Franciscan through and through and I think he tried to follow as closely as possible in the footsteps of St Francis. He too went to the extreme to get the message across, and so did John.'

John bought a few records with the money given him by Frau Pätz for this purpose, and wrote to thank her. He also wrote a letter-poem to Mrs Carey about Philo the leper, and sent a birthday card to his niece Pamela. As the cinema was going to show a film about

Jesus (probably *Jesus of Nazareth*, directed by Franco Zeffirelli, which came out in 1967), at Silveira House he met a nun and said to her: 'Sister, you must come with me to the cinema to see the life of Jesus. Will you drive me?' The nun did not have the time but he insisted, and who was she to resist, so they went to see the film together. In his last conversation with his Jesuit friend just before he left, John asked him: 'What shall I do if they come' – 'You should give them what they ask for. Don't die for five dollars' – 'Ah, no, it is leper money. I will give them coffee.'

Father Dove also promised that he would visit Mrs Bradburne in Devon. John then got down on his knees and asked his friend for his blessing. Before heading back to Mtemwa, he went to say hello to Father David Harold-Barry, entered his office, and asked him for a few stamps:

> I remember him saying to me, 'You are doing great work!' Jesuits are not good at saying that sort of thing to one another and so I was struck by it. It was no lightly mouthed pleasantry. It was a vocalisation of what he constantly did: he affirmed people. Meeting John, you always felt better about yourself. He was one of those people who lifted you.

Father Mukonori brought John back from one of his last visits to Salisbury and Silveira House. He would never forget the serious conversation which took place after about 60 miles:

> The day I was taking him back to Mutemwa, after about 60 kilometers, I say: John do you think you are safe? I don't think you are safe. – Well, I believe you know much better these things. What do you think? – You are not safe. – Why? – Right now you are open for anyone. – Why? – Because this area is no longer belonging to the Security Forces, they have been pulled out, it's no longer belonging to the guerrillas; so it becomes a frozen zone [A *frozen zone* in technical terms at that time in Rhodesia meant that that area would be occupied

by Zelous Scouts and they could behave as acting
guerrillas] which means that anyone with a lot of
arms, bandits and so on occupy that area, and it
is dangerous, and that's what happens in that area.
So, you are not safe. – What do you think? – I
really feel you should move out, but I don't think
you would. I feel I should move you out. – Yes.
What do you think I'll do? – I know you'll walk
back. – Yes, exactly. I'll walk back if you move
me out. I will accept you moving me out, but I'll
walk back. You see, I love these people. Maybe it
is selfish love, because before I met these people,
I did not feel I loved anyone, but the day I got in
contact with these people, I felt I loved somebody,
I felt that at last I contributed something to some
people who appreciated it. And this way I really
love these people.

They arrived at the spot where John had to get out of the car and
Father Mukonori said to him: 'John, goodbye. John, goodbye! I'm
sure before I go to London I'll come to visit you and hope we'll
meet again.' Back in Mtemwa, John wrote to Bruce Wilkinson on
the 16th about the Renewal:

I have been to one or two Charismatic Meetings.
They are not at all in my line but I am quite sure
that God blesses many people in their love of the
Charismatic movement.

His own vocation as he saw it was the one that he was sharing with
the Tertiary Franciscans, and to pray with the lepers that peace
would finally come.

John's family were also worried by what they were reading in
the newspapers about Rhodesia, and his brother Philip wrote
asking him to leave Mtemwa. But John was determined to stay.
He continued to pray, went back to the Centre, railed against the
absence of medication when one of the lepers fell ill, thanked
Stephen King for his parcels, and typed out his poems (186 at least
since the beginning of the year). The poems were beginning to

overflow everywhere in his hut, and John ordered a bookshelf to tidy them up and classify them. Was this not the opportunity to make a selection, as Father Dove thought he should do at the time, and get rid of some of them? He wrote to Father Harold-Barry, who recalled later:

> Only two weeks before he was killed, John wrote to me to say: 'Perhaps I shall put a match to my nonsensical writings before the shelf arrives.' (We were having a bookshelf made for all his writings.)

The problems with his neighbours continued to preoccupy him. To the stray cattle was added the problem of disappearing chickens, and trees continued to be cut down. John knew that the majority of his assistants were working hand in hand with the African farmers from the nearby village, and he guessed that if the Centre was going short it was not only because of the war that rations, blankets and clothes continued to disappear, and that part of the cattle ravaging the cemetery or the garden probably belonged to the same assistants. He felt like the black hen of St Francis' dream, and he fought back tooth and nail. When he became convinced that Phineas was involved in the theft, he shouted at him in front of all the assistants without worrying that these might be cousins or belong to the same family; he was aware that the guerrillas had promised them all the land, and therefore that the land belonging to the Centre would be theirs as soon as the Whites were expelled. He assessed the damages done by the cattle, and imposed a fine to reimburse the wrong done.

European authority was still quite strong, but resentment was on the increase: 'They had gone so far as to spread rumours about him, that he was a spy of the security forces', Heather Benoy said later. In the kraals around Mtemwa, word spread of the latest row, and this was eagerly picked up by the mujibhas. They too had an account to settle with him since the year before, when he loudly condemned them for killing the old man who used to attend Mass at the Centre.

John felt isolated in his fight for the lepers, especially because the Committee seemed to have lost all interest. After the death of

Alistair Guthrie, not one of the members was prepared to risk a visit to Mtemwa. John could only express his conscience freely in his correspondence with Father Gibbs. On August 13th he wrote to his mother, telling her about the tetracycline stratagem in the *Reader's Digest*: then remembering suddenly that Rhodesia was at war, and that mail was under surveillance, he continued:

> Would you please tell Mike in Artichokco that I would dearly love another Reader's Digest containing 500 Tetracycline, and that I feel quite happy about any risk that there might be to me on this side. If the Censor reads this letter I am offering him a Drink of Appeasement on the spot if not on the dot so that he may refrain from a Warning to the Excise and Customs Officers.

He also asked his mother to send him a photo of the Reverend Thomas Bradburne, his father, but not just any photograph:

> Could you let me have a photo of Fist in his prime – 45 or so – head and shoulders looking straight at me. Or even head to toes looking at chickens, in a biretta, or gardening in plus-threes!

On the 24th, he sent a card to Father Dove on which he wrote: 'I am trying to rely on the Lion of Saint Jerome & of Judah, & to be loyal. Have a super relaxing leave, & Guinness in Ireland.' On the 26th, he joked in a letter to Stephen King about their trips together on the Broads in East Anglia adding:

> For some odd reason no one has wasted a bullet on me yet... Though it may be in transit even now... The whole land is war sick. We keep on praying. Our own little Mtemwa Leper Colony has remained an oasis of peace, relatively speaking, thank God.

He finished the letter by writing that he was preparing to climb up a kopje from where he can salute the ocean and Stephen, but added a postscript: 'Met a legless chap who had to be taken home in a wheelchair, so I did not climb the kopje!' Those two lines say everything about his still intact devotion to the lepers. Since his return after his illness in 1978, his relationship with his leper friends had become more and more intense, and they recited together the prayer of Jesus to which he had now returned: 'Jesus of Nazareth, King of the Jews, we pray Thee that this war may end; please give peace in our land.'

Chapter 10

The Passion of John Bradburne, September 1979

There is no greater love than to lay down one's life for
one's friends.
(1 John 15.13)

Suddenly the prospect of an end to the war began to brighten. Shortly after the intervention of John Paul II, Britain decided to act, and the invitation sent on August 14th by Margaret Thatcher to all parties to the conflict received a positive reply from all except Robert Mugabe, whose friend Samora Machel, the Mozambique president, urged him to accept. At the end of their tether, the various factions involved were anxious for peace, each convinced they could win a post-agreement general election. Hope suddenly came to the kraals, the keeps, the farms, the villas, the hideouts in the bush, and the Centre at Mtemwa. On August 14th John wrote to his mother: 'In Mtemwa we pray and pray for this mad war to cease, and we believe that our prayers will be answered if we persevere well with humility.'

But for John himself, the darkness was closing in. On August 29th, Father Gibbs came to Mtemwa to celebrate Mass for the London talks. Pauline Hutchings arrived from her farm with her four children, and couldn't help noticing that in spite of the war there were twice as many participants at the Mass than when she first came. When the celebrations were over, they all decided to recite the so-called St Francis' prayer for peace ('Lord make me an instrument of Thy Peace...'), after which John helped those who couldn't walk to go home. He then invited his friends into his hut. Stanley, the Hutchings' cook, had prepared a meal of bread, butter and marmalade, and cake. Several lepers stood outside the hut, including an elderly couple who hadn't been able to register at the Centre, not having the necessary papers, and whom John had been sheltering in the meantime. John Dove had often scolded him for his inability to turn anyone away, warning him he would be segregated to a white leprosarium if he contracted the disease. (John took more care after that.)

Pauline gave John the bread and marmalade, and shared the cake among the group. She noticed that her friend changed places and put himself behind the open door, as if embarrassed that people outside might see Europeans eating food while they went hungry. This little scene revealed to her that he had no private life whatsoever. John was also worried about Father David Gibbs at All Souls, who was in regular contact with the guerrillas, but Pauline, like his other friends, was extremely concerned for John himself. As the Hutchings prepared to leave, 'he drew the Cross above the M (of Mary) in the dust on the back window of our truck. A fitting farewell.'

The next day, Thursday (or Friday, the date is not clear), John told Mai Coleta that he was not at peace in his hut, that evil stalked on all sides. Mai noticed that the hut had been invaded by a very aggressive species of red ant, which in Shona lore was a bad omen. That night John slept in the chapel. On Saturday September 1st, Mary's day, he was even more anxious, and asked Mai Coleta and the other lepers that he met to pray for him. Either they knew something, or had a premonition, and several begged him to leave Mtemwa immediately. At the end of the afternoon he climbed Chigona to pray. When he came down he seemed peaceful and told the lepers who had urged him to go that a great Angel had asked him to stay.

It appears his fate had already been sealed during meetings near Mount Mtemwa. Some of those who had been present later spoke to Brother Lawrence Makonora, after he had become Director of the Centre. Present were some farmers from the kraals who bore a grudge against John or the lepers, some mujibhas (two of whom were engaged in a reign of terror in the zone), and maybe one or two assistants from the Centre itself. It appeared the mujibhas had decided it was time to get rid of the murungu. The surprising thing was that they had taken so long to make up their minds. (Theresa the cook later said that she had received death threats because of her friendship with John.)

It was decided they would kidnap the white man and take him to the vakomana where he would 'meet his fate'. Then the cattle would be able to wander where they willed, because Phineas certainly would be no obstacle. Moreover the lepers would go away if they no longer had the protection of the white man, and the land would be handed over to the kraals. The mujibhas believed that if they took the white man to the vakomana they would gain favour with the local commander and maybe win the right to go to Mozambique. A pretext for the abduction was quickly devised: the white man was a spy; his radio was probably a transmitter for sending messages to the Rhodesian army. On the evening of Saturday September 1st, the mujibhas, who had gathered in Chimedza cave, near Hunhu, north-west of Mtemwa, decided to make their move the following day. On the same day, John Paul II was in Nettuno, where he presided at a Mass in honour of St Maria Goretti. In his sermon he exalted Christian martyrdom, and reminded the congregation that being a Christian was a lifelong struggle.

On the Sunday, Father Gibbs was unable to come to Mtemwa, and John organised a prayer meeting with Communion. He spoke of St Laurence Martyr, even though it wasn't his feast, and cited him as an example of courage and resolution. Should we conclude from this that John desired martyrdom? According to Father John Gough, 'John did not want to be a martyr just for the sake of it. He was convinced that was what he had to be, but he didn't like the means; he was afraid of death' (others have disagreed on this point). John did not return to his hut after the meeting, nor did he go to Chigona, but read the books of Judas and Esther, two stories of war in which the weak, with God's help, triumphed over the powerful. Then he told Mai Coleta to ask the lepers to come and pray with him.

Helicopters continued to pass over Mtemwa all day on anti-Terr operations, and tensions were high. When it was time to say the rosary, John was seized by an unquenchable thirst. He went to the tap, but there was no water. He then went to Mai Coleta and the other lepers to ask for water, but they didn't have any either. They watched him returning to his hut. For some time he had intended to move his hut nearer to the chapel, and it was perhaps for this reason that he began taking items of belongings from it. He then decided to sleep in the neighbouring hut, and settled in for the night.

On the same day, while the heads of the various factions involved in the war were preparing to leave for London, they all unleashed a series of murderous offensives to consolidate their strength at the negotiating table: the vakomana layed mines, attacked white farms, and executed 'traitors' (whom the mujibhas had denounced); the UANC militias and the African auxiliaries behaved as if they were in a conquered country; and the Rhodesian army, with the backing of the South Africans, got ready to launch Operation Uric, a grand offensive against the ZANLA training camps in Mozambique (due to heavy *guti* – 'misty showers' in Shona – their aircraft could not take off and the operation had to be postponed).

The abduction

After 1980, Father Dove, Father Gibbs, Father Lawrence Makonora, Andrew Whaley, Judith Listowel, Charles Moore and others opened inquiries into the abduction and death of John, collecting information from the actors and witnesses. Their accounts agree on the essentials but not always on the chronology and details. Most important points of disagreement will be indicated below. After the war, Denford Nyandimu took Father Dove to the cave in August 1988, and was subsequently beaten by Chief Ritsiko and other villagers, furious that 'the Whites had been on their mountain and had seen the H.Q. of the war heroes, and had to pay them a fine, one goat'.

It was around midnight on Sunday September 2nd when they arrived. There were between ten and fifteen in number, carrying sticks and bazdas, one of them with two hand grenades. They knocked at the door of John's hut. The two old lepers heard their arrival but were frozen in fear. They later recounted what they had heard, corroborated by one of the mujibhas: John was called outside and invited to pray. He got up, put on his Franciscan habit and his red headband, and opened the door. He told the group he was ready to pray but that they could do it there on the spot. They replied that it was too dangerous for them, that they must go to the bundu, and dragged him away while he repeated that they could pray where they were. The kidnappers then vanished into the night with their prisoner, having searched the hut and taken the radio. The two lepers remained hidden during all this time.

Soon the mujibhas tied his hands with a rope. John did not protest, but continued to repeat that they could pray where they were, asking: 'Is this the way you ask me to pray?' When he stumbled, the mujibhas loosened the ropes. He murmured that he had to go back to Mtemwa, and that in any case they had walked enough and could now pray without going any further. He had difficulty keeping up with his young kidnappers, and the formerly athletic John must have felt that night little more than an ageing man out of breath. Finally, having walked north-east about six miles and passed through Mafienzara, they arrived about two hours later at Chimedza cave in the Hunhu zone, where a group of 30 to 40 mujibhas, mostly boys, were waiting for them (another source spoke of hundreds, which seems unlikely for a small cave).

When they saw John arriving with his kidnappers, there were explosions of joy. When the commotion ended and he had been untied, John asked them again if this was really how they were going to pray and his question led to further hilarity. He would have prayer all right! The mujibhas began jostling and mocking him. One of them asked him if he had ever eaten shit, because he would soon have the opportunity to do so. He was forced to kneel and then pushed in front of one of the girls in the group and told to have sex with her, in the midst of laughter and sarcastic comments. The prisoner protested without crying out or trying to defend himself. Then they played records on a gramophone and shouted at him to dance. He replied that he liked dancing but not in these circumstances. The jeering continued all night long until his tormentors became bored. Then they again tied his hands and brought him to a neighbouring kraal, just as the day was dawning.

Here John was thrown into an empty hut where he spent the day. As elsewhere in the so-called 'semi-liberated zones', the village had its own ZANU committee. The mujibhas (perhaps accompanied by some villagers from Mtemwa) went to the chiefs and told them that they had captured a white man to deliver to the vakomana. When they said his name, they were reprimanded by the committee: the white man from Mtemwa was a good man; he loved the Africans and they had even seen him one day carrying a leper on his back all the way to the hospital at Mtoko. The mujibhas were disappointed, and promised to take him back to Mtemwa at nightfall.

Back at the Centre, the two lepers who had witnessed the abduction were still trembling, and spread the news: Baba John had been abducted. Phineas went to inform the authorities at Mtoko. The police arrived and locked the hut, then went away, leaving the key at the JOC (Joint Operations Command).

Trial

At Hunhu, night had fallen. The mujibhas had no intention of obeying instructions, and when they took John out of the hut bound hand and foot they went back to the cave at Chimedza hoping to find the vakomana. According to one of them, the ropes had not been removed this time, and John was frog-marched through the bush. There was nobody in the cave because the vakomana changed their hideout from day to day. But the mujibhas were familiar with other caves used by the guerrillas. One such was at Gwaze, near Mount Harare to the east. It wasn't in the guerrilla sector, and they had no right to go there, but they were not deterred; and moreover the commander in this region would not know the white man.

It was dawn when they arrived at the foot of the mountain beside the cave. (Andrew Whaley followed the same walk a few years later with Ernest Gwaze and a man called Chimedza, whose names were, maybe coincidentally, the same as the caves.) As they started to climb looking for vakomana, John fell on his knees, not because of exhaustion or lack of food but because he had seen Christ – in the form of a naive painting of Jesus on the side of the mountain. Having prayed, he got up again with difficulty and climbed with his kidnappers along a stony path between the rocks as far as the cave, which was hidden behind boulders on the side of the mountain. (A guide is needed to locate it – like many caves, this one was a sacred place for the local population, used to celebrate ceremonies in homage to their ancestors.) Before entering, John got down on his knees for a second time, and turned back towards the picture of Christ. So for the second night in a row he found himself in a cave – he who had come to Africa looking for a cave where he could pray. The cave was empty, and the mujibhas had no choice but to spend the night there. They untied the prisoner, who again prayed. (That same night, Father Dove, who was in Ireland, experienced a moment of agony which he felt was neither his own nor Christ's, upon whom he was meditating at that moment. 'But whose?' he asked himself.)

Brother Athanasius of All Souls Mission learned of the abduction when he called at Mtoko on Tuesday. He alerted Father Gibbs, who immediately drove to Mtemwa and found John's hut locked. He then went to Mtoko, got the key from the JOC, and came back to Mtemwa. The hut had not been ransacked. He set off again for Mtoko, where he met Pauline Hutchings. They returned to Mtemwa together and took away John's most precious belongings and prayer books. Father Gibbs stopped at Mtoko to return the key, and then went to All Souls, arriving just before the curfew. Father Mhishi, now the Superior of the Mission, went to Mtoko the same afternoon in search of information, without success. News of the abduction had also arrived at Silveira House and Salisbury. Father David Harold-Barry informed the Archbishop and tried to contact John Dove in Ireland.

John spent the day of the 4th in the cave at Gwaze. (This could have been Rutsito, according to another source which claims the vakomana were already in Gwaze cave on the night of September 3rd/4th, when John was first tried and 'released', then sent to Chief Rutsito, who was hostile to Europeans, and that he spent the 4th of September here before being taken to a morari near Mount Chitekwa then tried again. Apart from differing chronology, this version is not fundamentally different from the first.) Later that day a ZANLA commander arrived with 15 men (more would arrive later). The guerrillas were mostly young (almost three-quarters of the vakomana were under 25, after seven years of war), but carrying a Kalashnikov can do wonders for self-confidence. The commander met the prisoner and prepared to conduct a trial, as requested. Unfortunately for the mujibhas, he realised immediately that he was face to face with the famous white man of Mtemwa, whom he knew to be harmless. Moreover one of his men, Denford Nyandimu, knew John personally (a former pupil at All Souls, he had been forceably recruited with five others as ammunition bearers). He offered to go guarantor for John, saying that he had looked after poor African lepers.

The commander then asked the mujibhas why they had abducted their prisoner. Feeling wrong-footed, they had one argument which they thought would carry weight: the radio transmitter, which they alleged the white man used to pass information to the Rhodesian army. They produced the radio, adding for good measure that the white man had never spoken in favour of the war of liberation and had never helped them with provisions or in any other way. One of the mujibhas then made an allegation on the issue of religion: the white man did not follow the spirits of their ancestors. No mention was made of problems, such as stray cattle or theft, between the leper colony and kraals. The transmitter turned out to be no more than an ordinary radio. The commander delivered his verdict: the white man was not guilty and was free to go back to Mtemwa and continue his work with the poor Africans. This decision was not without precedent. Norma Kriger (in *Zimbabwe Guerrilla War*, 1992) cites the case of an African farmer abducted by the mujibhas and taken to the vakomana. The commander ordered him to be released as a friend of the guerrillas. The mujibhas obeyed his order, but later tied the man to a tree, beat him and left him for dead.

During all this time John had not spoken a single word. But at this point the commander's security adjutant intervened: the white man could not be released because he had seen their hideouts. Even if he promised not to reveal them, the Rhodesian security men would know how to make him talk. The two men discussed the situation at length, and the commander came up with a compromise: the prisoner would be sent to Mozambique to look after the refugees in the camps until the war was over. When they informed him of this decision, John refused to go: the lepers needed him. The commander, in a conciliatory spirit, then suggested that he go to Tanzania or even to China. But the prisoner was adamant: the lepers needed him and it was Mtemwa or nothing. He was then asked what he thought of the liberation of Zimbabwe. For answer he got down on his knees and recited the *Babu Vedu* ('Our Father...') and the *Kwaziwai Maria* ('Hail Mary...'). One of those present reported that all were deeply impressed by his serenity, as if these proceedings did not concern him at all.

'You will never see me again'

The commander had no more questions. His sympathy towards the prisoner was obvious, but he knew the laws of this war. He invited John to eat with him, offering sadza, a choice of tea or Coca-Cola, and bread. John ate some food, and the commander told him that they were going to take him to a morari. They walked for three to four miles east in the moonlight (full moon came two days later) and arrived at a large assembly of about 500 villagers. (According to another source, the walk was less than a mile and a half, with a much greater number of assembled villagers – three to five thousand.) John sat down in the midst of this great crowd and nobody seemed to take any notice of him. The revolutionary meeting proceeded as usual, with songs and slogans. At one point a woman called Dorica Mapfunde, came and sat beside John with her twin babies, who proceeded to sit in his lap, and quickly fell asleep. Later he gave them back to their mother and got up and said to her: 'Amai, you will not see me again but I will pray for you.' He then recited the *Babu Vedu* on his knees with his arms raised to heaven.

The morari came to an end late in the night, and the farmers went back to their kraals so as not to run into a Guard Force patrol (according to another source, it was then that the trial took place). The commander told the prisoner that he was free to go back to Mtemwa. John knew that it was a long way away but he had got used to walking. He joined a group of villagers who were headed on foot towards the Mtoko to Nyapamanada road, which was also the road to Mozambique. Two guerrillas armed with Kalashnikovs walked with them, and some others stayed a bit further back. John stopped twice to pray, sweating according to a villager in the group (despite the chilly weather and the southern winter). A cock crowed in the distance.

The presence of two armed vakomana in their midst made the group nervous. They finally arrived at the road about ten miles east of Mtoko near a stream running through a big pipe under the road, which was dry during this season. As the villagers crossed the road one of the vakomana took John by the arm, leading him to the side of the road into the bed of the stream, bordered by wild agave. (John Dove located the execution scene in a small garden, 70 yards below the road where the body was later brought. At this point, according to Denford Nyandimu, the assistant commander came up and said to John: 'Hey, John, you should have gone to Mozambique. Others did, and saved their skin, going back to England and so on...' John did not resist and fell on his knees. When he stood up a minute later the guerrilla behind him emptied his Kalashnikov into John's back. Who was he? Heather Benoy said: 'After the war, I was told that a man visited Father Dove to confess that he had killed John and that Father Dove had forgiven him... I am afraid that I could not have met him.'

The villagers, a few yards away from the scene, saw John fall on his knees and gently collapse to the ground without a word, as his blood flowed from his body – 'dying like a hwayana' (sheep), as one elderly man called Jairas, from the kraal at Kawazva, later reported to John Dove. Some 23–27 cartridges were later recovered from the scene. John died in the early hours of Wednesday, and his friends would have been quick to remember a poem, probably written when he was in Mtemwa in 1971, about the aria *Kommt Susser Tod* ('Come Sweet Death', BWV 478) by Johan Sebastian Bach:

> Come, sweet death, on Wednesday
> If you will and if you may.

In 1950, John had also written (in *Local Idiot* – *J.R.B.*):

> But what's the hurry? I do say;
> This might be my last Wednesday.

The villagers witnessed the scene with horror but, even more, panicking for their own safety. The guerrillas dragged the body into the middle of the road, scribbled a message, 'Victim of the liberation struggle', and disappeared into the bush. ('Brother John has suffered and this will happen to the auxiliaries', according to another source.)

Fearing that if the Whites discovered the body they would surely kill them, and not only them but everybody in the nearby kraals, the villagers set about hiding it. Some suggested in the big pipe under the road, others behind the bushes, on the rocky terrain on the far side. According to Jairas, when the villagers crossed the road to drag the body away, they suddenly heard chants in the distance. Startled, they dropped the body and hid in the bush. Sometime later they came back but could see nobody. The chants came again, this time even louder, and the villagers fled for a second time. Fear of the security forces being stronger than fear of the unknown, they came back once more to find a great white bird hovering above the dead body, rising and falling as if to protect the dead man. Again they fled, and again they came back. This time they saw three rays of coloured light, blue, red and white which seemed to come from the spot where the body was lying, converging in the air to become one. This time the villagers fled once and for all, and returned to their kraals.

What became of the Franciscan habit John had been wearing since his abduction? According to Denford Nyandimu, John had been wearing it right up to his execution, and was stripped after being killed (this hardly agrees with Father Gibbs' description of the body). The question remains open.

The gift to each of us and to all of us

At dawn on Wednesday September 5th the sky was clear, and Rhodesian and South African planes and helicopters were heading for Mozambique. Operation Uric lasted two days, but resistance was stronger than expected. Some 300 guerrillas were killed but also 15 Rhodesians, and the command structures of ZANLA remained intact. Mozambique President Samora Machel seized the opportunity to prevail upon Robert Mugabe to go to London and participate in the conference at Lancaster House.

In the meantime Father David Gibbs left All Souls in the Mission ambulance at about 6.15, followed by Hilary Wynne, a medical student who was at All Souls at the time, driving Luisa Guidotti's car. About a mile from the Mission they met an African, who told Father Gibbs: 'Father, they have killed a European. The Guard Force will go on the rampage and will fire at anyone they see.' The priest asked for more information, but the man didn't know who the

European was. However, Father Gibbs had already understood. Driving on towards Mtoko he came across John about 20 minutes later: 'John was lying half-on and half-off the tarmac on the left-hand side of the road, dressed only in his underpants. He had wounds in his legs and the lower part of his chest. The upper part of his chest, his arms, and his head were unmarked. He was lying on his back, his eyes wide open and his right hand was under his head, his left hand by his side. I closed John's eyes and spent a short time in prayer by his side.'

With help from Hilary Wynne he carried the body to the All Souls ambulance and drove to the JOC at Mtoko, the only place where there was a mortuary, left the body, and went to see the Hutchings. Pauline was shocked and grief-stricken. They climbed to a little cave on the kopje behind the family home, where Father Gibbs celebrated a Mass for the repose of John's soul. According to Pauline:

> that day a heavy pall of veld smoke settled over Mutemwa and the mountain was not visible again from here for over a month. It reminded me of Moses in the desert and the Cloud that covered the Tabernacle. I felt it almost an injunction telling me: 'While the cloud covers Mutemwa, stay quiet in your grief, paying worship to Yahweh and giving thanks for his beloved servant John Bradburne.'

Father Gibbs then went back to Mtemwa, announced the news to the lepers, and celebrated another Mass in the chapel before going back to All Souls. At the same time Dr Dell arrived at the JOC and took photographs of the body. Father Gibbs then telephoned Silveira House to tell them of John's death. The news arrived as members of the team at the Centre were beginning their day's work. A great sadness reigned in the community all day, and a prayer vigil was organised that evening. In Ireland, John Dove had finally been located by the Gardai on Wednesday at Ballyconneely, County Galway, and he telephoned London. Three minutes later he knew that his friend had been abducted. Shortly afterwards he discovered he had been killed.

The next day the *Rhodesia Herald* published, under the headline 'The friend of the lepers has been killed', a long article about John Richard (sic) Bradburne, lay missionary, murdered by the Terrs. It mentioned his eviction from Mtemwa in 1973 and noted that John had lived in a miserable hut. He was described as 'Mr Bradburne, a former teacher, street musician, stoker on a trawler, and soldier in the Gurkha Regiment, who enjoyed playing his recorder and writing poetry'. The paper quoted from John's own words, and Philippa Berlyn, obviously herself the source for the article, was also quoted:

> He was a complete man of God. I am very sad that
> he is dead. He gave up his total life for the lepers
> and he was also a very good poet. I am very sad
> that he is dead, but John himself, I am sure, would
> forgive those responsible.

She also said that she had received telephone calls from people who had known him at Mtoko: 'The whole of Mtoko, people of all races, are all angry and sad about his death.'

Like all John's friends, Anne Lander was deeply shocked by his death, but she had to leave for London the next day. Anxious to associate herself with the funeral Mass, she asked an Anglican friend, Jill McKay, to place three white lilies on the coffin with a card on which she had written 'Three-In-One', as a sign that her friend had truly lived the Trinity. She then left for London. Geraldine Morris, who lived in Salisbury and knew John by sight, reacted like many others: 'We saw him when he came occasionally into Harare, knew of him as someone deserving respect and honour for what he was and what he was doing. We were very shocked when we heard he had been shot.'

On Friday the 7th, the Doves-Morgan Funeral Services sent a hearse to Mtoko to bring John's remains back to the capital. When they arrived back the body was dressed in a calico robe, and placed in a coffin at 161 Salisbury Street. As reported later in the undertaker's Statement of Events: 'All wounds were checked and covered with cotton wool as a matter of formality.' At this stage, observations were made but not considered relevant at the time (they were recalled because of the subsequent events):

> 1. The remains were frozen. 2. The state of the cadaver was seen to be 'excellently preserved' with no putrefaction. 3. No skin slip. 4. No decomposition at all. 5. Wounds were clean, clear and dry (no blood was seen). 6. No discoloration.

Since Father Dove was in Europe, it fell to Father Harold-Barry to organise the funeral Mass – or rather the 'Resurrection Mass', as had been celebrated for other murdered missionaries. Archbishop Patrick Chakaipa, who had temporarily recalled Father Gibbs from All Souls, was to preside.

On Saturday the 8th the death notice was published, indicating that the funeral would take place at the Cathedral of the Sacred Heart on Monday September 10th at 11a.m., followed by burial at Mtemwa on the morning of Thursday the 13th. On the 9th there was much talk about John in the parishes of Salisbury and beyond, but also about the Lancaster House conference due to open the following day in London. Everybody was torn between hope and scepticism. John's friends gathered together, and the rector of the Cathedral arranged the finer details of the Mass with Silveira House. 'Angelical Angelina' typed out the protocol of the celebration.

On September 10th numerous Africans and Europeans converged on Sacred Heart Cathedral, as they had done two months previously for Luisa Guidotti; but no lepers were able to come from Mtemwa because of the curfew and the lack of transport. The hearse arrived at the Cathedral, and Father Webster welcomed the coffin. Kit Law played the *chaconne* and variations by Pachelbel, while her husband Arthur and others carried the coffin into the cathedral. The Rhodesville parochial choir sang the Irish hymn *Glory to the Lord* as Archbishop Chakaipa and his concelebrants ascended the altar. The Anglican Bishop of Salisbury, Paul Burrough, also attended. The Silveira House choir sang the *Kyriale* in Shona, which had so often been sung by John. Pauline Hutchings read chapter 46 from Isaiah on 'Fasting that pleases God'. The psalm was sung in Xhosa, and an African read from the Acts of the Apostles about

Peter at Jaffa. Then Father Gibbs proclaimed the Gospel of Jesus at the synagogue of Nazareth.

Father Harold-Barry began his sermon by citing those who could not be present: the dead man's family, 'his own special people, the people of Mtemwa, who suffer from leprosy – people so far from men but, as John used to say "so close to God"; all his friends, but especially John Dove, "who by God's special kindness is in England today to visit and console John's mother". He then spoke briefly about John's life, with a discreet allusion to the ordeal of 1973, mentioning a confidence that John had shared with him at the time: 'They think I am mad... perhaps I am!' He recalled how John, after the funeral of his friend Luisa Guidotti, was anxious and in a great hurry to return to Mtemwa, not wanting to sleep another night at Silveira House, 'hardening his face like Jesus going to Jerusalem'.

He then gave a picture of his friend as he had known him, 'always with a twinkle in his eye and always seeming to live without effort and constantly full of joy', adding: 'we were somehow tempted to think that it was easy for him – that life for him was just a long, peaceful river', but...

> We know that what John became was the flower and fruit of much inner silent generosity. Was it an easy thing to travel as he did with next to no money or provisions? Was it easy to live in a hut for so many years with little food and no running water? Was it so easy for him to live alongside the lepers and belong to them? Was it so easy for him to spend long hours in prayer? Do we not catch ourselves saying: 'but he loved that life.' Yes, he did. But let us be sure to remember that his life was the triumph of a generous response to God's love. Sure, God makes the road easy – for such generous people – and the burden light. But let us be very certain that there was a generous inner silent discipline in John. This is why I say John shows us the hidden life of Jesus. He chose a very clear manifestation of that hiddenness. We come today to show our sorrow, yes, but to show our joy

too at having known John. Let us flesh out that
knowledge in this way: by treasuring the hidden
life of Jesus.

He then recalled John's great love for the Virgin Mary, and his
poetry, and invited everybody to turn their thoughts to the lepers
of Mtemwa, for 'they have lost a father, a brother, a friend', waiting
and praying for John's remains to be brought back to Mtemwa for
burial. He asked: 'Who will now help them?'

Having briefly recalled other passions of his dead friend – the
Jews, his Ark, poetry, music – the priest turned towards Christ to
thank him for John and concluded his homily:

> And you, John, our dear friend, look after your
> people in Mtemwa still from where you are now.
> Make sure they lack nothing that will bring them
> too to the happiness of God's Kingdom and
> remember all of us on this day – you, who were
> so apolitical, pray for us that our leaders may find
> in their meeting a way to peace and that we may
> all of us – in the words of St Thomas More – meet
> again and be right merry in heaven.

In fact the war had never been more murderous than at that
moment, as the negotiations between factions were getting under
way in London. But the cathedral offered on that day the vision
of a peaceful multi-racial country, fraternal and united like the
image of the men carrying the coffin, the clergy, the readers and
the choirs. Father Webster remembered: 'The atmosphere was
somehow "special", since the murdered John was a very special
person' – a feeling shared by all those present.

A few drops and three wishes

The Archbishop then granted absolution, helped by Father Harold-
Barry and Father Webster. Finally Vaughan Williams' *Nunc Dimittis*
was sung by Rhodesville Parish choir to accompany the coffin as
it was being carried from the cathedral. At that moment however
a rumour had begun to circulate in the cathedral that blood had
begun to flow from the coffin.

What had happened? Jill McKay had brought the flowers and the 'Three-in-One' card on behalf of Anne Lander to the cathedral, but had been unable to get near the coffin because of the press of so many people. At Communion, she finally managed to leave the flowers on the coffin, with Anne Lander's card, but as she was about to move away she suddenly felt rooted to the spot, caught up in a 'spiritual whirlpool'. Soon afterwards Father Gibbs, a yard-and-a-half from the coffin, saw two drops of blood falling to the floor, as did Sister Felicitas and two coffin-bearers, Nashya Sherini and Simbarashe Muzuwa. Father Michael O'Halloran, master of ceremonies, was next to see them, and the first to react:

> At the time of the Holy Communion my eyes strayed to the coffin and I thought I saw under the coffin a very small pool of blood. I did not see any blood fall, still less did I see three drops of blood, although that has sometimes been asserted by others – even in print. My reaction was to make my way over to the credence to find a little finger towel to put over the liquid. This I did and I noticed that the cloth acted like blotting paper.

The Anglican Bishop Paul Burrough saw Father O'Halloran approaching with the purificator and he too observed the blood-stain, concluding that either blood had come from the coffin or one of the undertakers had cut himself. Father Harold-Barry had also seen it, and even thought to himself that it was not very respectful to wipe away blood with a purificator. Heather Benoy thought that it must be a Catholic rite. Margaret de Haast, in a wheelchair near the coffin, was bewildered, but didn't understand what was happening. Father Webster, who was about to assist the Archbishop with absolution, was standing in front of the coffin with the former Archbishop of Salisbury when he suddenly noticed a dark stain on the ground, very visible on the white tiles, just as another drop of blood fell. He then saw Father O'Halloran placing the purificator on the ground, and yet another drop of blood. He thought to himself that it must be John's blood, coming from the wound in his leg.

William Hamer-Nel, director of the funeral parlour, was also near the coffin. A quick glance at his watch had told him it was shortly after noon, and he began making his way forward to prepare the exit of the coffin from the cathedral. He saw Father O'Halloran taking the purificator and placing it below the coffin. Intrigued (never in 25 years as funeral director had he seen such a thing) he approached the coffin after the last rites were completed and immediately saw the blood which, as he described it in the Statement of Events, 'was crimson and looked fresh' – in his long experience this was impossible for a corpse after five days. He was all the more shocked because the blood had not been there at the beginning of the celebration, or he would certainly have seen it, because the cathedral was well lit and the blood would have been clearly visible on the white tiles. He knelt down, took the purificator, and placed it beside the flowers on the coffin.

After the service Father O'Halloran discussed the incident with the funeral director. He asked him if he had noticed anything, to which the undertaker replied: 'Yes, this is horrific', as what had happened 'would have indicated a lack of basic care on the part of the undertakers, an appalling professional lapse on their part'. He explained to the priest that after death, blood quickly congeals and no longer flows, and there was 'the additional fact that John's body had been in refrigeration for several days in the mortuary'. Father O'Halloran concluded: 'This was a strange and unaccountable thing. How then do we account for it?'

The remains were brought back to the funeral parlour, where the coffin was opened by the Director, in the company of Father Riederer. To their astonishment they discovered that there were no traces of blood either on the body or the coffin, inside or out, and that the body was completely dry. Where then did the blood come from? They were also struck by the impact of the bullets: the entry points were clear and clean, without the usual bruise marks, and John looked as if he were sleeping. Hamer-Nel kept repeating that he couldn't understand. In the afternoon Sister Margaret called with Jesuit Superior Father Ken Spence at the funeral home:

> I viewed the corpse and the inside of the coffin, but
> there was no sign of any fluid. The gunshot wounds

were completely dry and also the coffin itself. I did
notice that John was dressed in a white calico type
shroud that was used in hospitals before the family
dressed the body. At this stage John was supposed
to be going for burial. Whenever I saw John he was
always dressed in the habit, so I assumed that he
belonged to the Third Order of Franciscans. I was
speaking to the Jesuit Provincial later that day and
I made the comment that I was surprised that John
was not laid out in the Franciscan habit. I knew
from previous years when I nursed in Ireland that
people belonging to the Third Order were to be
dressed in the habit when they died. It was only
when I was given some photographs at a later date
of John laid out in the coffin that I knew that the
Provincial had contacted the Franciscan Fathers
for a habit after my comments.

Father Spence in fact made contact with the Franciscan Mission
at Waterfalls, and Father Desmond O'Malley, to whom 17 years
previously John had confided his three wishes – one of which was
to be buried in his Franciscan habit – soon arrived with one. The
body was dressed once more, the coffin closed, and John set off as a
Franciscan on his journey into eternity. The story of the bloodstains
under the coffin was soon published in newspapers, in Rhodesia-
Zimbabwe and abroad. Anne Lander, then in Britain, read about it
in a newsagent's shop: 'It was chilling', she would remember. Father
Spence asked for signed written statements about the events at the
funeral. Judith Listowel would do the same the following year, and
got signed statements by Nyasha Sherani, Bishop Burrough, Father
Michael O'Halloran, Father David Harold-Barry and Father David
Gibbs, as well as the undertakers' Statement of Events signed by
C. W. Hamer-Nel, R. A. M. Bury, C. Nel, K. Herbst, and Father
V. Riederer.

On the same day the constitutional conference on the future
of Rhodesia opened in the sumptuous surroundings of Lancaster
House, presided over by Lord Carrington, British Secretary
of State at the Foreign Office and Commonwealth affairs. The

three participants were Great Britain, as mediator; the Salisbury government with its African allies; and the Nationalists, represented by the Patriotic Front: Smith, Muzorewa, Sithole, Nkomo and Mugabe. Back in the rebel colony, all were fully aware of what was at stake: peace or the suicide of a nation, as the violence continued. Two Europeans were murdered on the 11th, and a third, Denis Claircourt, a Burma veteran like John, on the 13th near Umtali. But in the end the conference, which opened on the day of John's funeral, eventually led to peace, bringing to an end 15 years of civil war, a peace for which John had laid down his life. The Lancaster House Agreement was signed on December 21st. It made provision for elections on the basis of one man, one vote, with a constitutional guarantee for the rights and interests of the European minority for a period of ten years. From December 5th a ceasefire was effective and, on the 7th, Christopher Soames, a cousin of John Bradburne, was named Governor of Rhodesia, which reverted to the status of British colony for a period of four months. Soames governed the country, not without difficulty, until the election of March 4th 1980, from which Mugabe's ZANU emerged victorious. Zimbabwe was born.

On the afternoon of September 11th, Sister Margaret Murphy paid a visit to Dr Joan Lamplugh, whom John had known. She told her the story of the patch of blood, and gave her the purificator which Hamer-Nel had placed in an open brown envelope. The doctor immediately got in touch with Professor G. P. T. Barclay, a Scottish pathologist, and brought the envelope to his laboratory. The pathologist told her that he would need to cross match a sample of blood from the deceased, taken if possible from the heart, and gave her a suitable syringe and needle for the purpose. Dr Lamplugh immediately contacted the Jesuits and arranged a meeting at Doves-Morgan funeral parlour.

On the morning of September 12th, while the Rhodes Pioneers were starting their annual celebration for the last time in the history of the country, Dr Lamplugh and Father Spence were heading for the funeral parlour. The doctor had been unsuccessful in her attempts to obtain blood from either the heart or the carotid, but she was able to take a sample from a clot in the inner right calf. She also took a sample from the cotton wool taken from John's wounds, and found it to be of a brighter red than might have been expected, but she was not a specialist in post-mortem matters. That afternoon she brought all her specimens to Dr Barclay's laboratory. The next day she went back to her confrere:

> He said that the blood on the cloth was grossly hemolysed – that is the red blood cells were destroyed – making it difficult to cross match, but in his opinion, the blood was not from the same person.

In February 1980, Dr Barclay wrote to Judith Listowel:

> The stain which we tried to elute produced lysed material only and no acceptable conclusions could be drawn from our investigations. In other words, it was not possible to be unequivocal in the assertion that the blood was of human origin.

Since nobody asked Dr Barclay to preserve the cloth, it was thrown away, so the mystery remained unsolved. In the meantime rumours were rife in Harare and beyond, and on September 21st the *Rhodesia Herald* published its banner headline: 'Mystery blood not Bradburne's.' On the 27th a report on the matter was signed by four witnesses and Father Riederer. Its conclusion was terse: 'No Explanation'. As for Father O'Halloran, the meaning of the event was clear:

> My own thought has always been quite simply that God wished the coffin to be opened so that John, a good and faithful servant, could be dressed in death as he had always wanted to be dressed. John did remarkable things for God and his people and God did something remarkable for him. It seems that this is not the end of the story.

On September 12th the lepers of Mtemwa were preparing to welcome Baba John at their cemetery, but their wait was in vain. On the same day he was buried at the cemetery in the plot for murdered missionaries at Chishawasha, which he had visited on the very day he had arrived in Africa 17 years before. Phineas had phoned from Mtemwa to say that he had received death threats in the event of John being buried at the Centre, and had decided not to take the risk. Father David Gibbs, who had returned to Mtoko, agreed that it was not safe. One may wonder whether the threat was real, or whether it was a pretext on the part of Phineas and his friends, thinking that John's remains would be an embarrassing presence at the Centre. (According to another source, Father Gibbs was afraid that Phineas would desert if John was buried there.) An empty space was found at Chishawasha graveyard between Father Donovan and Father Pieper, and this is where John lies today. The white-painted metal crosses in the cemetery are identical. On John's we can read:

> John Bradburne of Mutemwa
> 3rd Order of Saint Francis
> Born 14 June 1921,
> Died 5 Sept. 1979

Soon rosary beads were draping the cross, and fresh earth was needed to replace that taken away for relics. Behind John's grave lies the grave of the young African Jesuit Francis Matsika, whom John had befriended in life. The spot exudes peace, the smell of pine and the gentle mercy of God.

Chapter 11

John after John

The name of Bradburne will ring down future centuries, and
that for the good.
(*Letter to Mother*, 3 June 1963)

The year 1979 came to an end in what was no longer Rhodesia
and not yet Zimbabwe, but it had been one of the bloodiest years
of the war: 160 Europeans (including 70 farmers), 2500 African
civilians, 4542 guerrillas and 146 soldiers of the Rhodesian army
had died. The ceasefire was more or less respected from the middle
of December, after which, according to a French mercenary at the
time, the paths of guerrillas and regular soldiers were more likely
to cross at football grounds. But revenge killings and banditry
continued, bringing the country to its knees. 'People have lost all
hope,' reported an official of the Salisbury Archdiocese who visited
the Mtoko area in July, where he saw people living out in the cold
because their former houses had been burnt by the army and they
were still building their new houses.

> Some people have had to move three times. A
> doctor from one area reported that people do not
> come for treatment when they are sick. They say
> they may as well die rather than live in such hell...

The elections of March 4th 1980 swept Robert Mugabe to an
overwhelming victory, and he seemed willing to honour the
promises of reconciliation that he had made at the independence
ceremonies at Rufaro stadium on April 17th. What followed, a
long descent into hell, especially since the end of the 1990s, is well
known. Mtemwa became Mutemwa. Father David Gibbs received
a note from the guerrillas expressing regrets for the death of his
friend. Sally Mugabe, the new First Lady, visited Mtemwa and

supported it up to her death in 1992. The Centre escaped the fate wished upon it by neighbouring kraals, and was not confiscated, thanks, in the minds of many, to John's protection.

But leprosy remained, as did the distress of the residents at having lost Baba John. Peter bewailed: 'There is no one to bathe me', and many others expressed their distress, though Mai Coleta insisted they could still feel his presence when loneliness weighed heavily upon them. On his return from Europe, John Dove brought the lepers to a gathering at the tomb of their friend at Chishawasha on November 10th. Brother Lawrence Makonora became Director of the Centre, and Caterina Savini took up residence there on her return from Italy. An ambitious project of 72 houses began in 1983, for which Ferdinand Spit obtained the backing of Amici dei Lebrossi and Aid to the Church in Need. In 1986 the lepers and their families moved into the new houses, and were provided with agricultural machinery and seed, but those who were severely handicapped remained in the central building.

In 1985 Father Dove became Director of the Centre and set up house in the old butchery. He was succeeded by an African deacon, Cyril Kawisi, who brought about some remarkable innovations until his retirement in 2004. John's friends continued to give their support to the Centre out of their own pockets. Father Gibbs remained very active until his accidental death in 2001, as did Father Harold-Barry, Anne Lander and Heather Benoy. The Hutchings became the backbone of the association of support, of which Paul Tingay was for a time president: he also went to live for six months in the old butchery.

In 2016 Mutemwa counted 43 residents, 24 of whom were leprous, as well as a number of elderly handicapped and impoverished people and 120 members of their families, and a staff of about 30. The clinic of the Centre treated some 112 people per month, including some people from the vicinity. The majority of residents were semi-independent, and at least 20 totally dependent residents lived in the central building. The spirit of John Bradburne lived on, according to Christine Pratt:

> Those who can see are the eyes for those who are
> blind, those who can walk do errands for those

who cannot, those who can use their hands will cook or weed for those who are unable to, and those who cannot do anything physical will keep each other company, tell stories and cheer us all up!

But not everything was rosy, and financial problems returned with the worsening of the problems of Zimbabwe. Carers spent most of their energy trying to ensure that both the residents and themselves got enough to eat, and services suffered as a result. Humour was a help, and sometimes a necessity, when wallets had to be replaced by wheelbarrows, to transport millions of worthless Zimbabwean dollars. In 2009 some of the buildings were damaged by storm; but the John Bradburne Memorial Society (see below) increased its aid, and an upward surge of generosity helped stave off disaster.

The objective is now to make the Centre self-sustaining in matters of food, and new irrigation programmes and the development of vegetable gardens have been launched. Today, the Franciscans have come to Mutemwa to administer there. An admirable initiative called Mother of Peace got off the ground near the Centre to help victims of the new African scourge: AIDS. Work on a new village started in 1994 on a patch of land measuring 182 hectares near Mutemwa dam, by two sisters, Mama 'Auntie' Stella and Mama 'Gogo' Jean, and their community, which began as a prayer group. They offer a warm welcome to visitors, with a lively show of singing and dancing. More than 70 headstones of the cemetery are clearly visible, a reminder of hardship suffered, but of a love which can transcend it.

Parallel with their support for Mutemwa, John's friends continued to promote his memory. When the war ended, they reinstalled the Ark in the tin hut. As the years went by, they came regularly to visit the hut and fight the rats, heat and dust, and some pilgrims went in search of relics. In 1995, the John Bradburne Memorial Society (JBMS) was established in Britain. The objects of the charity, as set out in its governing documents are:

> To relieve people in the area of Mutemwa, Zimbabwe, who are suffering sickness, hardship,

466 John Bradburne: Vagabond of God

and distress from leprosy or other causes, through
the provision of supplementary food, medicines,
medical care, clothing and shelter, with the object
of improving their conditions of life...

and to make known the life and message of John Bradburne.

It seems that this is not the end of the story

John's death might have passed unnoticed because of the news focus on the negotiations at Lancaster House, but this was far from being the case, and the prophecy of Father O'Halloran was borne out. The BBC, the South African press and the American information broadcasting services all carried the story. Margaret Smith heard it as she ate her breakfast and recognised her old suitor at Gaveney House. His niece and goddaughter Pamela recalls:

> Although I am not a Roman Catholic I went straight to Westminster Cathedral, where I knew John had spent some time working as a sacristan, where I did my best to pray for his soul. Being weak in faith and belief I prayed for a sign that all was well and when I opened my eyes the pillar directly in front of me was a place of dancing sunlight, when before it had been in shadow. While I do not claim this as a supernatural phenomenon it did have the effect of making me feel that John was contacting me to tell me he was where he had always wanted to be.

Little by little the name of John Bradburne became known. It was thus that Jean Vanier, after a visit to Zimbabwe in 1982, was prompted to write to Amis de l'Arche about the man whom he had just discovered, and whose message he had clearly understood (*Our Life Together: A Memoir in Letters*):

> After his death, and especially at his funeral, there were signs that showed he was deeply loved by God. I feel drawn to pray to him, that I, that we all, may remain faithful to our people. He was

a poor, hidden servant of those who were most abandoned. He lived with them and, little by little, he gave them a desire to live and a desire for Jesus. He really felt that the people with leprosy, often quite disfigured, were precious to the Father, that they were the most important people, that they were signs of God's presence.

For his part, Bishop Emmanuel Lafont, then parish priest in Soweto and later on Bishop of Cayenne (French Guyana), wrote:

I thank John for having lived the Gospel, which does not care about colour, language, customs and even less about 'what the neighbours say', which so often enslave us... God is a poet. John was a perfect reflection of him.

In 1980 Judith Listowel began writing a biography of John and contacted many witnesses, but when she died in 2003 she left behind two unfinished manuscripts. In 1983 John Dove published in Ireland *Strange Vagabond of God: the story of John Bradburne*, an irreplaceable testimony to the life of his best friend. The John Bradburne Memorial Society (JBMS) and later its Internet site continues to keep John's memory alive, and many articles continue to appear. Neither have books been wanting, and there has been a steady stream of personal reminiscences, pamphlets and extended studies. The most common labels that recur in the various publications are: eccentric, poet, vagabond, mystic, friend of the lepers, martyr, saint. A number of documentaries have been produced, composed mainly of interviews with friends of John, in places where he lived. There is a wonderful CD of his poems, prepared by Anne Lander, as 'John must speak for himself', mostly read or sung by himself, giving us the sound of his voice. Access can be had to his complete poetic output, thanks to the prodigious energies of linguist David Crystal and his wife Hilary at <www.johnbradburnepoems.com>, which also includes numerous letters. An abundant iconography and further information may be found at <www.johnbradburne.com>, the website of the JBMS. John's life has become an inspiration to novelists, poets, playwrights, sculptors and musicians. A recent example of him finding his place among great names of Catholic England is the anthology of J. Saward and others, *Firmly I Believe and Truly: the spiritual Tradition of Catholic England.*

In his lifetime a symbol of contradiction, so John remains in death. The purpose of this biography was not to inquire into the signs and miracles which have been attributed to him, but their number and variety cannot be passed over in silence (though the author does not propose to anticipate the judgement of the Church). The signs are in the first place the unexplained presence of bees or eagles. Shortly after John's death three swarms of bees arrived in the Benoys' house, and have been there ever since. In 1982 the journalist Angus Shaw, irritated by rumours of 'miracles' and 'stories of bees and eagles' circulating about John, decided to visit Mutemwa. When he returned to his car he discovered that it had been invaded by bees, as had his apartment when he returned to Harare. The episode had an effect on his life, though he remained an agnostic (a similar story was told by Rory Kilalea, after he had made a film about John). In the same year, John Dove and his guests saw two wild eagles perched for three-quarters of an hour near John's room at Silveira House just after he had said a Mass for him. Two days later he saw a bateleur eagle hovering over the spot where John was murdered, before heading off in the direction of the Centre.

In Harare Judy Joe, a single mother, was dying of cancer. Father Riederer met her and spoke to her about John. Judy returned to the faith, was cured, and married. She came to Mutemwa and Chishawasha to thank God, and brought home with her some stones from John's grave. She signed up to the Centre, organised the collection of second-hand clothes for the lepers, and accepted gifts on their behalf. Years later the cancer returned; she prepared herself to die with courage because, as she said, 'the lepers suffered far more'. In her last days she kept a photo of John with her. Later her mother, kneeling in front of the photo, prayed for a sign that her daughter was in heaven. At that moment a swarm of bees arrived and settled in the drawer where the stones from John's grave had been left. Judy's mother believed this to be a miracle and the press came running.

There have also been many instances of interventions such as a protective presence in situations of danger, moral healing, conversions and insights, following on prayers of intercession to John. Sixty-nine of these, many involving cures from health problems, can be found in the *Harare Herald* alone between 1981 and 1987. (Cases from Zimbabwe and elsewhere may also be found in Diana Mitchell's inquiry, in the Leominster John Bradburne Archives, in the JBMS Newsletter, and those that have been gathered for the diocesan Petition.) The most amazing relate to small children. Shortly after John's death a little girl was abducted at Borrowdale and held in a hut in an abandoned quarry. She was traced there by the police, unharmed, and related that she had been visited every day by a nice man dressed in a brown robe who spoke to her about Jesus, Mary and the rosary, and played, sang and prayed with her. When her mother showed her a picture of John in a newspaper she immediately said: 'Oh, that's him.' – 'But he is dead.' – 'No, he is not dead, he was with me every day.' Another girl, lost and found, said that a kind man with a dog had reassured her that she was safe. When shown John's picture she exclaimed: 'That's him!'

The first cure attributed to John was recorded as early as 1980, in Soweto. Winnie Mabaso was in the terminal phase of cancer at Baragwanath Hospital. Sent home to die, she prayed and offered a novena to John whom she had read about in a magazine, and soon after began to recover. Her parish priest heard about it and was interviewed by the South African press. It was the first in a long series of cures attributed to the intercession of John on several continents. Some of these involve people who knew John, like Father Pascal Slevin (brain tumour), but most of them concern other people. Cancer cures are numerous, but also other diseases considered incurable. The diocesan Petition records some 60 cases, and Diana Mitchell's enquiry and the Bulletin mention others. John Dove refers to miraculous cures in Westminster Cathedral obtained by touching sick people with John's headband. Sister Theresiana Muteme, Novice Mistress of the Congregation of Little Children of our Blessed Lady, is one of them. She was hospitalised in 1997 with breast cancer, which she had kept from others out of embarrassment and a certain acceptance of pain, until it became an open and purulent sore. It horrified Dr Saburi and Dr Nyakubu, who saw it the day she collapsed, overcome by pain, and she was considered to be a hopeless case. John's headband was applied to her and a novena to him and to Archbishop Chichester was started. The wound healed and Dr Saburi told her: 'I'm dreaming! Is it you or someone else?'

The best documented case concerns William Hamilton, hospitalised in Edinburgh in May 1994 with a malign tumour of the brain. Father Riederer, who had become chaplain at the hospital on his return to Europe began to pray with Mr Hamilton to John. On the morning set for the operation, the surgeon was obliged to cancel it when it was discovered that the tumour had disappeared. Professor Ian Whittle later wrote: 'I think it is fair to say that his cure was certainly miraculous and may indeed have been due to the prayers and to his faith.' Some witnesses have also spoken of remarkable natural phenomena linked to John. Diana Mitchell has recorded testimonies about phenomena of light and rotation in connection with the cross at Chigona, erected by an English person in thanksgiving for a cure from an eye disease.

As well as the gift of his life to the lepers of Mtemwa, these reported cures and other unexplained events attributed to John since the early 1980s have created a reputation for sanctity and a popular cult to John in Zimbabwe. (John's friends are divided on this point. For some, like Father Dove, these signs and miracles argue for a rapid recognition of John's sanctity. Others, without rejecting them out of hand, incline to prudence. For still others, John's greatest miracles were his lifelong spiritual combat and the everyday gestures during his ten-year stay in Mtemwa.) They even verge on the superstitious, such as when numerous participants at the funeral of Archbishop Chakaipa in April 2003 forsook the cortege to go and pillage stones from John's grave. A spontaneous cult quickly developed at Mutemwa, and the annual pilgrimage was encouraged by the bishops and clergy of Zimbabwe. Mount Chigona thus rediscovered a Shona tradition noted since the first Portuguese travellers: once a year the tribes came to the mountain where their founder was buried. A pilgrimage to Mutemwa developed spontaneously in the early 1980s, particularly on the anniversary of John's abduction and murder.

At the beginning of the 1980s a number of parishes like that of Father Tim Peacock would take truckloads of pilgrims to Mutemwa in a spirit 'rather penitential but very grace-filled'. But most pilgrims went of their own initiative. A peak of several thousand pilgrims was reached in the mid-90s, at which point Father Dove and Father Slevin decided, with the support of Archbishop Chakaipa, that they should be accompanied by pastoral backup. The twentieth anniversary of John's death in 1999 saw 15,000 pilgrims converge on Mutemwa, as a result of which the Archbishop of Harare officially declared Mutemwa an official pilgrimage site, and Mutemwa is now the most important place of pilgrimage in Zimbabwe. On the twenty-fifth anniversary in 2004, a shelter was built near the compound, and since then pilgrims arrive from all over Zimbabwe, some even from as far away as Soweto, despite poverty and the rigours of the journey. In 2015, Archbishop Robert Ndlovu handed over the pastoral care of the site to the Franciscan order.

In the year 2009, 15,000 pilgrims were present for the thirtieth anniversary of John's death, and 1000 for other feasts, to the tune of 100 a week, despite desperate conditions in the country at the time. The author of this book participated in the pilgrimage in 2010:

> Once more this year, here converge thousands of pilgrims, in overloaded cars, by bus, by trucks, on foot...

> Once more this year, here stretch out the long files of those waiting quietly for the sacrament of reconciliation all over the site and during the whole afternoon, and an even longer file in front of the Tin Hut, while the Rosary is prayed.

> Once more this year, here the patients of Mutemwa receive the visit of pilgrims and chat with them, while monkeys are playing in the jacarandas. And when the barrier of the language prevent much talk, shared smiles show they are worth a thousand words.

Once more this year, here comes with the evening the time of teachings and Holy Hour. 'Lord teach us how to pray' is the theme of the year, and prayers in answer are so fervent that they burst out in dance and shouts of praise and of joy.

Once more this year, here is now celebrated the night Mass, from 10 p.m. to midnight, in front of pilgrims so numerous that the sight of them on the lawn fades far away into the darkness.

Once more this year, here starts the procession on Chigona, with prayers, songs and Way of the Cross. At 2 a.m. our group is still at the bottom of the mountain while the first ones long past arrived on the top. The luminous points from the lamps climbing on the mountain side merge with those of the stars in the sky, and draw as a new constellation – we could call it 'the Holy Caravan' heading to the Holy Cross on top of Chigona.

Once more this year, here we spend now long night hours on the mountain, in praise, in singing and in prayers, and for some in sleep ... and also shivering because of the bite of the cold wind, until the day comes and reveals the splendour of the panorama and the glory of the rising sun.

Once more this year, here ends this pilgrimage with the morning Mass, at 6 a.m., livened up by the children of Mother of Peace, whose liturgical ballet evokes irresistibly what Our Lord says about their Angels 'who in heaven always see the face of my Father'.

Once more this year, here proceeds the long Offertory procession, the faithful bringing their offerings as they did during the first centuries of the Church – a bag of rice or groundnuts, a bottle of oil, a blanket, or a small bag of sweets, the mite of the widow (these offerings will be distributed between the patients of Mutemwa and the children of Mother of Peace).

And John in the midst of all this? This pilgrimage for the anniversary of John's abduction and murder has nothing to do with a 'bradburneolatry' of any kind. Of course, one who ignores the Shona language recognises his name from time to time during the teachings and the celebrations, but all the praise, the songs and the teachings are centred on God, on the Lord Jesus, on Our Lady. But you feel here strongly a peaceful trust in the intercession of a man who followed Christ and served his brothers up to giving them both the greatest proof of love, his life for them. In his Tin and Abduction Huts many souls discover or find again his moving spiritual presence, while they present their physical, mental, moral or spiritual problems or despairs to God or just tell Him 'Thank you' for the gift of a human life like John's. Surely, even if it is maybe better to come here another day to learn how Mutemwa daily life was in John's time, to participate in this pilgrimage gives you the key to understand his life and message.

Yes, the key, and even the keystone, like the ones which the builders of the cathedrals did put on top of their arches at the end of the construction, and which made the whole stand and get its proper meaning: the first truth about John you discover in Mutemwa is that nearly all the lines, all the threads of his life do converge here. As a precise example, let us focus on the 'thread' concerning lepers. As a little child, John used to listen to his mother who often read the story of the young Christian meeting a leper and carrying him on his shoulders until he discovers that he is in fact carrying Christ himself. This reading filled John with awe and dread. Later, when he discovered St Francis and became a member of the Franciscan Third Order, he learned of course of Francis' first meeting with a leper. When John studied for 18 months in Louvain, the House where he lived was very close to Saint Anthony's church where the future saint Damien of Molokai is buried, and he used to come and pray there in front of the 'Apostle of the lepers'. Then, when he arrived in Africa, the first of the three wishes he confided to Father Desmond O'Malley according to Father Dove's witness was 'to serve and live with lepers'. And now Mutemwa, at the end of the road! Similar itineraries throughout all his life, or at least a great part of it, could be followed, concerning his love of heights, his faith pilgrimage, his love of Our Lady, his poetry, music, his love of solitude, silence, prayer.

African pilgrims come to celebrate the memory of a European killed during the Liberation war. Why? One of them answered a week after this 2010 pilgrimage (in an Internet post signed Ngomakirura – a mountain near Harare):

> They came by foot, by bicycle, by open truck, by kombi and by bus. They came from Mutare and Bulawayo, from Kadoma, Kwekwe, and Harare as well as the areas round Mutoko. September 5th was the anniversary of the abduction and killing of John Bradburne of Mutemwa. 'Bradburne of Mutemwa'. It begins to slip off the tongue like Augustine of Hippo, Francis of Assisi, or Teresa of Calcutta. John himself would be horrified at being bracketed with such great people, but he is beyond the place where his protests are heard and whatever his reputation will be it will be. What

is sure is that thousands come spontaneously to that spot at the foot of Chigona hill where he lived among people with leprosy in the 1970s. No one is 'organising' Mutemwa. People just come and from different churches and maybe from no church. In the last five years their numbers have swelled.

Why do they come? Why do they spend scarce money on such a journey? We can be fairly sure of the answer. They come for healing. They do not seek dramatic cures, casting away crutches. There is no celebrity calling them forward to stand up and walk. They come mainly for inner healing. They come because they sense this place is holy. They sense that in this place someone wrestled with the evil one and triumphed; that this person became more human as a result and so approached the divine more closely. And they feel that this was not for himself alone but for all of us... What goes on in the heart of each one who comes to Mutemwa today will never be known. It will not reach the *Herald* or be shouted from the roof tops. But we can be sure that deep inner healing is silently taking place, and people know it and experience it. May ripples spread out and touch more and more people so that Mutemwa can contribute to the healing of our country!

Beyond Mutemwa, the memory of John is honoured in many places, both in Zimbabwe and in Europe. In September 2009 two impressive exhibitions were held on the thirtieth anniversary of his death, one in Westminster Cathedral in London, organised by the JBMS, the other in the Anglican Church at St Mary's at Ottery, organised by Jo Holloway – a clear sign of ecumenical concord. In Britain several prayer groups pray for his intercession and his beatification, as well as in other countries and Zimbabwe itself.

While the numerous miracles attributed to John can be considered to support his claim to beatification, the Church itself has tended to concentrate on the manner of his death. To invoke the term 'martyr' would be to anticipate any ultimate conclusion of the Church, which reserves the title for those who have been officially proclaimed such, but this indeed is what is at issue. Since 1982, the possibility of a canonical investigation, in cooperation with the Franciscan Secular Order (FSO), has been mentioned in correspondence between Harare and the general curia of the Franciscan order in Rome and CIOFS (FSO International Council). In the 1990s Father Pascal Slevin put together a diocesan file, declaring that he had 'no doubt that John died a martyr in his determination to serve his friends, the lepers'. According to Caterina Savini, 'you may call him a fool or a saint, but he was certainly a martyr'.

But a canonical procedure is necessary, and for that witnesses to his death and his life are needed. Of these there is no shortage, but collection and presentation of data would have to follow certain procedures. Thus in 2001 Father Slevin presented to Bishop Chakaipa a diocesan Petition of almost 100 pages, with an annexe of 150 documents. Delicate political issues aside, another unforeseen difficulty arises: John's renowned sanctity is such that many people take it for granted without realising the necessity to acknowledge the strict criteria of the Catholic Church in this domain. Furthermore, evidence would have to take written form, in a predominantly oral culture like Zimbabwe's. In fact, the cause of Luisa Guidotti, opened in 1996 by the Archbishop of Modena at the request of the diocese of Harare, has progressed much more rapidly.

Father Tim Peacock considers there are at least ten good reasons for beatifying John Bradburne, an opinion shared by many people (including the author of this book):

> 1. An example for us. 2. The first Zimbabwean saint. 3. He broke down barriers. 4. God calls all types of people. 5. His first love: In his love for God he continuously wanted to be alone with him. 6. His second love: His love for his neighbour knew no bounds. 7. His interesting character. 8. His spirit of self-sacrifice. 9. A martyr of love. 10. The graces he brings today.

Perhaps one day the man who wrote to his friend John Dove in 1952: 'Pray on for my sanctification too, because it would encourage so many souls if such a wreckage might come to canonisation, and I do so want to by-pass Purgatory!!' will be, who knows, the first Zimbabwean saint, for the Universal Church?

Prayer for the beatification of John Bradburne

God our Father, your servant John Randal Bradburne
showed the power of your love
by his life and death.
May his love of Christ and of Mary His Mother,
together with his selfless service to those considered
least in the world,
be a model for us to follow.
We therefore ask a favour through his intercession,
so that his generosity and holiness
may be recognised by the whole Church.
We ask this through Jesus Christ, our Lord.

Glossary

In order to avoid anachronism, place names have been written as they were at the time they are mentioned.

Enkeldoorn has now become Chivhu.
Fort Victoria: Masvingo.
Gwelo: Gweru.
Inangyani: Nyangani.
Melsetter: Chimanimani.
Mazoe: Mazowe.
Mtemwa: Mutemwa.
Mtoko: Mutoko.
Mrewa: Murewa.
Salisbury: Harare.
Selukwe: Shurugwi.
Sinoia: Chinhoyi.
Umtali: Mutare.
Wankie: Hwange.
Wedza: Hwedza.

The country has been known by several names:
1895 to 1964: Southern Rhodesia
1965 to 1978: Rhodesia
1978 to 1980: Rhodesia-Zimbabwe.
Since 1980: Zimbabwe.

Shona and Afrikaans terms used in the book

Amai, Mai: greeting addressed to a woman.
Ambuya, Mbuya: greeting addressed to a mother-in-law, a grandmother, an elderly woman.
Baba: greeting address to a man or a priest.
Bundu: wood, bush.
Chimurenga: rebellion, war.
Dare: tree where people gather to talk.
Dorp: village (Afrikaans).
Indaba: meeting.
Kashasu: very strong beer.
Kraal: a group of huts (Afrikaans).
Manheru: Hello!
Mondhoro: Lion (first ancestor of an ethnic group).

Msasa: brachystegia spiciformis.
Morari: revolutionary meeting in the bush.
Mubvee: sausage tree (kigelia africana).
Mudzimu: spirit of the ancestors.
Mujibha: young boy (used to describe ZANLA auxiliaries).
Muroye: witch doctor.
Murungu (or muzungu): European.
Muti: tree, dispensary.
Mwari: God.
Neepa: home-made alcohol.
Nganga: medium (by whom ancestors' spirits communicate with the present).
Pungu: wood, forest.
Pungwe: synonym of morari.
Roora: dowry.
Sadza: mashed corn, staple diet.
Sekuru: greeting address to an uncle, a grandfather, an elderly man.
Stoep: veranda.
Vakonama: boy (used to describe ZANLA guerrillas).
Veld: bush

Sources

Archives

The John Bradburne Archives at Leominster (John Bradburne Memorial Society), in the National English Literature Museum, Grahamstown (South Africa), in the Archdiocese of Harare, and on the poetry website: <http://www.johnbradburnepoems.com>.

Anthologies (*all published by the JBMS*)

John Bradburne's Mutemwa, in poems and pictures, edited by David and Hilary Crystal, 2000.
CD: *Alive To God,* Herald AV, Farnham, 2008.
Poems selected and edited by David Crystal
    Songs of the Vagabond, 1996.
    John Bradburne's Book of Days, 2004.
    John Bradburne's Birds, Bees and Beasts, 2007.
    John Bradburne on Love, 2009.

Personal recollections and testimonies

John Dove's *Strange Vagabond of God* (Gracewing, Leominster, 1997) was an essential source of information, both concerning events shared by the two friends and for other testimonies gathered (in particular from Fathers Sean Gildea, Paschal Slevin, Desmond O'Malley, David Harold-Barry, and David Gibbs, Heather Benoy, Arthur Law, Pauline Hutchings, Anne Lander, Andrew Whaley and William Hamer-Nel).

Judith Listowel's two valuable but incomplete typed manuscripts (*God's Jester: the Story of John Bradburne and the Black Lepers of M'Temwa* and *The Black Lepers of Mtemwa: the Story of John Bradburne*) are rich in recollections and extracts from letters, either of John or about him, especially from Mary Comber (Bradburne), Philip Bradburne, Michael Stern, Peter Comber, John Peacock, Alec Harper, Rex Newton-House, A. N. Shead, Joan F, Jack Dunn, Hugh Symons, Cecil Hardwicke, Adrian Hardwicke, Dom Bruno Sullivan, Dom Hugh Weld, Father Paul Waring, Dom Alfred Spencer, Adam Curle, Pamela Vermes, Darrell Blackburn, Father Brian Cavenagh, Edward Moberly, Sam Verrall, Archbishop Derek Worlock, Esme Bradburne, Mary Littledale, Shirley James, Heather Benoy, Pauline Hutchings, Elaine Barkess, Michael Gelfand, Coleta Mapfuta, Paul Barclay, Father Lawrence Makonora, Nyasha Shereni, Paul Burrough, Fathers Michael O'Halloran, David Harold-Barry and David Gibbs.

I would like to thank Lord Richard Grantley and the John Bradburne Memorial Society for allowing me to use these manuscipts.

The *John Bradburne Memorial Society Newsletter* has been publishing bi-annually since 1997 recollections, information and studies on John Bradburne and on Mutemwa. I had in particular access to recollections by Mary (Bradburne) Comber, Steve Benson, Tony Foster, John Hemsley, Parry Howell, Stephen King, Jack Dunn, Adrian Hardwicke, Teresa Thorp, Pamela (Bradburne) Kingsford, Nicholas Lowry, Bishop Robert Mercer, Wayne Perry, Perpetua Robert, Sister Angelina Katsukunya, Fathers Claudio Rossi, Colin Carr, and Paul Crane, Jerome Govere, Margaret de Haast, Mike Glenshaw, Father Sean Gildea, Fathers David Harold-Barry and John Gough, Pauline Hutchings, Sister Kathleen Keane and Cheryl Methven, as well as the studies mentioned below. I would like to thank the JBMS for having allowed me to use this material as well as unpublished recollections from the John Bradburne Archives, in particular Mary (Bradburne) Comber recollections, the family tree of the Bradburnes drawn up in 1993 by Michael Bradburne, and the file prepared in 1995 by Diana Mitchell, which contains other unpublished testimonies, in particular from Father John Dove, Howell Parry, Pamela (Bradburne) Kingsford, Ferdinand Spit, Frau Pätz, Alec Israel, David Savage, Winnie Mabaso and Father Michael O'Halloran. The diocesan *Petition*, compiled by Father Paschal Slevin, also contains a number of testimonies.

Books containing other recollections

AFMM, *Luisa Guidotti, Una vita per gli altri,* Milan, 2004.

Dove, John, *Luisa,* Mambo Press, Gweru, 1989.

Guidotti, Luisa, *Luisa agli Amici: Raccolta di Lettere, Societa editrice internazionale,* 1990.

Saunders, Stuart, *Vice-Chancellor on a Tight Rope,* New Africa Books, Johannesburg, 2000.

Towill, Bill, *A Chindit Chronicle,* Authors CP, San José, 1990.

Trethowan, Anthony, *Delta Scout: Ground Coverage Operator,* 30° South Publishers, 2008.

Vermes, Geza, *Providential Accidents: an Autobiography,* SCM Press, London, 1998.

Wortham, Christopher, *Fragments from Two Lives on Three Continents,* Strategic Book Publishing, 2009.

Other published accounts

Dove, John, *John Bradburne of Mutemwa, Three wishes fulfilled,* Mambo Press, Gweru, 1985.

Hacksley, Helen, *An Edition of a Selection of Poems by John Randal Bradburne*, Rhodes University, Grahamstown, 2006 (acceded at http://contentpro.seals.ac.za)

Maksjan, Anna, *The Mystical Dimension of the Poetry of John Bradburne and the Carthusian*, Analecta Cartusiana 247, Salzburg University, 2007.

Vose John, *John Bradburne: a Magnificent Eccentric*, JBMS, Leominster, 2005.

Articles in the JBMS Newsletter

Crystal, David, 'Beginnings and endings', Winter 2004, pp. 6–7.
    'Poetry data goes live', Summer 2006, p. 3.
    'If I could publish a slim volume', Winter 2009, pp. 8–10.

De Kerdrel, 'Stephen, Vagabonds and holy fools', Summer 2002, pp. 2–3.
    'John Bradburne, Wanderer, hermit, monk and hero', Summer 2003, pp. 5–7.
    'John Bradburne, a very English saint', Summer 2005, pp. 4–5.
    'John Bradburne and Our Lady', Winter 2002, pp. 5–6.
    'An introductory chapter to a potential new book', Winter 2008, pp. 3–4.
    'John Bradburne's importance for us', Summer 2009, pp. 7–8.

Elvins Mark, 'In the likeness of St Francis of Assisi', Winter 2005, p. 2.

Harold-Barry, David, 'Reflections on John Bradburne', Winter 2013, pp. 2–3.

McCarthy, Liam, 'Interview with Fr Sean Gildea, OFM', Autumn 2015, pp. 4–5.

Moore Charles, 'A martyr who turned love into the divine', Winter 2009, pp. 7–8.

O'Donoghue Patrick, 'John Bradburne', Summer 2005, p. 1.

Peacock, Tim, 'The benefits for John Bradburne to be eventually canonised', Winter 2006, p. 4.

Rance, Didier, 'Looking for John in England', Winter 2009, pp. 4–6.
    'John Henry (Newman) and John (Bradburne)', Summer 2010, pp. 2-3.
    'John at Chivhu', Summer 2011, pp. 4–5.
    'John Bee's buzz of bees', Winter 2011, pp 3–4.
    'John's mystical marriage in Santa Maria a Miano', Winter 2012, pp. 3–4.
    'John and St Damien of Molokai', Winter 2013, pp. 3–5.
    'John Bradburne's poetry', Summer 2014, p. 5.
    'John Bradburne at Westminster Cathedral', Summer 2012, pp. 2–5.

Articles and book extracts

Benson, Steve, *I Will Plant Me a Tree: an illustrated History of Gresham's School*, James, London, 2002.

Bingandadi, Francis, 'John Bradburne', *Catholic Church News*, December 2010.

Brigstocke, Celia, 'Hermit, vagabond... Saint', *Catholic Herald*, January 2010.

Crystal, David, *By Hook or by Crook: a Journey in Search of English*, Harper Perennial, London, 2007.

Crystal, David, *Just a Phrase I'm Going Through: my Life in Language*, Routledge, Abingdon, 2009.

Gibbs, David, 'John Randal Bradburne: missionary, poet, mystic, martyr, 1921–1979', *The Central African Journal of Medicine* 26 (2), 1980.

Hanley, Boniface, 'The Pilgrim', *The Anthonian* 56 (4), 1982.

Larby, Liz, 'John Bradburne, poet, naturalist, saint', *Old Greshamian Magazine*, 2008.

Moore, Charles, 'John Bradburne', *Daily Telegraph*, 29 August 1994.

Rance, Didier, *Prier 15 Jours avec les martyrs du XXe siècle*, Nouvelle Cité, Montrouge, 2004.

    John Bradburne, 'Le vagabond céleste ami des abeilles', *Ultreia*, Hiver 2015, pp. 196–208.

Scott, James, *The Life of Francis of Assisi: Is Franciscanism Relevant Today?*, Potchefstroomse Universiteit, 2002 (acceded at http://dspace.nwu.ac.za/handle/10394/828).

Vanier, Jean, *Notre vie ensemble*, Mediaspaul-Bellarmin, Paris-Montréal, 2009.

Films

Don't Let the Dream Die, Documentary on John Bradburne, JBMS, Leominster, no date.

Issues of Faith, Documentary on John Bradburne, JBMS, no date.

On Eagles' Wings: the Life and Death of John R. Bradburne 1924–1979, JBMS, 1999.

The Life of John Bradburne, as narrated by Ambuya Colletta Mafuta, Collen Magobeya, 2011.

Vagabond of God: the Story of John Bradburne, Norman Servais, Metanoia, Cape Town, 2001.

Varia

The life and death of John Bradburne have inspired poets (Brendan Kennelly, *Breathing Spaces*, 1992), playwrights (Rory Kilalea, *Friends*, 2007), novelists (Tendai Huchu, *The Hairdresser of Harare*, 2010), several essayists on Catholic England or figures of faith, musicians (Nicholas Wilton, *O Salutaris, Ave verum, Tantum Ergo*, 2001, and Gabriel Jackson, *In Nomine Domini*, 2010) and sculptors in Zimbabwe and Malawi (Church of the Mission at Mua).

Acknowledgements

I would like to thank all those who gave me their recolletions on John Bradburne or helped me (sometimes indirectly) for this book: (chapter 1) Alan Kitchen, Rev. Richard Moatt, Christopher Robson; (chapter 2) June Mitchell, Steve Benson, Liz Larby; (chapter 3) Peter Heppell, Frank Young, Captain B. K. Wilson; (chapters 4 to 6) Sister Camillia Walkin, Jo Holloway, Paula Parklyn, Patrick Hardwicke, Jack Dunn, Nick Salter, Harry Wheeler, Brother Nicholas, Michael Lowry, Brother Simon Brenann, Father Donizeti Ribeiro, Geza Vermes, Father Francesco Picciocchi, Guiseppe Alloca, Silvestro Peluso, Dom Aldhelm Cameron-Brown, Brother Anthony, Dom Damian Sturdy, CTSShop (London), Josette and Brian Swanson, Meg Whittle, Pamela Kingsford; (chapters 7 to 10) Father Sean Gildea, Father Tim Peacock, Heather Benoy, Sister Nora Broderick, Frank Guthrie, Rory Kililea, Agnès Mapfumo, Geraldine Morris, Sister Teresiana Mutume, David Paynter, Ferdinand Spit, Paul and Ann Tingay, Father George Webster, Pauline Hutchings, Caterina Savini, Anthony Trethowan, Andrew Whaley, Coleta Mapfuta, Sister Margaret Murphy, Cecilia Blight, Piet Both, Geneviève Lejeune, Helen Hacksley, Father Mark Elvins; (chapter 11) Mgr Emmanuel Laffont, Charles Moore, Norman Servais, Jean Vanier, residents and pilgrims of Mutemwa, Marge Chigwada, Rose Chihota, Stella Cornneck, Jean Cornneck and the children of Mother of Peace. I would like to thank especially Father John Dove, David Harold-Barry and Liam McCarthy, Lord Richard Grantley, David and Hilary Crystal, Heather Benoy, Anne Lander and, last but not least, Celia and Tim Brigstocke of the John Bradburne Memorial Society (JBMS), Christophe Rémond, first publisher of this book, Malachy O'Higgins, its incomparable translator into English, and Catherine, my wife, who all gave me unstinting support, and without whom this book would never have seen the light of day. And John, of course.